Comparative ethnic and race relations

South Asians overseas

Comparative ethnic and race relations

Published for the Centre of Research in Ethnic Relations at the University of Warwick

Senior Editor
Professor John Rex *Associate Director & Research Professor of Ethnic Relations, University of Warwick*

Editors
Professor Robin Cohen *Executive Director & Professor of Sociology, University of Warwick*
Mr Malcolm Cross *Principal Research Fellow, University of Warwick*

This series has been formed to publish works of original theory, empirical research, and texts on the problems of racially mixed societies. It is based on the work for the Centre of Research in Ethnic Relations, a Designated Research Centre of the Economic and Social Research Council, and the main centre for the study of race relations in Britain.

The series will continue to draw on the work produced at the Centre, though the editors encourage manuscripts from scholars whose work has been associated with the Centre, or whose research lies in similar fields. Future titles will concentrate on anti-racist issues in education, on the organisation and political demands of ethnic minorities, on migration patterns, changes in immigration policies in relation to migrants and refugees, and on questions relating to employment, welfare and urban restructuring as these affect minority communities.

The books will appeal to an international readership of scholars, students and professionals concerned with racial issues, across a wide range of disciplines (such as sociology, anthropology, social policy, politics, economics, education and law), as well as among professional social administrators, teachers, government officials, health service workers and others.

Other books in this series:
Michael Banton: *Racial and ethnic competition* (issued in hardcover and as a paperback)
Thomas Hammar (ed.): *European immigration policy*
Frank Reeves: *British racial discourse*
Robin Ward and Richard Jenkins (eds.): *Ethnic communities in business*
Richard Jenkins: *Racism and recruitment: managers, organisations and equal opportunity in the labour market*
Roger Hewitt: *White talk black talk: inter-racial friendships and communication amongst adolescents*
Paul B. Rich: *Race and Empire in British politics*
Richard Jenkins and John Solomos (eds.): *Racism and equal opportunity policies in the 1980s*
John Rex and David Mason (eds.): *Theories of race and ethnic relations*
John Solomos: *Black youth, racism and the state: the politics of ideology and policy*

South Asians Overseas
Migration and ethnicity

Edited by
COLIN CLARKE, CERI PEACH AND
STEVEN VERTOVEC

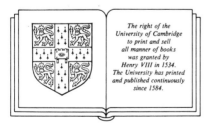

The right of the
University of Cambridge
to print and sell
all manner of books
was granted by
Henry VIII in 1534.
The University has printed
and published continuously
since 1584.

CAMBRIDGE UNIVERSITY PRESS

Cambridge
New York   Port Chester
Melbourne   Sydney

Published by the Press Syndicate of the University of Cambridge
The Pitt Building, Trumpington Street, Cambridge CB2 1RP
40 West 20th Street, New York, NY 10011, USA
10 Stamford Road, Oakleigh, Melbourne 3166, Australia

First published 1990

Printed in Great Britain by The Bath Press, Avon

British Library cataloguing in publication data

South Asians overseas: migration and ethnicity. –
    (Comparative ethnic and race relations series)
    1. South Asian emigrants, history
    I. Clarke, Colin C. (Colin Graham), *1938–*   II. Peach, Ceri
    III. Vertovec, Steven   IV. Series
    909'.04914

Library of Congress cataloguing in publication data

South Asians overseas: migration and ethnicity/edited by Colin Clarke, Ceri
    Peach, and Steven Vertovec.
        p.   cm. – Comparative ethnic and race relations
    Includes indexes.
    ISBN 0-521-37543-6 (U.S.)
    1. South Asians – Foreign countries. 2. South Asians – Ethnic identity. 3. South
Asia – Emigration and immigration. I. Clarke, Colin G. II. Peach, Ceri. III.
Vertovec, Steven. IV. Series: Comparative ethnic and race relations series.
DS339.4.S68 1990
305.8'914 – dc20   89-34308 CIP

ISBN 0 521 37543 6

CE

To Adrian Mayer

Contents

viii   *Contents*

Figures

Maps

Tables

Contributors

MUHAMMAD ANWAR is Director of the Centre for Research in Ethnic Relations, University of Warwick, having formerly been Head of Research, Commission for Racial Equality. He has an MA in Sociology, an MA (Econ.) and a PhD in Sociology. He has written extensively on ethnic and race relations. Dr Anwar's previous publications include: *Between Two Cultures* (Community Relations Commission, 1976), *Who Tunes In To What?* (Commission for Racial Equality, 1978), *The Myth of Return: Pakistanis in Britain* (Heinemann, 1979), *Votes and Policies* (1980), *Race Relations in 1981* (1981), *Young People and the Job Market* (1982), *Ethnic Minority Broadcasting* (1983) and *Ethnic Minorities and the 1983 General Election* (1984). He is co-author of *Participation of Ethnic Minorities in the October 1974 General Election* (1975) and *Television in a Multi-Racial Society* (1982). He is also the editor of *Muslim Communities in Non-Muslim States* (1980) and has written many articles in books and journals. His latest book, *Race and Politics*, was published by Tavistock in 1986.

ROGER BALLARD studied for his first degree in Social Anthropology at Cambridge and completed his PhD in Sociology at the University of Delhi in 1969. On returning to Britain he joined the SSRC Research Unit in Ethnic Relations, and in 1975 was appointed Lecturer in Race Relations at the University of Leeds; he now lectures in the Department of Comparative Religion in the University of Manchester. Taking a wide-ranging interest in the implications of the South Asian presence in Britain, about which he has published extensively, he has been particularly keen to explore the significance of settlers' continuing links with their homelands. His on-going research in Britain, mainly conducted in Leeds and Bradford, has been supplemented by visits to the Indian and Pakistani Punjab in 1972/3, 1981 and 1984/5.

JO BEALL is currently living in Britain where she is studying part-time and writing. Until the end of 1988 she was a lecturer in the African Studies Department, University of Natal, Durban, South Africa. Her disciplinary background is social and economic history and her research has concerned the history of women in Natal, South Africa. She has also written on contemporary South Africa, including papers and articles on women in South Africa's troubled townships and on the prospects and preconditions for achieving gender-neutral policy and planning in South Africa. From 1987 to 1988 she was national Vice-President of The Association of Sociologists in Southern Africa (ASSA). She was an organiser of a workshop, held at the University of Natal, on 'Regionalism and regionalisation in Natal/Kwa Zulu', which attracted both local and overseas delegates. She is an editor of the South African women's journal, *Agenda*.

SURINDER M. BHARDWAJ is Professor and Coordinator of Graduate Studies, and a former Chairman (1974–7) in the Department of Geography at Kent State University. He holds an MA from the Panjab University and an MA and a PhD from the University of Minnesota. His main interest is the study of religious circulation, and the role of religion in ethnic identity. His publications include *Hindu Places of Pilgrimage in India: A Study in Cultural Geography* (University of California Press, 1973), *Pilgrimage in World Religions*, co-edited with Gisbert Rinschede (Dietrich Reimer Verlag, Berlin, 1988), and several journal and encyclopaedia articles.

COLIN CLARKE is a University Lecturer in Geography and an Official Fellow of Jesus College, Oxford. He has taught at the universities of Toronto and Liverpool, where he was Reader in Geography and Latin-American Studies, and he has carried out numerous field investigations in Mexico and the Caribbean. His publications deal with race and ethnic pluralism, urbanisation, demography, rural change, and politics. He is author of *Kingston, Jamaica: urban development and social change 1692–1962* (University of California Press, 1975), *East Indians in a West Indian town: San Fernando, Trinidad, 1930–1970* (Allen and Unwin, 1986), and *Livelihood Systems, Settlements and Levels of Living in 'Los Valles Centrales de Oaxaca', Mexico* (School of Geography, University of Oxford, Research Paper 37, 1986); co-author of *A Geography of the Third World* (Methuen, 1983); and co-editor of *Geography and Ethnic Pluralism* (Allen and Unwin, 1984) and *Politics, Security and Development in Small States* (Allen and Unwin, 1987).

JOHN EADE is Senior Lecturer in Sociology and Social Anthropology at the Roehampton Institute, London. After reading modern history he completed a Diploma and M.Litt. in Social Anthropology at Oxford. His doctoral thesis undertaken at Birkbeck College, University of London, has been published through the Research in Ethnic Relations Series, Centre for Research in Ethnic Relations, University of Warwick, under the title *The Politics of Community: The Bangladeshi Community in East London* (Aldershot: Gower, 1989). His current research concerns national and local representations of Britain's Muslims and he is preparing papers given at an inter-disciplinary conference on pilgrimage at Roehampton for publication.

ELINOR KELLY is a lecturer in Applied Social Studies in Manchester University and specialises in work as a teacher, trainer, and researcher in racial and ethnic studies. Since 1971 she has concentrated on work in Manchester and Lancashire, focusing on migration and inter-ethnic relations. She has arranged courses and training with a number of local authority departments, and has carried out research enquiries into policy issues relating to the new minorities and their relations with the indigenous populations in Lancashire towns. She has been the academic director of three local studies and has written a number of policy reports and papers for local authorities, some of which are now being prepared for academic publication. In 1984 and 1985 she undertook field studies among migrant families in Gujarat, India, and since then she has visited Pakistan. The paper in this volume is the first outline of the transcontinental comparative perspective which she is now developing.

BÉATRICE KNERR is Assistant Professor in the Institute of Agricultural Economics and Social Sciences in the Tropics, University of Hohenheim, West Germany. She studied economics and oriental sciences at the Universities of Saarbrücken, Heidelberg, and Montpellier and did her PhD work at the University of Kiel where she worked as a lecturer and researcher. In 1984 she moved to the University of Hohenheim where she has specialised in international labour migration and its implications for developing countries. Her special regional interest is South Asia, where she has travelled and researched widely. She is the author of several papers on the economic consequences of labour export from developing countries, focusing on migration from South Asia.

VICTOR LAL is Research Fellow at the International Development Centre at Oxford University. A former senior sub-editor on the *Fiji Sun* newspaper in Fiji, he has written and commented extensively on Fijian

xvi   *Contributors*

politics. He is the author of *Fiji: Coups in Paradise* (Zed Press, 1990), which he wrote while holding a Reuters Fellowship at Oxford. He is currently completing a comparative book-length manuscript on Indians in Fiji and Natal in South Africa.

ANTHONY LEMON is a Lecturer in Geography at Oxford University and a Fellow of Mansfield College. He specialises in the social and political geography of Southern Africa, where he has held several visiting lectureships and research fellowships. His publications include *Apartheid: a Geography of Separation* (Saxon House, 1976), *Studies in Overseas Settlement and Population*, with N.C. Pollock (Longman, 1980), and *Apartheid in Transition* (Gower, 1987). He has also published numerous articles on elections in South Africa and Zimbabwe, and on various aspects of the geography of apartheid in South Africa and its regional significance. His current research interests include ethnic residential segregation and local government reform in apartheid cities.

CERI PEACH is a Lecturer in Geography at Oxford University and Fellow of St Catherine's College. His field work on urban ethnic segregation has taken him to India, South Africa, Australia, the United States, and Europe. He has held visiting fellowships at ANU, Yale, and Berkeley. He is author of *West Indian Migration to Britain* (Oxford University Press, 1968); editor of *Urban Social Segregation* (Longman, 1975); co-editor of *Ethnic Segregation in Cities* (Croom Helm, 1981) and *Geography and Ethnic Pluralism* (Allen and Unwin, 1984).

N. MADHUSUDANA RAO is a Lecturer in General Studies at the University of Akron, Ohio, USA. He holds an MPhil from the Centre for the Study of Regional Development in the Jawaharlal Nehru University, New Delhi, and a PhD in Geography from Kent State University, Kent, Ohio. His main research interest is in current trends and patterns of ethnicity in the United States with a special focus on Asian Americans. He has published articles related to ethnicity and medical geography. He has taught Computer Cartography and his specialities include the application of quantitative methods to qualitative data. He is currently completing a book on *Ethnogenetic Processes of Asian Indians in the United States*.

VAUGHAN ROBINSON is Lecturer in Geography at University College Swansea. Formerly he was a Prize Research Fellow in Race Relations at Nuffield College, Oxford, where he was also awarded the University's Frere Exhibition in Indian Studies. He has been a visiting lecturer in India, Pakistan, and Poland. His main interests are urban social geography, particularly the position of ethnic minorities in Britain. He wrote *Transients, Settlers and Refugees: Asians in Britain* (Clarendon, 1986), and co-edited *Ethnic Segregation in Cities* (Croom Helm, 1981). He is currently completing the manuscript of *The Geography of Race in Post-War Britain* (Clarendon, 1990).

SINGARAVÉLOU is Professor of Tropical Geography at University of Bordeaux III, and Director of the Centre for Studies in Tropical Geography, CNRS, Bordeaux, France. He was previously Professor and Head of the Department of Geography at the University of the French West Indies, Martinique, and Director of the Centre for Caribbean Studies, Guadeloupe. He is currently in charge of a research program on regional development in South India, and of a geographical atlas of Mauritius. His main interests are the Indian diaspora, and the social and cultural geography of the Caribbean and the Indian sub-continent. He has published recently a book in French on the East Indians in the Caribbean (L'Harmattan, Paris, 1988, 3 vols.).

HUGH TINKER is Professor Emeritus of the University of Lancaster, and formerly Professor of Asian Politics, London University (School of Oriental and African Studies). He was also Director of the Institute of Race Relations and member of the Council of the Minority Rights Group. Among his books are *A New System of Slavery: the export of Indian labour overseas 1830–1920* (1974), *Separate and Unequal: India and the Indians in the British Commonwealth, 1920–1950* (1976), *The Banyan Tree: overseas emigrants from India, Pakistan and Bangladesh* (1977), *Race, Conflict and the International Order: from Empire to United Nations* (1977). His latest book is *Men Who Overturned Empires: fighters, dreamers and schemers* (1987).

MICHAEL TWADDLE teaches politics and history at the Institute of Commonwealth Studies in the University of London. Hitherto, most of his publications have concerned black rather than brown Africans, and between 1974 and 1986 he edited *African Affairs*, the quarterly journal of the Royal African Society. However, during the interval between taking his BA degree from Cambridge University and researching a PhD in African politics at SOAS, he was a sixth-form teacher in an urban and predominantly South Asian secondary school in East Africa, and in 1975 he published *Expulsion of a Minority: Essays on Ugandan Asians* (London: Athlone Press). He is currently completing a book on East African Asians during the last hundred years as well as working in collaboration with Dr Christopher Abel of University College London on a study of South Asian settlers and others in the Caribbean during the last 150 years.

STEVEN VERTOVEC received degrees in Anthropology and Religious Studies from the University of Colorado and, under a Regents' Fellowship, the University of California, Santa Barbara, as well as a doctorate in Social Anthropology from the University of Oxford. He is author of *Hindu Trinidad* (Macmillan, forthcoming) and other articles on religion and ethnicity, and is editor of *Oxford University Papers on India (vol. 2)*. He currently teaches in the Department of Humanities at Brighton Polytechnic while also engaged in ethnographic research among Hindus in London.

PNINA WERBNER lectures in Social Anthropology and Sociology, and is currently a Research Associate in the Department of Sociology, Manchester University. She has conducted extensive research among British Pakistani immigrants in Manchester. Her major interests include urban ritual and religion, gift exchange, social networks, labour migration, urban ethnic politics, and ethnic economic entrepreneurship. She is currently directing a research project on Personhood and Moral Conduct among British Muslims, supported by the ESRC. Her major publications include *The Migration Process: Capital, Gifts and Offerings among Overseas Pakistanis* (Oxford: Berg, 1989); *Black and Ethnic Leaderships in Britain*, edited with Muhammad Anwar (Routledge, 1990); *Pakistan and Pakistanis: Culture and Change in a Modern Islamic Society*, edited with Hastings Donnan (Macmillan, 1990). She has also contributed articles to major journals and edited collections.

Preface

Development of the world capitalist economy during the last two centuries has brought together far-flung factors of production – including South Asian workers, the topic of this book – at economically advantageous locations: here, tropical plantations in the nineteenth century and cities of the developed world in the twentieth. These inter-continental movements of South Asians are only a small sample of the variety of labour migrations which have operated at global scale under the influence of capitalism, beginning with the African slave trade and later involving indentured Indians and Chinese, white convicts, and free labourers of many national origins, religions and races.

South Asians overseas represent only a small fraction of the ethnic populations displaced by imperialism and more recently by modern capitalism; likewise the complex overseas societies in which they have settled are only a sub-set of a larger body of racially and culturally pluralistic societies – all products of migration – which are scattered across the globe. Study of South Asians overseas therefore involves consideration of social issues such as the salience of race and culture versus class, the role of race and religion as keys to identity, the scope of civil rights as the basis for ethnic incorporation, and the relationship of gender roles to class and race differentiation. All these themes are discussed in this book, a major feature of which is the comparative analysis of South Asians in colonial and post-colonial contexts – largely the result of indentured emigration, and South Asians in western and Middle Eastern countries – the products of recent free movements.

This volume is the outcome of a symposium on South Asians overseas, funded by the Centre for Indian Studies, St Antony's College, Oxford, and the Economic and Social Research Council of the United Kingdom. It was held in Oxford in March 1987 and brought together scholars from Social Anthropology, Economics, Geography, History, Law, Psychology and

Sociology: many participants felt that it was one of the most fruitful conferences that they had experienced. The symposium involved fifty-five participants and thirty-five papers. The academic level of the contributions was very high, and the editors of this book have had great difficulty in selecting chapters from the wealth of material that was submitted. The editors would like to take this opportunity to thank the Centre for Indian Studies, St Antony's College, and the ESRC for their funding, Dr T. Raychaudhuri for his encouragement, and Professor Adrian Mayer for his support and advice, particularly regarding the choice and editing of the materials in this book. We should also like to thank Barbara Hird for the excellent index she prepared

We have tried to produce a volume with a coherent but comparative theme – migration and ethnicity as they relate to South Asians overseas. We have arranged the contents to illustrate the two basic locales in which South Asian communities have developed, and have written an introduction which highlights crucial themes in the general literature and provides a context for the contributions made by individual authors. In addition to the main introduction to the book, we have produced brief introductory notes to each of the two major sub-sections. Readers may wish to read the introduction in conjunction with these notes to get a preliminary view of the way in which material in different chapters ties together and the way various case studies are related to the more general issues embedded in the notions of migration and ethnicity.

Colin Clarke, Ceri Peach, Steven Vertovec

Introduction: themes in the study of the South Asian diaspora

Colin Clarke, Ceri Peach and Steven Vertovec

The total number of people of South Asian descent who are living outside South Asia is quite small compared to overseas communities of other origins. Exact figures are hard to obtain, due to major national differences in census taking and to the rapid fluctuations of some migrant populations, but a current date total for South Asian peoples living outside Pakistan, India, Bangladesh, Nepal and Sri Lanka is about 8.6 million (Table Intro. 1). This is fewer than 1% of the current combined populations of these South Asian countries, which is some 1,000 million. Much higher ratios of overseas to home-based populations are recorded by Jews (over 11 million worldwide, while only 3.5 million live in the state of Israel), Chinese (some 22 million overseas with 1,000 million living in China), Africans (estimated at 300 million outside Africa compared to 540 million in Africa itself), and Europeans (perhaps 350 million around the world with 700 million in Europe). Yet while their relative numbers are considerably less than for others, overseas South Asians are more dramatically spread around the world – especially in English-speaking countries (Map Intro. 1). Moreover, due to diverse contexts of migration and settlement, a variety of factors have differentially contributed to South Asian community development overseas. Sometimes overseas South Asians have socially fragmented and at other times they have been consolidated; in some places South Asians have disregarded many of their cultural traditions, in other places these are steadfastly maintained. The divergent histories of overseas South Asian communities have much to tell about international migration processes, social and cultural change, political development and ethnicity.

For more than 2,000 years, people from South Asia have travelled and established themselves abroad. Buddhist pilgrims and missionaries penetrated most of Central and East Asia, merchants from the subcontinent forged economic ties along the coast of East Africa, and various Indian

1

Table Intro. 1. *Overseas South Asians by major area, by country: 1987*

UK	1,260,000		United Arab Emirates	382,302
Netherlands	102,800		Oman	190,000
France	42,000		Kuwait	355,947
Germany (FRG)	32,335		Yemen (PDR)	103,230
Spain	10,000		Iraq	85,000
Portugal	7,300		Saudi Arabia	79,987
Sweden	7,046		Qatar	51,500
Austria	3,131		Bahrein	48,050
Norway	2,900		Yemen	14,000
Switzerland	2,863		Lebanon	15,000
Denmark	2,552		Iran	6,300
Other	9,107		Jordan	4,506
Total Europe		1,482,034	Other	319
			Total Middle East	1,317,141
Mauritius	700,712			
South Africa	350,000		Trinidad	430,000
Kenya	70,000		Guyana	300,350
Reunion	65,000		Surinam	140,000
Tanzania	40,000		Jamaica	33,600
Libya	35,500		Guadeloupe	23,000
Malagasy	21,250		Martinique	10,000
Zambia	20,900		St Vincent	6,000
Mozambique	20,850		Grenada	4,000
Zimbabwe	16,000		St Lucia	3,840
Nigeria	14,000		Panama	2,100
Seychelles	5,200		Other	4,440
Malawi	5,000		Total Caribbean	
Liberia	3,066		and Latin America	957,330
Algeria	3,003			
Ethiopia	3,000		USA	500,000
Zaire	2,711		Canada	228,500
Other	13,260		Total North America	728,500
Total Africa		1,389,722		
			Fiji	839,340
Malaysia	1,170,000		Australia	99,200
Burma	330,000		New Zealand	15,000
Singapore	169,100		Other	569
Bhutan	70,037			
Afghanistan	45,600		Total Pacific	954,109
Indonesia	30,000			
Hong Kong	20,180		Grand Total:	8,691,490
Philippines	12,100			
Thailand	6,802			
Brunei	5,500			
Japan	2,685			
Other	752			
Total Asia		1,862,654		

Sources: see facing page.

dynasties held sway over much of Indonesia and Southeast Asia. However, although these examples of hegemony, travel and trade left many cultural marks abroad, no sizeable South Asian communities were established. It is only since the nineteenth century that substantial numbers of South Asian peoples have migrated throughout the world and established themselves in new settings.[1]

Modern mass migrations from South Asia have taken place within two broad periods or sets of circumstances (Jayawardena 1973), and it is according to these that we have structured this book. The first is a phase conditioned by imperialism, in which large numbers of South Asians – particularly Indians – were transported in the late nineteenth and early twentieth centuries to various colonial territories around the world, where they would serve mostly as indentured labourers; others followed freely as traders and administrators. The second, current, phase has occurred since early this century, in which persons of South Asian descent have travelled freely and in increasing numbers to western countries and the Middle East to undertake occupations of all kinds – unskilled, skilled, entrepreneurial and professional.

Most overseas South Asian populations have followed a similar trajectory, which is akin to those for other migrant groups. One descriptive scheme, devised by Speckmann (1965) to outline the history of Asian Indians in Suriname, can serve to summarise the development of a number of South Asian communities outside South Asia. This consists of five stages: (1) immigration (causing social disarray and anomie); (2) acculturation (a reorientation of traditional institutions and the adoption of new ones); (3) establishment (growth in numbers, residential footing and economic security); (4) incorporation (increased urban social patterns and the rise of a middle class); and (5) accelerated development (including greater occupational mobility, educational attainment, and political representation). The sequence – reminiscent of Park's (1950) race-relations

Sources: Figures in this table are based largely on Arthur Helweg, *Statistical Information on Overseas Indians Worldwide*, mimeo, compiled 1987, no place or date of publication. Exceptions are given below.
Figures for the UK are based on the *Labour Force Survey, 1987*, published by the Office of Population Censuses and Surveys, HMSO, London.
Figures for Saudi Arabia and the United Arab Emirates are derived from Knerr's chapter in this volume.
Figures for Kuwait are derived from the 1985 *Year Book* of Kuwait.
Figures for Singapore are derived from the 1987 *Year Book* of Singapore.
Figures for Thailand are derived from the 1987 *Year Book* of Thailand.
Figures for Reunion, Guadeloupe and Martinique from Singaravélou's chapter in this volume.

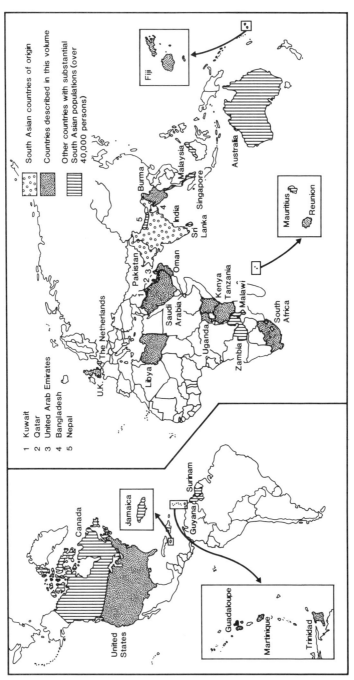

Map Intro. 1   Sources and destinations of South Asians overseas

cycle – represents more of an ideal type than a truly analytical model. In most contexts of South Asian migrant settlement, a host of independent factors have intervened to influence community development.

By referring to an interdependent set of themes or issues, patterns of similarity and difference can be more readily discerned among the many overseas South Asian communities established during the two general periods of South Asian migration. These themes and related issues, which recur throughout this volume, are outlined below under four rubrics.[2] In the following sections, aspects of the development of overseas South Asian communities within the two periods are summarised according to these themes.

(1) Migration processes and factors of settlement

The themes grouped under this heading are drawn initially from Jaya-wardena (1968), who saw them as variables directly channelling socio-cultural change among South Asians overseas (these are reiterated by Vertovec in chapter 4 to emphasise certain issues affecting South Asians in contemporary developing countries):

(a) *type of migration:* indentured or otherwise bound by contract, free passage (for purposes of education, employment or business), or political refugee; related to these types are the motivating conditions (so-called 'push' factors) in areas whence migrants came; whether migrants move with intentions of permanent settlement or hold a 'myth of return' (Anwar 1979);

(b) *extent of ties with South Asia:* presence or absence of kinship and marriage networks; property and other economic ties (including remittances); political involvement and organisational affiliation in country of origin; ability to visit the homeland for social, economic and religious purposes;

(c) *economic activity in new context:* type of employment and contract; degree of ownership or unionisation; extent of assets and investments; degree of ethnic economic specialisation, encapsulation and interaction *vis-à-vis* other ethnic groups;

(d) *geographic features of settlement:* predominance in urban or rural areas; isolation, segregation, or dispersal (Robinson 1986); proximity to other ethnic minority communities; location of important community centres;

(e) *infrastructures of host society:* existence of governmental migrant or refugee settlement policies; availability of housing, loans; existence of government authorities to monitor race relations or special interests of the minority South Asian community.

(2) Cultural composition

The composition of overseas South Asian communities is largely influenced by the factors listed in sections (a) and (b) above. Fundamental bases of differentiation within any South Asian population will include:

(a) *religion:* proportion of main faiths (Hindu, Muslim, Sikh, Jain, Christian); presence or activities of sects or movements within these traditions (such as Swaminarayanis or Sai Baba devotees among Hindus, Sunni or Ismaili Muslims, and moderate or pro-Khalistan Sikhs); extent of organisation; existence of centres of worship; prevalence of priesthood abroad;

(b) *language:* the extent to which Urdu, Hindi, Bengali, Tamil, and other languages such as Punjabi and Gujarati are used in the new context; the creation of a creolised South Asian language or use of a non-South Asian lingua franca; availability of literature in specific South Asian languages;

(c) *region of origin:* involving differing ethnic, religious, and linguistically plural backgrounds; cuisine, dress, folk traditions and art forms; pattern of domestic makeup; extent of urban or rural traits;

(d) *caste:* including influence of regional traditions or ritual and occupational specialisation; specific religious orientations; predominance and place in original local hierarchies; extent of the attenuation of the caste system and caste conciousness;

(e) *degree of 'cultural homogenisation':* or creation and use of a generalised (non-regional) corpus of South Asian cultural phenomena (including terminology, cuisine, dress, Hindu religious practices).

(3) Social structure and political power
The topics under this heading are inter-related, and stem subsequently from themes outlined under both headings above:

(a) *extent of ethnic pluralism:* number of ethnic groups and relative proportions within total society of immigration; economic niche associated with each ethnic group; period of arrival of South Asians *vis-à-vis* other migrants;

(b) *class composition:* whether the South Asian community spans a number of class groupings or is characterised predominantly by a single class makeup; presence or nature of solidarity with non-South Asian members of class;

(c) *degree of 'institutionalised racism':* existence of patterns of discrimination by public authorities or legislation militating against incorporation of migrant community; nature of stereotypes of South Asian minority by others and extent of media involvement in stereotyping; existence of widespread 'blame' placed on migrants during periods of national economic recession;

(d) *involvement in party politics:* nature of state constitution and franchise (facilitating or militating against fair migrant participation); extent of membership or representation of South Asians in prominent political parties; existence or nature of South Asian dominated parties; existence or nature of coalitions between South Asian parties and others; weight of South Asian community vote in elections.

(4) Community development
Finally, the effective development of community activity, collective sentiments, and a strong ethnic identity consequently depends on virtually all of the issues suggested above. Other critical features are:

(a) *organisations:* political, union, community, religious, cultural; their history, objectives, and efficiency; existence of community media;

(b) *leadership:* nature of charisma or message; patronage networks; ability to bridge cultural divides within South Asian community; effectiveness of liaising with non-South Asian leaders; legacy of corruption;

(c) *ethnic relations:* nature of social 'boundary' markers (Barth 1969); history of conflict or cooperation; nature of formal and informal socio-economic networks among ethnic groups; whether ethnic groups interact only in specific contexts (Furnivall 1939); extent of differentiation of social institutions; and role of the state in formalising ethnic relations or differentially incorporating ethnic groups into state systems (Smith 1969);

(d) *scale:* size, distribution, and composition of overseas South Asian community *vis-à-vis* others; effects of continued immigration on fusion/ fission tendencies of migrants (see chapter 9 by Bhardwaj and Rao).

In comparing the two main phases of South Asian migration, colonial and contemporary, the patterns which emerge from an observation of the above themes and sub-themes differ considerably. It is useful to review, in a general fashion, the developments stemming from these two sets of migration in order to set the stage for the more detailed analyses of specific contexts provided in this volume.

Colonial and post-colonial contexts

The large-scale emigration of South Asians, predominantly as indentured labourers, in the nineteenth and early twentieth centuries can be interpreted as a significant feature of the vast colonial expansion in that period, especially represented by the British Empire. South Asians (namely, Indians), themselves drawn from a colonial territory, travelled to other colonies far afield under various schemes and circumstances. Many remained in these colonies, from which they and their descendants entered the post-colonial era of independence and Third World development. Their histories and current situations are widely varying, as a thematic summary reveals.

(1) Migration processes and factors of settlement

Four *types of migration* characterise South Asian transplantation in the nineteenth and early twentieth centuries. That which resulted in the largest and most widely dispersed settlement of South Asians abroad was the indenture system, which functioned between 1834 and 1917.[3]

With the Act of Emancipation of 1834, slavery was abolished throughout the British Empire. In tropical colonies worldwide, owners of sugar and cocoa plantations desperately sought cheap labour. Through arrangements with British colonial authorities, a system of indentured Indian immigration was established, based in Calcutta and in Madras. (Similarly, following the abolition of slavery in their own colonies in 1846 and 1873 respectively, French and Dutch planters reached agreements with British authorities in India to obtain labourers under the same system.) Recruiters were sent into the hinterlands to acquire potential emigrants, who in turn signed contracts of indenture to serve on plantations abroad for a period of at least five years; during this time, indentured workers received a basic pay, accommodation, food rations and medical facilities, and, depending on the contract, free or partly paid return passage to India. The territories, numbers, and years pertaining to the system, under which some 1.5 million persons migrated, are listed in Table Intro. 2. Economic opportunities in the receiving colonies following the expiration of indenture contracts saw to it that only about one-third of these migrants chose to repatriate; subsequently, the descendants of those who remained have multiplied to become communities of substantial size – some, even national majorities or the largest racial block (Mauritius, Guyana, Fiji).

A second type of South Asian contracted labour migration took place to Southeast Asia and Ceylon (Sri Lanka). This involved two similar systems of recruitment, both of which used a network of middlemen and debt relationships: the *maistry* system used to acquire labourers for plantations in Burma (Chakravarti 1971), and the *kangani* system which gained workforces to tap rubber in Malaysia (Arasaratnam 1970) and to pick tea in Ceylon (Kondapi 1951). Davis (1951) estimates that between 1852 and 1937, 2.5 million Indians went to work in Burma, 2 million to Malaysia and 1.5 million to Ceylon. However, the short-term (even seasonal) nature of the work schemes and the proximity of these territories to India meant that the vast majority of these migrants returned home rather than settling abroad.

South Asians travelling to foreign colonies for purposes of commerce constituted the third type of migration in the late nineteenth and early twentieth centuries. It has been mentioned that Indian merchants had for many centuries engaged in trade along the East African coast; with the

Table Intro. 2. *Indentured Indian immigration by colony in the nineteenth and early twentieth centuries[a] and Indian population by country, 1980[b]*

Colony (country)	Period	Indian immigrants	Indian pop. (est.) 1980
Mauritius	1834–1912	453,063	623,000
British Guiana (Guyana)	1838–1917	238,909	424,400
Natal (South Africa)	1860–1911	152,184	750,000
Trinidad	1845–1917	143,939	421,000
Reunion	1829–1924	118,000	125,000
Fiji	1879–1916	60,969	300,700
Guadeloupe	1854–85	42,326	23,165[c]
East Africa (Kenya/Uganda)	1895–1901	39,771	79,000/430[d]
Jamaica	1854–85	36,420	50,300
Dutch Guiana (Suriname)	1873–1916	34,000	124,900
Martinique	1854–89	25,509	16,450
Seychelles	1899–1916	6,319	n.a.
St Lucia	1858–95	4,350	3,700
Grenada	1856–85	3,200	3,900
St Vincent	1861–80	2,472	5,000

Sources:
[a]Deerr 1938: 98; Davis 1951: 101; Roberts and Byrne 1966: 129; Gregory 1971: 53; Tinker 1974: 104; Lal 1979: 18; Singaravélou n.d. For various reasons (cited by the source authors), these figures are not entirely accurate. However, they do provide a relative indication of proportions. Further, it should be noted that these figures do not represent net immigration.
[b](Except for Guadeloupe) Tandon and Raphael 1984; *The Economist* 1984; Singaravélou n.d. Data not available are designated 'n.a.'
[c]This total is for the year 1967 (Singaravélou 1975: 86).
[d]These figures are much lower, of course, than those prior to the expulsions of 1972 (see Twaddle 1975; Tandon and Raphael 1984). In 1970, the Indian population of Kenya was 182,000 while that of Uganda was 76,000.

increase in transportation, urbanisation and administration which accompanied colonial expansion, these merchants were able to push their trade further into the interior or into urban markets (Twaddle, chapter 7; Gregory 1971). Other Indian merchants, too, quickly came to undertake business in colonies which hosted their indentured counterparts, particularly Fiji, Mauritius and Natal (South Africa).

Finally, Tinker (chapter 1) points out that Indians were also used by colonial authorities for clerical and administrative duties in overseas territories. This was especially so in Southeast Asia, and East and South Africa.

These various types of migration had direct consequences for the following three aspects of settlement. *Ties with South Asia* were at a minimum for indentured labourers, since they were on average geographically furthest from South Asia, were highly restricted in their movement and activity while under indenture, and were doubtless resolved to the severance of their ties to their homeland once they had decided to remain abroad following the termination of their indentureship. *Maistry* and *kangani* contracted labourers remained most strongly linked to South Asia, since their short-term migrations allowed them to return home as they wished. The commercial migrants – and to a lesser extent, the 'imperial auxiliaries' – remained well connected to their areas of origin through economic and marriage networks, frequent social, religious, and business visits, and property or business ownership.

The *economic activities* of the migrants were largely a function of their original migrations, too, and have only gradually changed in nature among their descendent communities in recent decades. Among each migration type and in each geographical context, South Asians occupied an ethnically based economic niche.[4] For example, indentured Indian immigrants to the West Indies, Mauritius, Fiji and South Africa became the rural labourers and independent farmers, especially in the sugar industries. Indian businessmen in East and Central Africa constituted the majority of the commercial middle class, while many Indians in Southeast Asia were associated with privileged civil service positions.

Indians' *settlement geography* followed their occupational specialisations, and was often related to the *host society's administrative infrastructure* for overseeing the welfare of the migrants. While under their indenture (or other) contracts, South Asian labourers in overseas colonies were restricted in their residence to the plantations. Eventually, they were permitted to settle elsewhere, but always within the vicinity of the estates, in order to provide a permanent supply of labour. Varying patterns and processes of settlement ensued in the different colonies, but almost everywhere the result was the isolation of the South Asian community in rural enclaves. In Trinidad, the ex-indentured Indians had considerable freedom to establish their own villages and lifestyles (Richardson 1975), while in British Guiana (Guyana), though hampered by the limited inhabitable space available along the coastal strip, they were none the less segregated (Despres 1969). In Mauritius, the migrants devised a means for collectively purchasing plots and founding villages (Benedict 1961), but in Fiji a unique colonial policy sought to ensure the indigenous Fijians' welfare by delimiting the area and tenancy permitted to Indian settlement off estates (Mayer 1953; 1961). In South Africa, legislation specifically restricted the movement and settlement of Indians, such that 80% came to live in Natal, where they were permitted to purchase only 0.01% of the land (Kuper 1960; 1969). Only in Jamaica were ex-indentured South Asian migrants widely dispersed – though rurally – because their collective settlement was spatially diluted by a large and rurally well-established African ex-slave population (Ehrlich 1971). In East and Central Africa, conversely, where South Asians were nearly exclusively merchants (and there were restrictive local settlement policies), the migrants were almost entirely to be found in cosmopolitan, urban settings (Morris 1968; Dotson and Dotson 1968; Ghai 1970). A similar settlement pattern applied to the Indian administrators in Southeast Asia, in contraposition to Indian labourers on rubber plantations (Jain 1970).

As far as a colonial management system for South Asian migrants was concerned, little infrastructure existed. In each colony a Protector of Immigrants was supposed to look after the welfare of the South Asians. Whether concerning the contract labourers, merchants, or clerical personnel, the colonial attitude toward South Asian migrants was generally one of favouritism towards what was perceived as a useful segment of the population. Overall, however, there was an 'assimilationist philosophy' among the imperial powers (Tinker 1982), and they usually paid little heed to overseas South Asians' grievances or aspirations (Tinker 1975). Indian authorities, though, did display much interest in the plight of their overseas sons and daughters: Indian nationalists played a large part in the abolition of the indenture system recommended by specially commissioned reports (MacNeill and Lal 1914), and after India's independence in 1947, Indian commissioners were sent to Trinidad, Mauritius and Fiji.

(2) Cultural composition

The population involved in each type of migration during the colonial period was quite diverse. In terms of *religion*, the great majority (perhaps 85%) of indentured and other contract labourers were Hindu – though this was complicated by internal traditions of Vaishnavism (predominantly North Indian), Shaivism (predominantly South Indian), and Shaktism (mainly Bengali and South Indian), as well as by numerous sects. Although Sunni Muslims comprised a smaller proportion of contract labour migrants, many traders and administrators were of this faith. Sikhs were brought under indenture to East Africa to construct the Kenya–Uganda railway; those who stayed were joined by Sikh traders and others who served the colonies in the police and militia.

The range of *languages* spoken by South Asian emigrants was very broad, and was, of course, determined by their regions of origin (Map Intro. 2). Most indentured workers who embarked for foreign colonies came from Hindi-speaking North India, especially Bihar and the Northwest Provinces (today's Uttar Pradesh); there, a large number of lesser

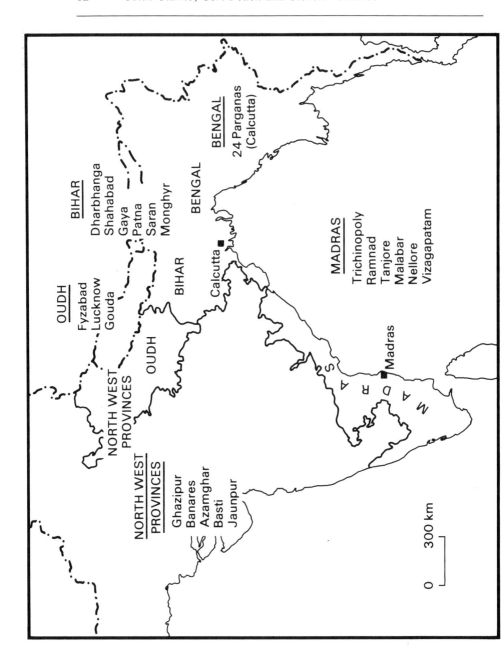

languages and dialects predominated from region to region (such as Varendra, Bhojpuri and Magahi). A smaller proportion of indentured migrants, but practically all of the *maistry* and *kangani* labourers, were from Tamil or Telugu-speaking South India. (Tamils were also the main migrants into the French islands, as Singaravélou explains in chapter 3.) South Asians who settled in East and Central Africa were overwhelmingly Gujaratis and Punjabis, as were many of the traders who travelled to South Africa, Mauritius and Fiji. In many places where North Indians predominated, a blending of languages produced a creolised 'plantation Hindustani' (Domingue 1971; Durbin 1973; Tinker 1974). In the years since their transplantation, however, most South Asian languages have fallen into disuse in favour of creole variants of French or English.

Over the years many South Asian communities have experienced a high *degree of 'cultural homogenisation'*, due to the clustering together of once regionally distinct peoples and their residence in comparative isolation from non-South Asians. This has been especially marked among North Indians in the case of religion (Vertovec 1988b; van der Veer and Vertovec n.d.). A cultural divide has often remained between North and South Indians in places where they arrived in comparable numbers, such as Fiji (Mayer 1961), though among both groups traditional customs and traits have attenuated overseas and elements of local culture have been adopted.

The *caste* composition of South Asian migrants in the nineteenth and early twentieth centuries was highly complex, due to the vast territories from which they were drawn. Regarding indentured migrants, however, most scholars agree that their caste makeup well reflected that of their regions of origin (Smith 1959; Lal 1979). In practically every context of post-indentured settlement, the caste system disintegrated and caste consciousness waned (Schwartz 1967). The reasons for this are manifold, but some of the most critical factors include: the absence of occupational specialisation, precise ritual roles, and inter-caste dependence (*jajmani*) in the new setting; the confusion of purity–pollution notions due to caste co-residence and commensality on estates; and, perhaps most importantly, the inability to recreate local caste hierarchies because of the breadth of the geographic area from which migrants came. Yet among the urban-based merchants and civil servants in Africa, caste consciousness remained high even though a system of caste-based interaction and exchange ceased to function. This fact led Kuper (1960: 30) to argue that caste awareness can survive if members: '(1) can maintain a ritual exclusiveness from the time they leave India; (2) hold a privileged position in the economic organization and avoid proletarianisation; (3) retain ties with a protected caste nucleus in India, and (4) isolate their women from intimate cross-caste contact'. Such conditions were only pertinent to the urban traders and administrators (Twaddle, chapter 7), as opposed to contract labourers and peasants, and these principles apply equally for the South Asian migrants in the contemporary period.

(3) Social structure and political power
Following their respective courses of migration, South Asian peoples have found themselves in a variety of *ethnically plural* contexts. South Asians comprised 2% of the total population of Kenya, but 70% of that of Mauritius; in Suriname, they share the country with at least a half dozen other ethnic groups, yet in Fiji, the population has been virtually bifurcated between South Asians (49%) and indigenous Fijians (46%). Moreover, South Asians overseas have generally been associated with an economic niche, as, indeed, have other groups in these plural societies. Besides occupation, other roles have been determined by migration and ethnicity among South Asians, notably those doubly subordinate gender ones played by indentured women (Beall, chapter 2; Lal 1985; Emmer 1986).

In most colonial and post-colonial societies, *class composition* has fitted within the framework of ethnic pluralism. Wherever South Asians have migrated as contract-bound manual workers – subsequently becoming rural agriculturalists – they have been relegated to the bottom of the local class hierarchy. Hence, Indian-dominated trade unions have had an impact on events in Trinidad, Guyana, Mauritius, and Malaysia (Tinker 1977). Where Gujarati and Punjabi merchants have travelled, they have become the established urban middle class – often acting as 'buffers' between the white upper class and the autochthonous working class, as in Africa. Occasionally, overseas South Asians have even formed part of the elite in colonial territories: before the Second World War, Indian 'imperial auxiliaries' in Burma accounted for well over half the country's doctors and bankers, and a third of its public administrators (Chakravarti 1971).

Regardless of South Asians' class designation, many societies have practised *institutionalised racism* against them. This has ranged from generally subtle forms – as in Trinidad, where discrimination has been identified in many public sectors (Harewood 1971) – to the most blatant discrimination encountered, predictably under *apartheid* in South Africa (Palmer 1957). Other examples of measures taken to curb overseas South Asians are the spin-offs from national policies introduced to favour 'sons of the soil' (such as Africanisation in Kenya and Uganda, and *bumiputra* in Malaysia). In this volume, Lal (chapter 5) gives a detailed account of the disadvantaged situation of Indians in Fiji – both before and after the coups of 1987 – the object of which was to exclude them from government.

With the exception of the middle-class Indian minorities in East Africa and Malaysia (Tinker 1977), access to representation and power through *involvement in party politics* has been the strategy of many overseas South Asians. They have experienced both successes and failures (Milne 1981; Vasil 1984). Indian-backed parties sprang up in many colonial territories following the Second World War as constitutional decolonisation began. However, since then, many Indian parties have struggled almost as much with internal communalism (especially along lines of religion) as with their programmes and campaigns. Some were doomed to eternal opposition (the Democratic Labour Party in Trinidad), some tasted victory only fleetingly (the People's Progressive Party in British Guiana), others eventually came to power on their own (the Labour Party in Mauritius), or in coalitions (the Verenigde Hindostaanse Partij in Suriname, and the United Labour Front in Trinidad). Everywhere, the nature of South Asian political involvement has had ramifications for their development as distinct ethnic communities, and this is true also of South Africa, where, as Lemon shows (chapter 6), Indians have refused to comply with the tri-cameral legislative system introduced by the National Party government.

(4) Community development
A collective sense of ethnic identity has been cultivated by, and imposed on, communities of South Asians in their various colonial and post-colonial contexts. Competition for control over resources, geographical segregation, political organisation, and efforts to maintain cultural traditions in alien milieux are some of the important elements contributing to the migrant communities' development. A variety of *organisations* or associations have been founded among South Asians in each setting to provide religious activities and guidance, to establish ties and networks of all kinds, to arrange savings schemes and funeral societies, to build recreational and social centres, to produce South Asian cultural events, to promote links with South Asia, and to liaise with non-South Asian organisations. Among South Asians overseas, such organisations can be seen as 'the main units making for internal cohesion in a minority group' (Kuper 1960: 84), representing legal and responsible modes of activity in the eyes of others, while serving as 'rallying points of communal sentiment' (ibid.: 85; Mayer 1956; Benedict 1961; Morris 1968; Malik 1971). Vertovec (chapter 4) describes how community religious activities are institutionalised among Indians in Trinidad and provide the basis for a flourishing of ethnic pride.

Through South Asian organisations, major *leaders* have emerged to stimulate and coordinate community pursuits and interests; by the same token, however, leaders have sometimes deeply divided their communities

by advocating communalism or factionalism within their ranks (Firth *et al.*
1957; Milne 1981). No less a personality than Gandhi (in South Africa)
made his career as a South Asian leader; prominent but lesser lights include
Ramgoolam of Mauritius, Lachmon of Suriname, and Jagan of Guyana.
Ethnic relations in colonial and post-colonial contexts have fluctuated in
locus, content and intensity. Like all migrants, South Asians overseas
have been treated as outsiders because of their different habits and beliefs.
The manner in which ethnicity is expressed among overseas South Asians
– their social boundary markers – are conditioned by a number of factors.
Jayawardena (1980) has suggested that Indian ethnicity is more 'public' in
Guyana, where they live in close contact with Creoles and others, whereas
in Fiji it is more 'private', since their relative isolation from ethnic Fijians
has called for little display of symbols of difference. In contrast, Tinker
(chapter 1) notes that due to tense ethnic relations in Burma, the
remaining Indians in Rangoon have deliberately concealed most outward
signs of ethnic identity and have become an 'invisible community'. In rigid
plural societies, such as in East and South Africa or Malaysia, ethnic
relations have been minimal save for economic interaction. In others, such
as in the Caribbean, both urban and rural settings have seen daily
interaction between Indians and African- or Chinese-descended peoples.
Almost everywhere, mutual suspicion characterises the generalised
opinion of Indian and other ethnic groups about one another, but
interpersonal relationships are usually friendly. Yet, South Asians have
also been the victims of race violence: in Guyana in the early 1960s, in
Malaysia in the late 1960s, in Uganda in the early 1970s, and in Fiji during
the late 1980s.

Finally, the *scale* of overseas South Asian communities has played a
major part in their historical development in each setting. Among
ex-indentured populations, their rapid natural increase deeply concerned
administrators and raised fears among non-South Asians of demographic
'swamping' – a factor negatively affecting ethnic relations. Among the
merchant migrants, their numbers remained few, but they were concentrated in urban areas: for example, though they accounted for only 2% of
Kenya's population, Indians still managed to provide 30% of Nairobi's
total. Generally, communal fissioning has taken place only to a limited
degree among contract-bound labourers and their descendants; these
divides have been mainly along Hindu–Muslim lines and between those of
North and South Indian origins. Among the merchant migrants, however,
much more sectarian and particularly caste-based community fission has
occurred. Morris (1968) has attributed this latter situation to four factors:
(1) proximity to India (allowing for easy communication and links with
specific social groups there); (2) a favourable political atmosphere allow-

ing for consolidation of smaller groups; (3) the existence of a 'pace-making' group who organise themselves communally, thus motivating others to do so; and (4) the ambitions of leaders (who promote their own ends by way of advocating communal interests).

A brief comparison of all these factors with more recent migrations of South Asians reveals many striking contrasts.

Contemporary western and Middle Eastern contexts

The contemporary period of South Asian migration and overseas settlement began early this century, but accelerated especially after the Second World War. While much of the actual movement of South Asian peoples abroad has slowed considerably during the last few years, their variegated development as ethnic communities continues dynamically. Much research has been published and is currently under way concerning contemporary overseas South Asians, and the following summary only points to some of their most salient features.

(1) Migration processes and factors of settlement

Unlike the migrations in colonial times, the main *types of migration* in the contemporary period have been more sequential. The first trickle of South Asians to places like Britain occurred during the period of the Raj and involved sailors, students and emissaries (Visram 1986). However, major influxes of South Asians to Britain did not take place until the 1950s and early 1960s, when emptying cities and an expanding economy called for more labour (Robinson, chapter 12; Robinson 1980). The Ballards (1977) have outlined a general sequence of South Asian settlement in Britain for this period, in which individual male 'pioneers' came and found work, lived together in shared houses, gradually brought over their family members, and eventually re-established their families and accumulated material assets in the new context. Chain migration was the key feature of South Asian transplantation in this period (Dahya 1973).

Towards the end of the 1960s and during the early 1970s, a comparatively new kind of overseas South Asian community arose, that of the 'twice migrant' (Bhachu 1985).[5] The bulk of these were South Asians who had lived for decades or generations in East Africa, but who were induced or forced to leave *en masse* due to radical Africanisation programmes introduced by the Kenyan and Ugandan governments (Twaddle, chapter 7 and 1975; Tandon and Raphael 1984). Also at this time, many Indians from other post-colonial settings migrated to western countries for economic reasons, especially to Canada from the West Indies (Ramcharan

1983) and from Fiji (Buchignani 1983), and to the Netherlands from Suriname (van Amersfoort 1970). Following the oil boom period of the mid-1970s, the Middle East has witnessed a massive injection of South Asian workers, a phenomenon Knerr explores (chapter 8). Also, beginning in the 1960s, but increasing dramatically in the 1970s and 1980s, a new type of South Asian migrant population has come to the fore, composed of well educated, highly professional and affluent South Asians who have made their way to the United States (Bhardwaj and Rao, chapter 9), Canada (Buchignani and Indra 1985), and Australia (Helweg n.d.). Yet given the world recession since the early 1980s (and given mounting racism or ethnic unrest), most Western countries have recently clamped down on the immigration of South Asians and, indeed, all foreigners.

In contrast to the ex-indentured populations, South Asian migrants in contemporary times have been able – because of their comparative affluence and world-wide improvements in communications – to maintain extensive *ties with South Asia*: marriage arrangements, kinship networks, property, and religious affiliations keep many migrants well-linked to their places of origin in the sub-continent, especially as a large number are still first-generation migrants. Kelly for example (chapter 11) has provided a detailed account of family connections between Gujarat and Lancashire. The benefits of migration, in the form of remittances, also play a significant role in keeping many overseas South Asians connected to persons in the homeland; in fact, remittances from abroad can even represent critical aspects of the local economy in parts of South Asia itself (Knerr, chapter 8; Helweg 1983).

Economic activities of contemporary South Asians are only gradually changing from their original post-migration patterns, and much the same can be said of their *geographical features of settlement*. Robinson (chapter 12) describes the trends in immigrant employment and South Asian settlement in Britain during the eras of postwar economic expansion and recent collapse, pointing out that British South Asians thus far have moved only marginally out of conurbation-centred, manual-labouring livelihoods (especially in textiles, steel, and transport). Restricted availability of housing has been a major factor in the segregated settlement of South Asians in Britain (Robinson 1986). Indians in the USA contrast markedly with their British counterparts. These widely dispersed South Asians are probably the most affluent ethnic group in the USA, and are largely professionals concentrated in medicine, engineering, and the natural sciences (Saran and Eames 1980). Recent South Asian migrants to Australia and Canada follow a similar occupational pattern, though their place of residence is more markedly clustered in the largest cities than it is in the USA. In the Middle East, the need for unskilled South Asian labourers has been eclipsed by the requirement for skilled ones, but for both groups spatial segregation has been enjoined. The 'twice migrants' from East Africa, now settled in Britain and elsewhere, have fared well in urban, middle-class occupations such as shopkeeping; many arrived with experience in this field, plus the capital to invest in businesses.

National *infrastructures* pertaining to the migration and settlement of South Asians have varied from country to country and over the years. Various Immigration Acts in Britain, particularly in 1962, 1968, and 1971 served in many ways to curtail the rights and status of South Asians seeking to migrate or actually moving to the United Kingdom (Marrington 1987). Only for Ugandan Asians, following their expulsion by Amin in 1971, was a special body created to serve in their settlement (Swinerton, Kueppert and Lackey 1975). Both Canada and Australia have, more actively than Britain, pursued policies aimed at integrating South Asian migrants into their societies (Buchignani and Indra 1985; de Lepervanche 1984). Migrants in the Persian Gulf, on the other hand, have been influenced in their migration – and in their residence and rapid turnover – more by the nature of their contracts than by governmental structures (Owen 1985).

(2) Cultural composition

Contemporary South Asian migrants have in many ways paralleled their nineteenth-century colonial counterparts in terms of their cultural complexity, but they have been drawn from very different regions of the sub-continent (Map Intro. 3) and have tended to settle more often in discrete regional-linguistic groupings rather than in heterogeneous enclaves.

As in the South Asian sub-continent, *religion, language*, and *region of origin* are closely intertwined among South Asian migrants (Knott n.d.). Of Britain's 1,271,000 South Asians, Muslims account for 44% and two-thirds of them are Urdu-speaking Pakistanis. The balance is made up of Bangladeshis and Gujarati or Punjabi Indians in almost equal numbers. Similarly, the 30% of British South Asians who are Hindu are over two-thirds Gujarati (the remainder is composed of equal proportions of Punjabis and other Indians). Sikhs – practically all Punjabi – comprise just over 20% of the British South Asian population. To complicate matters, many of the above are 'twice migrants' with experience in East Africa (most are Gujarati and Punjabi Hindus, or Gujarati and Punjabi Muslims and Sikhs). The complexity of South Asian community composition has led Robinson (1986) to define no less than twelve religious-ethno-linguistic groups present in the UK.[6] Ballard (chapter 10) demonstrates how two

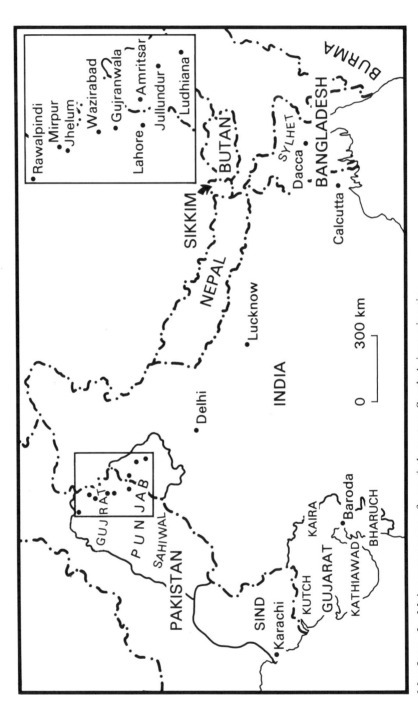

Map Intro. 3   Main source areas of twentieth-century South Asian emigration

culturally differing groups (though originating less than 200 miles apart) have experienced very different patterns of migration and settlement, while Bhardwaj and Rao (chapter 9) show that the new, highly professional immigrants to other Western countries come from an even more complex set of backgrounds.

Caste has remained an important source of identification for some groups in the modern South Asian diaspora (largely for reasons suggested above by Kuper). While a functioning system of caste-based relationships no longer exists overseas, awareness of caste membership is maintained either through self-proclaimed pride or through accusations about other people's low status (Michaelson 1979; Bhachu 1985). Caste affiliation, religious sectarianism, and regionalism have usually undermined tendencies toward *cultural homogenisation*. Although some blending of regional traditions within Hinduism has occurred in Britain (Knott 1987), Canada (Wood 1980), and the United States (Bhardwaj and Rao 1983), exclusive practices and associations have nonetheless developed among overseas Hindu groups (Bowen 1987; Barot 1987). In relation to this theme, Werbner (chapter 12) critically discusses the meaning of ethnic 'community' and ethnic divisions among British Pakistanis (Dahya 1974).

(3) Social structure and political power
The nature of *ethnic pluralism*, the political responses of governments to the existence of plural societies, and the place of South Asian communities within them have varied considerably among the receiving countries.[7] In Britain, Canada, and Australia, steps toward 'multiculturalism' have been taken officially; in the United States, experts have begun to reassess the 'melting pot' ideal of that society, though some believe the new immigrants will ultimately not differ in settlement behaviour, social integration, and spatial de-segregation from immigrants in former periods (Fuchs 1984).

Migrants to Australia, Canada, and the USA have tended to be characterised by high-status occupations. Most South Asians who initially came to Britain in the 1950s and 1960s were manual labourers, though their occupational distribution now resembles more closely that of the white British population (Peach *et al.* 1988). However, *institutionalised racism*, particularly in housing (Brown 1984), has meant they have been associated with a low position in Britain's *class structure*, and therefore confront great difficulties in achieving other forms of social mobility. The role and status of South Asian women are also greatly affected by this state of affairs (Saifullah-Khan 1975; Ghosh 1983), as are the possibilities facing second-generation South Asians, who are also confronted with difficult, culturally conflicting lifestyle choices (Thompson 1974). The basis for the close association between race and class among South Asians in Britain is widely debated among social scientists, but the issue is too complex to be drawn out here; some attribute it to local settlement histories, others to the nature of late imperialism and the demands of the international division of labour (Rex and Moore 1967; Rex and Tomlinson 1979). Robinson (chapter 12) touches on these themes in his treatment of the place of South Asians in the expansion and contraction of the British economy.

Though still somewhat limited, the political participation of British South Asians seems more pronounced than in other contexts of contemporary migration (Anwar 1986), and this may be due in no small part to their present low status (as opposed to the affluence of other overseas South Asians). Steps are being taken by British South Asians to increase their *involvement in party politics*, and Anwar (chapter 13) provides a national overview, while Eade (chapter 14) gives a complementary account of political dynamics among South Asians (Bangladeshis) at the local level. Among all South Asian communities – including those in post-colonial contexts – socio-economic repression has stimulated political involvement and opposition while middle-class or elite status has abated it (Hintzen 1983). Indeed, Tinker (1977: 14) has written:

> The diversity – and to some extent division – of Asian communities overseas, emphasized by religious and linguistic differences, is accentuated by economic differentiation: the aims and interests of the prosperous, urban, middle-class Asians are quite different from those of poor workers – labourers and artisans. The first group are likely to adopt a social and political philosophy of accommodation and adjustment to Western norms; the mass of the poor, especially the rural poor, will live in conditions of isolation which can only be ameliorated by protest or even revolt.

(4) Community development

Regardless of their activities in political spheres, contemporary South Asian migrants have almost without fail established a range of *organisations* wherever they have settled. Most of these, however, have taken considerable time to evolve, and several have gone through phases of expansion, contraction, division and merger, whether instituted for purposes of religion (Bowen 1987), community service (Buchignani and Indra 1985) or labour relations (John 1969). Arising from such community organisations, important *leaders* have come to the fore. Recognition and status within traditional spheres, as well as a genuine concern with community interests, often provide motivations for such potential and actual leaders (Shaw 1988, n.d.). Werbner (chapter 15) gives useful examples of problems surrounding British Pakistani organisations, leaders, and Community Relations Councils. She also notes how such organisations and leaders can become involved in conflict-ridden *ethnic relations*. In all major cases of contemporary overseas South Asian settlement – in Britain, Canada, Australia, and the United States – South Asians have not escaped racial discrimination and abuse. In Britain, moreover, they have themselves been party to racially instigated riots (Peach 1986). Multicultural policies may in the long run assist in the process of fair and equal incorporation of immigrants (Rex 1987), but the current state of poor ethnic relations in Britain requires much more than legislation to change it.

One method by which South Asian groups have protected themselves against abuse has been through social and geographical clustering (Gordon 1986). This has had a large impact on the *scale* of South Asian communities found in Britain today.

> Asians still remain tightly residentially clustered in cities such as Bradford, Blackburn and Leicester, and where systematic diach-ronic analysis has been undertaken, results indicate rising levels of segregation in the early and mid-1970s, and only slightly reduced levels since. Clustering serves not only a defensive function against racial harassment, but also provides a market for community services such as Mosques and Gurdwaras, ethnic food stores and other specialist retailers. It also allows the re-creation of dense traditional social networks with all the implications this has for quality of life and transmission of culture. It is hardly surprising that attempts to disperse the Asian population have not been successful.
>
> (Peach *et al.* 1988: 592)

Conclusion

Although the total number of overseas South Asians is modest by international comparison, they are found in a wide array of geographical, social, economic and political contexts. The various overseas communi-ties, which in a few receiving countries now form the largest racial group, have evolved differently from one another and from distant kinsmen in their original homeland. This introductory chapter, and indeed the whole layout of the book, has been structured around the broad differences between nineteenth-century colonial and twentieth-century western migrants from South Asia. However, a set of even more general propositions are implicit in the study of the South Asian diaspora, and merit re-statement.

Key overarching variables which condition the outcome of South Asian migration are: the nature and period of migration; the size of the migrating group relative to others comprising the receiving society; the internal complexity of the South Asian group; their consolidation in enclaves or otherwise; the fission or fusion of South Asians in their subsequent social organisation, cultural practice, and quest for political power; the politico-legal approach of the dominant community toward the incorporation of South Asians; and the social distance between the South Asians and other segments of the receiving society.

The diverse combinations of these dependent variables have collectively produced a fascinating set of world-wide cases, which challenge students to assess the relative strength of the forces that have facilitated or stifled ethnic community development among South Asians overseas. The studies brought together in this book enable the reader to compare similarities and differences arising from the South Asian diaspora with particular reference to the two basic themes of migration and ethnicity.

Notes

1 General and comparative overviews of the South Asian diaspora since the nineteenth century include Gangulee 1947; Kondapi 1951; Cumpston 1953; Jayawardena 1968; Tinker 1974, 1976, 1977.
2 The following comparative framework is based on Vertovec 1988.
3 There is a great deal of scholarship and documentation pertaining to indentured migration from India, including materials on political manoeuvres of planters and colonial administrations, public opinion, recruitment and contract procedures, shipment, plantation conditions. A few of the most comprehensive sources include the Protector of Emigrants Annual Reports, the Sanderson Report (British Parliamentary Papers 1910); Erickson 1930; Cumpston 1953, 1956; Saha 1970; Tinker 1974; Lal 1980; Carter 1987.
4 Important discussions and analyses of the contrasts between South Asian contract labourers and free merchant migrants are given in Kuper 1960, 1969; Morris 1968; Dotson and Dotson 1968; Tinker 1977; and Lemon 1980.
5 The South Asian 'twice migrant' was not so new when one considers the movement of Indians from Fiji to New Zealand, which had taken place since the end of indentured migration in 1917 and continues up to today (Tiwari 1980).
6 These are: Rural East African Gujarati Muslims, Urban East African Gujarati Muslims, Rural Indian Gujarati Muslims, Urban Indian Gujarati Muslims, East African Urdu-speaking Muslims, Indian Urdu-speaking Muslims, East African Gujarati Hindus, Pakistani Urdu-speaking Muslims, Urban Pakistani Punjabi Muslims, Rural Pakistani Punjabi Muslims and Punjabi Sikhs. Moreover, this is certainly not an exhaustive list of possible South Asian migrant categories in Britain.

7 A special issue of *New Community* (vol. 14, no. 1/2, 1987) reviews legislation, policies, and research on ethnic groups in Britain, and includes comparative treatment of parallel phenomena in Australia, Canada, and the United States.

References

Anwar, Muhammad 1979. *The Myth of Return*, London: Heinemann.
1986. *Race and Politics*, London: Tavistock.
Arasaratnam, Sinappah 1970. *Indians in Malaysia and Singapore*, Bombay: Oxford University Press.
Ballard, R. and C. 1977. 'The Sikhs – the development of South Asian settlement in Britain', in *Between Two Cultures*, ed. James L. Watson, Oxford: Blackwell, 21–56.
Barot, Rohit 1987. 'Caste and sect in the Swaminarayan movement', in *Hinduism in Great Britain*, ed. Richard Burghart, London: Tavistock, 67–80.
Barth, Fredrik 1969. 'Introduction', in *Ethnic Groups and Boundaries*, ed. Fredrik Barth, Oslo: Universitetsforlaget, 9–38.
Benedict, Burton 1961. *Indians in a Plural Society*, London: HMSO.
Bhachu, Parminder 1985. *Twice Migrants: East African Sikh Settlers in Britain*, London: Tavistock.
Bhardwaj, Surinder M. and Madhusudana N. Rao 1983. 'Religious reknitting of ethnic Hindus in the "new world"'. Paper presented at the annual meeting, Association of American Geographers.
British Parliamentary Papers 1910. *Report of the Committee on Emigration from India to the Crown Colonies and Protectorates* (a.k.a. the Sanderson Report), 27 (c. 5194).
Brown, C. 1984. *Black and White Britain*, London: Heinemann.
Buchignani, Norman 1983. 'Determinants of Fijian Indian social organization in Canada' in *Overseas Indians*, ed. G. Kurian and R.P. Srivastava, New Delhi: Vikas, 68–89.
Buchignani, N. and D.M. Indra 1985. *Continuous Journey: A Social History of South Asians in Canada*, Toronto: MacLelland & Steward.
Carter, Marina 1987. 'Indian labour migration to Mauritius and the indenture experience', D.Phil. thesis, University of Oxford.
Chakravarti, N.R. 1971. *The Indian Minority in Burma*, London: Oxford University Press.
Cumpston, I. 1953. *Indians Overseas in British Territories 1834–1865*, London: Oxford University Press.
1956. 'A survey of Indian immigration to British tropical colonies to 1910', *Population Studies*, 10: 158–65.
Dahya, Badr 1973. 'Pakistanis in Britain: transients or settlers', *Race*, 14: 241–7.
1974. 'The nature of Pakistani ethnicity in industrial cities in Britain', in *Urban Ethnicity*, ed. Abner Cohen, London: Tavistock, 77–118.
Davis, Kingsley 1951. *The Population of India and Pakistan*, Princeton University Press.
de Lepervanche, Marie M. 1984. *Indians in a White Australia*, Sydney: Allen & Unwin.
Deerr, Noel 1938. 'Indian labour in the sugar industry', *International Sugar Journal*, 40: 94–8.

Despres, Leo 1969. 'Differential adaptations and micro-evolution in Guyana', *Southwestern Journal of Anthropology*, 25: 14–44.

Domingue, Nicole 1971. 'Bhojpuri and Creole in Mauritius', Ph.D. thesis, University of Texas, Austin.

Dotson, Floyd and Lillian O. Dotson 1968. *The Indian Minority of Zambia, Rhodesia, and Malawi*, New Haven: Yale University Press.

Durbin, Mridula Adenwala 1973. 'Formal changes in Trinidad Hindi as a result of language adaptation', *American Anthropologist*, 75: 1290–304.

The Economist 1984. *The World in Figures* (4th edn), London: *The Economist*.

Ehrlich, Allen S. 1971. 'History, ecology, and demography in the British Caribbean: an analysis of East Indian ethnicity', *Southwestern Journal of Anthropology*, 27: 166–88.

Erickson, Edgar S. 1930. 'East Indian coolies in the West Indies', Ph.D. thesis, University of Indiana.

Firth, Raymond, David Pocock, H.S. Morris, Adrian Mayer, Burton Benedict 1957. 'Factions in Indian and overseas Indian societies', *British Journal of Sociology*, 8: 291–342.

Fuchs, L.A. 1984. 'Cultural pluralism and the future of American unity', *International Migration Review*, 18: 800–13.

Furnivall, J.S. 1939. *Netherlands India*, Cambridge University Press.

Gangulee, N. 1947. *Indians in the Empire Overseas*, London: New India.

Ghai, Yash 1970. *Portrait of a Minority: Asians in East Africa*, Nairobi: Oxford University Press.

Ghosh, Ratna 1983. 'Sarees and the maple leaf: Indian women in Canada', in *Overseas Indians*, ed. G. Kurian and R.P. Srivastava, New Delhi: Vikas, 90–9.

Gordon, P. 1986. *Racial Violence and Harassment*, London: Runnymede Trust.

Gregory, Robert G. 1971. *India and East Africa*, Oxford: Clarendon.

Harewood, Jack 1971. 'Racial discrimination in employment in Trinidad and Tobago', *Social and Economic Studies*, 20: 267–93.

Helweg, Arthur 1983. 'Emigrant remittances: their nature and impact on a Punjabi village', *New Community*, 10: 435–44.

n.d. 'Indians in Australia: theory and methodology of the new immigration', in *Aspects of the South Asian Diaspora, Oxford University Papers on India*, vol. II, no. 2, ed. Steven Vertovec, New Delhi: Oxford University Press (forthcoming).

Hintzen, Percy 1983. 'Bases of elite support for a regime: race, ideology and clientelism as bases for leaders in Guyana and Trinidad', *Comparative Political Studies*, 16: 363–91.

Jain, Ravindra K. 1970. *South Asians on the Plantation Frontier in Malaya*, New Haven: Yale University Press.

Jayawardena, Chandra 1963. *Conflict and Solidarity in a Guianese Plantation*, London: Athlone.

1968. 'Migration and social change: a survey of Indian communities overseas', *Geographical Review*, 58: 426–49.

1973. 'Migrants, networks and identities', *New Community*, 2: 353–7.

1980. 'Culture and ethnicity in Guyana and Fiji', *Man* (ns), 15: 430–50.

John, D.W. 1969. *Indian Workers Associations in Great Britain*, London: Oxford University Press.

Knott, Kim 1987. 'Hindu temple rituals in Britain: the reinterpretation of tradition', in *Hinduism in Great Britain*, ed. Richard Burghart, London: Tavistock, 157–79.

n.d. 'Bound to change? The religions of South Asians in Britain', in *Aspects of the South Asian Diaspora, Oxford University Papers on India*, vol. II, no. 2, ed. Steven Vertovec, New Delhi: Oxford University Press (forthcoming).

Kondapi, C. 1951. *Indians Overseas 1838–1949*, Bombay: Oxford University Press.

Kuper, Hilda 1961. *Indian People in Natal*, Durban: Natal University Press.

1969. '"Strangers" in plural societies: Asians in South Africa and Uganda', in *Pluralism in Africa*, ed. L. Kuper and M.G. Smith, Berkeley: University of California Press, 247–82.

Lal, Brij V. 1979. 'Fiji *girmitiyas*: the background to banishment', in *Rama's Banishment*, ed. Vijay Mishra, Auckland: Heinemann, 12–39.

1985. 'Kunti's cry: indentured women on Fiji plantations', *Indian Economic and Social History Review*, 42: 55–71.

Lemon, Anthony 1980. 'The Indian communities of East Africa and the Caribbean', in *Studies in Overseas Settlement and Population*, ed. A. Lemon and N. Pollock, London: Longman, 225–41.

MacNeill, J. and C. Lal 1914. *Report on the Condition of Indian Immigrants in the Four British Colonies: Trinidad, British Guiana or Demarara, Jamaica and Fiji, and in the Dutch Colony of Surinam or Dutch Guiana*, Simla: Government Central Press.

Malik, Yogendra 1971. *East Indians in Trinidad*, London: Oxford University Press.

Marrington, Dave 1987. 'From primary right to secondary privilege: an essay in British immigration law', *New Community*, 14: 76–82.

Mayer, Adrian 1953. 'The organization of Indian settlement in Fiji', *Man*, 53: (Art. 284), 182–5.

1956. 'Associations in Fiji Indian rural society', *American Anthropologist*, 58: 97–108.

1961. *Peasants in the Pacific*, London: Routledge and Kegan Paul.

Michaelson, Maureen 1979. 'The relevance of caste among East African Gujaratis in Britain', *New Community*, 7: 350–60.

Milne, R.S. 1981. *Politics in Ethnically Bipolar States*, Vancouver: University of British Columbia Press.

Morris, H.S. 1968. *The Indians of Uganda*, London: Weidenfeld & Nicolson.

Owen, Roger 1985. *Migrant Workers in the Gulf*, London: Minority Rights Group.

Palmer, Mabel 1957. *The History of the Indians in Natal*, Cape Town: Oxford University Press.

Park, Robert E. 1950. *Race and Culture*, Glencoe, Ill.: Free Press.

Peach, Ceri 1984. 'A geographical perspective on the 1981 summer riots in England', *Ethnic and Racial Studies*, 9: 396–411.

Peach, C., V. Robinson, J. Maxted and J. Chance 1988. 'Immigration and ethnicity', in *British Social Trends*, ed. A.H. Halsey, London: Macmillan, 561–615.

Ramcharan, Subnas 1983. 'The social, economic and cultural adaptations of East Indians from the British Caribbean and Guyana to Canada', in *Overseas Indians*, ed. G. Kurian and R.P. Srivastava, New Delhi: Vikas, 51–67.

Rex, J. A. 1987. 'The concept of a multi-cultural society', *New Community*, 14: 218–29.

Rex, J.A. and R. Moore 1967. *Race, Community and Conflict*, Oxford: Oxford University Press.

Rex, J.A. and S. Tomlinson 1979. *Colonial Immigrants in a British City*, London: Routledge and Kegan Paul.

Richardson, Bonham 1975. 'Plantation infrastructure and labor mobility in Guyana and Trinidad', in *Migration and Development*, ed. Helen Safa and Brian M. DuToit, The Hague: Mouton, 205–24.

Roberts, G.W. and J. Byrne 1966. 'Summary statistics on indenture and associated migration affecting the West Indies 1834–1918', *Population Studies*, 20: 125–34.

Robinson, Vaughan 1980. 'Correlates of Asian immigration to Britain', *New Community*, 8: 115–23.

    1986. *Transients, Settlers and Refugees: Asians in Britain*, Oxford: Clarendon.

Saha, Panchanan 1970. *Emigration of Indian Labour 1834–1900*, Delhi: People's Publishers.

Saifullah-Khan, Verity 1975. 'Asian women in Britain: strategies of adjustment of Indian and Pakistani migrants', in *Women in Contemporary India*, ed. A. de Souza, New Delhi: Manohar.

Saran, P. and E. Eames (eds.) 1980. *The New Ethnics: Asian Indians in the United States*, New York: Praeger.

Schwartz, Barton M. (ed.) 1967. *Caste in Overseas Indian Communities*, San Francisco: Chandler.

Shaw, Alison 1988. *A Pakistani Community in Britain*, Oxford: Blackwell.

    n.d. 'The making of a Pakistani community leader in Britain', in *Aspects of the South Asian Diaspora, Oxford University Papers on India*, vol. II, no. 2, ed. Steven Vertovec, New Delhi: Oxford University Press (forthcoming).

Singaravélou 1975. *Les Indiéns de la Guadeloupe*, Bordeaux: Imprimerie Deniaud.

Smith, M.G. 1969. 'Some developments in the analytical framework of pluralism', in *Pluralism in Africa*, ed. L. Kuper and M.G. Smith, Berkeley: University of California Press, 415–58.

Smith, R.T. 1959. 'Some social characteristics of Indian immigrants to British Guiana', *Population Studies*, 13: 34–9.

Speckmann, Johan D. 1965. *Marriage and Kinship among Indians in Surinam*, Assen: van Gorcum.

Swinerton, E.N., W.G. Kuepper and G.L. Lackey 1975. *Ugandan Asians in Great Britain*, London: Croom Helm.

Tandon, Yash and Arnold Raphael 1984. *The New Position of East Africa's Asians*, London: Minority Rights Group.

Thompson, M.A. 1974. 'The second generation – Punjabi or English?', *New Community*, 3: 242–8.

Tinker, Hugh 1974. *A New System of Slavery: The Export of Indian Labour Overseas 1830–1920*, London: Oxford University Press.

    1975. 'Indians abroad: emigration, restriction, and rejection', in *Expulsion of a Minority*, ed. Michael Twaddle, London: Athlone, 15–29.

    1976. *Separate and Unequal: India and the Indians in the British Commonwealth 1920–1950*, London: C. Hurst & Co.

    1977. *The Banyan Tree: Overseas Emigrants from India, Pakistan and Bangladesh*, Oxford: Oxford University Press.

    1982. 'British policy towards a separate identity in the Caribbean, 1920–1950', *East Indians in the Caribbean*, eds. Bridget Brereton and Winston Dookeran, London: Kraus, 33–47.

Tiwari, Kapil N. (ed.) 1980. *Indians in New Zealand*, Wellington, NZ: Price Milburn.

Twaddle, Michael (ed.) 1975. *Expulsion of a Minority*, London: Athlone.

van Amersfoort, J.M.M. 1970. 'Hindostaanse Surinamers in Amsterdam', *Nieuwe West-Indische Gids*, 47(2): 109–38.

van der Veer, Peter and Steven Vertovec n.d. 'Brahmanism abroad: The development of Caribbean Hinduism' (forthcoming).

Vasil, Raj K. 1984. *Politics in Bi-Racial Societies*, New Delhi: Vikas.

Vertovec, Steven 1988a. 'Indian ethnicity outside India', Paper presented at the Institute of Commonwealth Studies, University of London, 22 November.

 1989. 'Hinduism in diaspora: the transformation of tradition in Trinidad', in *Hinduism Reconsidered*, ed. G.D. Sontheimer and H. Kulke, New Delhi: Manohar, 152–79.

Visram, Rozina 1986. *Ayahs, Lascars and Princes: The Story of Indians in Britain 1700–1947*, London: Pluto.

Part I
South Asians in colonial and post-colonial contexts

Introduction

Colin Clarke, Ceri Peach and Steven Vertovec

The first movement of indentured Indians overseas to British colonial territory took place to Mauritius in 1834 and to British Guiana (now Guyana) in 1838 – in the immediate aftermath of British slave emancipation. During the second half of the nineteenth century, thousands of indentured Indians were destined each year for sugar plantations established on virgin land only recently incorporated into the British tropical empire (Trinidad, British Guiana and Mauritius); for long-established estates still judged by the sugar planters to be short of labour (Jamaica, the French Antilles and Reunion); for agricultural labour (Fiji and Natal, now South Africa) and non-agricultural tasks (Natal and Kenya) in British colonies acquired during the course of the nineteenth century; and even as non-indentured (sometimes white-collar) workers and retailers (Burma and East Africa).

Only in Mauritius, British Guiana and Fiji did Indians eventually form the largest segment of the population: elsewhere, they were sizeable elements (Trinidad and Suriname) or small rural or urban enclaves (Burma, Natal, Jamaica, Reunion and the French Antilles). Everywhere, however much they facilitated British, French or Dutch capitalism and British administration, they were spurned by locals as outsiders and often placed at a constitutional disadvantage after independence (for example in South Africa and Fiji); discriminated against *de facto* in some instances where they have been the majority – as in the case of Guyana; or expelled as undesirable (economically successful) aliens (Uganda and Burma). In short, while Indians overseas added to the complexity of many colonial societies by their very presence, resolution of cultural plurality since independence has seen Indians discriminated against or exiled, except in Mauritius, where they account for over 70% of the population, or those territories, such as Jamaica, Reunion and the French Antilles, where they are insignificant numerically and

33

economically, and, in the case of the French territories, where decolonisation has involved departmental incorporation into France. Indians' experience in Burma, as Tinker shows, was rather unusual: Burma is adjacent to India; it was conquered by the Indian army; and Indian immigrants (1880–1934) were free (not indentured) workers. Sometimes they acted as agents of British imperialism, filling middle-ranking positions on the railways, in the telegraphic service, on steamships, in rice mills, and in manufacturing. Indeed, Burma was governed as a province of British India from 1826 to 1937, and liberated from the Japanese in 1945 by an Indian–British army.

The privileged position of the Indians during British colonialism was totally reversed after Burma's independence in 1948. Burma Indians thereafter were politically powerless and subject to severe immigration rules, though until Ne Win seized power in 1962, they were generally treated with tolerance. After 1962, all Indians in prominent positions – doctors, lawyers, bankers and teachers – were summarily expelled, but humbler Indians survived by becoming 'invisible' – assuming Burmese names and dress and speaking Burmese outside the home. Today, in Rangoon, they keep a low profile, but in Mulmein there are still Hindu and Sikh temples and other Indian social centres.

Tinker compares the experience of the Indians in Burma with their counterparts in Malaysia and Singapore. The Chinese, to the Malays, are a menace; in contrast, Indians are 'small people' – largely plantation workers or, increasingly, an urban underclass, who only become a threat if they ally themselves with the Chinese. Singapore is virtually a Chinese city, but it has to function in a Malay world; so a multi-community image is fostered which satisfactorily incorporates Indians, most of whom are westernised to the point of speaking English at home. Throughout Southeast Asia, irrespective of whether political and economic circumstances are favourable or adverse, Indian communities are in decline; their subsidiary role in British imperialism is defunct.

Natal is arguably more typical of the experience of Indians overseas, in that it involved indentured labour – normally a five-year contract – on sugar plantations cut from the bush. However, indentured Indians also worked in coalmines and on estates. Indian women, the focus of Beall's chapter, were brought to Natal only with reluctance, and simply because the government of India had fixed the female quota at 29% some years before indentured immigration to this particular destination started in 1860. Nevertheless, Indian women's labour power was harnessed at certain crucial stages in the development of Natal's economy, and they were among the most exploited members of the proletariat; both their productive and reproductive labour facilitated capital accumulation, particularly on the sugar estates.

As Indians they were unwelcome and subjected to derogatory stereotyping; as Indian women they were seen as responsible for the increase in the size of the Indian population and symbolised its potential permanence; as women they had to struggle against two converging constructs of gender relationships – one among the immigrants, the other imposed by colonial rule – in both of which women were subordinate to men. Indian women responded by devising strategies for bare survival inside and outside the bounds of marriage and patriarchy.

Indian indentured emigration was not confined to the British Empire but spilled over into the French sugar territories of the Indian Ocean and the Caribbean – Reunion and Martinique and Guadeloupe. Singaravélou calculates that nearly 190,000 immigrants – mostly Tamils from South India – disembarked in the French colonies during the second half of the nineteenth century. Today their descendants number more than 130,000 in the three insular French *départements d'outre-mer*, almost four-fifths of whom live in Reunion. In all three cases, there is a major distinction between rural Indians and urban Creoles, and isolation has facilitated the persistence of both Hinduism and some Tamil speaking.

Since the Second World War, Indians have penetrated all sectors of the departmental economies, though they continue in the sugar cane sector as farmers and field labourers, as well as rearing cattle and growing provisions for the markets. Indian movement into public service, commerce, teaching, transport and the liberal professions has generated upward social mobility. The caste system and extended family have disappeared, and Indians have westernised, Creolised and converted to Catholicism. However, there is also some evidence that Hindu cults attract lower-class Creole devotees, while in Reunion, proximity to South India and Mauritius has led to some reinforcement of Hinduism.

As in the French *départements d'outre-mer*, the Indian community of Trinidad – also descended from indentured immigrants, but here essentially of North Indian provenance – is largely rural in location. Indians comprise 41% of the population and are a major force in Trinidad life. Yet, twenty years ago, many predicted the demise of Indian cultural institutions under the influence of educational and economic change. Vertovec shows, however, that neither the oil and sugar booms of the 1970s, nor the economic recession which set in after 1982, have brought about the cultural erosion among Indians – Hindus especially – that was anticipated by social scientists and locals alike.

Instead, Indian villagers used their new-found wealth to elaborate their culture. Indian music, Indian films, formal weddings, collective Hindu celebrations, and family rites proliferated. Despite the economic cutbacks, these revitalised institutions and activities have been maintained on a cooperative basis within the community as expressions of a self-confident ethnic identity.

Clearly, ethnic identity in Trinidad has not been based solely on the reinforcement of Indian cultural institutions and values but has been forged, in part, in opposition to the identity of the dominant segment of the society, politically – Creole. Decolonisation and independence have quickened inter-ethnic rivalries via the creation of, and competition between, political parties in many societies with a substantial Indian presence, and nowhere more controversially so than in Fiji, where two armed coups in 1987 underscored the unacceptability to Fijians of Indian access to political power via a coalition government, following the general elections.

When Fiji became independent in 1970, Lal notes, the departing British bequeathed power to the Fijians. Since then the Fijians have used their dominant position to defeat or deflect the demands of the Indian community – already the biggest group by 49 to 46% – for political and social equality. The constitution of Fiji, in effect, allowed for minority rule. Limitation on land purchase by non-Fijians has left the smaller once-dominant Fijian segment with 87% of the agricultural land. Moreover, hereditary Fijian chiefs have a veto in the upper house on any legislation affecting land ownership, Fijian custom or tradition. The civil service and the army, as in Trinidad, is non-Indian too. In Fiji, a system of unequal access to resources, though briefly challenged by the multi-racial government of 1987, has been reinforced by a Fijian military coup and the threat of a constitution that is racist, verging on South Africa's system of apartheid.

In South Africa itself, Indians have had to fit into a system of race relations structured around white dominance and African subordination. Beall shows that, although Indian indentured labour in South Africa was functional to white capital, the Indians themselves, even in the nineteenth century, were restricted in the property they could own, in the areas in which they could live, and in their movement between provinces. Officially, they were encouraged to return home after their indentures had expired. And, when the Nationalist Government passed the Group Areas Act in 1950, it was the Indians who suffered disproportionately from forced migration within the towns.

Anthony Lemon argues that, as a small and powerless minority, South African Indians long tended to rely on deputations and negotiations, at both national and international levels, to represent their views, though they did engage in passive resistance in 1903, 1913, 1946 and 1952. From the early 1950s, Indian radicals sought mass support and identification with the Africans, but the middle class, wanting to protect their commercial interests, aligned themselves with the whites. Since 1983 Indians have had a separate legislature in the tricameral parliament and control over their 'own affairs', but the Transvaal and Natal Indian Congresses have established a common cause with other races in the United Democratic Front, which spearheaded a successful boycott of the 1984 elections, and it is clear that there is widespread Indian rejection of a racial constitution which leaves Africans without the vote. Increasingly, South African Indians see their future as bound up with that of the African majority.

Indian experience in East Africa straddles indenture and free labour, the role of trader and imperial auxiliary: it therefore rather parallels the situation in Malaysia. Twaddle shows how the independence of Uganda, Kenya, and Tanzania in the early 1960s triggered a massive Indian exodus – especially from Uganda in 1972 under Idi Amin – back to India in a few cases and above all on to Britain. Nowadays, residual communities of Indian descent remain in Kenya and Tanzania of about one-quarter their size in the early 1960s, with even fewer staying in Uganda.

Indian experience of decolonisation in East Africa harks back to conditions in Burma (in both areas they were viewed by the locals as privileged and exclusive), suggests that South African Indians are wise to side with the black majority, and demonstrates that nineteenth-century emigration, whether indentured or free, was not a final movement to tropical colonies. Indians have moved on to metropolitan locales, and East African Indians now rub shoulders with recent South Asian immigrants in several British towns.

Dominance, subordination, incorporation or expulsion have all been experienced by one or another of the overseas Indian communities brought about by nineteenth-century emigration, typically under indentured contracts; much has depended upon the size of the community, its economic viability and its capacity for political organisation. Only in Mauritius where they are the vast majority, or Jamaica and the French *départements* where they are insignificant, miscegenating and Creolising, are the descendants of the nineteenth-century emigrants secure. Even where they are the major segment, as they are in Guyana and Fiji, Indians are differentially incorporated and lack many civil rights; in South Africa, where they are a sizeable minority, they are systematically disadvantaged by apartheid. Only in Trinidad, so far, does the large (but minority) segment of Indians compete on grounds of equality with Creoles, and enjoy (since 1986) access to power through a coalition of parties.

1

Indians in Southeast Asia: imperial auxiliaries

Hugh Tinker

British Burma

The Burma Indians are the principal group examined in this chapter, with those in Malaysia and Singapore considered as comparisons. In Burma in the 1980s there are probably 300,000 persons whose origins were in the Indian sub-continent (not including Gurkhas, Nagas, and other marginal hill peoples). This is a residual community, the detritus of what was in the heyday of the colonial period, 1885–1942, a vital component in British control and development of this fertile land. Domiciled Europeans and Eurasians numbered at most 30,000 in 1941 when the Indian population was 1,017,825 out of the total of 16,823,798. Many of them were transients, for it was simple to get to Burma from Calcutta, Madras, and other east-coast ports, and the cost of the passage as a deck passenger was about £1. Yet the stable, permanent, or semi-permanent Indian population formed at least half this total. They controlled key areas of Burma's economic, administrative, social and political life. The Burmese are a proud people, with a long national history; they do not feel any esteem for foreigners apart from the Chinese for whom they reserve the term *tayyok* which may be translated 'cousin'. For others, including the British and Indians, they feel something akin to contempt. The Burmese term for foreigner is *kalā*, applied to Indians and Europeans alike. Its origin is disputed, but it seems most probable that its meaning is similar to the Indian term *kāla*, 'black man'. They increasingly resented the dominance of foreigners, in consequence of colonial occupation.

The leading Burmese historian writes of the 'golden age' of the British Raj, 1890–1920, when:

> British rule did not seem to affect the general structure of Burmese society . . . The British officials of this period also

39

showed sympathy towards the people . . . No social barrier was created between the ruler and the ruled. The British officials were so few in number that, except in Rangoon, they could not set up exclusive social clubs and had to mix freely with junior Burmese officials.

(Htin Aung, 1967: 268)

So few in number – that was the crucial factor. But the Indians were not few; they were numerous; they were visible; and so it was that they became the symbol of colonialism, of foreign exploitation, and when at last the Burmese again became the masters of their own house it was the Indians who felt the brunt of the nationalist backlash. The Burmese view of Indians was clouded by ambivalence inasmuch as India had witnessed the birth and life of Lord Buddha and the holy places associated with his enlightenment – Sarnath, Bodh Gaya and others – were in India. The Burmese historical tradition told them that their own ancestors had been *Kshattriyas* in North India. It is generally accepted that the Burmese migrated into Upper Burma, probably in the seventh century AD from Nanchao (Yunnan). Sir Arthur Phayre in his pioneer *History of Burma* (Trubner 1883) considered the Kshattriya tradition 'improbable', but found reasons why it might be possible. Coming to the present, Burmese nationalists revered Gandhi and Nehru as the champions of Asian nationalism. There was an ideal India which they venerated: and there were the Indians they encountered – coolies, moneylenders, rice merchants – whom they detested.

The Indian 'occupation' of Burma really began after the Third Anglo–Burmese War (1885), although Indian merchants and Brahmans had been in the country for centuries. Mandalay was occupied and the last Burmese king deposed by an expeditionary force of about 5,000 (mainly Indian) within fourteen days. However, subsequently a guerrilla revolt spread from Upper Burma down to the Delta, occupied thirty years earlier. Over 32,000 regular troops had to be employed, and in order to free them a new military police force of 35,000 was raised, largely from among Punjabi ex-soldiers. Although it was possible gradually to reduce their numbers, as the revolt was suppressed, in the 1930s there were still over 10,000 Indian military police – mainly guarding the frontier areas.

As the railway was pushed up into north Burma, the great majority of its employees were Indians; they were also numerous in the posts and telegraphs, the customs, the other government departments. Doubtless Burmans could have been trained for these jobs, but there were Indians available with the right qualifications; moreover, they were prepared to accept lower salaries than the Burmese. The whole system was rationalised by the British according to racial stereotyping; the Indians were indus-trious, tractable, reliable; the Burmese were happy-go-lucky (they were frequently called 'the Irish of the East').

The whole situation seemed to be accepted because Burma was, by comparison with India, a good land. Before the British occupation Lower Burma had been sparsely occupied; a land of jungles and creeks. Under British rule it was opened up to paddy cultivation on a large scale, mainly through immigration from Upper Burma. In 1855 there were 993,000 acres under cultivation in Lower Burma; by 1895 this had risen to 5,007,000 acres and by 1930, 9,911,000 acres were under cultivation. Almost all the peasant farmers were Burmese, though the more substantial began to employ harvest gangs of Indians who came over to cut and thresh the paddy. The Burmese prospered, and the land was dotted with pagodas, white, silver and gold as evidence of this prosperity. However, they achieved no transformation in their economic status; they remained peasants, even if prosperous ones. A network of rural credit was provided by the Chettiars, bankers from Madras, who were also involved in purchasing the paddy, and sending it to the big rice mills in Rangoon for the process of grinding, and grading the rice for export. The biggest mill-owners were Europeans, such as Steel Brothers, but the middling firms were Indian; only the smallest rice mills were Burmese owned.

The British annexed Burma in several bites, the first of which included the outlying province of Tenasserim, and the British made Moulmein their headquarters. Previously a village, in the 1820s it began to assume the appearance of an Indian port: Indians formed about two-thirds of its population. Moulmein's importance dwindled when Rangoon was occu-pied (1852). Because this had been a Burmese port, the foreigners were not immediately dominant. From the 1890s its Burmese character diminished; the Burmese were pushed out into the suburbs. There was no overt pressure, but the arrival of thousands of Indian labourers meant that the city centre became an overcrowded slum where the Burmese had no desire to dwell. After 1920, this Indian influx spiralled; in 1925, 330,212 persons arrived in the city while 301,846 departed. By the 1920s two-thirds of Rangoon's population was Indian. This total reflected the transient character of the immigration; the 1921 Census enumerated 154,537 Indian males and only 34,797 females. Hence, while Burmese males (52,398) made up only one-third of the Indian total, Burmese females (50,927) outnum-bered their Indian sisters.

For the coolies who provided the workforce in the docks, in the rice-mills, pulling the city's rickshaws and in all the menial tasks associ-ated with removing rubbish and filth (known by the euphemism of 'conservancy') there were squalid tenements where they camped while their brief time in Burma passed in drudgery, made tolerable only by the accumulation of petty savings. There were other Indian migrants who stayed longer, filling the lower positions in trade and in government service. Perhaps they had left wives in India, but during their time in Burma they acquired Burmese wives: the status of such a woman being at first acceptable in Burmese society. However, in the end the men returned to India; leaving their Burmese wives and offspring – probably, in most cases, adequately provided for. Increasingly the Burmese resented this exploitation of their women; as one nationalist leader said 'What use will Home Rule be to us if . . . the Burmese nation has become half-caste by gradual extinction?' (Tinker 1976: 122).

The old nationalism had never died, though suppressed by military action. A new political nationalism became powerful in the 1920s. Increasingly, it focused upon Rangoon University, founded as a separate institution in 1920. This was supposedly set up on the lines of 'northern English universities'; its staff were mainly British or Indian, and many of its students were young Indians domiciled in Burma. In 1923 they actually formed a majority, though by 1927 they were just 47% (ISC, XI: 137–8). The 1920s were a period of prosperity. Paddy production continued to expand, with India taking a major share. In 1926–7, Burma's exports to India had a value of £18,000,000 including £8,250,000 for rice and paddy. Indian exports to Burma had a value of £11,625,000. This favourable situation was suddenly overturned when, because of the world slump, the market price of paddy fell in 1930 from Rs200 to Rs55 per 100 baskets: the lowest price in living memory. The Burmese peasant had been accustomed to getting through the months between sowing and reaping by living upon loans taken from the Indian Chettiars. Now repayment was impossible and (without any particular enthusiasm, they were not landholders) the Chettiars foreclosed. Over 30% of the agricultural land in Lower Burma passed out of the hands of Burmese peasant farmers into Chettiar ownership (Tinker 1957: 224–5).

This grievance was to have long-term effects. There was an immediate explosion in Rangoon. Gandhi's salt *satyagraha* (civil disobedience), and his arrest on 4 May 1930, was followed by a general strike of the Indian labour force. In the docks, the employers responded by taking on Burmese labour. The Burmese were not accustomed to cooly work; but these were hard times, and they came in. The Indian strike collapsed rapidly; when they reported back at the docks, the Burmans were discharged. Angry that they had been used (as they had) the Burmese took it out on the Rangoon Indians. Within a few hours the city centre was a battlefield. First, 2,000 Indian rickshaw pullers had their vehicles destroyed; then the rioters turned on the Indian shops. Some 7,000 Indians were, temporarily, made refugees (Chakravarti 1971: 132–3). The community was scared, and there were 33,000 departures for India during June 1930. This trend continued during 1931, when there were 22,591 more departures than arrivals. Thereafter, the previous pattern of a surplus of immigrants reasserted itself.

However, Burmese politicians had discovered the potential power of the city mob. This was exploited in 1938 by the unscrupulous U Saw. Some time previously, a Burmese Muslim had written a work criticising the Buddhist religion. This had nothing to do with the Indians, but through his newspaper Saw worked up passions, first against the Indian Muslims then more widely against the whole community. Rioting broke out, and lasted from late July until mid-September, the Rangoon police proving singularly ineffective. Officially recorded casualties totalled 164 Indians killed and 711 wounded, with considerable damage to property (Chakra-varti 1971: 157–60). Paradoxically, just before this outbreak Aung San, the future prime minister, invited Nehru to address the All-Burma Students Conference, declaring 'that a leader of millions . . . should be standing amidst us and instructing us makes us feel depressed for Burma that is denuded of leaders' (Tinker 1976: 151).

The rioting spread to Mandalay and other towns and left the Burma Indians feeling insecure. By this time, Burma had been separated from India (April 1937) and, despite assurances in the House of Commons by R.A. Butler, the Burma Indians were much more vulnerable. Further rioting in April 1940 left 26 Indians dead and 170 wounded. Moreover, the menacing U Saw was now premier of Burma and to bolster his unstable ministry he brought forward measures concerning Indian landholding and immigration and hinted that 'cohabitation' between Indian men and Burmese women would be severely regulated. This was the uneasy situation when the Japanese launched their invasion into Burma in December 1941. Moulmein was occupied after the briefest resistance (30 January 1942) and the advance on Rangoon continued steadily.

The Indians panicked. The wealthier citizens had already taken ship to Calcutta and Madras. Now the whole Rangoon Indian population set out to flee overland. The entire functioning of the city's services depended upon them: the docks, transport, fire services, water, electricity, communi-cations. Senior British officials followed them and persuaded their leaders to bring them back in return for a guarantee that they would be evacuated if the city was threatened. The eventual British exit from the city was hurried (the city fell on 8 March) and the Indians were left to make their way out as best they might. There were two main routes: via Taungup pass to Akyab and then to India, and when that route closed, via the Chindwin valley and Manipur to India. Between 450,000 and 500,000 finally arrived.

No one knows how many died en route: a figure of 100,000 has been suggested, but the total was probably between 10,000 and 50,000 (Tinker 1975).

This was really the end for the Indian community in Burma. The Japanese occupation brought travail for those who remained. They were required to make compulsory contributions to the Japanese cause; some Burma Indians were recruited in Netaji's Indian National Army, and died in the desperate attempt to invade India; many more were conscripted into the 'Sweat Army' drafted to build the Burma–Siam railway and died in thousands in the jungle. When the British returned to Rangoon (3 May 1945) the Indians hoped to return to the *status quo ante*. But it was a new world. It soon became clear that despite their military triumph the British no longer had the stomach to keep an empire. Aung San was now the man making the running. When he was invited to London to negotiate independence in January 1947, he stopped in Delhi and took advice from Nehru. Yet, as he gathered power into his hands, he ensured that the Indians would no longer play a decisive part in Burma's future development. Several months before Burma achieved formal independence, he was making it clear to Nehru that despite their personal intimacy he would not return to the former situation where the Indians enjoyed a special position in the country's economic life: henceforward their entry would be strictly controlled (Tinker 1984: 596–7).

Independent Burma

However, after independence the Indians still had a place (though diminished) in the new Burma. One Burma-born Indian, M.A. Raschid, played a major part in pre-war nationalist politics. He was president of the Rangoon University Students' Union and then of the All-Burma Students' Union. He organised the first major strike in the oil refinery at Syriam. After independence he became the minister in charge of certain key economic departments. Another Burma-born Indian, N.R. Chakravarti, was the foremost financial expert in the government, Adviser to the Burmese Finance Mission in London, September–October 1947, which negotiated the financial settlement with Britain to establish the arrangements after independence. Mr (later Dr) Chakravarti went on to become a senior official of the World Bank. In retirement he wrote what is the most thorough study of his community: *The Indian Minority in Burma*. Although as individuals they had parts to play, as a community they were deprived of their former leading position in the economy. A Land Nationalisation Act was rushed through parliament in 1948, depriving all absentee landlords of their rights (including the Chettiars, against whom it was mainly directed). The act was never implemented, and was replaced by the 1953 Act which (following representations from the Indian government) conceded the principle of compensation. However, the Act was applied so slowly that the relative claims of former landlords and former tenants remained uncertain for years (Tinker 1957: 229–46).

Indians dribbled back into Burma, while those who had survived the Japanese occupation took up their former jobs if they could. The 1947 Constitution laid down conditions under which the majority could apply for citizenship. Not many did so: the process was tortuous and slow. In the mid-1950s official immigration figures showed 226,743 Indians and Pakistanis as resident aliens; unofficial figures put their combined numbers at 800,000. After 1941 it was not possible to conduct a simultaneous nationwide census, but a survey in 1953 in Rangoon computed a total of 140,346 Indians and Pakistanis out of a city population of 737,079 (Tinker 1957: 188).

U Nu, prime minister 1947–56, 1957–8, and 1960–2 enjoyed a close friendship with Nehru and was generally kindly disposed to the Indians, though even he could refer to 'the Chettiar with the bloated abdomen' (Tinker 1957). In 1951 it was ascertained that there were only 400 doctors in the public service compared to 650 pre-war: 300 were recruited from India and Pakistan on short-term contracts. A few others were recruited as university lecturers and high school teachers.

All this came to an end when General Ne Win took over in 1962 and launched 'The Burmese way to Socialism'. The philosophy was that all foreigners, even those working on technical programmes, had proved harmful to Burma. He gave instructions that all, no matter how long they had been residents, must depart. The Indians as the largest immigrant community were hardest hit. By May 1964, the Indian government had classified 300,000 recently arrived from Burma as refugees. Special ships and planes were chartered to bring them back. Those departing were stripped of all valuables: all currency notes of Rs50 and above were sequestrated; jewellery, cameras and watches were confiscated. Women were searched as thoroughly as men. It was all as traumatic as the more highly publicised expulsions by Amin from Uganda (Tinker 1977: 150–1).

However, the Indians are persistent people and those not too prominent in the public eye managed to cling on. Even in Rangoon there are still streets where the majority of the shops belong to Indians: but they have become invisible. Indian names are not displayed above the shops, they wear Burmese dress, they speak Burmese (at any rate, in public). They also have a share in the more lowly occupations, such as driving motor trishaws, and as labourers, coolies. They remain in unexpected places: General Ne Win's personal servant is a Tamil (he is said to have been given the army rank of captain). In Moulmein, their first port of call, they are much more visible. Hindu temples and *gurudwaras* (Sikh temples) remain open for worship. Indian shopkeepers do not disguise their racial origins. They certainly do not possess the dominant position they once held in the town's commerce, but their role is not insignificant.

The last exodus from Burma to be recorded was that which took place in 1978 from border areas in Arakan back into Bangladesh. This has long been an area of coming and going. Some Buddhist Arakanese migrated across the Indian border long ago into the Cox's Bazaar–Chittagong area; they are called *Maghs* by the majority population. Muslims moved into the Akyab district of Arakan where they were termed *Yakhaing Kala* (Arakan Indians). The shortage of land in Bangladesh led to outward movements into Assam and Tripura and another large-scale movement into Arakan gathered momentum in the 1970s, beginning with the turmoil of the 'War of Liberation' (1970–1). Numbers can only be guessed at: from 250,000 to 500,000? Secessionists plotted to take the Akyab district into Bangladesh, and the Bangladeshi Military Attaché in Rangoon was involved. When all this was uncovered, people were expelled into the Cox's Bazaar area at the rate of 4–5,000 per day. The exodus was marked by armed clashes between the Burma Army and Muslim militants (*The Observer* 4 June 1978).

The troubles of the Burma Indians may not be over, for like all people driven out of mainline occupations they have taken up some shady activities. The British finally departed from Burma in January 1948, yet, forty years later the post-colonial epilogue still runs on.

Malaysia and Singapore under the British

What of the Indians in Malaysia and Singapore? In Malaysia, in the 1980s, the Indian population numbers 1,171,000 (1980) out of 14,200,000, while in the total Singapore population of 2,444,000 there are about 155,000 Indians. However, in Malaysia the Burmese view of *tayyok* has no place. The Chinese, to the Malays, are a menace: by comparison the Indians are 'small people' who only become a threat if they form alliances with the Chinese. Singapore is virtually a Chinese city, but because it has to function in a Malay world – both to north and south – there is a motive for de-emphasising Chinese predominance and fostering the image of a multiracial community. In this context, although it is the Malay minority which is the main concern of larger neighbours, those of Indian origin also feature as partners in multiracialism.

Britain secured a foothold in Malaya with the founding of Penang in 1786, though the action of Raffles in planting Singapore in the heart of Dutch colonial possessions in 1819 was to have much greater consequences. Malacca was transferred by the Netherlands to Britain in 1824, and, with the addition of small land areas adjacent, these three ports made up the Straits Settlements which formed British Malaya until the latter part of the nineteenth century. Like Burma, British Malaya was an outlying territory of the Indian Empire and from its earliest days Penang took in Indian traders and labourers. Most were Tamils, known to the Malays as *Klings*. The Indian population of Singapore was augmented by convicts, sentenced to transportation for severe crimes, mainly murder. The convicts were employed on public works and it was their labour which built St Andrew's Cathedral and Government House among many other buildings. The convicts could earn what amounted to freedom by good behaviour (these exemplary prisoners only had to report to the authorities once a month). In addition to the convict labour and the merchants there was a small Indian garrison, usually made up of two battalions of Madras Infantry. The population of Singapore increased from 11,500 to 90,700 between 1824 and 1864; in the same period, that of Penang increased from 48,500 to 126,700 (Table 1.1). In these early years the Indian component of the population was considerably greater than it was to be later.

Singapore rapidly became the principal entrepot in Southeast Asia, with a substantial population of European merchants who resented their subordination to far-off Calcutta. From the beginning, Penang and Singapore were free ports but the East India Company enjoyed a monopoly of the through trade between China and Europe. This monopoly was abolished when the Company's charter was renewed in 1833, and the Indian Government ceased to have any real interest in this distant possession. The European merchants agitated against control from India and in 1867 administrative supervision passed from the India Office to the Colonial Office. In the following decade the 'Forward Movement' began, leading to British dominance over the Malay states of the interior by means of British Residents whose powers were greater than those of their counterparts with the Indian princes.

In general, British penetration was achieved by negotiation, but where force was involved the soldiers were all Indian sepoys. There was the so-called Naning war, 1831–2, when pressure was put on a small state subordinate to Malacca by a force of 150 sepoys, while the much more important move into Selangor in 1873 was carried out by a force of mercenaries recruited in India (Pathans, Punjabis, Sikhs) who forced their way into the interior. Much later, a contingent of military police was recruited – mainly Sikhs – to provide a military reserve; these were called

Table 1.1. *Ethnic populations of Singapore and Penang 1864*

	Singapore	Penang
Indians	12,700	14,000
Chinese	58,000	39,000
Malays	13,500	55,000
Total population	90,700	126,700

Source: Cameron (1865: 109,149)

the Malay States Guides and came into being when in 1895 four of the west-coast states accepted British supervision as the federated Malay States.

However, Indian immigration into the interior was mainly to provide a labour force for European-owned plantations. The first demand came from the sugar and coffee plantations and the indenture system – introduced in more distant sugar colonies, such as Mauritius, Reunion and the West Indies – was the main means of recruitment. During this phase the Indian population greatly increased: thus, in the state of Perak there were 837 Indians in 1879 and 34,710 by 1901. This increase was dwarfed by the numbers of Chinese pouring in: of these there were 20,373 in Perak in 1879 and 149,375 by 1901. The British authorities saw in the Indians a potential counter-weight to this influx, whose secret societies made for a danger to British control. Thus, in 1887 the Governor of the Straits Settlements, Sir Frederick Weld advised London: 'The great preponderance of the Chinese over any other race in the Straits Settlements and to a larger and marked degree in some of the Native States under our administration should be counter-balanced as much as possible by the influx of Indian and other nationalities' (Despatches 1887). In 1887 the Indian government abolished the registration and supervision of non-indentured labourers and there was even greater emphasis on the *Kangani* system of recruitment whereby an Indian returning home was commissioned to recruit labourers from his home district. The *Kangani*, ganger or overseer, then hired his gang to a planter, collecting their wages and subtracting his not inconsiderable commission. This system was greatly boosted by the action of the Malayan government in giving subsidies to the shipping companies operating from South Indian ports, especially Negapatnam. From 1905 the British Indian Steam Navigation Company received a subsidy of Straits $250,000 per annum (say £60,000) and provided deck passages from India to Penang at Rs11 and Rs16 to Singapore. From this time onwards the main plantation production was switched to rubber, and the scale of operations vastly increased. By 1931 there were 703,535 acres planted with rubber trees and the estate population had grown to 237,000 of whom 144,000 were Indians.

One by-product of Malaya's transfer from the India Office to the Colonial Office was the development of a closer connection with Ceylon. Both the planters and government departments required subordinates able to communicate with their employees and proficient also in English. A ready supply was available in the Tamil community of Jaffna who had made great strides in English education, thanks largely to American missionary encouragement. Because their barren peninsula offered few opportunities, and openings in government service in Ceylon were limited, they readily responded to the invitations of planters and officials (particularly in the technical departments) who knew Ceylon and were now employed in Malaya. At first they filled clerical and subordinate technical and medical posts, but from these they moved up into the professions. When a railway system was constructed in Malaya, progress was slow and the so-called Ceylon Pioneer Corps was lent to Malaya to build railways and roads. The clerks, surveyors and engineers were 'Jaffnese'; the labourers were all South Indians. When the railways began to operate these same Tamils became the backbone of the railway staff.

The stereotype which the British had formed of the Malays was even more negative than that of the Burmese: they were idle, unreliable, backward, given to inexplicable violence (*amok*). The Chinese were acknowledged to be hardworking and enterprising but also they were unpredictable and potential trouble-makers. The Tamil labourers were steady workers and also docile and uncomplaining. The British planters therefore exploited the Indians to an extent they did not dare with the Chinese.

In 1910, the advantages of the *Kangani* system were officially recognised when indenture was abolished: pressure from India was also a factor. By 1921 the Indian community in Malaya and Singapore numbered 472,000 out of a total 3,327,000 (Malays 1,623,000; Chinese 1,172,000; others 60,000). The manner in which census statistics were collected blurs the question of whether the Jaffna Tamils were included in the Indian total or whether they appear among 'others'. (Their annual migration could not have exceeded 6,000.) They were concentrated in the (western) Federated Malay States where rubber cultivation was carried out. Population growth among the Indians was less than might have been expected, because so many labourers left their families in South India and returned thence when they had made some savings. In 1921 there were only 405 Indian females per 1,000 males and only 12% of the Indian population had been born in Malaya – mainly those in the long-settled communities of Penang and Singapore.

The world slump had a major effect upon the Malayan rubber industry; the planters lowered wage rates from 50 cents a day (about 6p) to 42 to 45 cents a day. The Indian labourers responded by departing: whereas there had previously been a substantial surplus of arrivals over departures, in 1928 and 1930–2 there was a massive exodus – a net loss of 180,000. Not until 1934 was assisted migration resumed. Even then the (British) United Planting Association of Malaya refused to restore the old rates. In June 1938 the Indian Government ended the migration and closed down the Emigration Depot at Negapatnam, despite howls of protest from the planters.

When war came to Malaya in 1942, the main impact was upon the 70,000 strong Indian Expeditionary Force who endured the long retreat down the peninsula and then, with the British and Australian troops, disappeared behind barbed wire. During the next three years, for a minority of the Indians there was a new prestige and status. The Japanese attempt to subvert the Indian soldiers met with only limited success, despite the harsh treatment meted out to any who actively resisted Japanese propaganda. The situation was transformed by the arrival of Netaji, Subhas Chandra Bose, who inspired the Indians by his rhetoric. Among the military prisoners many Sikhs now joined his Indian National Army (INA). They were joined by the local Sikhs of the military police, who employed particularly nasty methods against those who still actively resisted. Numbers were still inadequate, and the more robust estate Indians were recruited into the INA.

For many others a quite different fate awaited. Thousands of the Tamil coolies were forcibly enrolled in the 'Sweat Army' despatched to labour alongside British, Australian and Dutch POWs on the Death Railway. Many perished. An informed estimate suggests that 60,000 young labourers did not return (Arasaratnam 1970: 30). Those who returned (30,000?) were suffering from beri-beri, ulcers and other incurable maladies. Whereas, pre-war, the Indians formed about 15% of the total population, afterwards they numbered only 11–12%. Between the Census of 1931 and the next taken in 1947 there was an absolute decrease in the Indian population of 22,000 whereas in the previous decade the increase was 231,000. There was much bad feeling against the Jaffna Tamils, said to have worked as recruiting officers for the Japanese while exempt from labour on the Death Railway. The total failure of the INA in their attempt to penetrate over the Indian border in 1943 completed the humiliation of the community. Many would insist that the Malayan Indians have never recovered from the traumas of the Second World War.

Post-independence Malaysia and Singapore

There followed the communist campaign to drive the British out of Malaya (1948–60). Most left-wing Chinese were involved in this jungle war. So were a few Indian activists; but in general the vast majority of Chinese were trapped between the insurgents and the colonial power. The Indians on the rubber estates were the prime target for the jungle fighters, and were hopelessly vulnerable. The Chinese were identified with the 'terrorists' and were re-located in the 'New Villages'; the Malays were able to live down their wartime records as Japanese collaborators by forming the bulk of the government's local anti-terrorist forces. The Indians simply groped along, their community virtually leaderless, and with no further support from Mother India. Not only was immigration prohibited, but those who returned to India could not come back. The only positive aspect to this isolation was the creation of a settled Indian community, taking its marriage partners from local Indian women. The sex imbalance of earlier years began to be adjusted. By 1957 there were 746 Indian females per 1,000 males and 64.5% of all Malayan Indians were locally born.

Following the abortive Malayan Union scheme, Singapore was separated from the Federation of Malaya in 1948, and thenceforward they functioned as two separate political entities. The agitation against the Malayan Union had politicised the Malays, and belatedly the Chinese and Indians realised that pre-war political isolationism – the Chinese adhering to either Kuo Min Tang (KMT) or (amongst a few) the Communist Party in China, and the Indians looking to the Congress in India – would no longer suffice. The Malayan Indian Congress (MIC) was founded in August 1946 and was at first dominated by middle-class lawyers and doctors, mainly from North India. The first president was John Thivy, son of a Malayan Indian planter, later appointed by Nehru to be India's Commissioner in Malaya. It was not until 1955 that the MIC elected V.T. Sambanthan, a trade union organiser and a Tamil, as president, and the Indians acquired a leader who could speak to the estate workers. In its early years the MIC was associated with the left in Malayan politics, but in 1955 they joined the Alliance Party, led by Tungku Abdul Rahman, a Malay aristocrat, and the Malayan Chinese Association (MCA) led by Tan Siew Sin, a businessman. The MIC jumped on the Alliance bandwagon just before the first Federal election in 1955. Indians had been slow to put their names down on the electoral register, having been told by the MIC previously that this would facilitate their deportation. In 1955 they formed less than 4% of the electorate. They were allocated 2 seats to contest by the Alliance, compared to 35 for Malays and 15 for Chinese;

this more than reflected their electoral unimportance. For the following election in 1959, and subsequently, Indian registration was more in line with their population strength (1959: Indians formed 7.4% of the electorate). They fielded four candidates for the Alliance and nineteen for parties on the left (Ratnam 1965).

Politics made little difference to the great majority of the Indians toiling on the rubber plantations. In 1960 there were 2,306 estates with 285,300 employees, of whom 60,740 were Malay, 85,540 were Chinese and 138,500 Indians. The latter formed the vast majority on European-owned estates, where the only non-Indian workers were Malays employed as guards for protection against the jungle fighters.

Malaysia came into existence in 1963 as an independent entity formed out of Malaya (already independent from 1957), Singapore (fully self-governing from 1959) and the British territories in Borneo. Within two years Singapore had been separated from Malaysia and formed an independent republic. The great majority of the Malaysia Indians live in what was formerly Malaya, now called West Malaysia. From the 1960s onwards, the London-based rubber companies began to sell out to local syndicates. These companies sub-divided the plantations and sold off small plots to individuals. Government policy after the termination of colonial rule in 1957 favoured bringing up the Malay community, mainly fishermen and peasant farmers. They were the principal beneficiaries of the new policy. Thousands of Indians lost their jobs. There was also a switch from rubber to palm oil production on several estates, requiring a smaller workforce.

During the benevolent premiership of Tungku Abdul Rahman it may be said that Malaya was run by the Alliance – consisting of Malay aristocrats and bureaucrats, Chinese tycoons and British expatriates. All this came to an end after the 1969 election in which the Alliance sustained severe setbacks. Following the expansion of Malaya into Malaysia and the adherence of the Borneo territories, the legislature was expanded to 103 seats. The senior Malay partner, United Malay National Organisation (UMNO), lost 7 of the 58 seats previously held. Gains were made by the right-wing Pan Malayan Islamic Party and by an assortment of left-wing parties. Among them was the largely Indian People's Progressive Party whose strength increased from 4 to 12 seats. The 8 Indian MPs were led by two brothers, D.R. and S.P. Seenivagasam, who were Jaffnese lawyers, much respected for their efforts for poor clients.

Despite these setbacks the Alliance still had a clear working majority. However, the discredited leader of the Malay Chinese Association (MCA), Tan Siew Sin, announced they would withdraw from the governing coalition. Much too quickly, the opposition took out a victory parade.

This provoked a massive Malay backlash and the rural Malays came into Kuala Lumpur to launch a pogrom against the Chinese in the capital. Looting, killing, and burning ensued virtually unchecked. The only members of the government to respond were Sambanthan and Manicka-vasagam, both ministers, who volunteered to try to pacify the rioters. The efforts of the police were not very successful, but when the military were brought in – soldiers of the Malay Regiment – the consequences were disastrous, for the Malay soldiers openly sided with the rioters. When the carnage eventually burnt itself out, over 800 – mainly Chinese – had been killed: Chinese compelled to leave their homes and temporary refugees numbered 6,000 (Slimming 1969).

The 1969 riots effectively terminated the multi-racial Alliance policy of the previous twelve years. The avuncular Tungku resigned; the crisis had destroyed his style of government. He was succeeded by Tun Razak, another Malay aristocrat and former administrator, but a much harsher figure. Thenceforward, multiracialism gave way to Malay nationalism. Tun Razak seemed stalwart, but his health collapsed, and he died: he was succeeded by Mahathir Bin Mohammad. This was a shift not only in the generation to which the new premier belonged, but also a shift of class and outlook. Mahathir Bin Mohammad was a relatively young man (born 1925) and also middle class, a strong Malay nationalist, set apart from the aristocratic ex-administrators, such as Tun Razak. He made his position eminently plain in his book *The Malay Dilemma*. His predecessors were pro-British. If not anti-British, Dr Mahathir was highly critical of the former colonial power for creating a plural society in Malaya, taking from the Malays their birthright. Curiously, he also accepted the racial stereo-types employed in British times:

> It is not the choice of the Malays that they should be rural and poor. It is the result of the clash of racial traits. They are easy-going and tolerant. The Chinese, especially, are hardwork-ing and astute in business. When the two came in contact the result was inevitable.
>
> (Mahathir 1970: 85)

He insisted that the Malays ought to be treated differently from the non-Malays:

> The Malays and the Red Indians of America are more or less in the same category. Malays are accepted as the indigenous people of the country, but the country is no longer exclusively theirs . . . The claim that the Chinese and Indians are responsible for the development of Malaya still does not confer on these immigrants

the same status as the indigenous Malays . . . Immigrants may say that Malaya is their country. They were born in Malaya, they have worked here and they have property here . . . But the fact remains that should a Malay and an Indian be forced to leave Malaya, the Indian can settle down in India and be an Indian whilst the Malay cannot.

(Mahathir 1970: 69, 132)

This, then, is the climate of thought in the Malaysia of the 1970s and 1980s. Although the Indian population continues to increase, their proportion of the total population is slowly declining (11.3% in 1957, 10.7% in 1970, and 10.2% in 1980). The Indian population was 707,000 in 1957, 936,000 in 1970, and 1,171,000 in 1980 (Jain 1987). The total population in 1981 was estimated at 14,200,000 and the Indian proportion was then given as 9.1%. The winding up of the former estate system means high unemployment among Indians. In 1957 this was a mere 1.8% of the working population; by 1970 the figure was 8.8% (compared with a national unemployment level of 5.6%). Those without work drift into the urban areas forming squatter colonies: by 1980, 41% of Indians were classed as dwelling in the towns where they formed an underclass in this comparatively prosperous society. Despite relinquishing their former share of political power, the Chinese remain economically successful. For them there are ample compensations, but for the Indians, increasingly marginalised, the future offers a meagre prospect.

By contrast, the Singapore Indians have received fair treatment. Their political leadership has also been identified with the left, and when the People's Action Party (PAP) of Lee Kuan Yew split on ideological lines most of the Indian politicians went along with the radical minority. For example, J.J. Puthucheary was gaoled first by the British and then by the PAP government. While in prison he wrote *Ownership and Control in the Malayan Economy* (Singapore 1960) a work highly regarded by development economists. However, some have remained close to Mr Lee, notably S. Rajaratnam, a Jaffnese who was Singapore's Foreign Minister for many years.

It has been calculated that 30% of the Singapore Indians are now middle class, and along with their traditional control of the textile business they are important in the professions, particularly in higher education. Yet this very success is contributing to a process of denationalisation. Singapore uniquely has four official languages: English, Chinese, Malay and Tamil; most public signs are printed in these four languages. About 60% of the Singapore Indians are Tamils, and there are Tamil language schools. All students in secondary schools are required to learn two languages; in theory, non-Indians might take up Tamil, but whereas all the other three languages provide access to different areas of opportunity, Tamil takes nobody anywhere (except back to South India). Hence the professional Indians employ English as the language of the home, as well as in the office or the department. These professional Singapore Indians are no longer Indian in a deep, cultural sense. Also, they are becoming an ever smaller proportion of the total population as in Malaysia: 8.5% in 1961, 7% in 1971, and 6.4% in 1981. The Malaysian trend may be attributed to impoverishment and dislocation; that in Singapore seems to be an indication of improved material circumstances.

Conclusion

Throughout many areas of the world expatriate Indians are rapidly growing in numbers and importance. In Southeast Asia, whether political and economic circumstances are favourable or adverse, an irreversible decline seems to have set in. Introduced as a subsidiary component of British imperial expansion, when the British Empire in Asia was phased out they were unable to adapt to a different role.

References

Arasaratnam, S. 1970. *Indians in Malaya and Singapore*, London: Oxford University Press.

Cameron, John 1865. *Our Tropical Possessions in Malayan India*, London: Smith, Elder & Co.

Chakravarti, N.C. 1971. *The Indian Minority in Burma: the rise and decline of an immigrant community*, London: Oxford University Press.

Despatches 1887. Governor of the Straits Settlements to Secretary of State for the Colonies, No. 307 of 24 September 1887.

Htin Aung, Maung 1967. *A History of Burma*, New York: Columbia University Press.

Indian Statutory Commission 1930. *Memoranda submitted . . . by the Government of Burma* (Report, vol. XI), cited as ISC.

Jain, Ravindra K. 1987. 'Overseas Indians in Malaysia and the Caribbean: comparative notes', Paper presented at the Oxford Conference on South Asian Communities Overseas.

Mahathir Bin Mohammad 1970. *The Malay Dilemma*, Singapore: Asia Pacific Press.

Ratnam, K.J. 1965. *Communalism and the Political Process in Malaya*, Kuala Lumpur: University of Malaya Press.

Slimming, John 1969. *Malaysia: death of a democracy*, London: John Murray.

Tinker, Hugh 1957. *The Union of Burma: a study of the first years of independence*, London: Oxford University Press.

    1975. 'A forgotten long march: the Indian exodus from Burma, 1942', *Journal of Southeast Asian Studies*, Singapore, 6: 1.

1976. *Separate and Unequal: India and the Indians in the British Empire, 1920–1950*, London: C. Hurst.

1977. *The Banyan Tree: overseas emigrants from India, Pakistan and Bangladesh*, London: Oxford University Press.

1984. *Burma: the Struggle for Independence, 1944–1948*, vol. 2, *From General Strike to Independence*, London: HMSO.

2

Women under indenture in colonial Natal 1860–1911

Jo Beall

Introduction

A study of the experience of Indian women under contract as indentured labourers serves not merely to write women back into that particular episode in Natal's and, indeed, South Africa's history, but illustrates how the materialist-feminist discourse can point to crucial issues in a broader analysis of relations not only of gender, but of race and class as well. Materialist history writing has had to be alive to non-class aspects of social reality. For most people in South Africa, racial oppression has been the most important issue, but not the only issue, and it has not been experienced uniformly by men and women.

Most analyses of the process of class formation in South Africa assume that the experience of proletarianisation and racial oppression has been the same for men and women. Even when this has not been the case, there has been little recognition of gender relations rising not out of production but out of reproduction. Materialist–feminists, on the other hand, either in their efforts to demonstrate the way in which capitalism has increased the subordination of women, or in their assertions regarding the universality of women's subordination over time and space, have tended to ignore the specificity of women's oppression in particular historical configurations.

While it is true that the common history of struggle against both exploitation and oppression has united women and men workers in South Africa, it is also important to understand the social construction of gender identity and the development of unequal gender relations. This in turn can facilitate a broader understanding of the development of South Africa's political economy. It is possible from this perspective to understand the experience of Indian women brought to Natal, how their labour power was harnessed at certain stages in the development of Natal's economy, and how, at certain times, their unproductive labour and their reproductive functions facilitated capital accumulation in the colony, particularly on the sugar estates.

Both domestic and broader social relations of gender intersected as forces in the overall construction of gender relations. This played itself out either as conflict or collusion between male workers, overseers and employers for control over women. The presence of Indian women in the colony underscored, for the white settlers, the permanence of the Indian population which in turn had political ramifications. The 'boats not votes' sentiment extended well beyond the colonial period, and it was not until the 1960s that Indians were accepted as a permanent part of the South African population.

For the indentured women themselves, life meant a struggle against two similar but culturally different constructs of gender roles and gender relations, determined also by class position. Under indenture itself, Indian women devised a range of survival strategies and made a variety of choices. But these strategies and choices, far from indicating an unbridled independence, were made within certain structural constraints which need to be understood and which seriously curtailed their freedom and potential autonomy.

Indentured women and production

According to Brookes and Webb (1965: 85) Indians were 'the only part of the population of Natal which came by special and urgent invitation'. However, the invitation was not extended to Indian women. They were imported into the colony only grudgingly. To the chagrin of the planters, the Indian government had evolved a network of regulations governing the export of Indian labour well before importation to Natal began in 1860. This included a female quota of 29%. Women were deemed by the planters to be of little use in the sphere of production. Moreover, their role as reproducers was regarded with suspicion and resentment. The planters saw the system of indenture itself as the means by which the labour force should be replaced over time. The other colonists felt that the introduction of Indians into the colony on a permanent basis was an unnecessary complication to Natal's social fabric. Ultimately (and they were joined by the sugar planters in this), they saw the proletarianisation of the African population as the solution to Natal's labour needs.

From the outset, therefore, the quota of women was seen as dead stock, the planters wanting only strong, healthy men who could do the work necessary to create massive and orderly plantations out of the virgin, subtropical bush. Unlike other importing countries, such as British

Guiana, Natal did not recruit Indian women, nor did the planters pay for their introduction into the colony. The system dictated that one-third of the cost of indentured immigration was to be borne by the employer. By the end of the nineteenth century the planters had ensured that this did not apply to the quota of women assigned to them.

Nevertheless, this did not prevent the estate owners from realising the value of utilising women as a source of labour power. Their main tasks in the field were hoeing, weeding, planting beans and cowpeas between the cane rows and cutting plant cane. Remuneration for men was to be the rate of 10s per month for the first year of indenture, rising by a shilling a month for each successive year. Women who worked were to receive half the amount paid to men, and children were to be paid in proportion to their age. The law provided that married women were not obliged to work and that employers were still compelled to provide them with accommodation, rations and medical care. No mention, however, was made of single women or women whose unions did not conform to the legal definition of marriage in the colony. As the majority of women fell into the latter categories, sufficient confusion ensued to pave the way for a system of abuse which was never eliminated.

By the end of the first phase of indentured immigration in 1866, it was already clear that *all* women and older children were denied rations on many estates unless they worked. The issue of whether or not women should be compelled to work was not particularly pressing as at this stage women were not valued as workers. Planters had to be induced by law to provide women and children under 10 years with half rations if they were unable or unwilling to work.

Between 1866 and 1874 Indian immigration ceased temporarily, partly because of the depression during the second half of the 1860s (from which the sugar producers were not immune), partly because of resumed attempts to induce African cultivators into wage labour, and partly because, by this time, complaints of illtreatment and contract violations had reached the ears of the Indian government. It was, as a result, reluctant to allow continued emigration to Natal until provisions had been made to improve the conditions facing indentured immigrants.

The confusion which attended the regulations governing the employment of women persisted during the second phase of immigration and capital was made of this by employers. In truth, there was no blanket ruling on the matter of whether or not women could be compelled to work, although significantly, on the pre-1866 indentured contracts, opposite each woman's name were the words 'if employed', whereas after 1874 these words were omitted from the contracts. This led to a ruling by resident magistrates that women could be compelled to work unless protected by a medical certificate.

By this time, the understated but very clear objectives of the planters were that women should be paid if they worked and that they should in fact work. Not only does this indicate the growing realisation of the importance of women's productive labour, but it also illustrates their expectation that 'the family' would act as a material safety net for indentured women. This provided a rationalisation for paying indentured women at half the rate of men in the first place. The preference of many employers for 'task work' (piece work) for women labourers indicates that it was expected that the subsistence needs of women and those of their younger children, would be met from the wages of the men. This was an unrealistic expectation and had severe implications for the construction of gender relations within the indentured contract system.

Women were not equally useful in all sectors employing indentured labour and therefore it is not possible to generalise about their role in production or the extent of their exploitation. They worked most extensively as labourers on the coastal plantations. Their experience elsewhere serves as a contrast to this.

The largest official employer of indentured labour was the Natal Government Railways (NGR) which from the late nineteenth century was engaged in construction work linking the Witwatersrand with the coast of Natal. It ran its construction and maintenance gangs along the lines of an army, moving them from one site to another as the need arose. Comparatively, conditions on the NGR were quite good, but because of the nature of the work, there was no room for women. Consequently, women who were assigned to the NGR were not provided with work and received no rations. In the larger urban centres like Durban and Pietermaritzburg, many women were able to subsist by selling goods such as basketware. In the smaller towns, however, such as Ladysmith and Howick, the situation was so severe that 'in some instances men [used] to send their wives away from the line as they plead (and rightly) that a 12 lb ration is insufficient for two people to live on'. The Deputy Protector of Indian Immigrants who reported this added that he was 'besieged' by starving women, when he visited the inland lines, begging him to do something for them (Natal Archives, Indian Immigration Files [hereafter NA/II] 1895: 1/77).

A small but not insignificant number of indentured Indians were allotted to farmers and smallholders in the Natal Midlands, where they were used as farm labourers and domestic servants. They were usually employed in small numbers and this region had no equivalent of the large coastal employers of indentured Indians. Indeed, 98% of all upcountry farming enterprises using indentured workers had only four workers on average in their employment, as they relied in the main on the seasonal hiring of African 'togt' or day labour.

However, it was in this small farming sector that women were particularly welcome. They were most often used as domestic servants, though they had to engage in farm work as well. Employers usually requested that they be assigned men with families so that they could deploy the labour of the children round the farm and the women around the house. Indentured women were subjected to the long hours and isolation characteristic of domestic service. In addition, they were often treated with great harshness, something of which can be established from their complaints to the Deputy Protector. One woman, for example, complained of being made to stand on a barrel all day for refusing to work because she was in an advanced stage of pregnancy (NA/II 1916: 1/191).

The coal mining industry in Natal proved an important source of demand for Indian labourers as well. From their inception in the 1880s, the collieries faced competition for labour from the surrounding agricultural districts as well as from the recruiters representing the Rand mines. For a period around the turn of the century, they came to rely on indentured and ex-indentured or 'free' Indian workers. Mine labour was not popular among Indian immigrants, despite the fact that the wages were somewhat higher than for fieldwork. Ostensibly, Indian immigrants could only be drafted for mine work if they consented. In practice, the coal mines had no difficulty in recruiting sufficient Indian immigrants, and between 1903 and 1913, they made up nearly 40% of the labour force.

The number of women in the mines was relatively small. The fact that their number fell short of the official quota is explained by the fact that the substantial number of ex-indentured or 'free' Indians employed on the mines did not come with a statutory quota of women. Nevertheless, there was a place for women labourers, as they were used for surface work, picking and sorting the coal by hand from a mechanical screen. Perhaps more important then their role in the labour process was the way in which the scarcity of women was used by employers, managers and overseers to control the labour and mobility of men. There is strong evidence to suggest that it was not uncommon for mine managers to sell women to the men as 'wives' to prevent men whose contracts had expired from leaving, and for the same woman to be sold several times over (NA/II 1904: 1/130).

The Deputy Protectors who were responsible for indentured immigrants in the inland regions of the colony generally demonstrated more compassion or at least diligence in the recording of complaints. For this reason it is easy to gain the impression that labourers were treated worse there than on the coastal estates. However, even given the lack of meticulous records, it is possible to demonstrate that the poor conditions of indentured workers on the coastal estates totally eclipsed those in other sectors. Not only were conditions worse on the estates of the coast, but it was here that the greatest number of indentured immigrants were employed.

Among the properties in the sugar-belt, seventeen large plantations had developed, and they, together with the NGR, though constituting less than 10% of the employers in the region, engaged 64% of the indentured labour force on the coast. There was also a small intermediate group of medium-sized estates and a number of lesser enterprises which accounted for approximately 17% of all employers and 26% of the regional workforce.

The smaller enterprises and estates provided living conditions for tiny groups of workers fairly similar to those found in the interior of the colony. The large plantations, on the other hand, which dominated the economic landscape of Natal, were organised along quasi-industrial lines. Here workers were accommodated in barracks, which were badly ventilated, poorly lit and appallingly overcrowded. The unhealthy living conditions, when combined with the rigours of labour on the plantations, gave rise to a high incidence of occupationally and environmentally related diseases and a high mortality rate. In 1904 it was observed by the Protector that the mortality rate on the large estates was higher than elsewhere (NA/II 1904: 1/130). This is significant in that the 1913 Tuberculosis Commission observed that 'The authorities state that the extent of the sickness and death rate has proved a most reliable index of the conditions and treatment of coolies by different employers' (Tuberculosis Commission 1913: 92).

Women's productive labour was extensively harnessed and more actively employed on the estates than elsewhere. Although difficult to quantify, women were vital to the labour process on the estates for much of the period, serving to enhance the profitability of the sugar industry through their direct exploitation, and maintaining at a low level the overall costs of production under conditions of indentured labour.

The most intensive use of female labour was on the tea estates situated on the north coast of Natal, many of which were owned by planters who also had interests in sugar production. Mechanisation was impossible on the steep slopes where the crop was grown, and the profitability of the industry was too slim to sustain high production costs. When indentured immigration was terminated in 1911, tea cultivation faced a premature demise and the plantations were converted to sugar.

Indentured women were considered vital to tea cultivation precisely because their labour was ultra-cheap, though the preference for women workers was usually expressed in terms of stereotypes such as their greater dexterity (ability to pluck without damage the tender tips of the tea plant), or the fact that women were more suited to the demands of tea-picking which required powers of endurance rather than strength. Tea planters attempted to import immigrants from the tea-growing region of Assam and always requested families or women. Men were put to work clearing the fields and doing heavy factory work. Children were engaged in light factory tasks such as sweeping. But it was the women who were the most strenuously worked in the fields.

During the picking season, which lasted for nine months of the year, they laboured in the fields for eleven to thirteen hours a day. They were also engaged in ordinary cultivation work, such as weeding and digging up the ground between the young tea plants with hoes. They were paid half the male rate and received half the male rations. When they did not work they were not paid and received no rations. This led women to push themselves to work whether sick, pregnant or even in labour. It was not unknown for women to drop dead at their work.

The worst time for women on the tea estates was the six weeks following the long picking season when their labour was not required. During this period they were sent to the barracks without food or wages. In a complaint to Hindson and Company Limited the Protector wrote of such women: 'Those who are without husbands or men to look after them are compelled to beg for food, which they do, or obtain food by more objectionable means'. Hindson eventually agreed that he would give the women a fortnight's break with rations following the picking season, but not without a fight in which he threatened to have the medical officer who reported him removed for incompetence and the Protector dismissed from his post (NA/II 1904: 1/130).

On the sugar estates the women also engaged in field work. They did not cut the cane but worked as ordinary field hands. During the planting season, which began usually between October and November, women were put to weeding. This was conducted along the lines of task work, and women were frequently kept in the fields at unfinished jobs until long after dark. Although weeding was classified as light labour it was extremely back-breaking and monotonous. In addition women were also employed in cutting plant cane, which was used to establish new cane fields at the end of a number of years of ratooning. This was a semi-skilled task, as the pieces of cane to be used had to be carefully selected and handled so that the eyes from which the new shoots would grow were not damaged: then the women would lay the plant cane in furrows prepared by the male workers. This was the only skill acquired by women on the sugar estates. In Natal the harvesting and planting seasons overlapped to a considerable degree, and as the new fields were planted every year in rotation, this work involved women on a fairly regular basis for significant periods. However, when they were not thus engaged, they were invariably laid off without wages or rations.

The great advantage to the planters of women workers, therefore, was this ability to draw them into the workforce whenever their labour was required (usually at a daily rate of 6d and half rations) and to send them back to the barracks when it was not. For the planter, this alleviated the burden associated with captive labour such as slavery or indenture; namely, that of having to support permanently a labour force required only seasonally.

Despite the realisation that women's work was valuable to the running and profitability of the estates, it was the women who were first phased out of the estate labour force during the transition from indenture to other forms of labour utilisation. From the turn of the century, ways were sought to base the northwards expansion of the sugar industry into Zululand and even beyond, on the harnessing of local or regional African labour. While not immediately successful (Africans in Natal were able to resist long-term labour contracts in the colony until the second decade of the twentieth century) local Africans did engage in day labour. But it was the unskilled work of the women that was substituted by African 'togt' labour rather than that of Indian men. Indian men had achieved a level of skill rising out of five years (or longer) under indentured contract in various branches of sugar production. In 1920 it was reported that Indian men 'were found very handy at the mill, to be good cane cutters, and very useful in making drains and roads, but the kaffirs were found best for ordinary field work' (SA *Sugar Journal* 1920–1: 184).

The shift to African labour was in accordance with long-term planning and visions of expansion, but was also a response to the greater avail-ability of African 'togt' labour and the fact that African wages had dropped from around 10s per month in the 1850s (comparable with indentured wages) to around 9s at the turn of the century. Moreover, under the provisions of the Masters and Servants Act of 1894, Africans could be employed under twelve-month contracts on the estates, and Section 19 of this act provided that the wives, and children over sixteen, of the workers were also bound by the contract, thus eliminating some of the disadvantages associated with employing 'togt' labour (SA *Sugar Journal* 1920–1: 154).

Ultimately, in the presence of an alternative source of cheap labour which became increasingly available during the course of the twentieth century, all indentured immigrants were gradually phased out of the plantation labour force. The effect on women, however, was more immediate and more dramatic. Indian men were able to remain on the estates in conditions other than forced labour by virtue of the skills they had acquired under indenture. This was not the case for women for whom the most menial tasks had been reserved. Moreover, many of these skills served men in carving out a life for themselves outside wage labour altogether, and many began to work on their own account. Women terminated their indentured contracts ill-equipped for anything, and thus, as under indenture, were ultimately dependent upon developing relationships with individual men willing to support them.

The question arises as to whether women resisted their exploitation as indentured labourers. There is ample evidence to suggest that they did. To do so, however, meant risking physical assault either by employers or overseers, deprivation of wages and the withholding of rations. There is evidence that women deserted, occasionally joining African communities. Others set fire to cane fields and engaged in various forms of passive resistance. On the whole, however, this resistance was largely individual and defensive. For indentured labourers as a whole, the extent of collective resistance and worker consciousness is an issue which has been extensively debated and perhaps even exaggerated (see, for example, contributions in Bissoondoyal and Servansing 1986). With regard to women, it did not take an overt, collective form, and very often their individual acts of resistance increased women's vulnerability and reinforced their tendency to remain silent.

Indentured women and the reproduction of the labour force

As well as being directly exploited as workers, women were subjected to extreme forms of oppression in their capacity as reproducers of labour power. Both women's productive and unproductive labour was harnessed by employers and served to hold down indentured wages generally. This was particularly obvious on the coastal estates. Women's cultivation of garden plots partly met their own subsistence needs as well as those of their children and of the indentured men. This, together with their domestic work in the barracks, served to reproduce labour power on the estates on a day-to-day basis.

In the sphere of the proverbial double shift, indentured women were subject to extraordinary burdens. When not in the fields themselves or during their breaks, they were required by their male partners or the men to whom they were somehow indebted or obligated, to take them a midday meal in the fields or at the mill. In the evening they were expected to engage in food preparation, cleaning, washing and sexual activity. Given the disproportion of the sexes, they were frequently required to perform such tasks on behalf of not one but several men. This was often done in return for rations or other favours such as clothing or even protection. The precariousness of their remuneration for fieldwork increased women's dependence on men.

Initially, the planters did not recognise the value of indentured women as reproducers of labour power on a generational basis, as they saw the system of indenture itself as replenishing their workforce. However, by the turn of the century, and in the wake of complaints regarding the continued importation of Indian immigrants, attempts were made to reduce import-ation and to promote reindenture. In terms of Act 17 of 1895 which became effective in 1901, an annual £3 tax was imposed on all Indians coming out of indentured contracts who refused to reindenture or return to India. Although sold as a repatriation device to the anti-immigration lobby, the effect of the tax was to promote a high rate of reindenture and to ensure a continued supply of cheap and captive labour. The rate of reindenture reached its peak in 1912 when it was 95%. As the Protector explained, 'Even an optimist would hardly have anticipated such a large percentage of reindentures, 70% being the highest even looked for. This result has greatly helped in maintaining the labour supply of the province, especially in certain portions of the coast district' (NA/II 1912).

This shows not only the effectiveness of the tax as a coercive measure, but indicates how reindenture came significantly to supplement import-ation in the early twentieth century, as the economy expanded in the years before the African population became fully proletarianised. For this period, therefore, more than at any other time, the reproductive function of indentured women became important to capital which required that the indentured labour force be reproduced within the colony. This was particularly crucial to the planters given the constant threat to end indentured importation which in fact was implemented in 1911.

That the importance of the indentured women's reproductive function was transitory is attested to by the fate of women coming out of indentured contracts after 1911. There were hosts of cases of destitute women wandering about without employment or support. These women were classified as 'free' Indians because, according to the Protector, 'a destitute Indian cannot be under indenture' (NA/II 1913: 11/189). Employers were not interested in having them live on their premises if they did not work for them. Women in these circumstances were frequently repatriated to India. Women could be repatriated on a number of grounds: for example, if they applied for exemption from the £3 tax, were old, found begging, reported for medical treatment, had no family to support them, or resisted and showed defiance.

While all indentured workers, male and female, who were pauperised, in ill-health or who displayed unacceptable behaviour ran the risk of repatriation, it is significant that, given the sexual imbalance within the Indian population, proportionally almost as many women as men were repatriated. The ratio of men to women in 1911 was 100: 66 and yet of the 152,641 immigrants introduced into Natal, 24% of the males and 22% of the females had returned by this time. By 1927, 42% of the male immigrants and 39% of the female immigrants had returned (compiled from Reports of the Protector of Indian Immigrants 1911, 1920 and 1927). This seriously places in doubt the conclusion that women's scarcity value earned women independence and bargaining power under conditions of indenture, as has been argued in other contexts (Moore 1984). Their experience varied according to a number of factors such as their age, health, looks, vigour, personal relationships and personal history. For example, many of the women who were repatriated were widows, the Hindu taboo against widow remarriage persisting.

Indentured labour and gender relations

The Indian immigrants brought with them a culture with a different expression of gender relations from those prevailing among the African and white populations of the colony. Moreover, the retention of cultural values often served as a defence in a strange and hostile environment and frequently this found expression in the sphere of gender relations. Yet although the form of expression of gender relations was culturally specific, much of its ideological content was confirmed and reinforced by the dominant ideology of gender among the ruling white settlers. At the workplace there was both conflict and collusion between male workers and employers for control over Indian women. At a more general level there was congruence between white colonial perceptions and Indian expectations in terms of the proper ordering of relations between the sexes.

To take the most obvious manifestation of oppressive gender relations, that of physical and sexual abuse of women, the files of the Protector are replete with complaints of this nature. Very typical is the case of a woman called Vellach, employed by a Mr Hulley in the Pietermaritzburg district. She complained to the Deputy Protector's office thus:

> About ten days ago whilst in my master's bedroom regulating it, he came in, striking his pocket and saying that he would give me three pounds if I were to lie with him, as the mistress and her family had gone to town. I refused saying that my husband would beat me. He said he would not tell him.
>
> (NA/II 1880: 1/7)

In his response, Hulley used the gilt-edged defence exercised by so many employers accused in this way, pointing to the promiscuity of the woman and the incidence of venereal disease among the Indian population. He convinced the Deputy Protector of his innocence by saying: 'Putting aside her personal appearance which is not very attractive, is it likely that I, a married man, knowing what had been the matter with her . . . would be guilty of such a charge . . . ?' (NA/II 1880: 1/7). Vellach's request to be assigned to another employer was refused, again a common response to what was seen as a ploy by Indian women to leave positions they did not like.

Sexual harassment was not confined to employers. It was common for planters to rely on sirdhars to oversee the women in the workplace and the barracks and they frequently used the position to their own advantage. The way in which women were used and abused on the plantation has been clearly summarised by Tayal:

> [They] were treated almost as chattels, and even marriage was regarded with contempt in some quarters. On one of the biggest plantations, women were routinely used to punish recalcitrant male labourers . . . thus a situation was created in Natal which permitted the whites to believe that Indians were incapable of sustaining bonds of mutual affection and responsibility.
>
> (1980: 337)

To maintain a relationship was difficult in conditions devoid of leisure and privacy and where couples could be separated at the will of the employer. The Wragg Commission of 1885–7 noted: 'We regret to observe that too little regard is paid to this very essential requisite towards purity of life. There is a general huddling together of the sexes, of all ages, much to be deplored' (Meer 1980: 302). Yet when objections were made by single women to having to sleep under the same roof as single men, the response was generally an echo of that of the Protector who argued that there was 'nothing whatsoever to prevent the complainants from keeping themselves apart if they so wished, from the single men . . . ' (NA/II 1900: 1/197).

Life on the estates was not as simple as that for women who were forced to be dependent on men for food, clothing, a sleeping place or protection. The case of *Regina* vs *Mulwa*, who murdered his common law wife, Nootini, on the Blackburn Estate in April 1890, suggests that it was common practice for women to be shared as a cook, housekeeper and sexual partner with other men who could give a couple access to sleeping quarters or extra rations. In this case, Mulwa could not accept the situation and said in his statement before sentence: 'I killed her because she went with other men.' This case, in which a man was hanged for the murder of his partner, was just one of many on the estates, which involved murder, suicide, violence and abuse. It was common for women to be bought or sold for a shilling, with the tacit approval of employers, sirdhars, the male workers, and sometimes the women themselves. The tragedy of Nootini's situation can be seen from the evidence of a witness at Mulwa's trial. On the morning she was murdered she was heard pleading with her sick husband to go to work saying, 'if you don't go to work who will give us food?' It was that same morning that Mulwa found her 'lying' with another man (NA/II 1890: 1/57).

In the face of the marked sexual imbalance in the Indian population, and the benefits derived by men from, among other things, the sexual division of labour, indentured men were most vigorous in asserting their claims over women. Where possible, marriage was entered into, but the £5 fee required for legally recognised marriages was out of the reach of most indentured immigrants. Marriage by customary religious rites, Hindu or Muslim, was not considered valid in the colonial courts. This did not prevent Indian men from recourse to colonial justice, however, in their attempts to assert control over women. Cases of desertion, adultery and breach of promise to marry were brought before the Protector, and such cases were invariably decided in favour of the men. This was the same Protector who in terms of labour relations invariably decided in favour of employers!

Giving evidence to the 1872 so-called 'Coolie Commission', Rangassamy, an Indian hotel-keeper from Verulam, outlined his views on the problems created by the scarcity of women and the need for legislation to control them:

> As to marriages among the coolies we first imported too many males [who] were single and the scarcity of females causes [sic] many debauches and in many cases they committed suicide: therefore I consider to stop this, when they agree to marry, the agreement should be drawn by the Coolie Agent, in the Coolie Office. After they agree to marry; if either party refuse to marry, the Coolie Agent should punish the guilty person.
>
> (Coolie Commission 1872)

The various punishments suggested by Rangassamy were far harsher for women than men; although not followed to the letter by the colonial authorities, they were accepted in spirit. There was frequently a congruence in the male construction of gender roles and relations, even if there were differences as to how control over women should be ensured. The authorities gave to Indian men a more sympathetic hearing when they reported their anxieties regarding problems arising from the imbalance between the sexes. For women, whether control came via the law, through physical abuse, or ideological conditioning, it was pernicious and unrelenting.

Despite the effort to exert control over women by legalising unions under indenture, marriage was more of an issue for Indians outside indentured contracts. It seems that once Indians were free, marriage and the creation of a stable and 'traditional' family life became a priority. It was, perhaps, not only a personal response, but a defensive reaction to Indians's somewhat uncomfortable location within the social fabric of the colony, wedged between the politically and economically dominant minority of whites, and the numerically vast, subjugated African population.

The practice of child-marriage brought from India was given a particularly unsavoury flavour through the sexual imbalance among Indians in the colony. There is evidence that young brides could be purchased from their parents and that some unscrupulous guardians sold them several times over. Recent interviews with Indian women in Durban give some insight into how this practice was perceived by the young girls themselves:

> The practice of child-marriage, as practiced quite extensively in India was more characteristic of the period following indenture . . . Of all the women interviewed all those who had been married had no choice or say in who their husband was to be . . . Velimah: 'Father chose the husband, they won't let us go and choose, they'll give us a hiding . . . If he feels it OK we got married, never mind if he's a drunkard'.
>
> (Williams 1986: 17)

This control, although acquiesced in, was nevertheless perceived, if not as oppression, then at least with resentment. Despite this, and despite the assault on domestic relations experienced under indenture, it is clear that ex-indentured or 'free' Indians, both men and women, invested heavily, both materially and emotionally, in the establishment of household units and family lives. This needs to be explained, and may best be done by placing this South African study within the context of other writings on the position of women under the indentured labour system.

Women under indenture in comparative perspective

In a paper which sought to explore the condition of women under indenture in Fiji, Brij Lal concluded that:

> Women, it has been shown here, generally suffered greater hardships than men. They shouldered the dual burden of plantation work, the double standards of morality, and carried the

blame for many of the ills of indenture. To be sure, they were not
the chaste heroines of Indian mythology that the Indian nationalists made them out to be, but neither on the other hand, were
they the immoral 'doe rabbits' of the overseers' accounts.

(1985: 71)

The conclusions of Brij Lal for Fiji differ very little in substance from
those of this study. His investigation, however, is confined to the effects on
women of the indentured labour system without extending it to an attempt
to unravel the complexities of gender roles and relationships between
indentured men and women.

An attempt to do this is made by Brian Moore writing on sex and
marriage amongst Indian immigrants in British Guiana during the nineteenth century. He suggests that the paucity of women gave them a
considerable bargaining power which, together with their independent
earning capacity, 'enhanced their independence of the man or husband'
(1984: 12).

If conditions in any way paralleled those in Natal, it is suggested that
Moore's notion of female independence must derive from an uncritical
reading of official sources (avoided, for example, by Brij Lal). It also
suggests an acceptance by Moore of prevailing attitudes, liberally sprin-
kled with his own brand of sexism, illustrated below:

> Women shifted their allegiance with consummate ease to
> whichever male was prepared to make them the best offer. It was
> reportedly not uncommon for a woman to desert a man with
> whom she had cohabited for another, then for a third and perhaps
> a fourth, and sometimes even return to one of those whom she
> had previously left – and with apparent impunity.
>
> (1984: 4)

and:

> It was thus reportedly fairly commonplace for three or four men
> to live with one woman. A few men who were not afflicted by the
> prevailing virus of jealousy even exploited the female shortage by
> hiring out 'the partial use of' their wives, though this must have
> incurred the enormous risk of permanent loss.
>
> (1984: 5)

It hardly needs pointing out that the notion of sexually powerful and
manipulative women being hired out by their not too jealous partners
contains a contradiction. Women as property of men is taken as understood, and the implicit assumption here is that the lack of sustained

relationships was due not to the conditions under which indentured labourers lived and worked, but to the permissiveness and ambition of the women.

This is not to deny that women moved from one partner to another. It has to be questioned, however, whether manoeuvrability under the structural constraints imposed upon them constituted independence. One has to ask, for example, how independent Nootini was, in deciding to be lover both to Mulwa and Sahabdeen? One has to question the so-called bargaining power of the little girl referred to by the Inspector of Nuisances in Natal who wrote to the Protector in 1904 asking what to do about this child who lived in one of the NGR barracks. She was not employed and not permanently attached to anyone. She had 'no regular sleeping place but finds any place she can for the purpose' (NA/II 1904: 1/126).

Rhoda Reddock, in a paper on Indian women in Trinidad, which she subtitled 'Freedom denied', argued that women derived benefits from indentured immigration. In it they found an escape from starvation or widowhood or a possible life of prostitution. She goes on to say that 'the decision to emigrate in itself was a sign of the independent character of these women and the decision to emigrate alone and as individuals was a sign of their strength' (1984: 13). It is agreed that emigration may have been an attractive alternative to options such as widowhood or prostitution in India. It is not in dispute that the decision by Indian women to emigrate was a very brave one. However, looking at the evidence for Natal at least, some of Reddock's conclusions must be questioned. She sums up:

> This paper has sought . . . to return to Indian women their proud history of independence and struggle for some degree of autonomy over their lives. This history of struggle from the initial decision to migrate to the rigours of the plantation is one which unites them with oppressed and exploited women the world over who when necessary and where possible have resisted their oppression and fought for their autonomy as women and as members of exploited classes.
>
> (1984: 45)

Reddock has exaggerated the level of resistance and particularly *collective* resistance exercised by women under indenture. It is undoubtedly true that women fought to maintain control over their lives and were not passive objects of history, but it is difficult to conceive of women finding for themselves *independence* and *freedom* under conditions of forced labour!

Reddock also claims that, under indenture, Indian women 'probably for the first time in their lives, got an opportunity to exercise a degree of control over their social and sexual lives', but that this was lost once Indian women were 'firmly under the control of the men through the reconstruction, albeit in a different setting of the Indian patriarchal family system' (1984: 39). Firstly, the evidence of collusion amongst employers, sirdhars and male workers over the control of women under the indentured system means this argument does not hold – in the case of Natal at any rate. Secondly, it is an error to present the 'Indian patriarchal family system' as a static institution. For better or for worse, the experience of indenture had an impact on domestic relations and on the reconstruction of the 'traditional' family amongst Indians in Natal.

As Hazel Carby has suggested with regard to blacks in America and other people under colonialism, it is possible for the family to become the site of both political and cultural resistance (1982). In the South African case, the resultant emphasis on communalism has been politically both a progressive force (for example, the role of the Indian Congresses in the Congress movement) and a conservative force (for example, the participation by some Indians in the ethnically divided tricameral parliament). Whatever the political implications, it is true that the persistent potency of cultural values (particularly in the sphere of gender relations) has served as a source of social cohesion for Indians in South Africa. To see the Indian family as the central site of women's oppression is to extrapolate uncritically from specifically western feminist insights. This is not to deny that the 'Indian patriarchal family system' exists or that it has constituted a site of gender oppression. What is at issue here is that the system of indenture did not offer women a temporary respite from the hardships and oppression of an unchanging institution, nor did it offer women an opportunity to flourish as autonomous and independent social and sexual beings.

Conclusion

Indian women were brought to Natal with reluctance. Their labour power was nevertheless harnessed at certain stages in the development of Natal's economy, when they were among the most exploited members of the colony's proletariat. Both their productive and reproductive labour facilitated capital accumulation, particularly on the sugar estates. As Indians they were unwelcome and subject to obnoxious stereotyping. As Indian women they were seen to be responsible for the increase in the size of the Indian population and symbolised, for white settlers, its possible permanence. As women they had to struggle against two different but converging constructs of gender relations, in both of which, women were subordinated to men: one was that prevailing within the Indian immigrant population itself, and the other was the broader relations of gender which were developing under colonial rule in Natal. Undoubtedly women devised a variety of strategies for survival sometimes within and sometimes without the 'Indian patriarchal family system'. For many, marriage was not an option, particularly for widows or those who had been passed around the barracks from man to man and who bore the scars, both physical and psychological, of that experience. Above all, recognition is necessary of the constraints under which Indian women made the choices they did.

References

Primary sources
Colony of Natal Blue Books
Coolie Commission, 1872
Natal Archives, Indian Immigration Files (NA/II)
Reports of the Protector of Indian Immigrants
Union Government 34-1914: Tuberculosis Commission
South African Sugar Journal 1920–1

Secondary sources
Brookes, E.H. and Webb, C. de B. 1965. *A History of Natal*, Pietermaritzburg: University of Natal Press.
Bissoondoyal, U. and Servansing, S.B.C. (eds.) 1984. *Indian Labour Immigration*, Moka, Mauritius: Mahatma Gandhi Institute.
Carby, H. 1982. 'White woman listen! Black feminism and the boundaries of sisterhood', in *The Empire Strikes Back: Race and Racism in 70s Britain*, ed. Centre for Contemporary Cultural Studies.
Lal, Brij V. 1985. 'Kunti's cry: indentured women on Fiji plantations', *The Indian Economic and Social History Review*, 22, 55–71.
Meer, Y.S. (ed.) 1980. *Documents of Indentured Labour, Natal 1851–1917*, Durban: Institute of Black Research.
Moore, B. 1984. 'Sex and marriage among Indian immigrants in British Guiana during the nineteenth century', Paper presented at the Third Conference on East Indians in the Caribbean, Trinidad.
Reddock, R. 1984. 'Indian women and indentureship in Trinidad and Tobago, 1845–1917: freedom denied', Paper presented at the Third Conference on East Indians in the Caribbean, Trinidad.
Tayal, M. 1980. 'Gandhi: the South African experience', D.Phil., Oxford University.
Williams, M. 1986. 'Echoes from the past: race, class and gender, Indian women in the 1930s and 1940s', University of Natal Research Project.

3

Indians in the French overseas departements: Guadeloupe, Martinique, Reunion

Singaravélou

Slavery was abolished in the French colonies in 1848. It gave rise, among other things, to a serious manpower shortage, brought on by the departure of large numbers of freed black slaves who left the plantations to work in the towns or cultivate the hillier parts of the islands which until that time had not been exploited. The manpower shortage was only one of many factors which gave rise to a general slump in the sugar-producing economies of the Caribbean and the Mascareignes during the first half of the nineteenth century. Other contributory factors were either linked with the internal disorganisation of the plantation economy or resulted from the international economic situation.

Immigration had been considered long before 1848 as a solution to a possible manpower shortage both in the numbers and quality of workers required. After several attempts, immigration from India was judged the most satisfactory. The British colonies paved the way for recruitment into the French colonies. Reunion received the first influx of immigrants and the island served as a model and rival for Guadeloupe and Martinique. At first, recruitment of Indian coolies took place at the five French trading posts, especially Pondicherry and Karikal, but it was later introduced throughout British India, after the signing in 1861 of the Franco-British Convention (Singaravélou 1975).

The vast majority of Indian immigrant coolies were of Tamil origin: practically all in Martinique, 87% in Reunion, 60% in Guadeloupe. In the two latter islands, the remainder of the indentured immigrants were from Northern India and were called 'Calcutta' after their port of embarkation. Immigrants from Southern India were generally called 'Malabars'. The number of immigrants brought in varied from one colony to another (Table 3.1), as did the number of repatriations (Table 3.2), but, as a generalisation, the nineteenth-century Indian population in Reunion reached a peak in 1860 and in Guadeloupe and Martinique about twenty years later (Figure 3.1).

Table 3.1. *Total number of Indian immigrants in the French islands*

Island	Period	Number
Guadeloupe	1854–89	43,326
Martinique	1854–89	25,509
Reunion	1829–1924	118,000

Source: Singaravélou (1975); Dupon, J.F. (1967)

Table 3.2. *Total number of Indian repatriations from the French islands*

Island	Period	Number
Guadeloupe	1861–1906	9,460
Martinique	1858–95	11,077
Reunion	1835–1930	88,000

Source: Singaravélou (1975); Dupon, J.F. (1967)

Indentured immigration from India was suspended in Reunion in 1883 and in Guadeloupe and Martinique in 1885; it was halted definitively in 1917. We know little about the numerical evolution of the Indian population during the first half of the twentieth century. However, given the high mortality rate and the large number of repatriations, we can estimate with some confidence that the number of Indians has continually decreased over this period.

As well as the indentured Tamil immigrants, Reunion received a minority of voluntary Indo-Muslim immigrants. Until the end of the nineteenth century, their numbers were fairly small. The major immigration of these Muslim populations, which originated from North-West India (Sind and Gujarat), and were called locally *Z'arabes*, was between 1920 and 1935 (Dupon 1967). Thus, on the eve of departmentalisation in 1946, the Indian component was quite an important ethnic element in these colonial island societies.

Demographic growth and distribution of the Indian population since 1946

It is also difficult to study the numerical growth of the Indian population since the Second World War, as French census returns and all official documentation make no mention of ethnic origins. Thus any

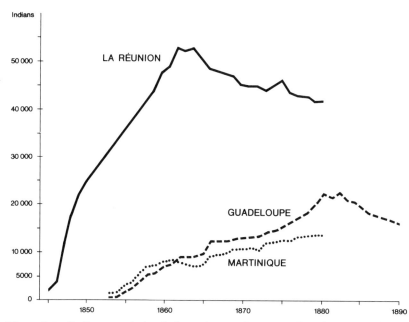

Figure 3.1   Indian population in late nineteenth-century Reunion, Guadeloupe and Martinique

evaluation of the Indian population has to be approximate and contains a fairly wide margin of error. Even the definition of an Indian is not straightforward. Somatic criteria coupled to cultural intermingling with the black Creole populations often produce surprising results. An Indian with fairly pure features may behave like a Creole, while a rural-dwelling mixed Indian with negroid features may participate fully in Indian culture.

From the 1967 census, we have estimated the number of Indians in Guadeloupe to be about 23,000 or 7.8% of the population. The true figure is certainly greater, especially if we add to this the mixed Indians (Singaravélou 1975). The Indian population in Martinique is even smaller. In the 1970s it was estimated at about 10,000 or 3% of the total population. In Reunion, the Indian population is much larger. A 1965 estimate suggested 65,000 Indians, or 16% of the island's total population (Dupon 1967). A more recent estimate, dating from the early 1980s, suggests about 67,000 or 13% of the total population, to which should be added 7,100 Indo-Pakistanis who represent 1.4% of the total population. Clearly, from information currently available, we have no way of deciding which of these two figures is the more accurate, but we should mention that other less-well argued estimates have been put forward and suggest there were 100,000 Tamil Indians in Reunion in the 1960s. This would put the Malabar population today at about 125,000 or almost 25% of the island's total.

Generally speaking, the Indian population in all three territories has gathered in the rural areas, around factories and close to large estates. This legacy from the plantation economy has been supplemented by settlement in a series of smallholdings and small farms run on a share-cropping system. Today this distribution has hardly changed, except for a noticeable tendency to move into the towns. Essentially, however, the Indian in the overseas departments remains a rural dweller.

In Martinique, the Indians and the mixed (or *chappé-coulis*) are to be found in particular in the northern communes of the island, often in the very places where their ancestors first began work in the sugar cane fields. Macouba and Basse-Pointe are the most Indianised communes in the island, followed by Trinité and Sainte-Marie. The Indians are small-holders or agricultural workers, usually living in the more remote areas of these rural communes, rather than in the towns.

In Guadeloupe the vast majority of Indians and mixed (or *bâtard-zindiens*) have gathered in the communes to the windward side of the volcanic island around Capesterre, on the plateaux in the east and in the plains in the north-west of Grande-Terre. More than four out of five Indians live in fourteen of the island's communes. In the commune of Moule one inhabitant in five is Indian, and in Petit-Canal and Port-Louis this figure rises to one in four. Saint-François is the most Indianised commune, with 40% (Map 3.1). Elsewhere, the Indians are fairly widely scattered, and it is unusual to find Indians in any area where there is no sugar cane.

Let us make a more detailed analysis of the 'sections' or remote rural areas. In each commune there are 'Indian sections'. In Saint-François, for example, the inhabitants of the Blonval section are 54% Indian; Pombi-ray, 63%; Dubédou, 77%; Dévarieux, 89%; in these four sections are gathered 30% of the Indian populations of the commune (Singaravelou 1975).

Just as in the other islands, the Indian population in Guadeloupe has become slightly urbanised. In 1967, in the two towns of Basse-Terre and Pointe-à-Pitre, there lived only 5% of the Indian population of the department. They represented only a fraction of the urban population: 3% in Basse-Terre and 2.2% in Pointe-à-Pitre. It seems, however, that for a few years now, the number of Indians living in the urban area of Pointe-à-Pitre has been increasing more rapidly than in the past, and these Indians are participating more and more frequently in tertiary sector activities.

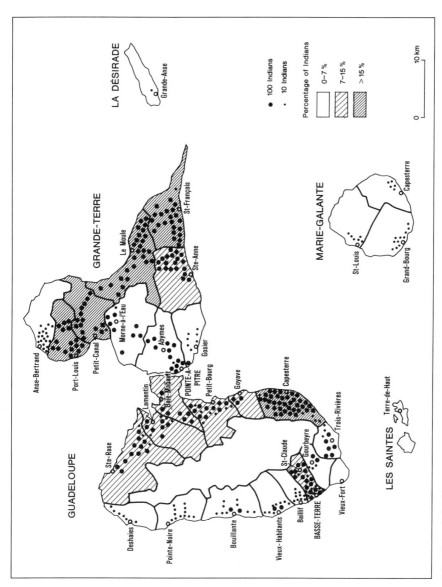

Map 3.1   Distribution by communes of the Indians in Guadeloupe, 1967

In the island of Reunion, there are a great many Malabars on the windward coast, from Sainte-Marie to Saint-Benoît in a virtually continuous concentration. Between Saint-Paul and Trois-Bassins there are some less dense and scattered groups at Saint-Leu, Saint-Louis and Saint-Pierre. They are hardly represented at all in the south-east of the island, between Sainte-Rose and Saint-Pierre, and this is due mainly to the lack of major sugar plantations in this difficult and sparsely populated forest region.

Socio-economic integration of the Indians

Being essentially rural, the Indian population continues to live mainly from the cultivation of sugar cane, and also from bananas and market-garden crops. However, thanks to a recent economic diversification, since the 1960s, Indians have begun to penetrate more and more often into the tertiary sector and are enjoying a rise in their social and economic status, based on improvements in education and an opening up of the towns.

In Guadeloupe, the occupational distribution of the Indian population is 59% in the primary sector, 10% in the secondary sector, and 31% in the tertiary sector, which includes, in particular, transport, domestic service, commerce and public utilities. By far the majority are wage-workers – 70.5% of the working population.

The Indians in all three *départements* are basically farmers working in the sugar cane fields. They are agricultural labourers on the land around the factories, sharecroppers on land belonging to the factory, or smallholders cultivating cane or raising cattle. One of the most important ways of rising socially is still to purchase land. In Guadeloupe, and likewise in Reunion, there have been major Indian landowners farming hundreds of hectares. Land ownership also fulfils a need for property and a place to put down roots.

A small number are fortunate enough to work in the sugar factories and rum distilleries. It has taken a long time for the Indians to penetrate this sector which for so long had been monopolized by the black Creoles. Since 1946 this trend has increased, and now several dozen Indian workers are in the factories and distilleries in Guadeloupe, Martinique and Reunion. Most, however, are unskilled workers, paid by the hour or by the day.

The Indians have also invested in agricultural sectors other than cane. In those areas which were most affected by the slump in the sugar market and where other cash crops for export were planted instead, the Indians, for the most part, remained on the land as farm workers or farmers. One typical example of this substitution is the recent development of banana cultivation in northern Martinique and in the Capesterre Belle-Eau region of Guadeloupe.

Very few Indians living in the country areas do not have their own garden, where they grow vegetables and root crops for their own consumption, and from which they sell any small amount of surplus in the local markets or from roadside stalls. There are regions, however, where vegetables and food crops are grown on a large scale, and the produce is sold in the major urban markets. In the Haut-Matouba-Papaye area, clinging to the side of the Soufrière volcano from which they are under constant threat, lives one group of Guadeloupean Indians which has made its mark in this way on the surrounding countryside (Lasserre 1962).

Rapid economic development among these Indians dates back to departmentalisation, urban growth in Basse-Terre, and especially Pointe-à-Pitre, improvements in road transport and a great increase in home consumption of vegetables. The basis of this development, however, has been a great deal of hard work, in difficult conditions and with no guaranteed results. These farmers laboured in the face of many difficulties, and are often held up as an example for their success. Large families continue to live on tiny smallholdings, but their desire to keep their own land is overwhelming. Their methods of cultivation are still very rudimentary, and they have problems in the commercial market because of quality and competition.

Compared with agriculture, which remains the Indians' favoured sphere of activity, the other sectors are not very well represented. Manufacturing industry is not highly developed in the overseas departments. The tertiary sector, on the other hand, has been opening up for several years, and there are some areas which are very promising for the prospects of the younger generation of Indians – transport, commerce, teaching and the liberal professions.

First, the ox-drawn cart, and for the last twenty years or so, the van, has represented a means of rising up the social and economic ladder for the Indian rural dweller. Many Indians in Guadeloupe and Reunion have invested money in passenger transport. Several dozen bus routes are operated by Indians in the two islands, serving first and foremost the Indian sectors.

Since departmentalisation, the number of Indian shopkeepers has continually increased, especially in the larger villages and the towns. They own small corner stores selling all kinds of foodstuffs and standard consumer goods. They even serve drinks and sandwiches. There is fierce competition with the Chinese and the black Creoles in the general-dealer and a bar section. On a higher level, though still in the distribution trade, the Indians own 'superettes' or mini-markets where everything from hardware to fruit and vegetables is sold.

The establishment of Indians in public and private service sectors dates from departmentalisation and is mainly due to improvements in educational standards. Until the Second World War, the illiteracy rate among Indians was very high. In 1967 more than 46% of Indians in Guadeloupe were illiterate. Even in the 1960s, it was unusual to find Indian pupils in the schools. Today, colleges and schools are welcoming them in ever growing numbers. In higher education establishments, the number of Indian students, though still limited, continues to increase.

Progress in the education of Indians is due to efforts made since departmentalisation. New primary and secondary schools have been built in the small towns and rural areas; tracks and roads have been improved so that they are now passable all year round. All these measures have made it possible for the Indians in rural and isolated areas to attend schools. Compulsory schooling until the age of sixteen, and social benefits linked with departmentalisation have enabled the young Indian to improve his level of training. Psychological prejudices, however, have not been completely done away with; absenteeism is still high during the season of the cane harvest; and Indians are still disadvantaged at school, especially in the literary subjects, because of the cultural backwardness of their rural and illiterate upbringing.

Improvements in schooling over the last thirty years have provided Indians with access to the liberal professions, to teaching and to qualified posts in the upper tertiary sector in banks and insurance companies. Unlike the English-speaking Caribbean countries, such as Guyana and Trinidad, there is no ethnic discrimination against Indians in the public service sector, and posts are awarded according to competitive examination. In this way, the best candidates are selected, regardless of their ethnic origins: many people from poor backgrounds have been able to rise to the highest positions in the public (and private) sector (Singaravélou 1988).

In Reunion, the behaviour of the Hindu Malabar population is similar to that of the Indians in Guadeloupe. The main original feature here is the presence and behaviour of the Indo-Muslim community, the *Z'arabes*. They are mainly present in the tertiary sector, and one of their monopolies is trade, especially in non-food products – fabrics, clothing, hardware, building materials, and furniture. More than two thirds of jobs in the trade sector are filled by Indo-Muslims. Although there is no strict division of labour between the ethnic groups, the Hindu Malabars are basically rural farmers and the Indo-Muslims are mainly urban tradesmen.

There is also a remarkable number of Indo-Muslims in the liberal professions: 5% of doctors, 4% of pharmacists, 4.5% of dentists and 10% of lawyers are Indo-Muslims. Departmentalisation has enabled this minority, which had grown rich through trade, to move into professions which until then had been the monopoly of the white bourgeoisie. This aspect of Indo-Muslim behaviour is similar to that of the Chinese minority.

The Malabar Indians enjoy a more balanced range of tertiary sector activities, although their numbers in the liberal professions, which are not insignificant, are nevertheless far below what one might expect. They account for 4% of doctors, 2.2% of dentists, 7% of pharmacists and 10% of lawyers. These public sector employees represent a quarter of the Malabar working population, but only 10% of the total number of workers in this category.

The social and economic integration of the Indians in the overseas departments is still not complete, though well on the way to being so. Another key indicator of their level of integration is the participation by Indians in local and national politics. Their numerical inferiority, their historical inheritance, and the psycho-sociological blocks they have experienced are all factors which go a long way towards explaining the Indian's reluctance in coming forward. However the political situation has developed quickly since departmentalisation, especially since the 1970s.

Several communes have town councillors or deputy mayors of Indian origin. In Guadeloupe and Reunion, there are general and regional councillors who are Indian. Since 1981, Guadeloupe has had one Indian deputy; and Reunion has one deputy and two senators who are Indian – 50% of the nationally elected representatives, as well as two mayors. Attempts to create an Indian party have failed, and there is no true 'ethnic' vote, as in other countries, but there is, nevertheless, an ethno-political awareness in the overseas departments. During election campaigns, the old prejudices and the stereotypical images resurface, bringing Indians, black Creoles and whites into conflict. This ethno-political awareness has been well and truly stifled in Martinique and weakened in Guadeloupe, but it is alive in Reunion.

Today, Indians are divided over the same issues that divide other groups of the population: progressive or conservative; for or against departmentalisation. On the whole, the majority of Indians favour maintaining the political status quo. As well as the social, economic and cultural reasons that are valid for all populations in the overseas departments, this ethnic minority is also justifiably afraid of losing French political protection, which it sees as a guarantee of ethnic justice.

The social and cultural assimilation of the Indians

I have examined the demographic growth of the Indian populations in overseas departments and their attempts, which are often successful, at economic diversification and integration. However, their Indian cultural heritage, now cut off from the roots, is being eroded, and their social institutions are in decline, under pressure from the society and culture of Creoles and westerners.

In the overseas departments the caste system has lost all social significance and does not influence the status hierarchy. The extended family has disappeared, to be replaced by the nuclear household. Occasionally, however, members of one family may collaborate in their agricultural work, buy land jointly, or farm inherited family land together to avoid dividing it up. But while the Indians lose certain socio-cultural features inherited from their tradition, they take on others and are then better able to integrate themselves into the host environment. There are also socio-cultural features which are retained, and even strengthened, and then serve as a point of resistance, a rallying flag for their 'Indianness'. And it happens more and more that the Indians convert Creoles to their traditions and values, especially in matters of religion.

The religious evolution

Religious and cultural life, and related institutions, have adapted to transplantation better than the social type of institution. The most common Indian religions in the French Antilles and Reunion are those linked with popular Hinduism. They are dedicated to the Mother-Goddess and a host of village deities transplanted from India to the colonies. The cults of Mâriammann, Madouraiviran and Kálimaï are practised, mainly by the Indians of Tamil origin. Blood sacrifice forms part of these cults, as does climbing on cutlasses in Martinique and the fire-walk in Reunion. Indian priests are 'Sunday priests' and generally have another job. Although they are all Indian, the congregation is by no means so. Black Creoles attend in ever-growing numbers, coming at first as amused onlookers, and then becoming faithful believers. This trend represents an Indianisation of the Creoles, which is growing all the time.

Popular Hindu religion is far from being authentic, however. It has become highly contaminated by Catholic ritual and theology. In the absence of a well-developed religious system, Christianity lent an arsenal of theological reinforcements and its indispensable support. In the Antilles and Reunion pressure from the Catholic Church easily overcame the weak resistance offered by the defenceless ethnic minorities. Today almost all Indians are nominally Christian, and it is unquestionably this large-scale conversion to Christianity which has been a major factor in speeding up assimilation of western values and the Creolisation of the Indian populations.

In the French Antilles, popular Hindu religion has survived, but Reunion has witnessed, since the 1970s, the emergence of a Brahminic Hinduism. Temples on the island dedicated to Siva and Vishnu are growing in numbers and the officiating priests are Brahmin. Vegetarianism is now a recognised precept. It is mainly the well-off, town-dwelling Indians who have adopted this Brahminic religion, as they wish to resist Creolisation and to differentiate themselves from the coolie culture of the plantations, and from the popular Hinduism which they judge to be obscurantist. Brahminisation has tended to spread in the Indian country areas, and its development is in relation to the socio-economic mobility being enjoyed by the Indian population of Reunion today.

In Reunion the Muslim minority has escaped the fate of the Hindus. The Muslims resisted better the forces of conversion to Christianity. Their networks of relationship, especially with the Indian region of Gujarat, the close solidarity of their community, the use of the Urdu language, their economic specialisation and their social mobility, are all factors which have strengthened the group and preserved it from the detrimental effects of assimilation.

Linguistic evolution

The disappearance of Indian languages and the acquisition of Creole are characteristic processes in the cultural assimilation that took place long before departmentalisation. A type of linguistic erosion occurred which led to the disappearance of Tamil, the predominant language among the immigrant Indians in the overseas departments. The reason for this was a deliberate attempt on the part of a great number of Indians not to teach their native language to children born in the colony, in order to facilitate their integration into the host society.

Today, such elements of the Tamil language as have survived play an indisputable role in maintaining Indian ethno-cultural identity in opposition to Creole culture. In the context of religion and ritual, prayers are said in Tamil, despite the fact that neither priest nor congregation understands a word. The sacred quality of the language thus becomes all the more obvious. The loss of Tamil has been accompanied by the acquisition of Creole, at first the language of communication on the plantation, and later, a true mother tongue. As we have already seen, departmentalisation enabled French to become more widespread among the descendants of Indian immigrants. Thus, linguistic assimilation has occurred in two stages: first creolisation, followed by gallicisation.

French policy of assimilation

The policy of the colonial power has played a significant role in speeding up the cultural integration of these ethnic minorities. Since 1848, it has been French policy to make no distinction by race and religion in its long-established colonies in the Caribbean and the Mascareignes. In the name of equality and fraternity between people, France has always chosen to gallicise dominated groups and diminish their social and cultural differences, and so cast them in the mould of French civilisation. The idea of equality was accompanied by the wish to assimilate.

Since 1946, when the three colonies became overseas departments, the policy of integration has gained in strength, first in the social and political spheres, and more recently in the economic and cultural spheres. Without specifically favouring the Indian minority, the benefits of this policy have enabled the Indians to integrate much more readily into the economic life of the departments and a new kind of competition has developed between Indians and Creoles for the urban professions and the tertiary sector. Paradoxically, it is in this final phase of France's policy of socio-economic integration and socio-cultural assimilation that the latent ethno-cultural antagonisms within the ex-colonial societies have emerged, notably between the Creole majority and the Indian minority.

Conclusion

The period from the 1970s to the present day has seen an easing off of the extreme form of integration policy which led to the development of a countervailing regionalism in Reunion and the Caribbean. This was based on the emergence of the Creole language and culture, on demands for economic self-sufficiency and for autonomy or political independence. What role can 'Indianness' play in the new regional identity that is being forged? Should it be submerged by this new entity or does it form an essential part of it? What will be the balance of power between the 'Creole nation' and the 'Indian nation' within these still developing island societies?

The answers to these questions vary, depending on the island under consideration. In Martinique, the small Indian minority has lost all signs of its individuality, except for a few traces of the Hindu religion. Economic integration is well advanced, and cultural assimilation is practically complete. The main reason is the small number of Indians involved. In Guadeloupe, where the Indian population is greater than in Martinique, they have been able to preserve some of their cultural traditions and integrate themselves more readily into the island's socio-economic structure, while diversifying their activities. But, as in Martinique, there is a high rate of mixing and the integration policy is beginning to bear fruit.

Reunion is a case apart. Here, the number of Indians and the ethnic density are much higher, and the distribution of the ethnic groups is much more uniform. The proximity of India and of the island of Mauritius, has meant that links with the society and culture of origin have been maintained, whereas in the case of the Antilles the break was much more brutal. In Reunion socio-economic integration is well under way, but cultural assimilation has been tempered by a revival of Hindu culture. Another original aspect of Reunion is the presence of an Indo-Muslim minority who are town-dwellers, tradesmen, and highly enlightened. At the present time, the ethno-cultural pluralism which is developing in Reunion has not reached the stage of communalism which is to be found on the island of Mauritius, although this does not rule out occasional outbursts of ethnic tension.

References

Dupon, J.F. 1967. 'Les Immigrants Indiens de la Réunion', *Cahiers d'Outre-Mer*, 20, 77: 49–88.
    1977. *Insularité et fait colonial dans les Mascareignes et les Seychelles*, 4 vols., Atelier de Reproduction des Thèses, Université de Lille III; Librairie Champion.
Lasserre, G. 1953. 'Les Indiens de la Guadeloupe', *Cahiers d'Outre-Mer*, 6, 22.
    1961. *La Guadeloupe*, Bordeaux: UFI.
Singaravelou 1975. *Les Indiens de la Guadeloupe*. Bordeaux: CEGET.
    1988. *Les Indiens de la Caraïbe*, 3 vols., Paris: l'Harmattan.

4

Oil boom and recession in Trinidad Indian villages

Steven Vertovec

The South Asian communities which took root and grew in colonial territories – today's 'Third World' – have been subject to conditions affecting traditional social and cultural life which are considerably different from those in which South Asians in modern western countries have found themselves. The four variables channelling socio-cultural change among South Asians overseas which Jayawardena (1968) has outlined differ fundamentally between these two contexts:

(1)   type of migration: migrants to colonies were mostly indentured labourers,[1] with the notable exception of isolated entrepreneurs who went to places like East Africa, South Africa and Fiji; most of those South Asian migrants to Western countries have been students, professionals, businessmen and semi-skilled labourers;

(2)   extent of ties with South Asia: indentured migrants on colonial estates found contacts with South Asia exceedingly difficult to sustain, as opposed to their counterparts in the modern West, who manage to maintain links of many kinds;

(3)   type of economic activity:[2] those in the colonies were originally plantation labourers, later becoming mostly peasant farmers or agricultural workers; in the West, industrial, business, or technical employment has been the norm;

(4)   structure and polity of host society: these, of course, varied significantly both historically and geographically; generally, South Asians in colonial societies were isolated on estates or in rural areas and were at the bottom of the local social structure, while legislation providing equal rights was long withheld; in contemporary Western countries, South Asians have not always been the lowest in social status, and more equal rights have existed, often from the beginning of their immigration. Yet in this

89

latter context, South Asians have nonetheless remained socio-culturally 'encapsulated' within many Western societies (Robinson 1984).

Other important factors which affect the nature of post-migration socio-cultural change among South Asians overseas include: proportion of migrants from various districts in South Asia (with variegated mixtures influencing the extent or style of cultural homogenisation, religious syncretism, linguistic creolisation, caste composition and the maintenance of caste rules); labour organisation and political activities among migrants and their descendants; degree of ethnic or religious intermarriage and religious conversion, and other variable aspects produced by specific historical circumstances and events.

Since the colonial territories have become independent, the South Asian communities resident therein have been involved with or affected by processes of development and political emergence characteristic of newly independent Third World countries. This, too, is a feature significantly differing from western countries, where South Asians have been transplanted into more economically and politically 'established' contexts. How does social and economic development in the Third World alter the lifestyles of overseas South Asian communities? The small republic of Trinidad and Tobago provides an exceptional test case to examine this question. Not only is it home to a substantial South Asian (Indian) population, but Trinidad and Tobago have recently been the setting for some of the most rapid and extensive socio-economic changes occurring in any developing country today.

Indians in Trinidad[3]

Trinidad is an island fifty miles long by thirty miles wide, which lies only six miles from the coast of Venezuela. Although it is so close to Latin America, Trinidad is wholly Caribbean in culture, widely renowned for its steelpan and calypso music, cricket and carnival. Its population is one of the most diverse in the Caribbean. In 1980, within a total population of 1,055,763, Indians comprised 40.7%, while Africans accounted for 40.8%, people of mixed race (generally African combined with white and Chinese – not much with Indian) 16.3%, white 0.9%, Chinese 0.5%, and others 0.8%.

The island was a British colony from 1797 until independence in 1962. Throughout most of its modern history, Trinidad has been devoted to sugar cane, and to a lesser extent, cocoa cultivation. Originally, the colonial plantocracy depended on African slaves for labour; but following the emancipation of the slaves between 1834 and 1838, the sugar industry throughout the British Caribbean was short of cheap labour. Schemes to introduce Portuguese, Madeirans, Chinese, and free West Africans to Trinidad failed to boost the industry, but consequently added considerable heterogeneity to an already diverse island population of Spanish, French, French Creole, Venezuelan, emancipated African, Amerindian, and English inhabitants.

Following the relative success of Indian indentured migration to Mauritius (after 1834) and British Guiana (after 1838), the colonial authorities began the importation of Indians to Trinidad in 1845. This system continued until 1917, bringing more than 143,000 Indians to the island (of whom only 29,448 returned to India). Over three-quarters of the immigrants were from what is now Uttar Pradesh, with most others from Bihar; at different times throughout the period, lesser numbers came from, among other places, West Bengal, the Native States, the Punjab, and South India (especially Madras).

The indentured Indians were housed on estates, where they laboured for at least five years. After their contracts had expired, many re-indentured themselves or worked part-time on the plantations. During the 1860s, Crown Lands became available, originally in exchange for the return passage to India promised in indenture agreements, and later for lease or sale. These lands, located mostly in the vicinity of the 'sugar belt' of western and southern Trinidad, were quickly acquired by ex-indentured Indians. Virtually homogeneous Indian villages had been established before the turn of the century, and Indians soon became independent cane farmers who produced a substantial part of the island's sugar crop. Although a certain number of Indians prospered as small businessmen, the post-indenture Indian community of Trinidad was one characterised by agriculture and rural residence; it continued to practice relatively the most alien sociocultural activities within the pluralistic society; and was relegated to the lowest position in the island's racially-ascriptive social status hierarchy (Crowley 1957). Braithwaite's *Social Stratification in Trinidad* (1953) underscored the continuity of a system of racially ascribed social status after the Second World War; this was to change little over the next two decades.

The distribution of wealth and poverty over the years in Trinidad is revealing of ethnic disparities. Urban incomes have been almost twice as high on average as rural ones. Indians have continued to be the most prevalent segment in rural areas – 83% of Indians resided in rural areas in 1964 (Malik 1971: 12), and this geographical inequality of income is reflected in distribution of wealth by race. In 1960, the per capita income per annum for whites was £1,250, for blacks £260, and for Indians £195 (Cross 1972: 11).

The first of a series of five-year national development plans was introduced by the Trinidad government in 1958. Policies were aimed at improving the island's infrastructure, diversifying the economy and fostering industries for export. Each of the three five-year plans which followed were deemed as total failures by most observers (Vertovec 1987: 211–14). By 1972, when 70% of all incomes were under the national average and one-third of the population were assessed as living in 'real poverty,' rural people and particularly Indians were shown to represent the highest proportion of all the poor nationally (Henry 1975: 17–21). Indians were also found to have a greater gap between rich and poor than any other segment in the country (ibid. 9–10). While a nascent Indian middle class (primarily composed of Christians) had made some inroads into higher levels of social status (LaGuerre 1974), the Indian community overall was least represented in the professions and civil service, and had the highest number of unskilled workers of any ethnic group in the island (see Cross and Schwartzbaum 1969: 202; Malik 1971: 15–16; Lowenthal 1972: 167; Dookeran 1986; Clarke 1986: 35–6, 80–5). Economic constraints on social mobility throughout Trinidad were made worse by clear signs of racial discrimination in many areas of employment (Camejo 1971; Harewood 1971).

Poor conditions and social disparities in the late 1960s fuelled tense ethnic relations and political upheaval (Hintzen 1981: 308–18; 1985; Craig 1981). The situation reached a climax in 1970 with the Black Power movement, a radical consortium of university students and disaffected urban blacks.[4] Viewing the country's then current plight in terms of a heritage of colonialism and slavery, the movement sought revolution in the form of a removal of all vestiges of white elitism and foreign domination. Certain members called for Indian support to do so, and various spirited marches and rallies were held. The results achieved were quite different from those desired. Chaos ensued in many quarters, the military attempted a takeover, and the prime minister declared a state of emergency. Rural Indians reacted in their own way by consolidating and reasserting many ethnic values in opposition to the African community's growing atavism. The greater proportion of Indians proceeded to protest at the poor economic conditions, assertion of African community values, and government clampdown by boycotting the 1971 national elections.

One form of panacea which prime minister Eric Williams and his African-dominated People's National Movement (PNM) offered to many was the creation of the Development and Environmental Works Division (DEWD). This programme provided considerable public funds for casual employment on various projects such as road construction and maintenance. However, it proved to be a 'money for votes' venture, in which most projects benefited PNM-dominated areas and most jobs were given to African, PNM party members. Hintzen (1985: 128) describes the programme as 'no more than an expansion and formalization of racial patronage' (Sutton 1984).[5] Only 5% of DEWD's funds were spent on roads for Indian-dominated agricultural areas (Craig 1985: 183). Thus, racially polarised politics continually acted to maintain economic distinctiveness.

In the early 1970s, therefore, Trinidad's socio-economic situation was severe. The island had seen a dwindling of productivity and a shrinking of foreign reserves, discrimination in public and private employment, racially-inspired unrest, an attempted coup and a state of emergency, boycotted elections, and the perpetuation of widespread poverty within inner urban and especially rural areas. Rural Indians felt themselves to be particularly alienated from the rest of society. The economically exacerbated tensions in Trinidad might have led to even greater social fragmentation and potential violence had it not been for sudden changes in the international economy, described later (pp. 95ff). But what of the Indians as a group?

Indians in Trinidad have been the focus of many sociological and ethnographic studies (Niehoff 1959; Freilich 1960; Klass 1961; Schwartz 1964; 1967b, c; Nevadomsky 1980, 1982a, b). Most of these studies have concentrated on degrees of cultural retention or cultural persistence among Trinidad Indians. The cultural forms and social institutions held by Trinidad Indians can be seen to be amalgamations of many North Indian patterns which have subsequently been modified or elaborated since the days of indenture (Vertovec 1987, 1988). A creolised Bhojpuri form of Hindi was quickly created to serve as a lingua franca among the initial Indian immigrants and the West Indian dialect of English became a standard language for interaction with non-Indians. While Islamic phenomena have altered least, Hinduism has been transformed from a composite of 'little tradition' forms practised by villagers in India to a single 'great tradition' in Trinidad centred on the ideals of *bhakti* (devotion) and Vaishnavism. The caste system has dissolved save for status attributions on the extreme ends of the Brahmin–Chamar scale. Although nuclear families are the most prominent forms, initial virolocality, settlement on family compounds, segmented households, ultimogeniture, patrifocality and patrilineality distinguish Indian families from most others on the island. Other aspects of culture have persisted in the Indian conceptual or value system, including behavioural restrictions between affines or fathers and sons, beliefs about the causality and cure of disease or misfortune, and the subservient status of women.

While poor economic conditions afflicted many rural Indians from their introduction to the island until recent times, important changes have affected their community in terms of educational advances and increases in occupational mobility. Furthermore, they have become less isolated as transport improvements and extra-village employment have served to expand their socio-economic networks. Examining such shifts in lifestyle and their effects on traditional Indian social institutions and cultural patterns became a natural focus of social scientists.

A number of observers have predicted that a distinct Indian culture in Trinidad would decline and disappear in the face of development (economic growth, occupational change, modernisation and westernisation). Most of these describe an impending absorption or assimilation of Indians into a single, nationwide cultural and social system (a process often deemed 'creolisation'). With regard to the longstanding differentiation between Africans and Indians, LaGuerre (1974: 106) stated, 'Economic development and the re-allocation of economic resources between and among groups will erode the traditional relationships.' Dookeran (1974: 80) believed, 'an economic system that creates the need for a trade-off between cultural persistence and economic betterment accepts implicitly a strategy for the absorption of the sub-culture into the dominant cultures'. Deosaran (1978: 9) set this gradual domination in terms of 'an unwieldy mixture of American influence with African support'. Indian youth, Nevadomsky (1980) observed, is particularly susceptible to such acculturation.

Various reasons have been put forward to justify this assimilationist perspective. Schwartz (1964; 1967b) has suggested that Indian villagers' incorporation into a cash rather than a subsistence economy has caused various changes in the institutions of family (tending from a joint to a nuclear type), caste (breaking down the final vestiges of endogamy), and communality (particularly caused by a shift from collective labour to individual wage earning).[6] Schwartz (1967c) has also claimed that increased concerns with social prestige, economic advancement, and immediate material rewards have been leading to the general demise of religion (especially Hinduism) among Trinidad Indians.

The Indian community in Trinidad has been described as having generally higher aspirations than any other group (Rubin and Zavelloni 1969; Baksh 1979). Nevadomsky (1981, 1983) has pointed out that as the socio-economic context in Trinidad develops, group aspirations have led to a greater prestige value being attributed by Indians to certain types of jobs, larger incomes, and higher levels of education. Occupational mobility has ensued: as Indians have moved up the social hierarchy, Nevadomsky claims, their distinct cultural dimension falls by the wayside. He, too, foresees the end of Indian religious traditions, suggesting the 'obvious irrelevance of many Hindu rituals to the newly emerging lifestyles' (1983: 78).

In the 1960s and early 1970s there were only sluggish changes in Trinidad's economy and social structure; it is to these changes that the above writers allude in terms of transformations of Indian social and cultural phenomena. After 1973, radical development of the economy would shed quite a different light on their hypotheses about Indian assimilation.

Oil boom 1973–1982

Trinidad has been an oil producer since the beginning of the century. Oil exports have played a growing role in the country's economy as the international sugar market has wavered over the past century. Trinidad's onshore oil wells neared exhaustion as the country moved into the 1970s with an unsure economic future. Important offshore finds were made in 1971, but the high costs of drilling and production made their viability questionable. Meanwhile, in 1971 and 1972, on the other side of the world, the Organization of Petroleum Exporting Countries (OPEC) was holding talks which would soon change the structure of the global economy. The primary result of their meetings was that in December 1973, OPEC raised the standard price of Arabian crude oil from US$3 to US$5 per barrel; in February 1974 this price was increased to US$11.65 per barrel, and the world began to feel the impact of an international 'oil crisis'.

Although Trinidad had on several occasions unsuccessfully applied to join OPEC, the country followed other non-OPEC nations in adjusting its own oil prices in relation to those of OPEC. Whereas Trinidad asked only TT$1.57 per barrel for its oil in the late 1960s, the country demanded TT$21 per barrel by 1975 (contemporary exchange rate TT$2.40 = US$1). A global oil shortage meant that Trinidad could sell at a high price as much oil as it could produce; therefore, crude oil production in Trinidad (especially from the offshore reserves) nearly doubled between 1971 and 1978.

Since the greatest proportion of oil production facilities in Trinidad was in the hands of American companies, the government introduced new tax legislation to maximise national gains. In January 1973, foreign firms like Amoco paid tax and royalty of only US$0.50 per barrel produced. By December 1973, after the first major price hike, they were required to pay the Trinidad government US$4.69 per barrel produced. This tax rate nearly doubled again in 1974. This meant a virtually instant economic windfall for the small country. Whereas foreign reserves totalled US$45,500,000 in mid-1973, by the end of 1975 they topped US$750,900,000. World oil prices fell slightly between 1975 and 1978, then redoubled in 1979–80 to peak at US$35 per barrel. In 1970, before the boom, Trinidad's oil exports earned the nation US$29,000,000; by 1980 the figure reached US$920,000,000.

With its newfound wealth, the government of prime minister Eric Williams set aside the models of previous five-year plans. 'Rather than resuscitate its development programme, the regime made a decision to embark on a massive endeavour of industrial diversification spearheaded by the state in partnership with foreign investors' (Hintzen 1985: 116). The consequent crash industrialisation programme quickly saw plans for the creation of two petrochemical plants, a second ammonia factory, an aluminium smelter, an iron and steel works, additional fertilizer plants, and widespread electrical expansion. Most of the development was designed to be located at the industrial estate at Point Lisas, fuelled by a new natural gas pipeline. Most, if not all, of the projects got off the ground during this boom period of the mid to late 1970s. Further, the government began to nationalise the major industrial sectors, including the purchase of Shell Oil's operations in Trinidad in 1974.

Domestic relief was also high on the government's priority list during the days when Dr Williams boasted 'money is no problem': this included a comprehensive system of subsidies for food, fuel, and utilities, reduced taxes, and an expansion of public works programmes aimed at reducing unemployment (by 1976, in fact, over half of the country's labour force was employed in some branch of the public sector). The DEWD programme and similar schemes designed to strengthen African party patronage were greatly expanded, to the chagrin of many Indians.

Overall, the island seemed exceedingly prosperous. By the late 1970s, the Gross National Product (GNP) reached a remarkable expansion rate of 6% to 8% annually. The GNP per capita continued to rise after its initial doubling following the first oil-price shifts of 1973–4 (Table 4.1). For the average Trinidadian, the effects of the national windfall were not felt immediately. Unemployment reached 15% in 1975 before declining, and in that year there was a violent national dispute between a united labour front and the government (Baptiste 1976). Yet, gradually, unemployment began to fall and average weekly earnings in all sectors grew dramatically: they doubled between the end of 1972 and 1975, then by 1982, climbed to five times their 1972 mark (Figure 4.1).

Within a short time, the island society quickly became absorbed in an easy money, free-spending, consumption-dominated ethos which one popular calypso at the time described as 'Capitalism Gone Mad'. The number of cars in the country increased by 65% between 1974 and 1980, and the number of televisions trebled over the decade. Electricity was

Table 4.1. *Trinidad and Tobago: gross national product (GNP) per capita, 1970–83*

	(US$)
1970	960
1971	940
1972	970
1973	990
1974	1,680
1975	2,000
1976	2,240
1977	2,380
1978	2,910
1979	3,390
1980	4,370
1981	5,670
1982	6,840
1983	6,850

Source: World Bank *Annual Reports*

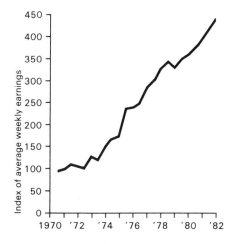

Figure 4.1   Index of average weekly earnings (all industries), Trinidad and Tobago, 1971–82

more readily available throughout the island, and refrigerators, stereos and other consumer goods became universal possessions.

In particular, manufacturing, construction, and transport grew rapidly through government contracts or as spinoffs from expansion in related, state-backed sectors of industry. Businessmen and entrepreneurs of all groups and areas prospered significantly during this period.

> [T]he black, coloured, East Indian, white and Chinese middle classes (the last three concentrated primarily in the private sector) have derived enormous benefits from the regime's chosen strategy for development, concentrating as it is on the use of foreign exchange and budgetary surpluses derived directly from international capital to expand the scope of participation of foreign investors in the Trinidad economy and to expand, develop, and strengthen the local business sector.
>
> (Hintzen 1985: 123)

The Ministry of Finance (1978: 131) noted that the main economic benefits of the boom were to be found especially in the urban zones. This concentration had several side-effects, including those described in a report on Trinidad's industrialisation programme by *The Economist* (13 September 1980: 91): 'This dash for heavy industry has sucked people in from the countryside to the city: 40% of the island's 1.1 million people now live in the miles of sprawl behind Port of Spain, producing urban squalor and a rash of arson in the city centre as suburbs expand.' The bulk of migrants who came from throughout the country to the city were African, thus serving to maintain the longstanding geographical differentiation between the largest ethnic groups. Although this kind of pre-boom ethnic pattern stayed the same, another changed fundamentally. During the decade of the 1970s, the Indian community as a whole rapidly achieved more prosperity and social mobility than it had during its previous 130 years in the island. They accomplished this through making educational advancements, by engaging in a great deal of capital investment, and by manipulating their own patronage networks. The majority of Indians continued to be rurally based, but came to engage in far greater extra-village employment due to the demise of the agricultural sector which ensued throughout the boom period.

The rural Indian community also received a substantial economic injection in the mid-1970s. In 1974, world sugar prices rocketed from £150 per ton to £650 per ton; cane farmers in Trinidad subsequently felt the shift when the amount of money paid to them more than doubled in a single increment in 1974–5.[7] Therefore, whether through employment in public or spinoff industries (primarily construction and transportation) or in sugar growing, rural Indians gained substantial material benefits throughout the decade of the 1970s and into the 1980s.

The years 1973–82 witnessed widespread and deeply-rooted socio-economic change in Trinidad. The enormous influx of wealth derived from oil exportation allowed the government to undertake large-scale industrialisation efforts as well as to bolster its clients – the working class African community – through selective public spending. Furthermore, the upper and middle classes of both major ethnic groups simultaneously received the ruling party's backing. Hintzen and Premdas (1984: 209–10) describe this dual policy which the government's newfound wealth afforded:

> The Trinidadian regime has used the legitimacy derived from its majoritarian base to cater to the interests of the upper and middle classes by adapting a capitalist development policy which emphasizes state participation. At the same time, it has preserved an ethnic 'definition of the situation' for electoral purposes. The combination of ethnic mobilization and elitist policies has resulted in the buttressing of the regime's power position while freeing it from the need to engage in a program of wealth redistribution.

Such a manipulation of interests ensured the PNM's return to power in the 1981 general election (La Guerre 1983). Moreover, Hintzen (1983: 379–80; 1985: 149) has suggested that within this context, ethnic communalist sentiments have been eroded among the middle and upper classes while ethnic identification has been reinforced in both the African and Indian working classes. This became evident in voting patterns and the general adoption of habits and values. The well-to-do of all ethnic groups took on the lifestyles that wealth provided for, especially in terms of material culture and an interest in the pursuit of commerce. On the other hand, the DEWD and other programmes under PNM patronage positively favoured and consolidated the African working class, while the decline in agriculture and other perceptions of economic discrimination against the rural Indian populace acted in a negative manner to promote their own forms of communalism.

However, rural Indians, as we have seen, did manage to benefit considerably during the boom years in Trinidad. As some community members achieved a degree of economic advancement, village or kin-based social networks often led to occupational opportunities for many other rural Indians (particularly in the construction and transportation sectors, which were not under direct management by the state). Sometimes the initial economic injections into rural communities came through the sudden rise in sugar prices after 1974; other times due to work programmes created by local, as distinct from national, government.

Thus, following the high degree of socio-economic alienation with which the rural Indian community entered the 1970s, the government's specialised use of economic gains after 1973 did little to amend the

Table 4.2. *Population by ethnic group, Penal Rock Road, Trinidad*

	African	Indian	Chinese	Mixed	Other	Total
1960						
male/female	174/165	1,301/1,346	6/1	95/100	13/4	1,589/1,616
Total	339	2,647	7	195	17	3,205
(%)	(10.6)	(82.6)	(0.2)	(6.1)	(0.5)	(100)
1980						
male/female	157/136	1,845/1,778	9/3	93/112	4/1	2,108/2,030
Total	293	3,623	12	205	5	4,138
(%)	(7.1)	(87.5)	(0.3)	(4.9)	(0.1)	(100)

Source: Statistical Office, Trinidad and Tobago (Censuses).

situation; in fact, it was exacerbated. The prosperity which rural Indians did manage to obtain through 'secondary' means did not act to dissipate their ethnic identity; nevertheless, many fundamental aspects of their village lifestyles were transformed. A brief examination of one Indian village provides evidence for these dynamics.

An Indian village in the boom years

The village of Penal Rock Road is situated in a relatively remote district of southern Trinidad, some five miles from the market town of Penal and approximately fifteen miles from San Fernando, the island's second largest urban area. The homes of its residents are scattered along one central road and among several small 'traces' which lead off the road into rolling hills. An equal proportion of the land throughout the village is devoted to sugar cane, rice and cocoa, while large gardens for subsistence and market crops lie adjacent to most homes. Table 4.2 gives the population and ethnic breakdown of the village for 1960 and 1980 (1970 data are unavailable on the enumeration district level). The village has been dominated by Indians (overwhelmingly Hindu) since its first settlement around 1910, and this pattern has changed little in the past few decades.

For most of its existence, Penal Rock Road was fairly isolated; its inhabitants grew cocoa, rice and cane for outside dealers, or perhaps a few seasonal crops to carry and sell in Penal. Penal was about as far as many villagers ever travelled; one forty-year-old man reported that he was over eighteen years old before he went even there. Yet by the time of Trinidad's independence in 1962, half of the working villagers had begun to obtain some form of employment in nearby areas, many serving as labourers on government-financed works. Table 4.3 shows the type of employment engaged in by villagers of Penal Rock Road in 1960 and 1980.

The first major economic event which had an impact on the village was not the oil boom and subsequent government projects. These took some years to be felt in Penal Rock Road. Rather, the sugar price rises of 1974 turned many cane-farmers into a local *nouveau riche*. Whereas farmers had been receiving TT$18.25 per ton of cane delivered to the scales in 1973, in 1974 they suddenly received TT$40.78 per ton (contemporary exchange rate approximately TT$4 = £1). The price continued to rise throughout the 1970s until it peaked at TT$104.69 per ton of cane in 1982. Cane farmers quickly began to earn several times their previous income simply for growing the same quantity of cane (or even less).

Almost instantly, farmers throughout the area went on a buying spree, not only to get tractors and vans, but luxury items. Tales are still told of this now almost mythic time: exaggerating somewhat, villagers say that you could drive your car into any cane-growing village or trace, sell it to the first farmer you met, and even receive the taxi fare home. Other stories are similar to the one about a fellow who, they say, took his first bountiful pay check in 1975 and excitedly bought a television and refrigerator . . . only to arrive back at home and recall that his area of the village had no electricity.

Numerous villagers who laboured seasonally for the farmers received more and more wages throughout the period after 1975. The cane harvesting season soon became not only a time of much work, but of much cash as well. The late 1970s and early 1980s was a period of 'en'less money', when a man could work in the fields for a few hours in the morning, eat well and relax in comfort at home for the rest of the day, and drink excessively in the rumshop all night.

By the late 1970s, in many parts of the country, a large proportion of the African working-class population was working for DEWD and similar state-organised schemes. A number of African villagers from nearby Morne Diablo at that time also gained employment through such programmes. No Indians from Penal Rock Road worked for DEWD, either due to ethnic discrimination on the recruiters' part or to ethnic pride on the Indians'. Instead, many workers from Penal Rock Road and other Indian villages in that part of the country went to work for St Patrick County Council. This local government authority provided similar job creation schemes for work on road construction and maintenance, bridges and drains, and landscaping.

The County Council had been an employer of some villagers since the 1950s. Yet the enormous increase in central government revenue in the 1970s also meant great increases in local government funds. Moreover, since 1977 St Patrick County Council had been under the control of an active opposition party, the United Labour Front (ULF). The ULF

Table 4.3. *Employed workforce by type of labour, Penal Rock Road, Trinidad*

	Agricultural	Manual	Non-manual	Total
1960				
male/female	230/18	316/25	63/10	609/53
(%)	(38/34)	(52/47)	(10/19)	(100/100)
1980				
male/female	154/6	586/16	129/72	896/94
(%)	(18/17)	(67/17)	(15/77)	(100/100)

Source: Central Statistical Office, Trinidad and Tobago (Censuses).

Council, one of the few in the island at that time, was strongly Indian-backed and therefore highly acceptable as an employer in the eyes of most Penal Rock Road villagers. In 1978–81 there was a massive expansion of the Council's work projects (a political move often perceived as a direct challenge to the crash programmes of the PNM central government). A number of these large projects, particularly road extensions and paving, were in the general vicinity of Penal Rock Road; gainful employment was obtained on these by scores of village men.

Thus, throughout the years of prosperity, the nature of employment in Penal Rock Road shifted substantially (Table 4.3). Agricultural employment dropped dramatically, while non-manual jobs gained moderately and manual jobs (especially in construction, transportation and light industry) increased most of all. More than three-quarters of employed women came to work in non-manual sectors (primarily in clerical, sales and medical-related occupations). Furthermore, notwithstanding the increased sugar prices, the cultivation of cane went into steep decline around the village, since labourers sought government- and county-sponsored work at twice the cane-cutters wage. Similarly, rice cultivation ceased almost entirely during the boom: families simply preferred to buy their rice rather than grow it. Meanwhile, the price of local produce and imported foodstuffs in local markets and shops soared.

The village has changed physically as well: cement and brick houses have replaced many of the wooden houses, and most have electricity. Cars and vans are found at many homes. Televisions, refrigerators, stereos, and even video recorders are now common household items. All along the main road of the village, various businesses have sprung up, including groceries, hardware stores, and, especially, rumshops. Within just a few years, at the height of the boom period, no less than seventeen rumshops opened within a one mile stretch in Penal Rock Road.

Conspicuous consumption and relative deprivation *vis-à-vis* neighbours brought about disruptions in home life, too. Once electricity arrived in the road, family members expected to have new material items, like refrigerators, TVs and stereos. The more money available, some say, the less harmonious a family became. New values and interests took hold of family members. The changing values of young people, in particular, who were better educated than their parents and who sought to identify with American or British pop culture, tended to create a sizeable generation gap. Many youths became critical of traditional lifestyles, labelling them as those of 'ol' time Indians' or lowly 'coolies'.

These shifts, however, did not dissipate Indian social and cultural institutions or values. Young married couples could now afford to build their own houses and maintain themselves as a nuclear unit – but these homes were usually within a few feet of the husband's father's house, and maintained a joint family compound with other brothers as well. Girls were educated to a higher standard and allowed to work outside the home or village – but tight reins were kept on them, and parents retained the final word in all marriage choices. Stereos and videos were utilised primarily for Hindi imports from India, creating more vivid models of 'Indian-ness' than ever before. Splendid sarees and embroidered kirtas became affordable dress for special occasions. And religion, far from dying, became a highly elaborated focus for cultural expression and social interaction.

Family-based rituals – especially Hindu *pujas* (ritual offerings) and *Ramayana* readings – proliferated in number, kind, and extensiveness during this period of prosperity. One type of Hindu celebration, the *yagna*, came to be of special importance in Indian villages like Penal Rock Road. *Yagnas* are nine or fourteen-day celebrations during which, daily, *puja* is performed, sacred texts are recited and interpreted by a pundit, and food is served to all in attendance. With the economic windfall, the village's *nouveau riche* increasingly sponsored these events for the spiritual merit of their families and the benefit of the entire community (as well as for their own prestige, since these celebrations cost many thousands of dollars). *Yagnas* propagate Hindu values and involve major collective activities during which villagers socialise, children learn, youths flirt, and cultural entertainment is provided through story and song.

Thus Indian social and cultural life not only survived rapid economic development, but actually benefited from it. The times of economic well-being were short lived, however.

Recession: 1982 to present

The economic well-being of Trinidad in the 1970s was based on oil. Enormous wealth gained so fast brought with it high lifestyles and big ideas, and many quickly overlooked the flimsy basis of the country's economy. The Permanent Secretary at the Ministry of Finance himself admitted that:

> The country was spoiled by a sudden injection of money which created a kind of euphoria. The Government after the first oil shock, found itself on a wave of affluence and embarked on a number of large capital projects. They lost sight of the fact that if anything went wrong with the revenue system there would be problems.
>
> (*Financial Times* 8 July 1985: 13)

The global 'oil crisis' was eventually resolved, and international adjustments over the years have led to a reduction in the oil prices which prevailed through the 1970s. OPEC began to cut its prices in 1981 and 1982, and smaller producers like Trinidad were forced to follow suit. World prices of crude oil tumbled from US$34 per barrel to US$29 then US$27. By April 1983, Trinidad had cut its price by 22%, and the country's earnings began to plummet. In 1982, foreign reserves totalled TT$7.6 billion; at the end of 1984 they had dropped to TT$2.8 billion. Oil production fell steeply, and in turn, other sectors began to feel an impending recession. Gross Domestic Product, which had reached unparalleled levels a few years before, grew at only 3.4% in 1981–2; in 1983 it actually declined by 5%, and by a further 7% in 1984. Trinidad's balance of trade also fell deeply into the red for the first time in 1982, and in 1983 the country showed a balance of payments deficit of TT$1.7 billion. A *Financial Times* Survey (1985) concluded that economically speaking 'the carnival is over for Trinidad and Tobago'.

As oil revenue declined, it became increasingly apparent just how dependent on this resource the country had become, and how badly the government had failed to use the boom wealth productively for economic diversification and stable job creation. At the beginning of the decade of the 1980s, the oil sector's contribution to the national economy was 'nearly three times the contribution of the next highest sector (transportation, storage and communication), nearly five times that of manufacturing excluding petroleum, and eighteen times that of agriculture' (Sutton 1984: 71). The crash industrialisation programme proved to be highly capital intensive (creating few jobs), often poorly conceived, and more often corruptly managed.

By way of example, 'the most telling criticism of government policy is what happened to the vanguard of the industrialisation drive, the Iron and Steel Company of Trinidad and Tobago (Iscott)' (*The Economist* 3 November 1984: 68). This massive plant cost US$458 million to construct, but has failed to find a secure market. It has therefore necessitated huge government support to maintain it as a political showpiece. Foreign observers concluded that Iscott 'continues to be a financial embarrassment to the government. . . . [By 1985] Iscott was costing the government nearly US$500,000 per day' (*South* September 1985: 245). Likewise, 'Fertilisers of Trinidad and Tobago Limited, a joint-venture project between the government and Amoco, was established at a cost of US$250 million, but suffered a loss of US$9 million in the first six months of 1983, with further losses recorded since' (ibid.). Overall, the manufacturing industries had never really become very well established as productive contributors to the national economy. 'In Trinidad and Tobago between 1973 and 1980, therefore, one had the classic boom conditions of a massive upward displacement of money income trends and income levels, euphoric expectations and little widening of the structure of real output' (Bourne 1985: 153).

As a recession gradually became widespread through all sectors, the well-paid jobs to which Trinidadians had grown so accustomed became fewer and fewer. Unemployment climbed from 10.3% in 1982 to estimates of some 22% by 1985; in 1984 alone there were 10,000 redundancies in the island. Manufacturing, transportation and construction were particularly hard-hit. Moreover, the government was forced to reduce subsidies for domestic energy consumption and other supports. These cutbacks have especially affected the working class. Agriculture was neglected throughout the boom, so that when it ended the island was importing 75% of its food requirements. The economic tide turned in Trinidad after 1982, serving to transform once again many of the socio-economic structures which had changed so rapidly during the boom years.

An Indian village in recession

Since virtually all extra-village jobs are gone – particularly the public work schemes which supported so many villagers – Penal Rock Road has fallen back on itself. There is a reluctant return to market gardening and even rice cultivation, yet cane cultivation still suffers due to a national dismantling of the industry. Young men, though, tend not to go back to agriculture: having been accustomed to a decade of easy money, they prefer to 'lime' (hang around on road junctions or near shops) rather than work in the fields or lagoons. The mile-long strip of now virtually empty rumshops is a telling metaphor for the village's boom and bust.

Nevertheless, the Indian activities boosted in the late 1970s and early 1980s have continued. Indian music blaring from expensive stereos and imported Hindi films on videos are everyday items bolstering ethnic identity throughout the village. Families have through necessity become even more tightly knit in structure and function. And ritual activities have continued in their revitalised forms: family *pujas* and local *satsangs* take place with the same frequency as they did in the 1970s (yet are conducted with less frills). *Yagnas* likewise are regular affairs – but with a significant difference.

As the economy declined, individuals were unable to sponsor *yagnas* as often as previously. Yet the institutions had quickly become the backbone of Trinidad Hinduism. Numerous groups were soon formed which raised money to organise and hold *yagnas* and other functions such as *Diwali* and *Phagwa* celebrations. Some are religious and cultural groups based around the two local *mandirs* (temples); some are travelling *satsang* or *bhajan* (hymn-singing) groups located in certain parts of the village and composed to a large extent of extended families; and some are simply youth organisations or cricket clubs.

Similarly, a new village welfare association has formed in opposition to the village council (which has been traditionally associated with the African-dominated PNM party). Its essential goals in these recession years are to promote community solidarity and to aid needy families in the village. Group-related activities have, consequently, come to be the prominent carriers of cultural continuity in contemporary Trinidad's Indian villages.

Conclusion

Before the boom, economic conditions were dire and Indians in villages like Penal Rock Road loathed the PNM government for being responsible for the erosion of agriculture, the lack of economic opportunity and racial politics. During the years of prosperity, village Indians made considerable economic gains, yet still opposed the African-dominated government by rallying around ethnic symbols: they felt that the PNM industrialisation programme and other budgetary expenditures were deliberately not intended to benefit Indians. Whatever wealth rural Indians did obtain, they believe, was through their own initiative and social channels. Finally, since the recession which followed 1982, Indians have pointed to the squandered national funds and marginally productive industries. 'Whey [where] de money done gone?' they ask, fully realising just how many billions of dollars the country once had. If the money had been invested in (Indian-dominated) agriculture, Indian villagers insist, the country would still be in good economic standing once the oil sector had collapsed. In this roundabout way, therefore, during the boom years Indian ethnic identification was reinforced; and these feelings have been bolstered even further in the recession years afterwards. Such findings contradict many of the previous studies and predictions regarding culture change among Trinidad Indians.

Socio-economic change need not bring about a decline in traditional religion or culture, nor a loss of communality among South Asians in developing countries. This was noted by Smith (1977: xviii) with reference to Indians in Guyana, where a similar geographic, historical and political context exists but where socio-economic development has been slow:

> Whereas a decade ago it seemed likely that there would be a progressive abandonment of the more orthodox forms of religion – Hinduism in particular – in practice we have seen a renewal of interest and an increase in ritual practice among those who are occupationally upwardly mobile. At the same time that Indo-Guyanese are moving in ever larger numbers into the city of Georgetown and adopting a 'modern' urban life style, there is a counter trend toward continuing residence in the rural areas (particularly those areas within commuting distance of town), and toward more active participation in religious and community organizations.

Furthermore, the perspective on overseas South Asians which sees assimilation as a necessary consequence of development suffers from a false notion of ethnicity. Ethnicity is not a quantitative matter: one is not 'more' or 'less' Indian if certain institutions are participated in more than others. Ethnicity is a matter of values surrounding self-identification, and socio-cultural institutions can both instil and express these values.

Among overseas South Asian communities, shifting social structures and economic advances or setbacks provide new contexts in which such institutions can be created or renewed to maintain collective unity and stability, regardless of the exact cultural forms taken. In the case of village Trinidad, new-found wealth provided not only certain comforts of modern life, but also the means of establishing new or altered socio-cultural patterns which remained after prosperity ended. Recognising this potential for adaptation is particularly pertinent for South Asians in Third World countries, where the context is subject to unpredictable change.

Notes

1 South Asian migrant labourers who went to Southeast Asia in the nineteenth and early twentieth centuries travelled mostly under the *kangani* and *maistry* systems of labour recruitment, whereby they made short-term contracts with local middlemen. The great majority of these migrants did not settle in Southeast Asia, but travelled periodically between the two land masses.
2 South Asians in East Africa displayed wholly different patterns of economic activity (merchant, administrative, and civil service occupations) from other colonial South Asian migrants. For general comparisons of contexts of South Asian colonial migration and settlement, see Gangulee 1947; Kondapi 1951; Tinker 1974, 1976, 1977; Vertovec 1987.
3 Though the nation is composed of two neighbouring islands, this article focuses on the major island, Trinidad. Tobago is much smaller in size and population (1980 – 39,524 of the Republic's total of 1,055,763), and is home for only a fraction of the country's Indian population (1980 – 648, or 0.15%). Much to Tobago's dismay, it saw little of the economic benefits of the 1970s which this paper describes.
4 For more on the Black Power movement in Trinidad and the crisis of 1970, see Nicholls 1971; Ryan 1972: 365–72, 454–62; Craig 1981; Sutton 1983, 1984: 45–6.
5 Craig (1985: 183–4) details the various improprieties which accompanied the DEWD programme. 'The very arbitrariness of the projects,' she writes, 'allows them to become the spoils of party patronage; at the same time, it leads to poor planning, improper accounting, bribery, corruption, low productivity and waste of resources.' Also see Taylor 1980: 14.
6 This thesis is similar to that proposed by Smith and Jayawardena (1959) and Smith (1963), in which changes in occupation among male heads of Indian households in Guyana are said to transform traditional family structures. Smith himself (1978) later refutes this.
7 This drastic rise was not only in response to the international sugar market, but also due to the impact of a series of strikes in the local sugar industry in 1974 centred on the creation of a new cane farmers' trade union.

References

Bahadoorsingh, Krishna 1968. *Trinidad Electoral Politics: the persistence of the race factor*, London: Institute of Race Relations.
Baksh, Ishmael 1979. 'Stereotypes of Negroes and East Indians in Trinidad: a re-examination', *Caribbean Quarterly*, 25: 52–71.
Baptiste, Owen 1976. *Crisis*, St Annes, Trinidad: Imprint.
Braithwaite, Lloyd 1953. *Social Stratification in Trinidad*, Kingston: ISER.
Bourne, Compton 1985. 'Banking in boom and bust economies: lessons from Trinidad and Tobago and Jamaica', *Social and Economic Studies*, 34: 139–63.
Camejo, Acton 1971. 'Racial discrimination in employment in the private sector in Trinidad and Tobago: a study of the business elite and the social structure', *Social and Economic Studies*, 20: 294–318.
Clarke, Colin G. 1986. *East Indians in a West Indian Town*, London: Allen & Unwin.
Craig, Susan 1981. 'Background to the 1970 confrontation in Trinidad and

Tobago', in *Contemporary Caribbean: a sociological reader*, ed. Susan Craig, Port of Spain: Susan Craig, vol. 2, 385–423.

1985. 'Political patronage and political resistance: village councils in Trinidad and Tobago', in *Rural Development in the Caribbean*, ed. P.I. Gomes, New York: C. Hurst & Co., 172–93.

Cross, Malcolm 1972. *The East Indians of Guyana and Trinidad*, London: Minority Rights Group.

Cross, Malcolm and Allen M. Schwartzbaum 1969. 'Social mobility and secondary school selection in Trinidad and Tobago', *Social and Economic Studies*, 18: 189–207.

Crowley, Daniel 1957. 'Plural and differential acculturation in Trinidad', *American Anthropologist*, 59: 817–24.

Deosaran, Ramesh 1978. 'Multiculturalism for democratic living', *Caribbean Issues*, 4: 3–21.

Dookeran, Winston 1985. 'East Indians and the Economy of Trinidad and Tobago', in *Calcutta to Caroni*, ed. John G. LaGuerre, St Augustine, Trinidad: Extra-Mural Studies Unit, University of the West Indies (2nd edn), 63–76.

Freilich, Morris 1960. 'Cultural Diversity among Trinidadian Peasants', unpub. Ph.D. dissertation, Columbia University.

Graham, Sara and Derek, Gordon 1977. *The Stratification System and Occupational Mobility in Guyana*, University of the West Indies: ISER.

Gangulee, N. 1947. *Indians in the Empire Overseas*, London: New India.

Harewood, Jack 1971. 'Racial discrimination in employment in Trinidad and Tobago', *Social and Economic Studies*, 20: 267–93.

Henry, Ralph M. 1975. 'A note on income distribution and property in Trinidad and Tobago', Port of Spain: CSO Research Paper No. 8, 1–20.

Hintzen, Percy C. 1981, 'Capitalism, socialism and socio-political confrontation in multiracial developing states: a comparison of Guyana and Trinidad', PhD dissertation, Yale University.

1985. 'Ethnicity, class and internationalist capitalist penetration in Guyana and Trinidad', *Social and Economic Studies*, 34: 107–63.

Hintzen, Percy C. and Ralph P. Premdas 1984. 'Race, class and development: toward an explanation of poverty and repression in less developed countries', *Plural Societies*, 15: 193–219.

Jayawardena, Chandra 1968. 'Migration and social change: a survey of Indian communities overseas', *The Geographical Review*, 58: 426–49.

Klass, Morton 1961. *East Indians in Trinidad*, New York: Colombia University Press.

Kondapi, C. 1951. *Indians Overseas 1838–1949*, Bombay: Oxford University Press.

La Guerre, John G. 1974. 'The East Indian middle class today', in *Calcutta to Caroni*, ed. John G. La Guerre, Trinidad: Longman, 98–107.

1983. 'The general elections of 1981 in Trinidad and Tobago', *Journal of Commonwealth and Comparative Politics*, 21: 133–51.

Lowenthal, David 1972. *West Indian Societies*, London: Oxford University Press.

Malik, Yogendra 1971. *East Indians in Trinidad*, London: Oxford University Press.

Ministry of Finance, Republic of Trinidad and Tobago 1978. Planning for Development: National Physical Development Plan, Trinidad and Tobago

110   *Steven Vertovec*

(Part 1: Survey and Analysis), Port-of-Spain: Town and Country Planning Division, Development and Planning Series TT2.

Nevadomsky, Joseph 1980. 'Changes in Hindu Institutions in an alien environment', *Eastern Anthropologist*, 33: 39–53.

1981. 'Cultural and structural dimensions of occupational prestige in an East Indian community in Trinidad', *Journal of Anthropological Research*, 37: 343–59.

1982a. 'Changing conceptions of family regulation among the Hindu East Indians in rural Trinidad', *Anthropological Quarterly*, 55, 4: 189–96.

1982b. 'Social change and the East Indians in rural Trinidad: a critique of methodologies', *Social and Economic Studies*, 31: 90–126.

1983. 'Economic organization, social mobility, and changing social status among East Indians in rural Trinidad', *Ethnology*, 22: 63–79.

Nicholls, D.G. 1971. 'East Indians and black power in Trinidad', *Race*, 12: 443–59.

Niehoff, Arthur and Juanita 1959. *East Indians in the West Indies*, Milwaukee: Milwaukee Public Museum Publications in Anthropology No. 6.

Pollard, N.J. 1965. 'The erosion of agriculture in an oil economy: the case of export crop production in Trinidad', *World Development*, 13(7): 819–35.

Robinson, Vaughan 1984. 'Asians in Britain: a study in encapsulation and marginality', in *Geography and Ethnic Pluralism*, eds. Colin Clarke, David Ley and Ceri Peach, London: Allen & Unwin, 231–57.

Rubin, Vera and Marisa Zavelloni 1969. *We Wish to be Looked Upon*, New York: Teachers College, Columbia University.

Ryan, Selwyn 1972. *Race and Nationalism in Trinidad and Tobago*, Toronto: University of Toronto Press.

Schwartz, Barton 1964. 'Caste and endogamy in Trinidad', *Southwestern Journal of Anthropology*, 20: 58–66.

1967a. (ed.) *Caste in Overseas Indian Communities*, San Francisco: Chandler.

1967b. 'The failure of caste in Trinidad', in *Caste in Overseas Indian Communities*, ed. Barton Schwartz, San Francisco: Chandler, 117–47.

1967c. 'Differential socio-religious adaptation', *Social and Economic Studies*, 16: 237–48.

Smith, Raymond T. 1963. 'Culture and social structure in the Caribbean: some recent work on family and kinship studies', *Comparative Studies in Society and History*, 6: 24–46.

1977. 'Introduction' in *The Stratification System and Occupational Mobility in Guyana*, Sara Graham and Derek Gordon, University of the West Indies: ISER, viii–xxi.

1978. 'The family and the modern world system: some observations from the Caribbean', *Journal of Family History*, 3: 337–60.

Smith, Raymond T. and Chandra Jayawardena 1959. 'Marriage and the family amongst East Indians in British Guiana', *Social and Economic Studies*, 8: 321–76.

Sutton, Paul 1983. 'Black power in Trinidad and Tobago: the crisis of 1970', *Journal of Commonwealth and Comparative Politics*, 21: 115–32.

1984. 'Trinidad and Tobago: oil capitalism and the "presidential power" of Eric Williams', in *Dependency under Challenge*, eds. Anthony Payne and Paul Sutton, Manchester University Press, 43–76.

Taylor, Jeremy 1980, 'Drowning in Petrodollars', *New Internationalist*, 94: 13–14.

Tinker, Hugh 1974. *A New System of Slavery*, London: Oxford University Press.

1976. *Separate and Unequal*, London: C. Hurst and Co.
1977. *The Banyan Tree*, Oxford University Press.
Vertovec, Steven 1987. Hinduism and social change in village Trinidad, D.Phil. thesis. Oxford University.
1989. 'Hinduism in diaspora: the transformation of tradition in Trinidad', in *Hinduism Reconsidered*, eds. Gunther-Dietz Sontheimer and H. Tulke, New Delhi: Manohar, 152–79.

Soures from which economic data derived

Barclays Bank 1985. *Abecor Country Report*, Trinidad and Tobago.
The Economist, 13 September 1980, 90–1.
The Economist, 15 August 1985, 9–10.
Financial Times Survey Trinidad and Tobago, 25 March 1977.
Financial Times Survey Trinidad and Tobago, 8 July 1985.
Keesings Contemporary Archives
Petroleum Economist 1979. *Latin America and Caribbean Oil Report.*
South Magazine September 1985, 231–47.
South Magazine August 1986, 114–15.
Taylor, Jeremy 1980. Drowning in Petrodollars, *New Internationalist* 94 13–14.
World Bank 1974–84 *Annual Reports.*
World Bank 1979–83 *Atlases.*

5

The Fiji Indians: marooned at home

Victor Lal

On 14 May 1987, the Fiji Indians awoke to mark the 108th anniversary of the arrival, aboard the sailing ship *Leonidas*, of the first Indian 'coolies' in Fijian waters. That day had an additional significance because for the first time the Indians were sharing power. The country was being governed by an Indo-Fijian dominated coalition government, formed a month before, after Fiji's fifth post-independence general election. In fact, that day was to see the arrest of all their progress. A group of ten masked and armed soldiers – led by the country's third-ranking Fijian soldier – Lt. Col. Sitiveni Rabuka – stormed parliament as the Government Buildings's clock chimed ten. In a swift and bloodless coup the troops arrested the newly-elected prime minister, Dr Timoci Bavadra, and his parliamentary colleagues, and put them into waiting army trucks to be taken into custody.

The general election had been held from 4 to 11 April 1987. When the final votes were counted, on 12 April, one of the longest reigning governments in the Commonwealth, that of prime minister Ratu Sir Kamisese Mara's Alliance Party, conceded defeat to a coalition of parties led by a 52-year-old medical doctor, Dr Bavadra, an ethnic Fijian. The coalition, made up of the Indian-backed National Federation Party (NFP) and the multi-racial Fiji Labour Party (FLP), won 28 of the 52 seats in the House of Representatives. The right-wing Alliance Party, which had ruled Fiji since independence from Britain in 1970 (mainly backed by indigenous Fijians), won 24 seats.

The overall election results established 31 new members in the House of Representatives; 21 former parliamentarians of whom 16 were members of the Alliance were also returned. Although Dr Bavadra became the second Fijian prime minister after independence, the Fiji Indians for the first time dominated the government: the NFP/FLP Coalition of 28 consisted of 19 Indians, 7 Fijians and 2 others.

Several factors contributed to the coalition's victory: one was the complex one man-four vote electoral system; another was the Fijian urban middle-class's challenge to the legitimacy of chiefly rule, coupled with the anti-Indian campaign launched by the Fijian Nationalist Party (FNP); third was the presence of a small but influential Western United Front (WUF), an anti-Alliance (splinter) Fijian party led by a high Fijian chief, Ratu Osea Gavidi; and most important of all was the fact that for the first time a Fijian, Dr Bavadra, was leading a major opposition party in a general election. Moreover, the Indians retained a remarkable degree of internal cohesion.

The outcome of the election seemed to promise a new era of multiracial politics in Fiji. But for many rural Fijians, the results signified the beginning of 'Indian rule', just as for many Indians it was a dream finally come true, a share in the political kingdom. Almost as soon as Dr Bavadra and his government were sworn-in, a Fijian nationalist movement called Taukei (native Fijian), led by Apisai Tora (a former cofounder of the NFP, and later an Alliance MP) and a few prominent Alliance personalities, sprang up. Tora said the group had been formed to mobilise the Fijian people and give them a more unified voice on national affairs in their own country. He promised a campaign of civil disobedience, calling for changes to the Fiji Constitution to guarantee Fijian chiefly leadership in government for ever.

At meetings and demonstrations he charged that the Bavadra government was a front for Indian interests and that their immediate objective was to rob Fijians of ownership and control of their land. He was joined by the Great Council of Chiefs – the sheet anchor of the Fijian way of life – and others, notably a group of Alliance ex-cabinet ministers. The public demonstrations were quickly followed by road blocks, attacks on Indian politicians' homes, and fire-bombings of premises owned by Indian businessmen. The politically orchestrated campaign plunged the Bavadra government into deep crisis, facilitating the process of military intervention in the politics of Fiji.

After placing the prime minister, Bavadra, his ministers and backbenchers under house arrest, Lt. Col. (now Brigadier) Rabuka claimed he had taken action to forestall threats to law and order and to pre-empt the possibility that, in the event of civil unrest, Bavadra's government would resort to calling on the Fiji army to maintain law and order. But within days it emerged that the coup was racially inspired: Brigadier Rabuka told a press conference that he had seized power to 'safeguard the Fijian way of life'; he wanted to impose Christianity as the official religion of Fiji, and to ensure that the country would never again experience a government dominated by the Indo-Fijian population.

This intrinsically racist announcement immediately attracted hundreds of Fijians, who converged on the quadrangle of the government buildings in Suva to celebrate the military takeover. The Indians began to leave the city as rumour, fear and confusion swept throughout the streets. Although Bavadra and his colleagues were released from detention on 19 May and the governor-general, Ratu Sir Penaia Ganilau, resumed authority as Fiji's chief executive, the state of siege was to continue for another eight months culminating in the second seizure of power by the army in September.

Brigadier Rabuka mounted the second coup to abort the formal announcement of a compromise reached by the rival parties to form a bi-partisan government. In a radio broadcast, he said the recent developments had made it clear that the objectives of the coup he led in May had not been achieved. In a tangled set of exchanges, the country saw the direct intervention of the Queen in the Fijian crisis, the governor-general's resignation to become the first president of the newly declared Republic of Fiji, and the return of his former political colleague and traditional high chief, Ratu Mara, to the premiership. Meanwhile, a new constitution was being drafted to entrench Fijian political paramountcy and institutionalise Indian political inferiority (Lal 1990).

The colonial period

Why the two coups took place will be debated for years. The racial character of the coups, however, highlight one aspect of politics in Fiji – the importance, and crucial factor, of race – a subject whose origins can be traced to the period of the British colony. The history of ninety-six years of British rule in Fiji is, broadly speaking, one of benevolent apartheid. It kept apart settler Europeans, the indigenous Fijians and the Indians, who were originally brought from British India in 1879 to work on the sugar plantations as 'coolie labourers'. Later, at independence, the Constitution of Fiji codified these vestiges of racialism. Today politics is race and race is politics among Fiji's multiracial population of 714,000, where the Fiji Indians (48.6%) slightly outnumber the native Fijians (46.2%) and minority Europeans, part-Europeans, Chinese and other groups (usually referred to as General Electors).

The ethnic groups have preserved many of the social customs, language, religion and etiquette of their forebears although, for the most part, adopting the English language and aspects of English manners. Ethnic affiliation, however, remains the main basis of social, economic and political identity. Fijian society is traditionally hierarchical in structure and the Fijians hold fast to their traditions, living in villages under hereditary chiefs. Fijians who no longer draw on their villages for their livelihood are employed mainly by the government, constituting an urban proletariat. But their penetration of the business sector, to date, has been minimal. The Fijians, however, communally own 83% of the land, dominate the Fiji army, and – before the two coups – the Great Council of Chiefs' nominees in the Senate had a veto over any Bill affecting Fijian land, custom or tradition.

The role of Fijian chiefs

The link with the British crown was forged on 10 October 1874, when a group of Fijian chiefs, led by the self-styled 'King of Fiji', Ratu Seru Cakobau, signed the Deed of Cession whereby Fiji became a possession and a dependency of the crown. But the Fijian chiefs, who had been the traditional rulers of the country from time immemorial, were recognised as such by the British government. So, through a system of indirect rule, separate Fijian institutions and the Great Council of Chiefs were established to govern the Fijians. These institutions, while creating a 'state within a state', gave the Fijian chiefs a free hand to rule their people, and deeply influenced the subsequent history of the colony. The fact that the Fijian community itself is not monolithic, as is supposed, permitted the emergence of the eastern chiefs (such as Ratu Sir Lala Sukuna) as power brokers in the control of the country. They demanded their land back when the British departed. For example, Ratu George Cakobau, the great-grandson of Ratu Seru Cakobau and the first local governor-general after independence in 1970, told the Fiji Legislature: 'I have nothing against independence. Let that independence come. But when independence comes, I should like this recorded in the House: Let the British government return Fiji to Fijians in the state and in the same spirit with which Fijians gave Fiji to Great Britain' (quoted in Anthony and Meller 1963: 103). Ratu Penaia Ganilau, his successor as governor-general, declared: 'The running of this colony must be handed over into the hands of the Fijians: by that I mean administratively and politically' (quoted in Watters 1969: 24).

Inevitably, the chiefs succeeded in extracting recognition from Britain as the authentic 'sons of the soil'. But the partnership between the chiefs and the colonial government not only enabled 'the domination of eastern chiefs particularly over the west, but it also resulted in the rise of a new type of bureaucratic chief, aware of the need to adjust to the demands of the colonial state if they were to achieve their class aims' (Robertson 1986). It was not surprising, therefore, that in 1987 the FLP symbolised for the Alliance a challenge by Fijian commoners to the entrenched Fijian chiefly system; this pertained especially to the rise of Dr Bavadra, a commoner Fijian, from long-neglected western Viti Levu, to the highest office in the land.

The Fiji Indians

The Indo-Fijians, in contrast to the indigenous Fijians, are 'all chiefs and no commoners'. They are more commercially minded, work the sugar farms, run the business enterprises and serve as lawyers and doctors. Briefly, the first contingent of 463 indentured Indians, whose origins lay in Britain's policy of transporting labour from India, arrived in Fijian waters on 14 May 1879 to work on the sugar plantations. Many of their fellow Indians had already travelled under similar contracts to several tropical destinations: Mauritius, Trinidad, Jamaica, British Guiana (Guyana), Natal in South Africa and Suriname. In all, from 1879 to 1916, some 60,537 Indians came to Fiji as indentured labourers on five-year contracts. They were not entitled to a free passage to India until they had lived ten years in the colony, and so there was no alternative but to find some employment during the five years after indenture; nearly two-thirds of them decided to enter farming or trade – becoming 'free Indians'.

Of the emigrants, approximately 75% boarded their ships in Calcutta and the rest in Madras. Among the migrants from Calcutta there were 85.3% Hindus, 14.6% Muslims and 0.1% Christians. The Hindus were from a variety of castes: Brahmins and other high castes comprised 16% of those who came to Fiji through Calcutta, the agricultural castes 31.1%, artisans 6.7%, low castes 31.2%. An analysis of age reveals 68.7% of those who left Calcutta were between 20 and 30 years old and 17.9% between 10 and 20; those between 30 and 40 comprised 4.9%; those over 40, 0.2%. After the indenture period, the so-called 'free migrants' arrived. These were Gujaratis and Punjabis from North-West India (Gillion 1962).

During the colonial period the Indians continued to labour for the Australian giant, the Colonial Sugar Refining Company, which virtually financed the colony. It may be noted here that the inhumane treatment the indentured Indians suffered at the hands of their white masters – an experience remembered in Indo-Fijian folklore as *narak* (hell) – permanently embittered the relationship between the Indians and Europeans. The bitterness of *narak* is best captured in the words of Walter Gill, an overseer during the last years of the system:

> The indenture they signed was for five years' slavery in the cane fields of his Britannic Majesty's Crown Colony of Fiji – to them it was *girmit*, an agreement – and it contained some of the most

pernicious clauses thought up by man. There were such things expressed and inferred as 'fixed immigration ratio of four men to one woman', no choice of place or method of employment; women to work in the fields for at least the first seven months of their pregnancy; housing conditions worse if anything than those from which they had escaped; working hours unlimited. And all for a few pence a day. (Gill 1970: 38)

The 'free' and politically conscious Indians' clamour in the 1920s for a common electoral roll and economic rights subsequently aroused strong political feelings. As one European politician, Henry Marks, remarked in 1929: 'We have the Indians here and we must make the best of it and teach them we are the colony and not the Indians' (quoted in Ali 1980: 136). The position of the Indian in Fiji was to be none other than a servant or a serf. Furthermore, the Indian stereotype of the Fijian as an irresponsible, childish, uncivilised fellow, or *jungli*, and the Fijian depiction of the Indian coolie as heathen and undersized, brought to work as a plantation slave, proved advantageous for the Europeans. In order to remain masters, the Europeans imposed their own racial segregation through separate halls, churches, voluntary associations, tennis clubs and Sunday schools. Although the position changed in later years, it was the Indians who faced the brunt of European domination (Mamak 1978). Yet the Indians continued to struggle for their advancement, and especially so after 1920, when all unexpired contracts of indenture were cancelled and the Indian population settled down as farmers and cane growers. They perceived that political activity held the key to further progress, and with increased determination they attempted to penetrate every sector of the political system.

Ethnic politics

In the face of increasing challenges, the Indians were finally granted communal franchise in 1929. For the next thirty years, they continued their fight for political emancipation, culminating in the formation of their own political party, the Federation Party, in the 1960s. They later merged with the small, but predominantly Fijian, Western Democratic Party, led by Tora, then a militant trade unionist, to form the National Federation Party (NFP).

The Alliance Party, formed in 1966, also showed strong ethnic leanings. Led by Ratu Mara, the Alliance was a coalition of three parties: the Fijian Association, which claimed the loyalty of the bulk of the native Fijians, the General Electors Association (GEA), and the Indian Alliance, which drew support from a small but significant section of the Indian community. The Alliance and the NFP were to guide the destiny of Fiji for many years.

While the Fijians remained cut off from mainstream national issues and infinitely loyal to their traditional political system, the Indians became formidable rivals to the Europeans in many spheres of life. But, although the Indians were becoming a force to be reckoned with, they were isolated from the running of the country because of their demand for a common roll, their repeated strikes in the cane fields and their refusal to support the war effort, though by 1946 they had become the colony's largest racial group.

As already noted, on 10 October 1874 a group of Fijian chiefs ceded Fiji to Great Britain. On 10 October 1970, Fiji became an independent nation in the Commonwealth. The ninety-six years between these two Octobers were years of considerable political, social and economic change. The relationship between the different communities greatly deteriorated. Ordinary political arguments became transformed into racial quarrels. The races drifted apart. The Indians maintained that only through common roll elections could Fiji emerge as 'one people, one country, one nation'. Common franchise had been idolised by Indians as 'the panacea that would provide them with security by ensuring them a permanent place in the Fijian sun' and equality they saw as 'a matter of *izzat* (self respect), and communal franchise as their stigma of inferiority' (Ali 1977: 19). The Fijians, on the other hand, were not going to concede a common roll; they maintained that if a common roll was introduced their status would fall 'from that of a nation to that of a mere community' (Vasil 1984: 116). The granting of the franchise to the Fijians in 1963, and the Fijian Association's victory in the general elections to the Legislative Council the same year, also encouraged Fijian leaders to appeal directly to Fijians for racial and electoral support.

When the respective parties finally met in London for the 1965 constitutional talks, the power struggle for the country was evident. The Indian delegation contended that the proper course was to proceed at once to elections by single member constituencies, on a common roll, with neither communal qualifications for elections nor communal reservations of seats for candidates. They made clear their view that, as the Indians constituted the majority of the population, they were entitled to a parity of representation with the Fijians: they also maintained that full internal self-government should be introduced forthwith. The Fijian leaders and the European oligarchy disagreed, insisting that a common roll was a desirable but long-term objective.

The result of the 1965 debate was the introduction of a partial communal roll and a new cross-voting system. An elected legislature, with a mixture of communal rolls and racially reserved seats, was created under the 1966 constitution, and it was this body of 36 members which constituted the post-independence parliament. The 1966 election results gave the Alliance 23 seats, but two victorious Independents and the 2 members of the Great Council of Chiefs also aligned themselves with it, to make its total 27. Thus the Alliance Party took over the running of the colony.

In this deeply divided society each community has its own party. In 1966, the Indians clearly identified themselves with the NFP, which was founded as a political organisation to champion their cause and aspirations. The Alliance, on the other hand, revealed itself as a predominantly, though not exclusively, Fijian party. The 1966 elections were simply another form of ethnic struggle (Ali 1977: 68). On 1 September 1967, the Executive Council was replaced by a Council of Ministers and Ratu Mara (a high chief and by now a knight) became chief minister. However, signs of trouble emerged when the nine NFP members (representing the Indian communal seats) condemned the 1966 constitution as iniquitous and undemocratic, and walked out.

Tension increased, especially during a 1968 by-election, but in 1969 a series of discussions took place between the Alliance and the NFP, led respectively by Ratu Mara and Siddiq Koya. These talks covered additional constitutional changes and, on 3 November 1969, the two parties agreed on most issues, except on the composition of the legislature and the method of election. The key difference was that while the NFP argued in favour of a single roll to create a united nation, the Alliance preferred to accept the divisions of race as the basic fact of life in Fiji. A Constitutional Conference was subsequently held at Marlborough House in London from 20 April to 5 May 1970. After a great deal of midnight oil had been burnt, on 30 April, Ratu Mara announced that agreement had been reached on an interim solution.

The constitution

In view of the multiethnic nature of Fiji society, the new constitution provided for communal representation. There were to be 27 communal seats, of which Indians and Fijians were allocated 12 each, while 3 went to the General Electors. The remaining 25 seats were national seats, which again, were allocated on a racial basis: 10 Fijian, 10 Indian and 5 other races. Many believe that the General Electors – most of whom have favoured the Alliance – were over-represented.

Fiji's voting system, among the most complex in the world, was such that for a communal seat only voters of a particular race could vote for a candidate of that race. Thus, every voter had four votes: one for a communal candidate of the voter's own ethnic group and three for national candidates of each of the three groups – Fijian, Indian and General Elector. Apart from the Lower House, there was also agreement that a Senate, constituting 22 members, be appointed by the governor-general on the basis of nominations distributed as follows: prime minister 7, leader of the opposition 6, Great Council of Chiefs 8, and the Council of Rotuma 1. The Upper House, in general, had powers only of delaying and amending legislation passed by the Lower House. Nevertheless, the Senate, which was created at the suggestion of the Indian delegates, was designed to serve as a protector of the land rights of the Fijians.

While the Indian leaders opted for a small piece of the political pie rather than none at all, the 1970 Marlborough House Conference represented a solid victory for the Fijians. The Fijians were a minority, but the constitution went out of its way to safeguard their interests. True, the 98% of Fiji-born Indians who accepted Fiji citizenship were protected under a Bill of Rights incorporated in the Fiji constitution: but this was, however, not a sufficient guarantee. Many Indians believed that with the passage of time their vulnerability would increase, and for examples they turned to the fate of other overseas Indians, particularly those in East Africa (Twaddle, chapter 7).

On 10 October 1970 Fiji became independent, bringing to a close, temporarily, all the social and political tensions generated by over three-quarters of a century of British rule. The country became a parliamentary democracy in which rival parties were to compete for power: the political leaders had signed a constitution which assumed the operation of representative and responsible government using the Westminster model. Whenever the question of constitutional reform had been considered during the period of British rule, none of the communities, including the Fijian, showed any hesitation in emphasising the need for Fijian rights to be entrenched. The principal aim of the Fijian and European leaders was the prevention of the 'Indianisation' of Fiji. Thus, racialism was to become the key to future policies in the country. The political demands of the Fijians were sharpened further by their special circumstances as a minority fighting to maintain a separate identity. The possibility of domination by Indians was, and still is, the nightmare of many Fijians and other ethnic groups. In particular, the Fijians did not, and do not, try to justify their own domination but most of them prefer it to the reverse.

Politics is about power. During the London talks, the principal issue had been about who was losing power and who was gaining it. A deeper study of the decision reached at the Constitutional conference shows that the fear that Fijians would be swamped by the majority Indians had been overplayed, because the two racial groups were equally large (effectively two 'majority' communities'), each large enough to view itself as capable of assuming a majority role, and thereby the right to rule. Yet, it seems that no consideration was given to future population trends which might lead to the Indians becoming a minority in Fiji.

This fact emerged in 1976 when, for the first time since censuses were conducted, those of Indian origin declined as a percentage of the total population, so that once again they constituted just under 50% of the total population. Projections were also made showing that by 1988 Fijians would overtake the Indians as the largest racial group in the country. Apart from its far-reaching implications, this change in racial proportions raised a fundamental question: which was to be treated as the minority, to be given constitutional and political safeguards? All the recent indicators suggest that the Indians are on their way to becoming a minority. The latest figures released in 1986 reveal that while the Fijian percentage rose from 44.2% in 1976 to 46.2% in 1986, the Indian percentage dropped from 49.8% in 1976 to 48.6%. The population gap between the Indians and the Fijians had declined from 5.6% to 2.4% (*Fiji Sun* 3 October 1986).

Independence in 1970 left in its wake a fear among the Indians about their security in Fiji, and a corresponding apprehension among the Fijians of the superior economic qualities and political aspirations of the Indian community. While the Indians outwardly displayed solidarity with the Fijians in securing a peaceful and bloodless transition to independence, within their hearts and homes they knew that their day of judgement had been merely delayed but not abandoned. There was euphoria mixed with sadness. Nevertheless, the Indians joined in the independence celebrations, hoping that common sense and fair play would prevail.

Politics since independence

The brief explosion of joy which marked independence, the political honeymoon between Ratu Mara and Koya, and the *rapprochement* between the Alliance and the NFP during the constitutional talks, came to a close after the first general election in 1972. The Alliance, led by Ratu Mara, easily won with 33 seats out of the 52 in the House of Representatives. The NFP took 19 seats. By the time of the 1972 general election communal polarisation between the different communities was complete. Although the predominantly Fijian Alliance government promised to carve out 'unity in diversity', the euphoria of independence was just the beginning of a long retreat that lay ahead for the Indians who had marched from plantations to politics.

In January 1974, the Fijian Nationalist Party (FNP) was founded. It began arguing that the Fijian's constitutional position was destined to be gradually undermined. Although the FNP did consider some form of common roll, this would have been accompanied by the reservation of 75% of seats and most ministerial positions for Fijians. In October 1975, the FNP caused a stir in the House of Representatives by calling for the expulsion of the Indian community. The minimum the FNP was prepared to accept was the clear subordination of Indian interests to Fijian ones. The expulsion motion was defeated but, by all accounts, it touched a deep nerve by articulating much that was normally left unsaid on both sides.

Among the Indian community there was a general consensus that their leaders had failed to ensure their security. The NFP's strength as a political force was felt in the April 1977 general elections, when it won 26 of the 52 seats; the Alliance won 24; FNP leader Sakeasi Butadroka, and an Independent, Ratu Osea Gavidi, (later the Western United Front (WUF) leader) won a seat each. But because of bickering over who should be prime minister, the governor-general, Ratu Sir George Cakobau, appointed the Alliance as the caretaker government and Ratu Mara as prime minister. The NFP split into two groups – the Dove (Muslim) and Flower (Hindu) factions – in the September elections of the same year. The results were disastrous. Its strength was reduced from 26 seats to 15: Flower got 12 and Dove took 3.

The factions patched up their differences later and fought the 1982 election in coalition with the Western United Front (WUF). Led by a moderate Indian lawyer, Jai Ram Reddy, they won 24 seats to the Alliance's 28. The elections of 1982 saw racial recriminations becoming the keynote of the political exchanges. The NFP accused the Alliance of hiring expatriates to prepare a 'How to Win an Election Kit', and alleged intervention by the American Central Intelligence Agency (CIA) in preparation for moves to destabilise any government formed after a successful NFP electoral campaign. Party members warned that such American intervention would have used the Fijian armed forces. The Alliance accused the NFP of receiving $1 million from the Soviet Union, and charged that Indian High Commissions in Fiji and Australia were being used to further Soviet interests in the South Pacific. Ratu Mara also accused India's High Commissioner to Fiji, Mrs Soonu Kochar, of interference in Fiji's domestic politics, and she was subsequently expelled from the country. A Royal Commission of Inquiry into the 1982 elections tore the races further apart.

Thus, the only silver lining to the clouds of political and racial uncertainty was the birth of the multi-racial FLP, which was officially launched on 6 July 1985. The FLP, which came into being after the Alliance government unilaterally imposed a wage freeze in November 1984, had promised to cut across the traditional, racially arranged voting system in a country where 'race is a fact of life'. Its stunning electoral victory in the April 1987 elections seemed to offer that opportunity.

In the words of a former NFP parliamentarian, Karam Ramrakha: 'A new marriage is taking place, a meeting of minds of the educated elite in Fiji, an elite which will bring in a new era to the country.' As for the change in the political landscape where the Alliance, comprising mostly chiefs, became the major opposition party with Ratu Mara as leader, Ramrakha further added:

> And the chiefs who have wielded so much power, and have made Fiji what it is today. Yes, they too have to recognise this change . . . a political adjustment has to be made. The genius of the Fijian people allowed them to cede their country and remain in charge of it. Their society has come down the centuries intact: their people still cling to their valued culture, traditions and customs.
>
> (*Fiji Sun* 13 April 1987)

In the wake of this assertion it becomes necessary to analyse the circumstances and conditions which led to the present state of affairs, and also to ask why, in 1987, after seventeen years of independence, Fiji still had a divided polity experiencing acute ethno-nationalist conflict between the Fijians and the Fiji Indians.

Land, education and other issues

The four most sensitive and divisive issues are the electoral system, the ownership of land, education, and the fact that the Fijians, even when special programmes have been established to initiate them into the commercial world, lag to a very large degree behind other races in their integration into the money economy. Two of these, land and education, generate the most intense debate, especially during election times. The land question is the single most divisive one. The Fijian regard it as the crucial axis of both economic and political power. To them it represents culture, identity and security.

Education is to Indians what land is to Fijians – the source of their existence. During colonial days, the planters were totally against the education of Indians, though the Christian missionaries were already committed to the education of the Fijians. The opponents of Indian education wanted them merely as agriculturalists. Today, many Indians believe that the key to the economic and political salvation of their children lies in their greater participation in higher education. In the words of Dr Ahmed Ali, who later became the Minister for Education in the Alliance government:

> the Indians contend that without education, their children will grow up untrained and will be fit only for manual labour. Hence, history will repeat itself: just as their ancestors had to indenture themselves to labour abroad so their children would be destined to do likewise. Without education, they would not even be able to emigrate from Fiji, and if evicted, what would they do abroad but become slaves of someone else, like their forefathers.
>
> (Ali 1980: 203)

Land is ever a contentious issue. Briefly, the owning of the land by the Indians in Fiji is a natural ambition. But the possibility has been seriously circumscribed everywhere by different land ordinances. It was Sir Arthur Hamilton Gordon (later Lord Stanmore), who, as first colonial governor of Fiji, left a bitter and intractable legacy by providing that land which was not yet alienated to Europeans, consisting of nearly 90% of the country, was to remain under Fijian ownership. Today, most of the land is Fijian owned; the freehold land is in European hands, and the Indians own barely 1.7% of the country. The Indian leaders, to reassure their Fijian compatriots that they did not want to threaten Fijian interests, agreed during the constitutional talks that the nominees of the Great Council of Chiefs in the Senate should hold the ultimate power of veto on land issues, irrespective of the government in power.

Ironically, many Indians, especially the farmers, feel that their political leaders sold out the community on the land issue. Indians feel extremely insecure and vulnerable because, as the former NFP leader, Jai Ram Reddy, has pointed out, 'many of them, particularly farmers, are mere tenants with very limited security of tenure – and they realise that it is in the nature of a lease that it will expire one day, be it 20 or 30 years'. He pointed out that while 'the tenant knows that he has a place to live, he is not sure that his dependent will when he is gone'. Land leases are granted to the Indians for a thirty-year period and are due to expire in the year 2000. There is no assurance that new leases will be entered into.

The Indian dilemma is aggravated further because: (a) the largest group of unemployed come from this sector, as they have no material security; (b) they are generally squatters and their mobility is severely limited; (c) they do not have a social security system to underpin their existence; (d) they cannot fall back on the land because they have none;

and (e) the greatest degree of undernourishment and poverty is to be found within this group.

Above all, the Indians do not have anything similar to the Fijian Administration (a system of local government for Fijians), the Fijian Affairs Board, the Great Council of Chiefs, Provincial Councils, the Fijian Development Fund Board, the Native Land Trust Board or the Native Land Development Corporation, through which they can articulate and marshal their opinions and grievances. No effort was made either by the British or the Alliance government to establish a Ministry of Indian Affairs (on the lines of the Ministry of Fijian Affairs) even as a symbolic gesture to indicate that the Indians were not, as some claimed, deliberately being treated as second-class citizens. Inevitably, the Indians could not but make empty protests:

> We do not enjoy any basic say in the centre of power, nor are we ever likely to do so. No community, no, not even a heavy-duty one like the Indians, can continue to nourish itself on the politics of protests; no community which contributes so much to the life-blood of the country can tolerate such isolation, or can be so forgotten. We must not be placed in a corner, but in the centre.
>
> (Quoted in Milne 1981: 210)

Economy

We must also put in perspective another erroneous and often repeated idea that Fijians hold the political power, while Indians hold the economic power. This can lead to the simple conclusion that since the Indians control the economy, it is they who are the wealthier group. There is a great deal of myth-making on this subject.

The economic imbalances among the ethnic groups can be traced to the period of British rule. Many researchers have shown how the colonial government's native policy was responsible for the post-war gap in resource distribution between the Fijians and those of other racial groups (Narayan 1984). In recent years some students of Fijian politics have blamed the present institutions, in-built customs and traditions, and the role of the Fijian chiefs which they claim hinder Fijian commercial enterprise. The Indians, on the other hand, learnt their lessons from the experience of indenture. The economic disparities and occupational distribution of the different racial groups have been thoroughly documented in studies of the period under review, notably by an Australian economist, E.K. Fisk (1970). Over the years, the income disparity between the two major races has narrowed, as is evident from a World Bank report

(*Fiji Times* 23 June 1986). The report disclosed that the income gap between the two groups in fact was relatively moderate. In 1977, the average income of an Indian family was $4,003, that of a Fijian family $3,398, while a family of other races earned on average $6,228 per year.

Furthermore, while the position of the employed Indians was better than that of Fijians, when it came to unemployment the situation was reversed. In 1976, Fijians were 46% of the unemployed, and Indians 48%, while people of other races accounted for the remaining 6%. But between 1976 and 1982, the number of unemployed Fijians declined from 46% to 34%; the number of unemployed in other races dropped from 6% to 3%; but the number of unemployed among the Indians increased from 48% in 1976 to 62% in 1982 – an increase of 14%.

Fijians also dominate the civil service, government, and the law-and-order institutions. The composition of the Fiji police and the military reveals a similar pattern. The disparity, however, is alarmingly sharp for the armed forces, the key instrument of power, and no doubt an essential element in any ethnically divided society. The armed forces comprise 1,852 Fijians, 88 Indians and 82 from other communities (1985 figures). The police force contains 755 Fijians, 684 Indians and 63 others. The Public Service includes 7,928 Fijians, 8,165 Indians, 94 Europeans and 956 from other communities. Among the Permanent Secretaries, 9 are Fijians, 5 Indians and 1 European. The conspicuous lack of Indian representation in the top tier of administration, and the fact that many candidates of Indian origin are well qualified (the percentage of Indian passes in internal examinations conducted by the Fiji Public Service Commission are significantly higher than among their Fijian counterparts) is another source of friction. The Mara Administration used to employ expatriate Indians (a Trinidadian in the Foreign Office, Sri Lankans in the judiciary) rather than Fiji Indians. In May 1982 James Shankar Singh resigned from the Alliance on the grounds of irreconcilable differences between himself and Ratu Mara. Singh recounted:

> It is my sad experience throughout the existence of the party that Indian leaders and members have been made tools or vehicles of convenience by the party leader, and once the general election is over and Ratu Sir Kamisese is conveniently seated in the Prime Minister's chair, he treats them like a bunch of coolies.
>
> (*Fiji Sun* 11 May 1982)

A general review of events shows that after independence in 1970, and shortly before the two coups in 1987, there was a marked widening of the communal divide. The society became increasingly divided along racial lines with the formation of the Fijian Nationalist Party: the Fijian population, which regarded Butadroka as a true 'nationalist', provided substantial support for his party, and anti-Indian propaganda began to find a sympathetic ear amongst certain sections. The Fiji Indians, on the other hand, who had been promised in the Salisbury Dispatch of 1875 that they would be 'in all respects free men, with privileges no whit inferior to those of any other class of Her Majesty's subjects resident in other colonies', came to the conclusion that another South Africa or Uganda was in the making in the South Pacific (Yarwood 1968: 201–18). Their fears were heightened after the 1982 general elections, when the Great Council of Chiefs called for the Fiji constitution to be amended much as the Fijian Nationalist Party had demanded: two-thirds of seats in the House should be reserved for Fijians; the prime minister and governor-general should always be Fijians. In all of this what was to happen after the 1987 election was foreshadowed.

The Australian historian, K.L. Gillion, in his study of the history of Indians in Fiji, concludes that their history shows how they 'continued to adapt to the land to which their great grandparents came under such unhappy circumstances. If they were not yet Fijians, they were certainly the Fiji-Indians' (1977: 198). The final picture that emerges of Fiji Indians in the 1980s is that of a community which is destined to rebuild its life within the Fijian version of apartheid. While the vast majority of Fijians seem to 'wander between two worlds, one dead, the other powerless to be born' (Matthew Arnold, 'Stanzas from the "Grand Chartreuse"'), their present chiefly leaders have demonstrated, through their actions, that they have not abandoned the dream of political paramountcy in perpetuity, while pursuing their traditional lifestyles.

The Fiji Indians, on the other hand, may remain in an inextricable bind. Those truly stranded are the overwhelming majority of Indians on the sugar plantations. Unlike their great grandparents, the majority are marooned in their own homes, sulking and pondering their future. The following declaration of an ex-indentured woman labourer, in 1979, Rangamma, whose parents had worked on a fruit farm near Cape Town in South Africa before arriving in Fiji in 1899, still applies to the Indo-Fijians today: 'Fiji is my place. There is nobody in India for me.'

Conclusion

The Fijian *coup d'état* of May 1987 has significance for the millions of South Asians overseas: how many years should they wait to become 'natives'? But, for the Fiji Indians, the coup, in what seems a cruel twist of fate, ousted their representatives from Parliament on 14 May 1987, 108 years to the day since their ancestors were first introduced to work on the sugar plantations, thus arresting the community's triumphant march from plantation to Fiji's parliament. Their history, however, will record that their own *displacement* from British India prevented the *dispossession* of the Fijians in colonial Fiji. Indeed by a happy irony the indentured Indian was uprooted specifically to prevent the Fijian way of life from disintegrating. In 1978, Dr Satendra Nandan, the poet/politician who was among those to be seized in Parliament on 14 May 1987, had reminded the nation:

> It is interesting to speculate if this peasant labourer had not come to Fiji at a critical time, not only the Fijian way of life but many island communities in the South Pacific would have been disrupted and perhaps permanently dislocated. The planters needed labour, the government wanted economic viability for political stability, and it is anyone's guess what they would have done to achieve this. Thus the displacement of the Indian prevented the dispossession of the Fijian. This may be the lasting and most significant contribution of the peasants from India. Without this the Fijian might have lost much of his land, and more tragically his self-respect. (*Fiji Sun* 10 June 1978)

References

Ali, Ahmed 1977. *Fiji: From Colony to Independence 1874–1970*, Suva: University of the South Pacific.
      1980. *Plantation to Politics: Studies on Fiji Indians*, Suva: University of the South Pacific and the *Fiji Times and Herald Limited*.
Allott, Miriam (ed.) 1979. *Arnold: The Complete Poems*, 2nd edn, London: Longmans, 301–10.
Anthony, J. and N. Meller 1963. *Fiji Goes to the Polls: the Crucial Legislative Council Elections of 1963*, Hawaii: East West Centre Press.
Fisk, E.K. 1970. *The Political Economy of Independent Fiji*, Canberra: Australian National University Press.
Gill, Walter 1970. *Turn North-East at the Tombstone*, Adelaide.
Gillion, K.L. 1962. *Fiji's Indian Migrants: a history to the end of indenture in 1920*, Melbourne: Oxford University Press.
      1977. *The Fiji Indians: challenge to European dominance 1920–46*, Canberra: Australian National University Press.
Lal, Victor 1990. *Fiji: Coups in Paradise*, London: Zed Press.
Mamak, Alexander 1978. *Colour, Culture and Conflict: a study of pluralism in Fiji*, Australia: Pergamon Press.
Milne, R.S. 1981. *Politics in Ethnically Bi-Polar States: Guyana, Malaysia, Fiji*, Vancouver: University of British Columbia Press.
Narayan, Jai 1984. *The Political Economy of Fiji*, Suva: South Pacific Review Press.
Robertson, R.T. 1986. 'Making new histories of Fiji: the choice between materialist political economy and neo-colonial orthodoxy', *Journal of Pacific Studies*, 12: 33–58.

Vasil, R.K. 1984. *Politics in Bi-racial Societies: the Third World Experience*, New Delhi: Vikas Publishing.
Watters, R.K. 1969. *Koro: Economic Development and Social Change in Fiji*, Oxford: Clarendon Press.
Yarwood, A.T. 1968. 'The overseas Indians: a problem in Indian and Imperial politics at the end of World War I', *Australian Journal of Politics and History*, 14, 2.

6

The political position of Indians in South Africa

Anthony Lemon

Uncertain beginnings: Indians in a 'European' society

Indians were the final element of South Africa's plural society to enter the country, and for a long time their permanence was questioned by Europeans. While this is no longer the case, Indians remain a small and virtually powerless minority. In 1985 they numbered 839,000, or 2.9% of South Africa's population (SAIRR 1987). Even this population share is declining, given a 1984 birth rate of 28.2 per 1,000 compared with an estimated African figure of 40 per 1,000. It is, however, in relation to the European or white minority that Indians have been politically subservient hitherto. They have shared this condition with the officially designated coloured (mixed-race) minority (9.7%) and the African majority (71.8%).

In the province of Natal, European planters at first sought a break-up of rural locations or reserves in order to force the indigenous Zulus to work on their new sugar and cotton plantations. When the chance of this faded they eventually turned to India, following the precedent set by sugar planters in Mauritius and the Caribbean. Thus the indenture system was extended to Natal, and between 1860 and 1911 some 140,000 Indians came. Some of the later immigrants worked on the railways, in the coal mines of northern Natal, and in domestic service. Many of those on plantations were offered land as an inducement to re-indenture, but as their numbers increased an earlier promise of citizenship was not fulfilled and the offer of land was subsequently withdrawn. Nearly all Indians nevertheless remained in South Africa, turning mostly to market gardening and trading in peri-urban and urban areas (Lemon 1980: 109).

Some 10% of Indians entering South Africa were 'passenger' immigrants who came at their own expense to trade and work in commerce, especially in the 1880s and 1890s. This group had a more balanced sex ratio than the indentured majority, hence the descendants of 'passenger'

131

immigrants comprise some 30% of all South African Indians today. Since 1913 Indian immigration to South Africa has been restricted to the dependants of existing residents, and by 1960 a mere 5.5% of Indians had been born outside South Africa (Sadie 1970: 7).

White attitudes to Indians have been characteristically ambivalent; employers found their labour useful, but traders and businessmen feared competition. Indians were excluded altogether from the Orange Free State between 1891 and 1985, and from northern districts of Natal between 1927 and 1986. In the Transvaal they were hedged-in by restrictions on property owning and employment, but many of these were either never fully enforced or successfully circumvented. The Cape was more permissive, but owing to its distance from Natal attracted relatively few Indians. Continued restriction of inter-provincial movement after 1910 maintained the concentration of Indians in southern Natal. Inter-provincial movement has been unrestricted since 1975, but strong community institutions and family ties have tended to discourage out-movement. Thus 82% of all Indians remained in Natal in 1980. In the absence of past restrictions, many more Indian businessmen and traders would almost certainly have found their way to the towns of the Transvaal and the Orange Free State. As it is, 73% of all South African Indians lived in the Durban–Pinetown metropolitan area alone in 1980; they constituted 37.5% of the total population in this region. Other major concentrations of Indians are found in the Pretoria/ Witwatersrand/Vereeniging area (99,000 – 12% in 1980) and Pietermaritzburg (51,000 – 6.2%).

Europeans found a new cause for grievance in the late 1930s as Indians began to 'infiltrate' predominantly white residential areas, especially in Durban, and trading areas in Transvaal towns. The white reaction was wholly disproportionate to the scale and nature of penetration, but led to restrictions on Indian ownership and occupation of property in 1943 and 1946. Indians further increased their unpopularity with Europeans by bringing their lack of citizenship rights to the United Nations in 1946, through the agency of the Indian government, an action which first drew international attention to South Africa's racial policies (Palmer 1957). Voluntary 'repatriation' schemes continued until 1975, although immigration has exceeded emigration since 1933; this, together with South Africa's extraordinarily belated recognition of Indians as a permanent part of her population in 1961, underlines the continuing ambivalence of white attitudes. These reflected the underlying conviction that Indians were 'alien' and 'unassimilable', a view based largely on visible symbols of pluralism such as religion, food and dress. In practice, cultural differences cut across such cultural categories, and Natal Indians, although certainly distinctive, have long been more westernised than any other overseas Indian community (Brookfield and Tatham 1957: 50).

Whites seldom recognise that Indians are themselves culturally diverse, especially in terms of religion. Hinduism is predominant in Natal, whilst Muslims (20% of all South African Indians) are more numerous in the Transvaal and the Cape, but these are umbrella terms which conceal great complexity. Only 16% of Indians are Christians, but religion is not necessarily so significant a barrier to assimilation as it seems. Hinduism is singularly eclectic (Kuper 1971: 250), and western influences are particularly noticeable in the Arya Samaj (reform movement). Religion is in any case a personal, private affair for both Hindus and Muslims, and as such it need impinge relatively little on everyday social relations with other races.

Despite the effects of residential resettlement under the Group Areas Act (1950), the extended family or *kutum* remains important for most Indians. It consists of all those with whom consanguinity can be traced through a common paternal grandfather or grandfather's brother, and it is 'the primary community which insulates Indians in South Africa from the rigours of the larger society' (Meer 1979: 136, 141). *Kutum* bonds lay the base for group solidarity and have come to extend across the barriers of religion, language, economics, and caste, resulting in relatively close-knit Indian community. While wishing to retain this composite identity, however, Indians do desire integration into the wider South African social system. Instead, their place in South African society, as traditionally viewed by whites, exemplifies Furnivall's characterisation of a plural society as a 'business partnership rather than a family concern' in which 'the social will linking the sections does not extend beyond the common business interests' (1948: 308). But for Indians the spontaneous expression of that social will is difficult if not impossible to measure, restricted as it is by both white laws and white attitudes.

The Indian economic position under apartheid

Agriculture was the largest single source of Indian employment in 1936, when it accounted for 37.8% of Indian workers, but today the corresponding figure is less than 5%. Urban growth has taken its toll: Indian smallholders have been displaced from areas such as Bayhead, Springfield Flats, and Chatsworth without the provision of any alternative areas of agricultural land. Much of the land farmed by Indian sugar cane producers is steeply sloping and would be rejected by white farmers. Structural problems including the small size of Indian holdings and lack of capital have been accentuated by widespread fragmentation, as no additional land has been made available for Indian agriculture; some former cane growers now work in sugar mills. Indian agricultural production could have been greatly increased given training facilities, easier capital availability, and more land.

Owing to the extent of their commercial involvement, Indians suffered disproportionately from the application of the Group Areas Act. Afrikaners have tended to regard Indians as non-productive and parasitical due to their association with commerce, and a prominent Indian South African, Fatima Meer, asserts that 'one of the prime purposes of the Group Areas Act is to eliminate, or at least to reduce to a minimum, Indian commerce' (1971: 23). Whether or not the intentions behind the Act were so blatantly anti-Indian, the effects are undeniable: of 2,765 traders removed between the commencement of the Group Areas Act and the end of 1984, 91.4% (2,530) were Indian; of these, 1,551 were in the Transvaal, 576 in Natal, and 403 in the Cape. Dislocation has thus been particularly great in the Transvaal and the Cape, where absolute numbers of Indians are relatively small but the proportion dependent on commerce was very high – as many as 87.6% of Transvaal Indians in 1963 (1971: 23). By 1966, only 7.5% of Transvaal Indians remained unaffected by the proclamation of group areas.

In the small towns of Natal and the Transvaal, many Indian traders lost their livelihood when they were removed to Indian group areas distant from most of their customers. Even in Pretoria where the proclamation left nearly one-third of Indian traders unaffected, the removal of African and coloured populations living in close proximity to the Asiatic bazaar made loss of business inevitable. In Pageview, near the centre of Johannesburg, the removal of Indian traders was eventually followed by the building of a R16 million Oriental Plaza a stone's throw away from former Indian shops, but with rents too high for many small traders who were unable to re-establish their businesses. In the Grey Street complex of Durban, the largest concentration of Indian trading in South Africa, conflicting impressions of official intentions created a climate of insecurity which made loans difficult to raise and deterred many owners from properly maintaining their premises. Only in 1973 was the Grey Street area proclaimed an Indian group area for trading and light industrial (but not residential) purposes.

In terms of the Group Areas Amendment Act of 1984, local authorities, other organised bodies, or the Minister may submit requests to have areas investigated for the purpose of having them declared free trade areas. The procedure is characteristically cumbersome, but by October 1985 a total of forty-six municipalities had applied for open trading areas, the first of which were declared in 1986. This new system will partially restore to

Indians the freedom to trade which they enjoyed before 1950, although it cannot of course undo the immense damage inflicted upon the Indian community by group areas legislation over the past thirty-five years, nor restore businesses to many who lost their livelihood as traders. The new policy is, moreover, a characteristically incremental reform, highly bureaucratic in its mode of operation and very much an apartheid measure in the race-conscious manner of its framing; it seemed anachronistic even before it had begun to operate. The experience of open trading areas will undoubtedly add to already growing pressures for the total removal of ethnic considerations from the statute book on urban trading.

Indian employment in manufacturing rose sharply in the 1940s, when large numbers of whites were in the armed forces. In the ensuing decades many Indians displaced from commerce by the effects of group areas legislation entered manufacturing. Indians are employed in almost all manufacturing sectors, but especially in those where Indian industrialists are more involved, which include clothing, textiles, footwear, food and drink, furniture, paper, and printing. Average wages of Indian workers are less than half those of whites in most manufacturing sectors, and fall to below a quarter in the largest sector, clothing, which employs many Indian women at low rates. In most sectors, however, Indians earn more than coloureds, often substantially so, whilst Africans trail far behind.[1]

Economic circumstances in the 1950s and 1960s virtually forced the Indian community to accept female employment, despite cultural constraints. The rapid economic growth of Natal since the mid-1960s created the necessary work opportunities. By 1983 the Indian activity rate of 32.9% was not far behind that of coloureds (35.5%), though still significantly below that of whites (42.2%).

The negative effects of the Group Areas Act encouraged those few Indians with capital and know-how to diversify into manufacturing. This was encouraged by the Department of Indian Affairs after 1961, and Indian industrial development areas were designated at Stanger, Tongaat, and Verulam on the north coast of Natal, and in Pietermaritzburg. Several industrial sites were also designated for Indians in and around Durban. The Industrial Development Corporation began to assist small numbers of Indian firms in the 1960s, and in the mid-1970s started to develop selected industrial sites for Indians. However, the relatively small areas of land allocated specifically for Indian use meant that prices were higher than for 'white' land in similar locations, which resulted in 'unit' factories for Indian tenants in areas of heavy demand. Some Indian industrialists found themselves in areas proclaimed white, which restricted their expansion and prompted them to search for new sites where practicable; others suffered from uncertainty in areas such as

Clairwood at the head of Durban Bay and Durban's Grey Street complex. Indian industrialists were the major beneficiaries of the Group Areas Amendment Act of 1977 which eliminated restrictions on ownership, occupation, purchase, and use of land and property by unqualified persons in areas zoned for industrial purposes. Although this did not apply to industrial areas sited in proclaimed group areas, many such areas were subsequently de-proclaimed, enabling Indians to compete on more equal terms with white industrialists.

The creation of the Department of Indian Affairs in 1961, the government takeover of Indian education from the provinces, and the extension of Indian local government all created wider job opportunities for Indians, although they would undoubtedly have entered administrative employment much earlier if competition had been unrestricted. The 1983 constitution will result in increasing Indian recruitment to jobs in national government where, in contrast to local authorities, their average earnings are close to those of whites.

Indians have enjoyed a degree of access to higher education since 1938, and all professions are now open to them. In 1985 over 17,000 Indians were enrolled at South African universities, including 5,925 at their 'own' university at Durban-Westville, and a further 8,210 registered for correspondence degree courses with the University of South Africa (UNISA). Proportionately, this represents more than three times the number of coloureds at universities. White university enrolment was 40% higher, proportionately, than that of Indians in 1985, but this gap is narrowing rapidly.

Early political developments

As a small and powerless minority in South Africa, Indians tended largely to rely on negotiations and deputations at both national and international level to represent their views. On four occasions, however, they engaged in passive resistance campaigns, the first two under the leadership of Gandhi. These campaigns show a gradual broadening of Indian political concern. In the first (1903), the resistance came from traders who were adversely affected by new laws in the Transvaal. The second campaign, ending in 1913, involved wider issues, directly related to indentured Indians; it emancipated Indian politics from the interests of the traders and paved the way for the rise of a political elite drawn from all sections of the Indian community (Kuper 1971: 264). Passive resistance was not tried again until 1946, when it was specifically directed at the 'Ghetto Act' (the Asiatic Land Tenure Act), though it had far wider implications. The leaders were young, educated radicals who formed themselves into a non-racial anti-segregation council and subsequently took control of the South African Indian Congress. A fourth resistance movement in 1952 expressed a further development of identification between Indians and Africans, and was indeed aimed at laws affecting Africans more directly than Indians.

Such Indian-African cooperation was a remarkable achievement coming only three years after the Zulu–Indian riots in Durban, when 50 Indians were killed and 503 injured. The Indian Congress on that occasion showed 'a forbearance and political wisdom which was almost super-human' (Brookes and Webb 1965: 292). Its leaders realised that the causes of the riots were deep-rooted, and that the hatred exhibited was partly due to frustration and partly due to the fact that the 'privileges' enjoyed by Indians, such as freedom from the pass laws, were not shared by Africans. However, as storekeepers and moneylenders occupying something of the position of Jews in Eastern Europe before the Second World War, most Indians must have been acutely aware of their potential vulnerability at the hands of an African majority.

From the early 1950s, Indians came to be organised on two distinct ideological grounds of protest and compromise. Interracial political action was represented by the policies of the South African Indian Congress, led by educated radicals seeking mass support and identification with Africans. The South African Indian Organisation, in contrast, saw African nationalism as potentially threatening to the hard-won position of the traders and merchants whose interests it articulated. It stood for compromise and accommodation with whites, and probably reflected the attitudes of most Indians at the time. Such accommodation arose from a position of weakness, however, and should not be confused with willing acceptance of the status quo.

Indian political structures: the dynamics of 'parallelism'

The constitutional development of Indians lagged behind that of coloureds but eventually followed a similar pattern. Pretoria had long accepted that what it regarded as the 'coloured problem' was incapable of a geographical solution on homeland lines: 77.0% of the coloured and Indian population was urbanised by 1970. This led to the concept of parallel development which was intended to meet the white government's basic demands of non-integration and non-domination. It involved pro-gressive elimination of the more odious forms of discrimination and the creation of coloured, and later Indian, political institutions which would be responsible for running the purely domestic affairs of these groups within the spatial and institutional framework of separate development.

At a national level the South African Indian Council (SAIC) was established in 1969, initially as a wholly nominated body. It was only in 1974 that half the members of the SAIC were elected for the first time, and then by Indians already occupying elected positions in local government. The SAIC did not become a fully elective body until 1981. It remained purely advisory until 1976, when it acquired executive functions in respect of Indian education and social welfare, but no legislative powers.

Indians (and coloureds) were also denied real power at local level. In the mid-1970s most Indian townships had only nominated local officers, management or consultative committees; the Indian local authority of Isipingo, near Durban, became a fully-fledged borough council in 1975, and town boards functioned at Verulam and Umzinto. By 1980 there was some increase in democracy if not in power: all Indian management and local affairs committees were fully elective, but they remained advisory. Local authorities (white) consulted them only rarely, and both Indians and coloureds increasingly demanded the abolition of management and local affairs committees and the establishment of direct representation on a non-racial basis on city and town councils. One city council, Cape Town, expressed its wish for such representation by all ratepayers in 1985, but this is not permitted under the Regional Services Council Act of 1985, which allows only indirect representation of racially structured, local authorities on a wider metropolitan body.

In both its national and local structures, parallelism thus constituted a very unequal form of partnership. Even the government appeared to see it as an interim policy, while publicly resisting any suggestion of socio-political integration, and firmly rejecting the recommendations of the Theron Commission for direct coloured representation in existing parliamentary, provincial and local government bodies (Theron Commission). Rhoodie (1973) foresaw that increasing sophistication at all levels of human endeavour would progressively enhance the bargaining power of coloureds in particular: 'brown power' was a function of white rejection (1973: 50), and thus in sociological terms a self-fulfilling prophecy. Given the impossibility of a coloured 'homeland', such power would ultimately have to be met with closer coloured-white association. While the bargaining power of Indians is far weaker, the similarity of their existing political structures to those of coloureds, and the fact that they are more highly urbanised even than whites (91% in 1980), made Indian inclusion in any new political structures inescapable.

A new constitution

In August 1977 a new constitutional plan was unveiled. Africans were totally excluded, but the plan contained limited elements of consociational democracy for other groups (Vosloo 1979). It was subsequently endorsed by the four provincial National Party congresses, but rejected by both the Coloured Representative Council and (unanimously) by the SAIC. Eventually a new President's Council was appointed in 1980, charged with conducting a constitutional investigation designed to give Indians and coloureds some form of political representation in a common state with whites. The reports of the Constitutional Committee of the President's Council in 1982 provided the basis for the Republic of South Africa Constitution Act which received the assent of the state president on 22 September 1983.

The new constitution retained many features of the 1977 proposals, but in place of three parliaments it created a single tricameral parliament consisting of the House of Assembly (white), the House of Representatives (coloured) and the House of Delegates (Indian). Representation is broadly proportional to population using a 4:2:1 ratio which actually favours Indians substantially (the actual population ratio in 1985 was 5.8:3.5:1). The same ratio is used for the electoral college which chooses the state president, for those members of the new President's Council who are designated by the three Houses, and for the membership of joint standing committees. Members of the electoral college are designated by resolution in each House, which effectively means that all will be members of the majority party in the House concerned. The majority party in the House of Assembly thus controls the election of an executive president whose powers are incompatible with a truly consociational democratic system.

The constitution makes a crucial distinction between the 'own affairs' of each population group and 'general affairs'. The former include, with qualifications, social welfare, education, art, culture, recreation, health, housing, community development, local government, agriculture, and water affairs. Each House controls these matters for its own people, with the major constraint that budgetary allocations fall outside its sphere of responsibility, since finance is classified as a 'general affair'. The practicability of the 'own affairs' concept effectively rests on the continuance of the Group Areas Act, which may help to explain current government reluctance to consider major modification of the Act.

There is a Ministers' Council for each population group and a cabinet consisting of the state president and ministers appointed by him. No racial quotas are specified for the latter, but the first cabinet included only one Indian; that he was designated minister without portfolio suggests that the government was not yet (and is not) prepared to see a department of state headed by a non-white.

To aid the three Houses in reaching consensus, joint standing committees meet to discuss 'general affairs' prior to the second reading debates in the respective Houses. Joint rules and standing orders for these committees, which are vital to the functioning of the system, are not laid down in the Constitution Act, but were approved by the white parliament in the final hours of its existence (Lemon 1984: 86). Opposition parties in each House may be represented in joint standing committees, but resolutions of such committees require majority support from standing committee members of the majority party in each House. This provision, like the whole tricameral arrangement and the preclusion of voting at joint sittings of the three Houses, is clearly designed to prevent a liberally inclined white minority from combining with Indian and coloured members to outvote a National Party government. In this sense 'the constitution is apparently designed to avoid consensus of a kind deemed undesirable by its architects' (ibid.). Austin (1985: 190) describes it as 'incorporation at arm's length'.

The Indian elections of 1984

The new constitution was submitted to whites in a referendum in November 1983. The overall 'yes' vote of 66.3% was higher than generally expected (given strong right-wing opposition) and viewed as a resounding success for President P.W. Botha. In the absence of referenda amongst Indians and coloureds, however, elections to the tricameral parliament inevitably became a test of the acceptability or otherwise of the new constitution.

Of the five Indian parties contesting the election, only the tiny National Federal Party (NFP) had fought an election before. The National People's Party (NPP) had controlled the SAIC since the first elections for that body in 1981, but the party was formed *after* the election by Amichand Rajbansi, chairman of the previous (nominated) Indian Council, who had drawn together a number of independents and two members of the NFP. The NPP contested 38 seats in the election for the House of Delegates. Its main rival, Solidarity, was formed only months before the election, but managed to contest all 40 seats. The Transvaal-based Progressive Independent Party contested 8 seats, including all 3 in Lenasia (Johannesburg), the NFP 3 and the Democratic Party 2.

During the run-up to the election of number of candidates defected to other parties after the offer of a seemingly more hopeful seat, which reflects the artificiality of the new party divisions. Such disaffections might also be seen as typical of the 'village politics' mentality, or they could be viewed as evidence that large parliamentary salaries were the prime motivation. The large number of Independent candidates could be viewed in similar terms. They included many with some claim, however slight, to community service or group leadership. Some stood as Independents after failing to secure nomination for a registered party. A number were former NPP members who had differed with Rajbansi, usually on small issues. Still others were wholly new to politics. The large number of Independents was thought likely to boost the percentage poll, and resulted in up to nine candidates standing in certain constituencies, some of them doing little or no campaigning.

The NPP's longer experience was a double-edged sword. The SAIC lacked legitimacy after its election in 1981 on a 10.5% poll, which included a large number of spoilt papers. With the delegation to the SAIC of powers over Indian education and social welfare the NPP had been strongly criticised for its handling of these matters. The Teachers' Association, for instance, had rejected any collaboration with the SAIC on the grounds that it was a government-controlled body with no professional skills (SAIRR 1984: 39). Rajbansi was personally distrusted by many for his handling of education in particular. Despite these shortcomings, the NPP entered the election campaign as the established Indian party with superior grass-roots organisation, and soon demonstrated the effectiveness of its special vote machinery.[2] It fought a less open campaign than Solidarity, holding far fewer public meetings, and thus tended largely to escape open confrontation with the boycott supporters.

Personalities were more important than parties and policies in the election. Both the NPP and Solidarity produced manifestos which, given the known needs of the Indian community, were similar in their material aspirations. In education, the NPP stressed equal, compulsory education for all and the elimination of separate schools and universities, whereas Solidarity, clearly with the SAIC's record in mind, demanded 'no political interference in the administration of professional matters, e.g. education and social welfare' (Reddy 1984). The NPP demanded repeal of the Group Areas Act, although in a speech Rajbansi referred to the more limited aim of creating 'grey' areas open to all races (*Daily News* 20 August 1984). Solidarity merely aimed for more land and houses at reasonable prices. The NPP mentioned individual rights to the protection of life, liberty, and property, and access to the judiciary in defence of these rights, as well as freedom of the media and freedom of expression. Solidarity's manifesto had a more economic emphasis, reflecting the concerns of Dr J.N. Reddy, its leader; it advocated the encouragement of economic growth through foreign investment and the 'removal of all racial constraints in the free enterprise system' (Reddy 1984).

On one crucial point the two manifestos were very similar. The NPP demanded 'the elimination of discrimination and the sharing of power by all citizens, but with safeguards against domination and oppression' (*Star* 24 August 1984), while Solidarity advocated 'peaceful change towards a just and democratic society with safeguards for minorities' (Reddy 1984). That both major Indian parties should mention safeguards has an obvious significance, coming from a 2.9% minority group in the population.

For a party so recently formed, Solidarity's status as a serious contender in the election was remarkable. Its strength depended upon the calibre of its leadership and of many of its candidates. Unlike the NPP, Solidarity attracted a small group of the Indian intelligentsia, which was otherwise more associated with the Natal Indian Congress. Its finances were aided by the affluence of some of its supporters. Its organisation was effective in Natal, but far less so in the Transvaal, where its leadership was poor; however, the NPP was weakly established there as well. Solidarity also had problems in the Cape, with only a handful of spare-time workers and widely scattered Indian communities in three vast constituencies. In Natal, the party was helped by control of one of the three weekly Indian newspapers, *The Graphic*, by its chairman Pat Poovalingam. The latter had gained credibility as a leader by keeping a promise to resign from the President's Council if Africans were not included on it within a year. During the 1984 election campaign he promised to give the new constitution a five-year trial (*Daily News* 10 August 1984).

Unfortunately, Poovalingam was considered somewhat aloof and remote from the people, a serious failing given the personal nature of Indian politics. This was certainly not true, however, of Dr Reddy, whose stature and economic abilities were admitted to the author even by his opponents. He had founded the New Republic Bank and chaired it for seven years; was on the Natal board of the Standard Bank; a member of the prime minister's Economic Advisory Council; and a director of many companies. He relinquished many of these business interests to lead Solidarity. His speeches were such as to establish him as a potential national leader, beyond the confines of 'own affairs'. Thus he outlined plans for industrial diversification, concentrating on export industries and more processing of South Africa's raw materials; he stressed the development of the informal sector; he emphasised the role Indian businessmen could play in industrialisation in Natal's Tugela Basin; and he stressed the need for peaceful change and economic strength in South Africa in order to provide the employment opportunities needed by Indians, coloureds, and Africans (*Graphic* 10 and 17 August 1984).

The election battle between Solidarity and the NPP was largely sub-merged by the more fundamental issue of participation. The boycott movement was spearheaded by the United Democratic Front (UDF), a non-racial body launched in 1983 in response to a call from Dr Allan Boesak when addressing the Transvaal Anti-SAIC Committee (TASC) six months earlier. The Natal Indian Congress (NIC) and Transvaal Indian Congress (TIC) both affiliated to the UDF, and played the major role in the boycott campaign amongst Indians. The NIC had been effectively silenced by a spate of bannings in the 1970s, but was revived from 1978 onwards and was active in the school boycotts of 1980 and the anti-SAIC election campaign in 1981. The TIC was revived at the January 1983 meeting of the TASC. Both the NIC and TIC share the same principles and had been federally united in the South African Indian Congress, but this body has not yet been resuscitated.

During the campaign, the NIC ninetieth birthday celebrations were attended by 8,000 people. The NIC also attempted to visit every Indian home in Natal to urge people not to vote. It nominated 'counter-candidates' in each constituency whose records of community service were claimed to outstrip those of the actual candidates (*Daily News* 2 August 1984). George Sewpersadh, the NIC president, argued that 'the people going in . . . have no history in the political struggle outside government institutions. They have no mass support. They have not worked with the people, and by going in they are making it easier for the government to entrench apartheid' (*Natal Post* 1–5 August 1984). The TIC publicity secretary, Cassim Saloojee, attacked the constitution for offering Indians 'a room next door' rather than genuine seats in parliament (*Star* 19 July 1984).

The long-term alternative offered by the UDF and the Indian Con-gresses was seldom spelt out in public, apart from references to the Freedom Charter of the African National Congress. In practice, the strategy appeared to be to follow up a successful boycott of the election with continued pressure at local and national levels, using every oppor-tunity until the government was forced to accept genuine negotiation in the form of a national convention. The participating parties regarded this as unrealistic, arguing that boycotts had achieved little in the past.

The small Indian Reform Party of Y.S. Chinsaamy also boycotted the election. Chinsaamy had discussions with Dr Reddy (a former vice-chairman of the Reform Party) about joint participation in the elections. He was deterred, however, by the hostility of Chief Buthelezi to participa-tion; instead he put his partnership with Buthelezi in the South African Black Alliance first, leaving Dr Reddy to become the leader of Solidarity.

The many religious bodies opposing participation included not only

Christian organisations but also the Islamic Council of South Africa and the Muslim Youth League. However the Jamiatul Ulema Natal, a body of Muslim theologians, left the matter to individual conscience. The major Hindu organisations also took no stand, and both the president and secretary of the South African Hindu Maha Sabha contested seats in the House of Delegates (*Leader* 24 August 1984).

The election results

The NPP and Solidarity received virtually the same number of votes (36.6% and 36.5% respectively). The NPP, with 18 seats to Solidarity's 17, subsequently managed to construct an overall majority by winning over three of the four Independents, one of whom was backed by the (coloured) Labour Party. The PIP, with one seat, was the only other party to gain representation. No clear regional division of support between the NPP and Solidarity emerged; given the very low voting figures most of the majorities were anyway very small. Even in the seats contested by party leaders the turnout was low: 22.3% in Glenview (Reddy), 14.1% in Arena Park (Rajbansi), and 13.2% in Reservoir Hills (Poovalingam). The official percentage poll figure was only 20.3% nationally; it was 19.6% in Natal but 23.4% in the Transvaal and 24.1% in the Cape. If participation is measured in terms of all eligible voters rather than those who actually registered, the national figure is reduced to only 14.25%. Official voting figures may also be inflated by abuse of the special vote procedure, intended for those genuinely unable to vote on polling day. More than one-third of all the votes cast for the House of Delegates were special votes, and in several constituencies they outnumbered votes cast on polling day itself (*Leader* 31 August 1984). The TIC and NIC collected a large number of affidavits to support allegations of abuse, including seventy from a single constituency, Actonville on the East Rand, where 59.3% of all votes were special votes. The Indian Congresses declared their intention of asking the Supreme Court to declare the House of Delegates elections invalid on the basis of such evidence (*Cape Herald* 8 September 1984).

Indian voters turned out in greater numbers in less highly urbanised areas (Table 6.1), but not to the same extent as coloureds. Their lowest percentage polls were recorded in the three Lenasia constituencies, of which one, Lenasia West, was the scene of some of the worst election day violence, and in Pietermaritzburg, where the SAIC poll in 1981 was only 6% and NIC organisation was strong. In the sixteen constituencies of Durban, the Indian heartland, the overall poll was 17.8%.

A number of factors help to explain why the Indian poll was even lower

Table 6.1. *Regional voting patterns for the House of Delegates, 1984*

Region	Registered electors	Votes polled	% poll
Chatsworth	89,015	16,404	18.4
Rest of Durban	98,488	16,906	17.2
Sub-total	187,503	33,310	17.8
Pietermaritzburg	26,941	2,618	9.7
North and South coasts	81,699	19,500	23.9
Natal 'country'	45,240	11,617	25.7
Cape urban	8,432	2,139	25.4
Cape 'country'	2,582	510	19.7
Lenasia	16,994	1,836	10.8
Other Transvaal towns	25,858	7,423	28.7
Transvaal 'country'	16,652	4,659	28.0

Note: 'Country' includes rural areas and smaller towns.
Source: The Government Gazette, 1984.

than that for coloureds (30.9% of registered electors, 17.8% of all those eligible to vote). One is the exceptionally high rate of Indian urbanisation, already mentioned: there was no Indian equivalent of the coloured farm workers of the Orange Free State, for instance, who tended to see the new dispensation as a major advance on anything they had known before. Secondly, the memory of the derisory poll in the 1981 SAIC elections was still fresh, and deterred most Indian leaders from participating in 'establishment' politics. The proximity of the Indians to the Zulu, and their awareness of the racial bitterness which participation would cause, was a third factor. This was emphasised by Chief Buthelezi's fierce hostility to the elections, underlined by his reminder of the 1949 Zulu-Indian riots and his threat of a consumer boycott of Indian shops (*Natal Post* 22–5 August 1984). Fourth, it must be remembered that the NIC, unlike the UDF, has a long history behind it and a traditionally central place in Indian politics. Its leaders are men of standing in the community, many of them 'graduates' of banning or house arrest. Its prominent use of Ghandi's name in the campaign, claiming that he would have boycotted the new dispensation, was probably effective, although the historicity of the claim was fiercely contested in the columns of the *Graphic* (see, for instance, 17 August 1984).

The NIC campaign was given a minor boost in its closing stages by the decision of the Rector of the University of Durban-Westville, Professor Jaap Greyling, to close the University in view of the prospect of student unrest during the election period (*Natal Post* 22–5 August 1984 and *Graphic* 31 August 1984). This had the effect of strengthening the manpower resources of the boycotters on election day.

Of vastly greater import, however, was the government's own action in detaining 18 UDF, NIC, and TUC leaders, including the president and vice-president of the NIC, under section 28 of the Internal Security Act. The detentions were ordered on 21 August, a week before the Indian election, and undoubtedly served to strengthen the boycott campaign by seeming to confirm that the new dispensation was simply old wine in new bottles. This probably helped the NPP, which could rely on the support of those who had voted in 1981, and therefore deprived Solidarity of victory. This was somewhat ironic, given indications (such as frequency of mention on radio and television) of government preference for a Solidarity victory, and for Dr Reddy as a cabinet member.

The indecisive result in the House of Delegates election was unfortunate in that it produced the unseemly spectacle of 'wheeling and dealing' by the NPP and Solidarity, each trying to woo the support of Independents and even, in the case of Solidarity, members of the other party. The NPP image was hardly improved by Rajbansi's request for more ministries, apparently on no better ground than the need to reward a large number of his own supporters. This request was not surprisingly refused, but Rajbansi managed to construct a majority with the backing of three Independents.

Conclusion

Events since 1984 fall outside the scope of this paper, but in general terms they have largely confirmed the impotence of Indian (and coloured) members of the tricameral parliament in securing fundamental reform. Paradoxically, the success of the boycotters did put pressure on the government to make some concessions, both economic and political, to those elected, in order to demonstrate the effectiveness of the new dispensation. Its ability to do so is constrained both by political pressures from the right and by an economy which is increasingly under siege as it emerges from recession. Within these constraints, but with little or no evidence of direct response to pressure from the new MPs, the government has pursued what it regards as a logical strategy in effecting reforms relating to Indians and coloureds.

It has, for instance, repealed the Mixed Marriages Act and section 16 of the Immorality Act (which forbade sexual intercourse between whites and other race groups), both of which are arguably inconsistent with the spirit of the new constitution. The repeal of legislation excluding Indians from the Orange Free State and northern areas of Natal was an even more necessary corollary of their supposed participation as equals with whites in the central government. The inclusion of Indians and other races on the new nominated executives which have replaced elected but all-white provincial councils, and in the new Regional Services Councils at metropolitan level, are both consistent with what appears to be the government's new direction. In both cases power is still concentrated largely in white hands, although the Regional Services Councils are at least structured so as to require a degree of consensus which goes beyond the white representatives; their objectives and funding are also intended to ensure a degree of redistribution of wealth between communites that has been absent from local government hitherto, and which is intended to contribute to the better provision of services in non-white areas (Lemon 1987: 289–94).

The 1984 elections have left bitter divisions in the Indian community. It is clear that the majority do not wish to see the new constitution succeed; and its exclusion of the African majority must anyway ensure that it can only be an interim measure. For Indians the enduring political significance of the constitution will be the unprecedented degree to which it brought them into the mainstream of political opposition to apartheid, above all through the Indian Congresses and their affiliation to the UDF. This clear identification of the larger part of the Indian community with the African majority was confirmed by a percentage poll of only 23.7 in the 1989 election. It is a trend for which Indians may have cause to be thankful when eventually apartheid gives way to some form of majority rule.

Notes

1 Such figures are necessarily crude: they conceal the occupational levels at which people of different race groups are employed, the qualifications held, and the existence or otherwise of different remuneration for the same job according to the ethnic classification of the worker. The latter is, however, decreasing.
2 A special vote may be cast in advance of an election by an elector who through illness, old age, absence from home on polling day, or other genuine cause is unable to reach the polling booth.

References

Austin, D. 1985. 'The Trinitarians: the 1983 South African Constitution', *Government and Opposition*, 20, 2: 185–95.
Brookes, E.H. and Webb, C. de B. 1965. *A History of Natal*, Pietermaritzburg: Natal University Press.
Brookfield, H.C. and Tatham, M.A. 1957. 'The distribution of racial groups in Durban: the background of apartheid in a South African city', *Geographical Review*, 47, 1: 44–65.
Furnivall, J.S. 1948. *Colonial Policy and Practice*, Cambridge University Press.
Kuper, H. 1969. 'Strangers in plural societies: Asians in South Africa and

Uganda', in *Pluralism in Africa*, ed. L. Kuper and M.G. Smith, Berkeley: University of California Press, 248–82.

Lemon, A. 1980. 'Asian overseas settlement in the nineteenth and twentieth centuries', in *Studies in Overseas Settlement and Population*, ed. A. Lemon and N.C. Pollock, London: Longman.

1985. 'The Indian and coloured elections: co-optation rejected?', *South Africa International*, 15, 2: 84–107.

1987. *Apartheid in Transition*, Aldershot: Gower.

Meer, F. 1971. 'Indian people: current trends and policies', in *South Africa's Minorities*, Johannesburg, SPRO-CAS Publication no. 2: 13–32.

1979. 'Portrait of Indian South Africans', in *South Africa: Sociological Analyses*, ed. A.P. Hare, G. Wiendieck and M.H. von Broembsen, Cape Town: Oxford University Press, 133–44.

Palmer, M. 1957. *The History of the Indians in Natal, Natal Regional Survey*, vol. 10, Cape Town: Oxford University Press.

Reddy, J.N. 1984. *Message to the People: solidarity for peaceful change*, Durban: Solidarity.

Rhoodie, N.J. 1973. 'The coloured policy of South Africa: parallelism as a socio-political device to regulate White-Coloured integration', *African Affairs*, 72, 286: 46–56.

Sadie, J.L. 1970. 'An evaluation of the demographic data pertaining to the non-White population of South Africa', *South African Journal of Economics*, 38, 1: 1–34; and 2: 171–95.

SAIRR (South African Institute of Race Relations) 1985 and 1987. *Survey of Race Relations in South Africa*, Johannesburg: SAIRR.

Theron Commission: Report of the Commission of Inquiry into Matters Relating to the Coloured Population Group, RP 38/1976, Pretoria: Government Printer.

Vosloo, W.B. 1979. 'Consociational democracy as a means to accomplish peaceful change in South Africa: an evaluation of the constitutional change proposed by the National Party in 1977', *Politikon*, 6, 1: 13–28.

7

East African Asians through a hundred years

Michael Twaddle

the past has boiled itself over
and we are the steam that must flee
(Jagjit Singh 1971)

Poetry is sometimes preferable to history as commentary upon the most tragic aspects of the human condition. History, Aristotle suggested many centuries ago, 'tells of what has happened', poetry 'the kinds of things that might happen'. Poetry was therefore to be considered 'more worthy of serious attention than history; for while poetry is concerned with universal truths, history treats of particular facts' (quoting translation in Dorsch 1967: 43). Even if we do not go all the way with Aristotle's relegation of history to narrative rather than analysis, there is something to be said for poetry as commentary upon the essential tragedy of the East African Asian predicament:

> for the sweat is dry
> that built the railways,
> and black blood must forget
> swamp sleeping savagery of greenness
> that burst into an indian bazaar,
> because the time and tide
> and the valour of your business mind
> condemned the brown jew
> to comb his days in commerce and trade
> . . .
>
> but my eyes shall burn again,
> a resurrection of brown pride
> for i see you now, my father,
> fling the victoria cross
> into dung-heap of the british empire.

Indeed, very shortly after the publication of these lines in *Poems from East Africa* (Cook and Rubadiri 1971), what might happen did happen: a wholesale expulsion of persons of South Asian descent, citizens and non-citizens alike, from Idi Amin's Uganda in 1972 (Twaddle 1975; Adams and Bristow 1979). Thirteen years later, in less organised fashion but with additional looting, Asian traders who returned to the same country after Amin's downfall were again relieved of much property in another military *coup* and this time many of them left Uganda voluntarily. In Kenya there was looting of Asian-owned shops in Nairobi in 1982, during an abortive military insurrection. A decade and a half earlier, increasing restrictions upon Asian traders who had not yet acquired citizenship in the newly independent state led to their increasing exodus from there too, particularly to Britain.

When Enoch Powell claimed that the resultant out-migration was too large, and that '200,000 Indians in Kenya alone have an absolute right of entry into this country', the British government of the time was panicked into rushing a bill through parliament to restrict further Asian entry into Britain (Fisher 1973: 296–7). Perhaps inevitably, immediately before the Commonwealth Immigrants' Bill became law in mid-1968, the Asian exodus from East Africa turned into something approaching a stampede. Moreover, when this particular British bill did become law, and Idi Amin shortly afterwards expelled virtually all Asians from Uganda, the exodus turned into the slower, much more complicated, but still painful process of quotas and vouchers that it remains to this day (Tinker 1977). Nowadays, within East Africa itself, residual communities of South Asian descent live on in Kenya and Tanzania, about a quarter of the size they were in the early 1960s (which represents roughly one-half of 1% of the current estimated total populations of these two countries), with of course fewer staying on in Uganda; while in the more southerly independent states of Zambia, Malawi, Zimbabwe and Madagascar, where South Asian settlers were always less numerous than in Kenya or mainland Tanzania, comparatively fewer also remain today (Balachandran 1981; Ghai and Ghai 1970; Nag 1979; Dotson and Dotson 1968; Patel 1973; Delval 1976; Tandon n.d.).

It was therefore understandable that in 1971 an East African Asian poet should have protested:

> now they shall look back in anger
> the mercedes-benz politicians,
> black suited, whisky voiced, swiss bank accounted,
> searching in vain
> for brown liberals behind the counter
> and taunt us about commitment –
> for the blood is dry
> that roused green savagery
> from the slumber of the swamps.

But how *accurate* was this protest? In the first quotation from the poem, the image of 'slumbering green savagery' clearly applies to the harassment of Asian traders by African politicians shortly after independence from Britain. But in the second one the image implies that East African Asians introduced trade into a region of Africa hitherto wholly ignorant of it. This, it is necessary to stress, was not so.

Before the British, French, German and Italian conquests of the late nineteenth century, indigenous East Africans were not wholly ignorant of trade (Gray and Birmingham 1970). But the external trade in which they engaged involved dealing in slaves and firearms, of which incoming European colonial powers publicly disapproved; indeed, 'anti-slavery' was one of the most eloquent ideological justifications for colonial conquest at the time. It was therefore *new kinds* of trade in which incoming Asian traders engaged, as the European imperialists pushed their way into the East African interior, and introduced railways and new monetised currencies in order to facilitate colonial tax-collection as well as to support incoming European settlers. Soon, earlier traders in places such as Uganda were joined by South Asian traders who acted as informal bankers for European colonial officials in the interior as well as importers of a wide range of fresh foreign goods. Soon, Christian missionaries, too, were depending upon the new Indian traders in the interior. Why did he import 'such miserably third-rate bicycles instead of getting some sound make'? asked one missionary of an Indian trader in the Ngora bazaar. 'His reply was, "I do not want to ride them; they are only to sell to the natives."' (Kitching 1912: 205).

Such traders operated on very thin margins of profit before the First World War, and in retrospect it seems unsurprising that a folk myth should have developed subsequently of South Asians wholly pioneering trade in a region of hitherto 'slumbering green savagery'. But the myth does mislead. Not only were there several sorts of both intra- and extra-regional trade in the East African interior before the arrival of the generality of South Asian settlers during the twentieth century, but much of the savagery associated with earlier trade was itself of comparatively recent origin. It was especially associated with the slave and gun trade of the middle to late nineteenth century. Furthermore, and not without a certain irony in light of the subsequent South Asian folk myth, this trade too was financed to a very considerable extent by an earlier generation of South Asian merchants living along the East African coast (Sheriff 1987; Gundara 1981; Iliffe 1979).

None the less, even this generation of Indian traders was by no means the first to establish settlements along the East African coast. For one of the essential characteristics of South Asian settlement in this particular region of the world is its antiquity. According to one Arab tradition, Aristotle himself advised Alexander the Great to establish a colony of ancient Greeks on the island of Sokotra off north eastern Africa; as a result 'they subdued the Indians who were established there, took possession of Sokotra and removed a colossal idol to which the Indians paid homage' (Pankhurst 1979). Indian traders, however, continued to visit, as they did at other trading centres along the East African coast, well into the first century AD, as the famous *Periplus of the Erythraean Sea* makes clear; and thereafter, as Hatim Amiji remarks, the abundance of Chinese blue-and-white porcelain that found its way to East Africa during the medieval period did so, for the most part, in Gujarati ships (Amiji 1983). None the less, very few of these ancient Indian traders seem to have ventured very far into the East African interior.

By the mid nineteenth century there were a number of South Asian trading communities living in East African coastal ports. Questioned by the Sanderson Committee in 1909, Sir John Kirk reported that on Zanzibar island South Asian settlers 'went back, generally, every seven or eight years, visited their wives and families [in India] and came back again to East Africa to trade. When they made large fortunes the Hindus went away and did not come back; but the Mussulmans settled with their families' (Parliamentary Papers 1910, Cd 5193: 242). Other witnesses confirm the concern amongst South Asians then living on Zanzibar island, to keep as strictly as possible to themselves and not to fraternise unduly with non-Indians; the leading Ismaili trader of the time apparently was not willing to eat in the American consulate for reasons of ritual purity (of course, this may not have been his *only* reason for such abstinence) (Gundara 1981: 40). However, by the late nineteenth century the Indian population of Zanzibar already ran into thousands, and India, after all, was only one monsoon away. Elsewhere along the East African coast, South Asians were settled less densely and numerously. In these smaller settlements, as on Zanzibar itself, Kirk reported that there lived 'the "Chotara", or a half-caste breed between the Indian and the Swahili' (Parliamentary Papers 1910, Cd 5193: 239). But doubtless, offspring of many cohabitations between African women and South Asian traders who were Muslims would have merged into the surrounding Islamic and predominantly Swahili-speaking population in less formal ways too, much as mating between Arabs and Africans itself created the Swahili population of the East African coast area over many centuries (Whiteley 1969; Iliffe 1979).

This is something which should be kept in mind when considering the start of the far greater South Asian penetration of the East African interior that occurred in the immediate aftermath of the European colonial partition, at the very end of the nineteenth century. As in previous eras on the coast, it was difficult for Europeans in the interior to distinguish between 'Indians' and 'Arabs'. This was especially the case where the Indians in question were Muslims, for British colonial officials did not easily distinguish between Arab and Asian Muslims. Furthermore, some South Asians at this time made differentiation more difficult by speaking Swahili fluently – much more fluently, seemingly, than their descendants nowadays (Neale 1974 and personal communication from Dr Joan Maw). Arabs as well as Asians, too, took advantage of incoming British, French, German, or Portuguese rule – but not Italian administration, it would appear, to any significant extent (Pankhurst 1979: 122) – in order to establish themselves as shopkeepers wherever the new conquerors moved. But there were rarely sufficient densities of either Arabs or Asians in inland East African townships before the First World War for there to be more than one mosque as a general rule; nor, even if most Indian traders settled locally were Hindus, for them to bother excessively about the finer points of caste between Hindus.

Take, for example, two townships in what are nowadays the Soroti and Mbale districts in Uganda. There were two of the most lightly administered areas in the Uganda Protectorate immediately before the First World War. In 1913 a wealthy trader called Lal Mahomed died intestate at Kaberamaido, then part of Lira district. His property consisted:

> almost entirely of trade goods and cattle . . . scattered all over the District. Part of the trade goods are in various shops licensed in the name of the deceased and part in the hands of itinerant hawkers trading on his behalf. Most of the cattle are in the custody of numerous Kumam headmen . . . The deceased undoubtedly owed thousands of rupees in various quarters, and he also had many outstanding debts to recover.
>
> (Lira Archives: Administrator-General's returns for 1913)

In this respect, the deceased trader resembled a number of other richer South Asian traders remaining alive locally. But the British official reporting his death described him as 'one of the leading Arab traders of the District' (ibid.). Oral testimony recorded shortly before Idi Amin's expulsion of Asians from Uganda, however, established that in fact he was a Baluchi hailing originally from the borders of what are nowadays Iran and Pakistan, as too were a number of other newly arrived traders in Kaberamaido and Mbale townships at this time (Najak 1965; Shakramali 1965). Now, to be sure, Baluchi merchants may have been atypical of the generality of South Asian traders in East Africa at this time, as subsequently, in speaking Swahili especially fluently; in being Sunni Muslims

like most African Muslims but unlike most other Muslim South Asian
traders; and in sharing ' other characteristics of cultural assimilation such
as dress, celebrations and dances' (Stroebel 1979: 28–9). But this raises a
crucial question: which community *can* be considered typical of East
African Asians at any time during the last hundred years?

Certainly not the Baluchis, for reasons already given. Baluchis were
recruited during the nineteenth century as bodyguards for Sultans of
Zanzibar and they were of roughly the same number as the Memons,
another Sunni Muslim South Asian community (Bagha 1970; Gundara
1981). Baluchis and Memons both outnumbered Parsis residing locally
(who were of course Zoroastrian in religious belief), but were themselves
outnumbered by various Hindu trading castes already operating along the
East African coast such as the Banias, Bhatias and Lohanas. They were
still further outnumbered by Muslim Shia sects, such as the Daudi
Bohoras, the Ismaili Khojas and the Isthnasteris (Gundari 1981). Ismaili
Khojas acknowledging the imamship of the Aga Khan were by far the
largest single South Asian community living in nineteenth-century Zanzibar (ibid.). This preponderance of Ismailis persisted throughout East
Africa until the First World War. Thereafter, Hindus, mostly moving into
the region as 'passenger migrants' and paying their own expenses for
travel across the Indian Ocean, increasingly came to outnumber Muslim
South Asians; by the end of the European colonial era in the 1960s,
Hindus accounted for around 70% of all East African Asians though
much basic statistical work remains to be done in this field (Ramchandani
1976; Tandon n.d.; Blacker 1972).

None the less, though losing out in comparative numbers to incoming
Hindus (particularly to Patidars) during the early twentieth century, the
Aga Khan's Ismailis retained the sociological initiative in other important
respects. This was because, largely as a result of their imam's distinctive
influence upon them, Ismailis were successfully persuaded to adapt to
changing conditions more quickly and more completely than any other
community of East African Asians. This made them even less typical of
the generality of South Asian settlers in East Africa than the Baluchis,
albeit with a paradoxical outcome. For through their establishment of
special cemeteries, educational facilities and community care, Ismailis
became veritable pacemakers for communal crystallisation amongst other
East African Asians too. Jains, Goans, Hindus of various kinds, Sikhs of
at least three categories, and several other Islamic communities of both
Shia and Sunni dispositions, were all stimulated to establish special burial
grounds, schools and recreational centres, in response to 'pacemaking'
activity in each of these spheres by followers of the Aga Khan (Morris
1968).

By the time British rule ended in Tanganyika, Uganda, Kenya and Zanzibar in the early 1960s, East African Asians were therefore divided into a complex mosaic of religious and caste associations, each concerned to safeguard its identity and persistence. This communalist zealotry was the despair of individual South Asians locally seeking to establish working relationships with the new African political leaders. As Yash Ghai noted at the time:

> The Asians wanted to be left alone to pursue their own traditional ways. Laws were enacted in East Africa for the application of personal, religious laws, e.g. marriage, divorce, succession, to the Asian religious communities. This helped not only to preserve the cultural identity of these communities, but also put obstacles in the way of inter-communal and inter-racial contacts. In addition, the Asians, by and large, continued to maintain links with their countries of origin . . . immigrants tended to come from certain specified regions of India, the Panjab and Gujerat . . . The effect of all this was to make the Asians a self-sufficient, ethnocentric community.
>
> (Ghai 1975: 132)

However, during the genesis of the major South Asian migration into the East African interior immediately before the First World War, communal consciousness amongst these particular immigrants had been much less marked. It was communalist pacemaking by the Aga Khan's Ismailis, combined with further immigration from the Indian sub-continent during the 1920s and 1930s which, amongst other things, prompted a whole range of South Asian communities to develop the 'critical mass' necessary to make funerary, educational, and recreational communalism viable in the East Africa of these economically depressed inter-war years (Morris 1968).

Of course, broader politics influenced these developments, too. Particularly important was the bitter wrangle over the denial of territorial and political rights to East African Asians at the same time that European businessmen and farmers in Nairobi and the western highlands of colonial Kenya continued to be as outrageously privileged as ever in these regards. The wrangle came to a head in the early 1920s, when some pro-Indian writers even demanded that parts of British East Africa should become a colonial dependency of India rather than Britain; when African nationalists divided into mutually antagonistic pro- and anti-Indian factions; and when white settlers agitated vociferously for a full-blown white-dominated order to be established on the South African model instead. Before the 1920s, British protectorate officials were reluctant to define the

roles and rights of South Asian settlers in East Africa too carefully, occupying as these settlers did so many differing positions in the infant colonial
administrations as artisans, police and railway personnel as well as
working as traders; so many different positions, in fact, that Herbert
Samuel remarked in 1902 that the 'progress of [that is, British colonial
takeover of] these portions of Africa would have been slow indeed, had it
not been possible to draw upon our Asiatic possessions for unlimited sup-
plies of subordinate labour with brain and hand' (quoted in Mangat 1969:
61–2).

But, at the close of the First World War, Indian nationalism in India
fused with resentments amongst Indians resident in British East Africa to
articulate public demands for reform. Following the sacrifices of Indians
as well as Europeans during the war, it was now demanded that brown
citizens of the British empire living in Kenya should enjoy the same privileges as white citizens regarding political representation, rural land-
ownership and urban residence. The ensuing controversy was extremely
bitter, and only partially quietened by a formal declaration by the British
Colonial Secretary in 1923 that, in any future dispute between Indians,
Europeans and the local African inhabitants, the interests of the natives
should remain 'paramount'. In practice, this meant that the existing
restriction of land purchase within the 'white highlands' of west-central
Kenya to Europeans would remain in place at least for the next thirty
years, as too would residential segregation by race, lesser legal privileges,
very limited political representation for British Indians compared with
Europeans, and mostly only middle-level administrative positions within
the local colonial bureaucracy (Mangat 1969; Gregory 1971; Tinker 1976).

During the 1930s, Indians' rights to trade outside major townships were
also severely curtailed throughout British East Africa (Spencer 1981),
while in the 1940s wholly unrestricted immigration from the Indian sub-
continent was brought to an end. At times, to be sure, the white settlers'
campaign to limit future Indian immigration verged upon the farcical.

> Illegal immigration from India, through passengers boarding B.I.
> line ships at the Kathiawar ports under the guise of seeing off pas-
> sengers and then failing to leave with the shore party [and] going
> ashore at Mombasa under the guise of being passengers in transit
> for southern ports led to demands that Kenyan colonial immi-
> gration and medical officials should scale ships' donkey ladders
> before ships finally docked at Mombasa.
>
> (Magor, Kenya National Archives)

However, the effects of this campaign, if not aspects of the campaign
itself, were serious for East African Asians. After the Second World War,

only those South Asian settlers wanted for jobs (for which there were insufficient qualified applicants available locally) could be recruited from outside – and this meant principally Sikh carpenters and other Punjabis employed in the construction industry (Maini, in Twaddle 1975). While there was some further South Asian immigration therefore after the Second World War, and overall South Asian numbers continued to grow, the major inward population movement of South Asians into East Africa was now at an end. Inevitably, this turned East African Asians still more visibly into an *urban* racial minority locally, and a politically very vulnerable one once British colonial rule ended. 'If the Indian presence, with all its outward diversity but basic racial identity, hit me in the eye', wrote one Indian high commissioner to Kenya during the 1960s, 'it was not surprising that the African's awareness was so much sharper. In the new world which the African was trying to create for himself, the Indians and Pakistanis stood out as discordant, unassimilable citadels of exclusiveness' (Bhatia 1973: 18).

The newly independent government of India tried to pressure East African Asians into allying with African nationalism during the 1950s, Apa Pant in particular being prominent during the Mau Mau emergency in attempting to persuade local Indians to back African demands. But European politicians like Michael Blundell also increasingly courted local Asian assistance as African majority rule became a serious possibility (Blundell 1974: 152–3); and the results in Uganda too, as Sir Amar Maini has remarked, were inevitable charges of hypocrisy when Asians tried to keep open as many options as possible and behaved inconsistently, 'when private actions did not (and could not) match up to public, stated aspirations' (Maini, in Twaddle 1974: 117–18; Gregory 1981). Some of the most influential studies of East African Asians were composed at this time and inevitably reflect these cross-currents. We have already quoted Yash Ghai's comment on the backward-looking character of East African Asian communalism. Subsequently, after the substantial exodus from Kenya in the late 1960s, and the wholesale expulsion from Uganda in 1972, he and other East African Asian commentators argued that, in effect, 'nothing could be done': it was British colonialism which in effect had invited South Asian settlers into East Africa and dictated their basically subordinate economic role there, and in time this role was bound to rouse black African hostility (Ghai 1975: 738–9). Basically that, too, had been Jagjit Singh's complaint:

> the past has boiled itself over
> and we are the steam that must flee.

But poetry by itself is not enough. There is still work to be done by social scientists in collecting and analysing oral and other information about

South Asian population movement both in and out of East Africa, and about successive communal crystallisations amongst them over the last hundred years. And here it is important to remember that Africans as well as Asians in East Africa were divided into a diversity of differing communal and other interests, and both sets of interests had critical implications for the destiny of East African Asians locally.

Take, for example, the wholesale expulsion of Asians from Uganda in 1972. That was prompted, not only by the advent to power of one of black Africa's most repugnant post-colonial dictators, but by a supporting Ugandan soldiery containing a critical constituency of Nubians extremely hostile to Asian traders. 'Nubians' were predominantly poor Africans living in slums in Nairobi as well as in Uganda. They were descended from the Sudanese mercenary soldiers employed by British colonial officials during the 1890s and 1900s and, by the time Amin seized power in Uganda, constituted a secondary ethnic category to which virtually any Africans speaking the Nubi version of Arabic and practising Islam according to the Sunni Maliki code could attach themselves. Clearly, such a residual – and by 1972 predominantly urban – social category of Africans had a very concrete interest in ousting Asian shopkeepers from Ugandan townships (Pain, in Twaddle 1975). And yet, before Amin seized power, Ugandan Asians had appeared in less danger of wholesale deportation than their Kenyan counterparts, though discriminatory legislation against noncitizen Asians continuing to trade in major township areas was quicky passed in Uganda as well as in other countries in East and Central Africa immediately after independence from Britain (Twaddle 1975).

In Kenya, too, Frank Furedi sees much of the additional discrimination against Asian traders there originating in the grievances of African traders earlier disadvantaged by Asian predominance in both wholesale and retail trade. Furedi sees a new class of African traders crystallising shortly after the Second World War which 'tried to compensate for their economic weakness by exerting its political muscle' through African nationalist organisations such as the Kenya African Union (Furedi 1974). KAU was the principal forerunner of the territorial political party which took Kenya into independence from Britain in 1963 under the leadership of Jomo Kenyatta. Kenyatta's own political career, incidentally, started as a failed African shopkeeper, and the history of Kenyan politics since independence has been punctuated by vitriolic outbursts against Asian traders by lesser African leaders, a number of whom were also earlier unsuccessful traders. A recent historian of Africa has remarked that African nationalism in East and Central Africa had a much sharper radical edge than in West Africa, in part to be accounted for by weakness within the local African bourgeoisie (Freund 1984: 218). However, far more important

even than that factor was 'the escalation of postwar capitalist development [under British colonial auspices], felt by [African] peasants and
workers with unprecedented force and identified locally, not merely with
the distant "government", but with racially defined minorities: white
settlers, Asian businessmen and, in Zanzibar, "Arab" planters' (ibid.).
   Where does this leave the study of East African Asians nowadays?
There have been two basic tendencies in the most recent scholarly
research. One has stressed the importance of communal crystallisation in
shaping both South Asian settlement patterns in East Africa and the
allegedly predominantly apolitical behaviour of most South Asian settlers
there. The other has taken the contrary view, that politics were in fact of
the greatest importance in shaping East African Asians' migrational
behaviour and in dictating their destiny.
   That is the perspective particularly portrayed by Mangat (1969),
Gregory (1971) and Tinker (1976). Mangat, in particular, argues that,
once the question of equality with white settlers had been raised and
settled so noisily and substantively in its disfavour during the 1920s, there
was little that the South Asian minority in East Africa could do about it
subsequently. For even in Kenya, where settlement has been much more
substantial than anywhere else in East and Central Africa – in relative as
well as in absolute terms – members of the South Asian minority have
never accounted for more than 2% of the total population (Bennett 1976).
   To Stephen Morris, however, the Asian question in colonial Kenya
during the 1920s seemed at best a 'slightly unreal drama' because:

> the failure of the few politically active Indian settlers to construct
> a united community – except on certain short-lived issues – also
> rested on a number of other equally important factors . . .
> inherent in the nature of [South Asian] immigration: the fact that
> it was voluntary; the size of the settlement at different times, a fact
> which affected its development; its composition in terms of
> religion, caste, sect, and district of origin in India, as well as the
> economic and political situation in Africa – all these factors
> limited the kind of society that the Asians could, and indeed
> wanted, to make in Africa. Their leaders spoke of 'apathy', when
> they themselves simply wanted to get on with the trade which they
> had come to pursue, and to save enough money to go home
> without having done themselves social harm by mixing too
> closely with inappropriate people abroad.
>
> (1970: 234)

Morris's analyses of the Aga Khan's Ismailis in Uganda, and his stress
upon the importance of population growth and the comparative proxi-

mity of the Indian sub-continent (by comparison with, say, either Fiji or Trinidad) for initially the crystallisation and subsequently the maintenance of communal identities amongst East African Asians have become the basic conventional wisdom of the second tendency.

The second tendency's stress upon South Asian immigration into East Africa as an essentially voluntary phenomenon has also become axiomatic. To the extent that the great majority of labourers recruited for railway-building in British East Africa from India during the 1890s and 1900s eventually returned to India, this stress upon the greater demographic importance of passenger migration is undoubtedly correct. However, the thousands of Sikh and Punjabi indentured workers who constructed the railway from Mombasa to Uganda in the 1890s and 1900s, and decided not to return to India afterwards, were by no means insignificant in number by comparison with the 'passenger Indians' also moving into the interior during these years, although, of course, they remained small fractions of both the 'passsenger Indian' community and majority of indentured labourers who did return to India after service in East Africa. None the less, despite some subsequent studies of Bohoras (Amiji 1975), Goans (Kuper 1979), Jains (Zarwan 1976) and Punjabi Hindus (Rothermund 1965), there have not really yet been sufficient studies of other East African Asian communities, in either number or depth, for it to be possible to say conclusively whether Morris's assumption of some fundamentally apoliticality among them (when compared with, say, the generality of East African Africans) should be accepted or not.

There also needs to be much more attention paid to those wider economic processes whereby the 'big push' by South Asian traders into the East African interior before the First World War turned into something both more permanent and more problematic after it. This was the time when, as John Lonsdale and Bruce Berman have pointed out, British colonial officials struggled to 'cope with the contradictions' of ensuring the survival of colonialist governance at the same time as attempting not only to introduce but also to manage more capitalist forms of agriculture amongst the majority African population (Lonsdale and Berman 1979). Ian Spencer has also indicated that the increasing restrictions on Asian trading activity in the Kenyan reserves after the First World War were dictated as much by British colonial officials' concerns about the developmental drawbacks of East African Asians' family trading practices as about the counterproductiveness or otherwise of Indian political demands for greater equality with white settlers during these years (Spencer 1981). There is also a need for research into East African Asian contributions to secondary industrialisation immediately before, during, and after the Second World War (Murray 1978).

None the less, in certain respects the most urgent research still required into South Asian movement into (and out of) the East African interior over the last hundred years is both the easiest and the most difficult sort possible: the study of communal crystallisation among East African Asian communities thus far unstudied from this particular perspective – easiest, because even the most elementary information about certain caste and sectarian organisations and associations in East Africa is presently lacking, and even secondary schoolchildren could assemble this. At the same time, it is extremely difficult, because such research also requires cunning and understanding of a very high level for its successful pursuit. Let me mention just one such (and, to my knowledge, thus far insufficiently studied) problem for further East African Asian research: the process whereby the descendants and co-religionists of Sikhs among the hundreds of indentured labourers who did *not* go back to the Punjab after constructing the railway from Mombasa to Uganda, crystallised into the communities of East African Sikhs who migrated to Britain during the 1960s and appeared 'more Anglicised than the migrants who came directly from India' yet paradoxically 'more inclined to wear the turban, to maintain religious practices, and to cultivate those cultural features which sustained that ethnic identity' (Banton 1983: 320). That is a research project which should prove of much more than antiquarian interest; upon which Bhachu (1985) has some interesting things to say regarding Ramgharias, to be sure, but on which much remains to be discovered both in East Africa and abroad!

Acknowledgements

This survey benefited from a research visit to East Africa in August–September 1987 financed by the Irwin Fund of London University, and from discussion of it at the European Science Foundation's colloquium on 'Migration' held at Gothenberg University in May 1988.

References

Adams, Bert V. and Mike Bristow, 1979. 'Ugandan Asian expulsion experiences: rumour and reality', *Journal of Asian and African Studies*, 14: 191–203.
Amiji, Hatim 1975. 'The Bohoras of East Africa', *Journal of Religion in Africa*, 7: 27–61.
1983. 'The Asiatic bias in the historiography of the East African Coast', *Journal of African Studies*, 10: 66–72.
Bagha, Yusuf A. 1970. 'History of the Memon community in Mombasa', B.A. thesis, Nairobi University.
Balachandran, P.K. 1981. 'An embattled community: Asians in East Africa today', *African Affairs*, 80: 317–25.
Banton, Michael 1983. *Racial and Ethnic Competition*, Cambridge University Press.

162   *Michael Twaddle*

Bennett, C.J. 1976. 'Persistence and adversity: the growth and spatial distribution of the Asian population of Kenya, 1902–1963'; Ph.D. dissertation, Syracuse University.

Bhachu, P. 1985. *Twice Migrants: East African Sikh Settlers in Britain*, London: Tavistock.

Bhatia, Prem 1973. *Indian Ordeal in Africa*, Delhi: Vikas.

Blacker, J.G.C. 1972. 'Demography', in *East Africa: its peoples and resources*, Nairobi: Oxford University Press.

Blundell, Michael 1964. *So rough a wind*, London: Weidenfeld.

Cook, David and David Rubadiri (eds.) 1971. *Poems from East Africa*, London: Heinemann.

Delval, Raymond 1976. 'The Indians in Madagascar', *Kroniek van Afrika*, 1976–7, 3.

Dorsch, T.S. 1967. *Classical Literary Criticism*, Harmondsworth: Penguin.

Dotson, Floyd and Lillian Dotson 1968. *The Indian Minority of Zambia, Rhodesia and Malawi*, New Haven: Yale University Press.

Fisher, Nigel 1973. *Iain Macleod*, London: Deutsch.

Freund, Bill 1984. *The Making of Contemporary Africa*, London: Macmillan.

Furedi, Frank 1974. 'The development of anti-Asian opinion among Africans in Nakuru district, Kenya', *African Affairs*, 73: 347–53.

Ghai, Dharam P. and Yash P. Ghai (eds.) 1970. *Portrait of a Minority: Asians in East Africa*, Nairobi: Oxford University Press.

Ghai, Yash 1975. 'Amin and the Asians', *Times Literary Supplement*, 4 July: 738–9.

Gray, Richard and David Birmingham (eds.) 1970. *Pre-colonial African Trade*, London: Oxford University Press.

Gregory, Robert G. 1971. *India and East Africa*, Oxford: Clarendon.

1981. 'Co-operation and collaboration in colonial East Africa: The Asians' political role, 1890–1964', *African Affairs*, 80: 259–73.

Gundara, Jagdish 1981. 'Fragment of Indian Society in Zanzibar: conflict and change in the 19th century', *African Quarterly*, 21: 23–40.

Hansen, Holger Bernt and Michael Twaddle (eds.) 1988. *Uganda now: between decay and development*, London: Currey.

Iliffe, John 1979. *A Modern History of Tanganyika*, Cambridge: Cambridge University Press.

Singh, Jagjit 1971. 'Portrait of an Asian as an East African', in *Poems from East Africa*, ed. David Cook and David Rubadiri, London: Heinemann, 156–9.

Kitching, A.L. 1912. *On the Backwaters of the Nile*, London: Fisher Unwin.

Kuper, Jessica 1979. '"Goan" and "Asian" in Uganda: an analysis of racial identity and cultural categories', in *Strangers in African Societies*, ed. William A. Shack and Elliot Skinner, Berkeley: University of California Press.

Lira Archives, Uganda 1913. Administrator-General's returns, LDMP, 92.

Lonsdale, John and Bruce Berman 1979. 'Coping with the contradictions: The development of the colonial state in Kenya, 1895–1914', *Journal of African History*, 20: 487–505.

Magor, E.W. 1948–9. Kenya National Archives, Nairobi: minutes of 9 October 1948, 14 November 1949, CS/2/2669 and 2670.

Mangat, J.S. 1969. *A History of the Asians in East Africa*, Oxford: Clarendon.

Morris, H.S. 1968. *The Indians in Uganda*, London: Weidenfeld.

1970. 'Review' in *Bulletin of SOAS*, 33: 233–5.

Murray, Robin 1978. 'The Chandarias: The development of a Kenyan multinational', in *Readings on the Multinational Corporation in Kenya*, ed. R. Kaplinsky, Nairobi: Oxford University Press.

Nag, Prithvish 1979. 'Asian settlement in Zambia', *African Quarterly*, 18, 4: 159–77.

Najak, Sachedena 1965. Interview at Lira, 9 November.

Neale, Barbara 1974. 'Kenya's Asian languages', in *Language in Kenya*, ed. W.H. Whiteley, Nairobi: Oxford University Press.

Pain, Dennis 1975. 'The Nubians: their perceived stratification system and its relation to the Asian issue', in *Expulsion of a Minority*, ed. Michael Twaddle, London: Athlone.

Pankhurst, Richard 1979. 'The "Banyan" or Indian presence at Masawa, the Dahlak islands and the horn of Africa', in *Actes* of the *Association Historique Internationale de l'Ocean Indien*, Paris.

Parliamentary Papers 1910. Report of the Committee on Emigration from India to the Crown Colonies and Protectorates, part II, minutes of evidence, Cd 5193, 242.

Patel, H.H. 1973. *Indians in Uganda and Rhodesia – some comparative perspectives on a minority in Africa*, University of Denver Centre on International Race Relations: Denver University Graduate School of International Studies.

Ramchandani, R.R. 1976. *Ugandan Asians: the end of an enterprise*, Bombay: United Asia.

Rothermund, Indira 1965. *Die politische und wirtschaftliche Rolle der asiatischen Minderheit in Ostafrika*, West Berlin: Springer.

Shakramali 1965. Interview at Soroti, 11 November.

Sheriff, Abdulm 1987. *Slaves, Spices and Ivory in Zanzibar: Integration of an East African Commercial Empire into the World Economy, 1770–1873*, London: Currey.

Singh, J. 1971. *Overseas Emigrants from India, Pakistan and Bangladesh*, Oxford.

Spencer, I.R.G. 1981. 'The first assault on Indian ascendancy: Indian traders in the Kenyan reserves, 1895–1929', *African Affairs*, 80: 317–25.

Stroebel, Margaret 1979. *Muslim Women in Mombasa 1890–1975*, New Haven: Yale University Press.

Tandon, Yash no date. *Problems of a Displaced Minority: the new position of East Africa's Asians*, London: Minority Rights Group.

Tinker, Hugh 1976. *Separate and Unequal: India and the Indians in the British Commonwealth, 1920–1950*, London: C. Hurst and Co.

1977. *The Banyan Tree*, Oxford University Press.

Twaddle, Michael, ed. 1975. *Expulsion of a Minority: Essays on Ugandan Asians*, London: Athlone.

Whiteley, W.H. 1969. *Swahili: the rise of a national language*, London: Methuen.

Zarwan, John 1976. 'The social and economic network of an Indian family business in Kenya, 1920–1970', in *Kroniek van Afrika*, 1975–6, 3.

Part II
South Asians in contemporary western countries and the Middle East

Introduction

Colin Clarke, Ceri Peach and Steven Vertovec

The first part of this volume dealt with the societies created by the movement of indentured and other forms of contract labour in the nineteenth-century colonial system. There was also free movement during this time, but this category of migration expanded dramatically in the period after the Second World War, especially through movements to western countries and the Middle East.

The postwar period was the era of decolonisation and it had two major effects on South Asian migration. The first was the Partition of the sub-continent into India and Pakistan in 1947, which caused a massive uprooting of population, particularly in the Punjab. It is estimated that by March 1948, about 6.5 million Muslims had migrated to West Pakistan and some 6 million Hindus and Sikhs had left it. In the east, partition and subsequent disorders led to probably 4 million refugees leaving the then East Pakistan (now Bangladesh) and about 1 million Muslims entering it (Spate 1963: 118–19). The Punjab, the area most affected by the refugee movements, was also the area which was to figure prominently in the subsequent overseas migrations.

The second effect of decolonisation was to expose the Asian minorities, introduced into other colonial societies, to the political pressures of the native nationalists. The most savage expression of anti-Asian policies was seen in Amin's 1972 expulsions from Uganda, but pressure had been applied in Kenya from 1965 and in Uganda in 1969, well before Amin seized power. By 1981 there were 155,000 South Asians of East African origin living in Britain (Peach et al. 1988: 566, 605–7). However, although East Africa was the first area to manifest the conflict of autochthonous nationalism with the immigrant South Asian communities, tensions were evident from the Caribbean to Fiji.

This period of upheaval and forced shifts of population was followed by a period of massive demand for labour in many of the metropolitan

167

countries of the west. This period of demand extended from the postwar economic recovery of the early 1950s to the oil shock and subsequent economic slump after 1973. Many South Asians, displaced or sensitised by the political tremors of the earlier period responded to the economic attractions of the later. There were major movements of population from agricultural areas in the Punjab and from the threatened entrepreneurial populations of East Africa to Britain, but in addition, the skilled population was more widely dispersed to the USA, Canada and Australia. By 1981 the Indian, Pakistani and Bangladeshi population of Great Britain numbered over a million, of whom about a third had been born in the country (Peach *et al.* 1988: 566).

While 1973 marked the oil crisis for the western world (see Robinson's chapter on the urban crisis in Britain) which stopped labour immigration into Europe in its tracks (Peach 1987), it had the reverse effect in the oil rich countries of the Middle East. The huge rise in oil prices stimulated demand for labour which led to a substantial influx particularly from Muslim areas in the sub-continent. Knerr's chapter traces the movement and shows that 2 million Indians, 1.5 million Pakistanis and 200,000 Bangladeshis were involved. Knerr also shows that overseas migrants make very substantial contributions to the economies of the sending countries. Overseas remittances were worth the equivalent of 44% of the goods imported into Pakistan in 1984, 21% of those in Bangladesh and 18% in India.

While the movement to the Middle East contained large elements of unskilled as well as skilled labour, South Asian movement into the United States was initially highly selective of skills. Although some South Asian presence had been noted since the end of the nineteenth century (Sikhs on railway gangs settled into irrigated farming in California) substantial immigration did not start until the relaxation of US immigration laws in 1965. Bhardwaj and Rao's chapter shows that by 1980 the South Asian population of the United States was just under 400,000.

Interestingly, because South Asian migrants were not part of some earlier chain-migration system, they show a high degree of regional diffusion. Europeans started on the East coast and spread west; Chinese and Japanese started on the west coast and diffused east. Indians arrived as part of a skilled student population and diffused down the urban hierarchy; over half of the South Asian population is concentrated in the fifteen largest metropolitan areas. Because of the high professional status of the migrants, they show low degrees of segregation within the urban areas. This is in marked contrast with the situation in Britain outlined in Robinson's chapter.

The chapters by Ballard and Kelly span the relationship between the

English and sub-continental ends of the migratory stream. Ballard argues that two-thirds of British Asians originate in the Punjab and that three-quarters of this number come from two small areas: the Jullundur Doab and the Mirpur District. Yet although these areas are less than 200 miles part, they represent totally different social worlds. Kelly, on the other hand, deals with the Gujarat and Blackburn ends of a migrant channel and shows that the migrant lives in the same religious- and caste-determined world despite the separation of 8,000 miles.

Ballard demonstrates that Sikhs and Muslims, despite starting at similar lowly points in the British economic system have described very different economic trajectories since then. He examines the popular conception of Sikhs as a dynamic thrusting group and Muslims as a more passive, inward looking group and shows that the situation is more complex. The starting point of the Sikhs in the irrigated and rich Jullundur Doab contrasts with the much poorer, rain-fed agriculture in the broken hill country of Mirpur. There were, thus, substantial differences between the two groups in wealth and education long before leaving the sub-continent.

However, there are also critical differences in social organisation between the two groups which are of greater significance than the prior economic contrasts. The critical social difference is in Sikh and Mirpuri Muslim marriage rules. The Sikhs favoured village out-marriage while the Muslims favoured cousin marriage. The result was that Sikh brides regularly moved out of their family villages on marriage, while Muslim brides typically stayed in their home village while moving to their husband's family house. Sikhs thus had a tradition of mobility and breaking away from old social networks, while marriage in the Muslim community reinforced existing networks and attachment to place. Sikhs migrating to Britain rapidly established their family units. The myth of return was much stronger for the Muslims and it was a longer time before they decided to establish their families in Britain rather than to return to them in Mirpur. Purdah among Muslim women in Britain reduced the social mobility and economic base of their families in contrast with the more outward-going position of Sikh women. Thus, differences in economic background and in social organisation have produced a steady differentiation of the Sikh and Muslim populations in Britain.

Kelly gives a humanistic, participant observer's account of transcontinental families. Her observations give a depth of evidence which can be seen to support Ballard's analysis. She describes life in a Muslim family in the Gujarat and in Blackburn. She points to the highly fissiparous nature of social organisation in Baroda and the surrounding countryside and points to a lifestyle circumscribed by religion and caste. She shows how envy, prompted by the Indian government's attempts to protect minority rights among scheduled castes, lapped over into Muslim sub-castes and eventually precipitated rioting by Hindus against Muslims. This, in turn precipitated the migration of her contact to Blackburn. She shows how her friend moved from social encapsulation in India to a similar enclave in Britain.

The last four chapters deal with British settlement exclusively and they confront, head on, the difficulty in conceptualising the South Asian community. South Asians do not exist as a concrete community. The group is dialectically rather than absolutely defined. Ethnic identity is contingent rather than categorical. The concept that is important to convey here is that South Asians exist as South Asians for some purposes but not for others. They exist as South Asians as opposed to West Indians or as opposed to whites, but for other purposes they dissolve into their sub-groups of nationality, religion, region, language, caste, sub-caste or *biraderi*.

Robinson's chapter attempts to mesh together the findings of different scales of academic approaches. He sets the South Asian population in Britain in the context of Britain's changing postwar economic position. He shows how the South Asian population was drawn in as a replacement population, particularly to manufacturing industries in the conurbations. He charts the subsequent decline of manufacturing jobs and the growth of service industries and shows the differential regional effect (broadly north–south), the differential urban effect (loss to conurbations and gain to smaller towns) and the gender specific effects (loss of male work, gain of women's part-time work). Many of these changes have acted against Asian interests. He argues that only 5% of the Asian population in Britain is found in cities with a twentieth-century industrial base. As in the United States, there is a high concentration of the Asian population into the largest urban areas: two-thirds are found in the six largest conurbations. However, unlike Bhardwaj and Rao's findings for the United States, there are high levels of segregation within those areas.

There is further evidence also, for Bhardwaj and Rao's fusion/fission analysis and for Ballard's divergence theory, with Bangladeshis showing poor housing conditions and high concentrations. On the other hand, over a third of British South Asians are living in comfortable semi-detached or better housing and, though high, levels of segregation are falling.

Anwar's chapter examines some of the political implications that follow from Robinson's analysis. Since Asians number about 1.5 million in Britain and are highly concentrated spatially, it allows them to exercise power in a few areas. He lists seventeen wards, where ethnic minorities, largely Asian, formed 50% or more of the population in 1981. He cites the

1986 figure of sixty-four Asian councillors elected in Greater London Borough elections as evidence of progress in representation. He shows that the Asian vote is strongly Labour, but not as strongly Labour as the Afro-Caribbean population, and speculates that the Asian political route might follow the trajectory of Jewish political representation. The Jewish population is much smaller than the Asian population, less than 500,000 (and probably closer to 300,000). Prior to the 1987 General Election, there were no Asian MPs while there were thirty of Jewish origin. Anwar shows that the Jewish population was overwhelmingly left voting at the beginning of the century, but had become more evenly divided between left and right over time. There is some evidence that the Conservative Party regarded Asian cultural values as making them a natural part of the long-term Conservative constituency.

The position of the Bangladeshis in the political system is examined in some detail in Eade's chapter. The 1981 census showed 48,000 persons born in Bangladesh living in Britain, although with the British-born Bangladeshi population, the figure was probably double that by 1988. Nearly 20% of the Bangladeshi population in living in a single London Borough, Tower Hamlets, where they form, perhaps, 13% of the population. Eade's chapter shows how cleavages have developed within the Bangladeshi population in factional struggles for leadership. The traditional leadership of the business community has been usurped by a younger group. As government agencies have channelled funds into community organisations, stricter accountancy of expenditure and controls have produced a cadre of professional activists. Sylheti background rather than the broader Bangladeshi origin is the key political factor and politics in Tower Hamlets is dominated by a homeland orientation.

The contextual rather than the absolute nature of ethnic identity is most fully articulated in the final chapter of the book, by Werbner. She sees three major axes of differentiation among the Pakistani population of Manchester. The first is descent (region, language and religion); the second is hierarchy (wealth, caste, occupation and education); the third is what might be called contingent geography (current residence, network clusters, economic enclaves). Werbner argues that the third mediates crucially between the lateral and hierarchic divisions within the ethnic group.

The Manchester Pakistani population is internally fragmented yet externally conceived of as homogeneous. There is therefore a struggle between the internal segments to represent the community as a whole. The 'community' is represented by opposed elites competing for local hegemony. The state, as the source of communal funding, operates with the fiction of communal unity and highlights internal divisions. However, it would be a mistake to view the Pakistani community as marginalised or colonised. There is a drive towards increasing cultural and economic autonomy on the one hand and increasing involvement in broader political structures on the other. Consolidation and expansion are thus key processes characterising Pakistani settlement.

References

Peach, C., V. Robinson, J. Maxted and J. Chance 1988. 'Immigration and ethnicity', in *British Social Trends since 1900*, ed. A.H. Halsey, London: Macmillan, 561–615.
Peach, C. 1987. 'Immigration and segregation in Western Europe since 1945', in *Foreign Minorities in Continental European Cities*, eds. G. Glebe and J. O'Loughlin, Stuttgart: Franz Steiner Verlag, 30–51.
Spate, O.H.K. 1963. *India and Pakistan*, London: Methuen.

8

South Asian countries as competitors on the world labour market

Béatrice Knerr

During the last fifteen years a new form of migration from South Asian countries, which differs markedly in its economic and social implications from the nineteenth and early twentieth-century movement of indentured labourers, has gathered momentum. This new phase of migration is based on fixed temporary contracts, which attract labourers from South Asia to work in the oil-rich countries of the Middle East. The economic development of Pakistan, Bangladesh and to a lesser extent, India, has become increasingly dependent on this type of labour export. Migrant workers' remittances of foreign exchange in 1983 paid for 55% of all merchandise imports of Pakistan, 42% of Bangladesh and 20% of India; they amounted to nearly 80% of Bangladesh's and more than 25% of India's merchandise exports and were nearly equivalent to those of Pakistan (Table 8.1). It is therefore not surprising that the governments of Bangladesh and Pakistan, having become aware of this most important source of foreign exchange, have tried to promote the export of their labour; additionally, they hope that this can help them solve their labour surplus problems. The question, however, arises as to whether they will be able to keep up with the changes in demand structure. Closely related to this is the question whether governments use the right marketing strategy. The national blend of expatriate labour in any host country is not only the result of market forces, but also of deliberate policy measures towards migration, in both labour-importing and exporting countries. This chapter will analyse the future opportunities of the Pakistani, Bangladeshi and Indian labour forces of finding employment outside their home country, in the face of growing competition from other countries' labour supply.

The first section of the chapter describes the changing structure of demand for labour in the main labour-importing region during the last fifteen years, and against this background outlines the advantages and

173

Table 8.1. *Workers' remittances to their home countries and their relation to export earnings and import expenditures, 1970–85*

	Pakistan	India	Bangladesh
Remittances in million US$			
1970	86	113	n.a.
1981	2,056	n.a.	386
1982	2,580	2,293	329
1983	2,925	2,617	629
1984	2,567	2,659	437
1985	2,526	2,291	421
Remittances as % of merchandise exports			
1970	11.8	5.5	n.a.
1981	71.4	n.a.	48.8
1982	107.4	27.1	42.8
1983	95.1	26.9	79.7
1984	99.0	28.2	46.8
1985	92.2	22.3	42.1
Remittances as % of merchandise imports			
1970	9.3	3.4	n.a.
1981	38.5	n.a.	14.8
1982	47.8	16.3	14.3
1983	54.7	19.3	41.8
1984	43.7	17.7	21.4
1985	42.9	15.7	15.2

Source: Calculated with data from The World Bank, *World Development Report*, Washington, various years.

disadvantages of South Asian labour in comparison with that of other competing countries. The following section tries to forecast changes in the extent and structure of labour demand which will probably take place in the importing countries during the next few years. On the basis of the lessons learned, the competitiveness of South Asian countries under changing conditions are examined.

The following observations are restricted to forms of migration where the migrant remains part of the economy of his country of origin; they therefore concentrate especially on contract migration, which is of major importance in the present international labour market and which, *ceteris paribus*, yields the highest return of foreign exchange to the home country. It should be emphasised that labour export is not to be viewed as an export of people but as an export of services carried out by migrants themselves. As far as governments promote this export, it is, under the circumstances of today, meeting the interests of the migrants and potential migrants.

Demand and competition in the international labour market

The framework within which manpower export occurs today is significantly different from that in recent years. I wish to concentrate on the movements which have occurred in the last fifteen years.

By far the most important demand for expatriate labour today originates in the oil-exporting countries of the Middle East which, according to estimates, currently absorb up to 2 million Indians, 1.5 million Pakistanis and 200,000 Bangladeshis (VIZ 1987). Inundated with capital, these countries embarked on ambitious development projects for which their own labour force was far too small. Consequently, large and increasing labour imports have taken place which are characterised by a very strong competition among the suppliers of expatriate labour. Employment of South Asians outside their home country is thus determined by the demand for labour with certain skills in the Middle East, which itself is influenced by developments in the oil market and the development priorities of the Middle East countries, as well as by the supply of labour from other countries and from the indigenous population of the labour-importing countries themselves. The position of South Asian countries can only be analysed in a dynamic context. This shows that a successful strategy for countries trying to export labour is not to expect a static demand for labour, but to maintain a high degree of flexibility in order to adapt to the changing structure of demand. For the individual worker, this means perhaps only a short working period in the importing country.

The structure of labour import in the years after the first oil boom
The year 1973 witnessed the beginning of a rapidly increasing demand for expatriate labour in oil-exporting countries of the Gulf region, Saudi Arabia, Kuwait, the United Arab Emirates (UAE), Bahrain, Qatar and Libya. Increasing demand for labour during the following years was determined by increasing oil revenues, and a development strategy adopted by all oil-exporting countries in the Middle East, which concentrated on the erection of physical infrastructure and therefore created a demand for labour, especially in the construction sector, and largely for unskilled manual workers.

This demand could not be satisfied by domestic supply because of: (a) very small domestic populations; (b) a low participation rate by the domestic population in the labour market which is caused especially by the traditionally low participation of women (except in the agricultural sector); (c) the traditional aversion of the indigenous population to blue-collar jobs, and at the same time, an obligation by governments to provide white-collar jobs for nationals who, thereby, were not forced to take up undesired employment (these jobs were also attractive due to high pay and many privileges); (d) lack of human capital especially in technical areas. This is closely related to the above-mentioned aversion to blue-collar jobs. Only those who had no chance to go to university would undergo technical education (Birks and Sinclair 1980).

Initially the gap was filled mainly by Arab workers from neighbouring countries, who migrated individually. This process had already started in the 1960s especially from Egypt, Yemen and Jordan. At the beginning of the 1970s there were only a few South Asians among the migrant workers in the Middle East. They had migrated individually and most of them came from India which has had a tradition of sending labour to the Middle East since the Second World War. At that period, however, South Asian labour could not successfully compete with Arab workers who were the ideal buffer for the Middle East labour market since: (a) Arabs are not regarded so much as foreigners in other Arab countries; (b) they live in close proximity to the labour importing countries; (c) language and cultural barriers are not difficult to overcome; (d) 'to-and-fro' migration is a century-old tradition within the Middle East and North Africa (MENA) region; and (e) the Arab states outside the oil region have relatively large populations, comparatively high rates of participation, widespread under-employment and low wages at home.

Therefore, workers from Arab countries were willing and able to fulfil the labour demand of their capital-rich neighbours for several years. In the middle of the 1970s, however, scarcity of labour began to be felt more and more within these countries; the number of expatriate workers in the oil-exporting economies of the Middle East which was estimated at 800,000 in 1972, had already doubled by 1975. Thirty per cent of Yemeni, 40% of Jordanian and 25% of Omani workers had emigrated (Serageldin *et al.* 1983: 72). Hence it became increasingly difficult to recruit Arab workers.

Large-scale imports from South Asia

By 1975 the mobile labour supply from Arab countries seemed to have been depleted. As some Indians and Pakistanis had already found their way into the rich oil-exporting states, these connections were used by friends and relatives when opportunities for employment of labour from outside the region improved. At the same time, private agents actively started to recruit workers for the Middle East in India and Pakistan and, later on, also in Bangladesh. Within a short time, emigration from South Asia to the MENA region gathered momentum and continued on a large scale. When the governments of Pakistan and Bangladesh became aware of the potential that this migration had for their domestic economies,

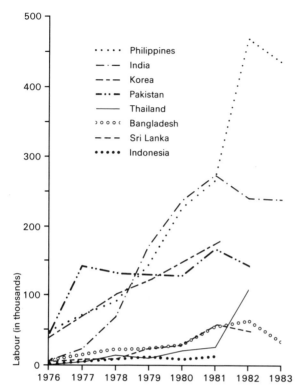

Figure 8.1   Annual outflow of contract migrants from selected Asian countries
Source: Abella 1984, and *Statistical Yearbook* of Bangladesh.

especially regarding the remittances which quickly amounted to hundreds of millions of US dollars, they tried to intervene in this process, not only to protect their own labour force from abuse but also to promote labour export.

In 1975, 71% of the expatriate labour in the Middle East were nationals of other Arab countries, and 20% were Asians, the majority of them coming from the Indian sub-continent (Table 8.2). The other Asians were mostly Malaysian, Nepalese, Filipino, Thai and South Korean (UN/ESCAP 1984) (Fig. 8.1). Non-Arabs stayed especially in Bahrain, Kuwait, Qatar and the UAE. This nationality structure, however, changed rapidly over the following years. South Asians had several advantages which made them competitive in the Middle East labour market: they were cheap and they were disciplined and hard workers (La Porte 1984: 701). Most of them came from Muslim countries – Bangladesh and Pakistan – or Muslim regions of India (Gulati 1986: 194); most were

Table 8.2. *Population by major sending region in the major labour-importing countries,*[a] *1975 and 1985*

Group	1975 Population (1,000)	%	1985 Population (1,000)	%	Annual increase 1975–85
Arab non-nationals	2,237.3	71.5	5,688.8	59.5	9.7
South Asians	559.5	17.9	2,410.6	25.2	15.7
East Asians	20.3	0.7	398.0	4.2	33.8
Other	309.3	9.9	1,066.3	11.1	13.2
Subtotal	3,126.4	100.0	9,563.7	100.0	11.8
Nationals	9,758.3	75.7	14,313.3	60.0	3.9

Notes:
[a]Algeria, Bahrain, Iraq, Kuwait, Libya, Oman, Qatar, Saudi Arabia, UAE.
[b]Figures for 1985 are forecasts made in 1983 by the World Bank. They are based on assumed growth rates of the output and productivities of 19 countries in the MENA region for the period 1976–85; they range from 1.1% (Lebanon) to 10.3% (Iraq), with 8.6% for Saudi Arabia, 9.4% for UAE, 4.7% for Kuwait and 8.7% for Libya.
Source: Serageldin *et al.* 1983: 60.

from Kerala, which is one of the Indian states with the highest proportion of Muslims (Raj and Tharakan 1983). They were often organised in groups through private agents who acted as intermediaries, and later on also by government agencies. Thus they could be contracted collectively and in advance, which facilitated planning by the employers. The South Asians, who were skilled, namely the Pakistanis, had long years of experience. Indians had the advantage of comparatively high educational levels. Individually, South Asians also had the possibility of entering Middle East countries illegally; for example, as *hajjis* (pilgrims) or by crossing the long uncontrolled borders, especially to Saudi Arabia, by land or by sea. Once they had entered the country it was not very difficult to find employment.

The workers from Bangladesh and Pakistan were increasingly supported by their governments. The Bhutto government actively promoted labour export to the Middle East as part of its foreign policy, in order to form links with other Islamic countries, especially the oil exporters, Saudi Arabia, the UAE and Kuwait. Pakistan has been able to provide highly skilled professionals who are urgently needed by the oil-exporting countries; it has also supplied military manpower to approximately two dozen countries, several of which are in the MENA region (La Porte 1984: 701). In order to respond to the demand structure in the Middle East, the

Table 8.3. *Main countries of destination of South Asian migrant workers, 1980*

In-migration country	Out-migration country						1984	
	Pakistan[a] number	%	India[a] number	%	Bangladesh[b] number	%	Bangladesh[b] number	%
UAE	137,000	36.87	109,500	39.04	4,847	16.26	5,302	9.69
Saudi Arabia	29,700	7.99	29,700	10.59	8,695	29.17	20,587	37.25
Bahrain	26,160	7.04	12,300	4.39	1,351	4.53	2,325	4.25
Kuwait	34,000	9.15	45,000	16.05	3,687	12.37	5,697	10.41
Iraq	7,500	2.02	2,000	0.71	1,927	6.46	4,701	8.59
Libya	65,000	17.49	32,000	11.41	2,976	9.98	3,386	6.19
Oman	44,500	11.98	35,600	12.69	4,745	15.92	10,091	18.44
Qatar	20,700	5.57	11,850	4.23	1,455	4.88	2,643	4.83
Jordan	4,000	1.08	500	0.18	127	0.43	1	–
Yemen	3,000	0.81	2,000	0.71	–	–	–	–
	371,630	100.00	280,450	100.00	29,810	100.00	54,733	100.00

Source:
[a]*ILO. World Labour Report*, 1986.
[b]*Statistical Yearbook of Bangladesh* and author's calculations.

government of Pakistan currently (late 1980s) undertakes vocational and other training activities through the establishment and expansion of training facilities designed to further improve the skill levels of potential overseas workers (La Porte 1984: 703). In Pakistan and Bangladesh the governments have established special agencies for the marketing of their labour force: in Pakistan the BEOE (Bureau of Emigration and Overseas Employment), founded in 1971, and the OEC (Overseas Employment Corporation), founded in 1979, have labour attachés in the Middle East and a network of roughly 500 private licensed agents processing state-to-state labour contracts (Tsakok 1982: 320). In Bangladesh, the BMET (Bureau of Manpower, Employment and Training) was very successful in the mediation of the labour force during the first years of its existence, but since then migrants have preferred private connections. Nevertheless, government migration policies support them to a certain extent. The governments of Bangladesh and Pakistan run special educational and training courses for workers who want to apply for jobs in the Middle East to increase their competitiveness in the Middle East labour market. The output of trainees from government institutions in Pakistan, for example, was planned to be 30,000 in 1985, which was a three-fold increase over the level of 1978/9; this just closed the gap left by migration (Tsakok 1982: 321). Through the years, migrant labour has become more and more an object of bilateral state agreements, and the governments of Bangladesh and Pakistan are alert to the need to contact labour-importing governments for this purpose.

During the first years of South Asian immigration most Bangladeshis, Pakistanis and Indians worked as unskilled labourers. The termination of the phase of infrastructural projects and the new emphasis on industrialisation in the Middle East changed the structure of demand for labour and the structure of supply obviously had to adapt. Before 1976, 1 million unskilled workers were employed in the labour-importing countries for the erection of overhead capital. Between 1975 and 1980 1 million more skilled workers had to be imported to manage and operate this new infrastructure (Shaw 1981: 637) (Table 8.3). The capital-poor Arab countries were not able to meet the growing demand for professional and, especially, technically skilled labour; this was not solely because their markets were already depleted by emigration, but also because these countries received grants-in-aid from the oil-rich states to build up their own development projects and this, in turn, required comparatively highly skilled labour at home. Some of the labour-exporting countries felt the effects of an increasing scarcity of labour and they themselves started to import labour for wage rates that were lower than those paid in the oil-rich states.

The East Asians: a new form of immigration

At the end of the 1970s some new developments strongly influenced the possibility for South Asians to find employment in the Middle East. There was growing social unrest among South Asian immigrant workers. Increasing hostility against employers in the host countries resulted in riots against bad working conditions and wage discrimination in Bahrain in 1974, in Saudi Arabia in 1976, and in Dubai in 1977 (Ling 1984: 21). This made governments of the oil-exporting countries increasingly aware of the long-term problems which rise out of large-scale immigration. As a steep reduction of imported labour was impossible for economic reasons, they started to change their immigration policy by looking for new sources of expatriate labour, and the possibility of isolating migrant workers from the domestic population.

East Asian companies entered the Middle East market with a completely new form of package migration which was well suited to the new migration policy of the importing countries. Under this system, workers with contracts for a fixed period of time are brought into the country (without their families) for the realisation of a certain project. They live in communal accommodation isolated from the host population. This kind of organisation has the additional advantage of being cheap. Package contracts of this kind brought workers from South Korea, Taiwan, the Philippines and the Peoples' Republic of China. The pioneers were, in particular, private Japanese firms which, however, were not accepted as employers by Asians. Very soon the first contracts were concluded between companies from labour-exporting countries, especially South Korea and the Middle East countries. In this way South Asian workers have lost part of their market share to East Asians. Companies from the Philippines and Indonesia followed the Korean strategy, sometimes engaging in co-ventures with domestic Middle Eastern enterprises. For several years, East Asian companies could draw their labour from a nearly unlimited pool. At the beginning of the 1980s, wages in the Middle East were twice those in Korea, three to five times those in Thailand, four to six times those in the Philippines and seven times those in China (Ling 1984: 24). Like South Asia, East Asia has the advantage of supplying labourers who are accustomed to 'working under harsh conditions, for long hours, separate from family and friends, and accustomed to the discipline required for the projects that have been undertaken in the MENA region' (La Porte 1984: 701). Moreover workers from East Asia have a comparatively high educational level which is of growing importance.

Korea's entry into the Middle East labour market started in 1973, when its first 300 construction workers were sent to Saudi Arabia and Iran (Kim and Lee 1983: 1). Since then, Korea has been extraordinarily successful.

Table 8.4. *Population and crude activity rate in the major
labour-importing countries by country of origin, 1975 and 1985*

Country of origin	1975		1985[a]	
	Population (1,000)	Crude activity rate	Population (1,000)	Crude activity rate
Egypt	620.3	60.0	2,016.1	29.9
India	205.7	69.0	819.8	35.3
Jordan	503.0	27.6	1,145.9	23.0
Pakistan	353.8	58.1	1,591.1	27.8
East Asia	21.6	94.9	398.1	92.8
YAR	607.6	54.1	751.2	50.7

Note:
[a]Figures for 1985 are forecasts made in 1983, see note to Table 8.2.
Source: Serageldin *et al.* 1983: 59.

The country developed its marketing strategy during the Vietnam conflict
when Korean construction firms began to organise package arrangements
for overseas work which comprised materials, design, supervision and
workers. Success in this approach encouraged the Korean government
actively to assist private domestic firms in the pursuit of other overseas
contracts. At that time – starting in the 1960s – temporary migration for
employment emerged. It marked the beginning of a systematic, national
effort by the Korean government to exploit an international opportunity
(La Porte 1984: 705). For the purpose of package migration, the Korean
government has devised several laws and regulations. It sanctions three
employment channels: local firms, foreign companies, and specific invitations from foreign governments. A model has evolved that relates to the
specifics of Korean culture and working habits. In 1981 construction
orders from the MENA region (about 1,100 in number) generated over
US\$ 40 billion (Kim and Lee 1983). Since 1977, however, shortages of
manpower have been observed within the Korean economy. The Korean
government, nevertheless, still seems to favour a labour export policy.

　There are still other reasons why the Middle East obviously has a strong
preference for East Asian labour. Middle East labour importers are highly
sensitive to the growth of migrant communities (Serageldin *et al.* 1983).
The main reasons for their resistance to further immigration by dependants are the danger that they could outnumber the nationals (with
associated political and social problems) and the high infrastructural costs
involved. 'The rapidity of the evolution of migrant communities has led

labour importers to view their management as one of the key domestic issues, if not the most important' (Serageldin *et al.* 1983: 58). Usually, the migrant communities consist initially mostly of young men. After a certain time, however, they assume more and more the composition of a normal population, as families are brought to the host country. This development is reinforced by the fact that migrant workers are within the most fertile age groups. There are, however, striking differences between the nationalities: South Asians are very quickly joined by their families, while East Asians bring very few dependants (Table 8.4). Between 1975 and 1985 the population of Indians, Pakistanis and Bangladeshis more than quintupled, though the number of workers from these countries increased by only 25%. This indicates the possibility that the South Asians will develop into minority groups within the oil-exporting Middle East states. In contrast to this, the East Asian group consists almost entirely of workers. This is mainly the result of the highly organised character of the labour import from this region, which is also the key to its rapidly increasing share of the labour market. Within the Arab groups, only the share of Egyptians has increased, mainly as a result of their professional qualifications.

Replacement migration: a new market for South Asians
    South Asians play an increasingly important role as 'replacement migrants'; that is, as immigrants who come into the country 'to fill a vacancy created by the departure of a national for employment abroad' (Serageldin *et al.* 1983: 83). This secondary labour migration has occurred especially in Jordan, Oman and the Yemeni Arab Republic (YAR). The country most affected by this so far is Jordan, with an estimated 75,000 replacement migrants in 1980, the majority of them being Egyptians, together with some 5,500 Asians (Serageldin *et al.* 1983: 83). Most of Jordan's secondary migrants are unskilled workers. Not only has Jordan lost much of its labour force to the oil-producing economies, but, as a result of labour emigration, new jobs were created within the country that could not be filled by nationals. This applied particularly to many of the less-skilled jobs, for example, in the building industry. Another consequence of labour emigration from Jordan has been an accelerated rural-to-urban migration within the country, which has resulted in an increasing shortage of agricultural labour. All this has caused an increase in real wages which has attracted workers from other countries, primarily Egyptians, who have not succeeded in finding jobs elsewhere in the Middle East. The structure of this secondary migration is determined by the (expected) productivity of the different nationalities.'The marginal productivity of most Jordanians is thought in the labour-importing

countries to be higher than that of the Egyptians who are replacing them. Hence the demand in the peninsula, in the first instance, is for Jordanians and not for Egyptians.' (Serageldin *et al.* 1983: 83). The replacement migration of Pakistanis into Jordan, which was initially spontaneous, is now organised and subject to government agreement, in contrast to the immigration of Egyptians into the Jordanian agricultural and construction sectors, which is usually on an individual basis. The former system is a response by the Pakistani government to a request from the Jordanian authorities to increase the flow of Pakistani workers in a regular and more orderly manner. Most of the Pakistani migrants into Jordan are unskilled workers.

The secondary migration taking place into the YAR involves different categories of highly qualified experts who are, however, few in number. Many (about 5,000) at the beginning of the 1980s, were teachers and nurses, and were almost exclusively Arabs. There are also workers from the Sudan, Somalia, Ethiopia and other countries around the Horn of Africa. The most recent arrivals are the Asians. They work in the construction sector, occupying jobs that were previously filled by Yemenis. The number of migrant workers in the YAR was estimated at about 25,000 in the spring of 1980. Of those who received work permits from the Ministry of Labour in 1979, 59% were Indian or Pakistani, and 11% were Korean (Serageldin *et al.* 1983: 85). The reason why oil-exporting countries prefer workers from Korea is also persuasive in other Middle Eastern countries. In the YAR, Asian labour involves low cost and is often organised. Therefore, penetration of the secondary migration market by this group is to be expected. A problem arises for the government as to whether Asian workers will stay permanently within the domestic labour market. 'Because these Asians are employed in urban centres and in the modern sector . . . their continued presence limits the participation of nationals in that part of the economy' (Serageldin *et al.* 1983: 85). There are, furthermore, indications that expatriate workers fill jobs that Yemenis themselves are capable of filling. Thus it may be that Asians are employed because they are cheaper, while Yemenis remain unemployed.

Replacement migration has also become more and more important in Oman. First this involved only people with higher skill levels, as is typical for capital-rich oil exporters. In 1975, however, 12,000 unskilled workers had already been brought into the country, and it is estimated that their number increased to 19,000 in 1985.

Development priorities and economic outlook for labour-importing countries

Development priorities

Current and future development priorities in the labour-importing countries can be read from their five-year plans. Since most Middle East countries do not publish them, their details however, are not always known.

The development plan for Saudi Arabia, which runs from 1985 to 1990 is formulated in a very flexible way, allowing for adaptation in the case of diminishing state revenues. It is based on the assumption of an average growth rate of GDP of 4% per annum. The budgets for the coming years were fixed at about 200 billion Saudi Rials per annum (BfAI/NfA(k), 1985). All sectoral growth rates – except the one expected for the industrial sector – are below those for the period 1980 to 1985. The Saudi Arabian development plan includes the following:

(a)   It declares the infrastructure as almost completed. Major goals are the privatisation of the economy, the promotion of agriculture, industry, mining, education and vocational training.

(b)   It is based on an increase in productivity of 4% per year resulting from changes in the labour market. A decrease is anticipated particularly in the construction sector; its growth rate is expected to be -2.8% per annum, against an increase of 15% in the industrial sector, and of 9% in the financial sector.

(c)   A minimum life standard for each Saudi Arabian citizen will be secured, comprising free schooling and medical treatment.

(d)   The private sector should be induced to invest within Saudi Arabia.

(e)   Islamic values should be preserved.

(f)   Within the period of the plan, 45 hospitals are to be constructed and more than 1,000 centres for first aid. Out of the 62.239 million SRIs assigned for social and cultural development, 57% will be spent in the health sector.

(g)   Productive investment will be promoted, and technologies with a high capital intensity will receive special priority. The plan stresses the government's intention of diminishing the number of non-Saudi workers and at the same time, improving the qualification structure of the labour force.

(h)   In order to develop agricultural production, subsidies will be given, for example, for the production of grain, fertilizer and dates.

(i)   New industrial development zones (so-called 'industrial cities') will be built in Medina, Assir, Mekka, Hail, Tabuk, Jizan and Najran.

The current plan has a target which cannot be found in former plans: the obligation to reduce the number of foreign workers by at least 500,000. It puts emphasis on the education of sufficient national workers. Out of the budget's 500 billion SRI, 27.2% is bound to be spent on the development of human resources (first of all education and vocational training); 26.1% on health and social services; 17.9% on traffic and telecommunications; and 13.5% on communities and housing. The share of health and social services exceeds that of the previous five-year plan by nearly 30%, but the share of infrastructure is being lowered.

The primary objective of the UAE's five-year plan (Statistische Bundesamt 1985) is a high rate of economic growth to be reached independently of oil exports. The sectors which enjoy priority are infrastructure, energy and health. Priority is also accorded to a decrease in expatriate labour and a better integration of those foreigners who will stay in the country permanently. Abu Dhabi, Dubai and Shardja, the oil-producing emirates, are striving hard for industrial development. Several large industrial centres were built or are being built at Rwais (Abu Dhabi) and Djebel Ali (Dubai), each with an investment ranging from hundreds of millions to more than US$ 1 billion.

Most governments in the Middle East would like to exert stricter control over migration than is actually possible. In recent years immigration policy has become tighter. Saudi Arabia and the Gulf States, for example, try to enforce regulations which require proper documentation for all migrant workers.

Economic outlook
The economic prospects of the labour-importing Middle East countries hinge on oil revenues. Therefore future oil prices are crucial for the demand for foreign labour. Their oil revenue which was at 14–15 US$ per barrel in 1986 is anticipated to rise to between 15 and 20 US$ per barrel in 1990 and between 25 and 35 US$ per barrel in the year 2000. World wide demand for oil is expected to increase from 45.7 billion barrels in 1986 to 52.0 billion barrels in 1990, and to between 54.7 and 56.3 billion barrels in the year 2000 (Schürmann 1986; Petroleum Economics 1986). About half this demand is expected to be satisfied by OPEC countries. If the Middle East oil exporters keep their market share, their economic situation will most probably remain stable. Against this background, a new oil boom with a tremendous increase in labour demand cannot be expected.

Future prospects for labour export from South Asia

The South Asian countries can calculate their chances in the Middle East labour market by comparing the advantages and disadvantages of their labour force with those of other competitors; by analysing the experience of the last fifteen years; and by looking at the development priorities and future economic prospects of the oil importing countries. By these means they can develop a strategy that will enable them to compete successfully in the international labour market.

From the development priorities of the oil-exporting countries the conclusion can be drawn that these countries will try hard to cut back on their use of expatriate labour, but it is debatable whether they will succeed. First of all they would have to substitute expatriate workers by capital and a domestic labour force. The replacement of labour by capital could partly be effected. As calculated by Serageldin *et al.* (1983) a 1% increase in social product would require a 0.3 to 0.5% increase in labour employment. Hence, if the region achieves the growth rate anticipated by Saudi Arabia, about 2% more workers will be needed (when an anticipated increase of labour productivity of 4% is taken into account, it will be a little less).

Some of the oil-producing countries already seem to have depleted their stock of domestic labour and will not be able to increase this supply even by ambitious educational programmes. The gap cannot be filled by domestic labour, even if the qualifications of the new entrants correspond to the structure of labour demanded. Yet this is not likely to be the case. The educational infrastructure of the Arab countries is inadequate to meet the needs of these rapidly expanding economies. In Saudi Arabia, for example, between 1970 and 1980 the share of foreigners among doctors rose from 87.2% to 95.4%, and among nurses from 74.0% to 85.5% (VIZ 1983). Although enormous efforts have been made to improve the quality of domestic labour in the oil-rich countries, it will be many years before significant results are apparent. The educational system in Arab countries of the region is often criticised because the universities produce too high a proportion of graduates in literary subjects. For example, at the end of the 1970s, 85% of the university students in Qatar and 70% of those in Libya were enrolled in the arts (Shaw 1981: 643). A very low percentage of the students is enrolled in vocational or technical schools. At the end of the 1970s, in Saudi Arabia 5.9%, in Kuwait 4.6%, in Libya 2.5% and in Qatar 2.5% of the students attended vocational or technical schools (Table 8.5). Some of the labour-exporting Arab countries, however, achieved a better performance: for example, in Egypt 18% and in Jordan 12.6% of the students were in vocational and technical schools. As Egypt has a large

Table 8.5. *Student enrolments in vocational and technical schools,*
1975–8

Country	Year	No. of students in vocational and technical schools (a)	(a) as % of all students in secondary level and above (b)	% of students in (a) that are females (c)
Bahrain	1976–7	1,976	10.4	24.0
Kuwait	1977–8	2,084	4.6	42.6
Libya	1977–8	4,990	2.5	0.0
Qatar	1975–6	82	2.5	47.6
Saudi Arabia	1977–8	5,169	5.9	0.0
Jordan	1976	9,437	12.6	26.7
Egypt	1976–7	403,541	18.0	35.0
Sudan	1976–7	12,104	4.3	24.4
Yemen AR	1977–8	522	3.8	0.0

Source: National *Statistical Yearbooks* and published bulletins of respective
Ministries of Education, in Shaw, 1981: 644.

Table 8.6. *Total and professional Arab immigrants admitted to the USA*
by country of birth, 1972–7

Country	Total no.	% in professional, technical and kindred category		
		1972–7	1975–6	1977
Oil-rich	11,740	14.0	12.1	15.7
Oil-poor	58,958	12.3	11.3	11.4
Bahrain	116	62.5	31.7	28.6
Kuwait	2,342	16.9	18.6	14.3
Libya	667	40.4	34.8	34.5
Oman	60	42.9	26.6	18.2
Qatar	79	35.7	45.2	13.5
Saudi Arabia	1,424	25.1	25.4	28.3
UAE	204	33.3	8.8	22.2
Egypt	10,763	28.6	29.4	18.7
Jordan	14,771	6.8	5.6	6.8
Sudan	197	17.7	21.4	5.1
Yemen AR	3,279	0.6	0.7	1.4

Source: Department of Immigration and Naturalization, US Government Micro-
fiche. ASI 1979, in Shaw, 1981: 646.

population, the supply of skilled and technical workers is accordingly high. Many Egyptian graduates, however, leave for the USA, which is one of the most important recipients of Arab skilled workers (Table 8.6). Between 1962 and 1977, for example, it absorbed about 18,200 professional, technical and kindred workers from Arab countries, including 2,500 engineers, 3,700 medical professionals, and 1,100 natural scientists (Shaw 1981: 645).

The stated shortages in the oil-exporting countries will persist for the next decade because a sufficient number of people must first pass through the school system, a system which has not yet sufficiently expanded, largely because of difficulties in the quantity and quality of domestic teachers. Furthermore, the emigration of highly qualified labour out of the region – especially from oil-poor Arab countries – will continue to 'undermine efforts to integrate educational output with future manpower needs' (Shaw 1981: 647). Many of those who study abroad, often with a government scholarship or funding, do not return to their home country. The brain drain from the region is persistent and 'implies that "Arabisation" of the labour force is at least 10–20 years off' (Shaw 1981: 651). For the oil-exporting countries these circumstances mean a lasting dependence on expatriate non-Arab labour for which the demand will consequently increase. Its structure, which in turn will influence the structure of immigrants' nationalities, will be determined by the development priorities of the oil-exporting countries. As shown above, they put increasing emphasis on industrial development, education and health.

Although the labour-importing Gulf states display a growing tendency towards a policy of reducing the share of expatriate labour, the practical possibilities involved in implementing it are limited. The dependence on non-national labour will increase, almost regardless of changing economic conditions. Therefore, it becomes a matter of increasing concern to politicians and planners in the labour importing countries. Not only does economic development make expatriate labour indispensable, but illegal migration across the long and uncontrolled borders is easy, by land or by sea, the latter being the method preferred by Pakistanis. Saudi Arabia has the additional problem of millions of non-Saudi Muslims who come to Mecca each year, which is used as a port of entry by illegal labour migrants. Private employers often actively recruit within the group of *hajjis*. Furthermore, even if no more foreign workers enter the country, demographic development alone will ensure an increase in the size of certain migrant groups, thus reducing the governments' freedom of access towards foreign labour.

For all of these reasons, expatriate labour will continue to increase in importance, despite the wishes of Middle East governments. In the long term the South Asians who have settled in the oil-exporting countries will not be able to compete with highly qualified Arabs because almost nowhere in labour-importing countries are non-Arabs offered free schooling; only a few private schools were founded in Kuwait – some of them run by Indians and Pakistanis – which receive government subsidies. In the UAE, where the South and East Asian component of the work force is particularly large, non-Arabs constitute only 2% of the non-national student body. Although they are well integrated into the UAE labour force, those South Asian families which have their children with them did not have them enrolled in the school system by the mid-1970s (Serageldin *et al.* 1983: 6).

The preference for industrialisation through the construction of large industrial complexes also works against South Asians because private firms or state organisations in Pakistan, India and Bangladesh are not yet able or willing to set up package projects; hence they have no chance against East Asians, especially South Koreans, whose national enterprises offer ready solutions for the implementation of industrial projects. Furthermore, temporary package migration is much more suited to the Middle East's strategy of enforcing 'a fairly rapid turnover of foreign labour in order to ensure a skill profile compatible with the needs of a very rapidly changing economy' (La Porte 1984: 502). Today, the significance of East Asians in the Middle East lies not in conventional manpower exports but rather in contracts – and attendant exchanges, such as banks, loans, investments – that are being negotiated between corporations and governments in the Middle East (Ling 1984: 35). Although Korean and Taiwanese companies find it more difficult to implement package programmes with rising wage levels at home, they can still draw on cheap labour from the Philippines, Thailand, Indonesia and the Peoples' Republic of China, which is aggressively promoting labour export. China is also trying to engage in complete package contracts.

The new skills required do not favour South Asians. This is not necessarily the consequence of their educational level being too low to satisfy the new needs of the Middle East labour market. Pakistanis were overrepresented in the skilled professions in 1975, but in the course of time this has evened out (Serageldin *et al.* 1983) (Table 8.7). In the higher-skill categories, Jordanians are clearly overrepresented and it can be predicted that East Asians, too, will increase their share within this group. It is the new sectoral priorities which are obviously working against South Asian labour. Within the service sector there is a tendency to employ Arab nationals, particularly Egyptians, as administrators and in certain government-administered spheres such as education and health. Pakistanis, in contrast, are overrepresented in the construction sector, which is

Table 8.7. *Employment of Pakistanis and all non-nationals in the major labour-importing countries, 1975, 1985*

	All non-nationals				Pakistanis			
	1975		1985[a]		1975		1985[a]	
Occupational level	number (1,000s)	%	number (1,000s)	%	number (1,000s)	%	number (1,000s)	%
Professional and technical	1.5	0.8	12.8	2.4	49.3	3.1	158.8	4.5
Other professional	5.5	2.7	17.9	3.3	95.2	6.1	253.4	7.1
Sub-professional and technical	12.6	2.3	38.2	7.1	54.1	3.4	173.6	4.9
Other sub-professional	4.6	6.1	21.7	4.0	66.0	4.2	207.7	5.8
Skilled office and manual	68.3	33.2	140.1	25.9	268.4	17.1	609.2	17.2
Semi-skilled office and manual	32.6	15.8	87.0	16.1	301.1	19.2	653.7	18.4
Unskilled	80.4	39.1	223.6	41.3	736.7	46.9	1,491.9	42.1
Total	205.5	100.0	541.3	100.0	1,570.8	100.0	3,548.3	100.0

Note:
[a]Figures for 1985 are forecasts made in 1983. See note to Table 8.2.
Source: Serageldin *et al.* 1983: 51.

Table 8.7. *Employment of Pakistanis and all non-nationals in the major labour-importing countries, 1975, 1985*

| | All non-nationals | | | | Pakistanis | | | |
| | 1975 | | 1985[a] | | 1975 | | 1985[a] | |
Occupational level	number (1,000s)	%	number (1,000s)	%	number (1,000s)	%	number (1,000s)	%
Professional and technical	1.5	0.8	12.8	2.4	49.3	3.1	158.8	4.5
Other professional	5.5	2.7	17.9	3.3	95.2	6.1	253.4	7.1
Sub-professional and technical	12.6	2.3	38.2	7.1	54.1	3.4	173.6	4.9
Other sub-professional	4.6	6.1	21.7	4.0	66.0	4.2	207.7	5.8
Skilled office and manual	68.3	33.2	140.1	25.9	268.4	17.1	609.2	17.2
Semi-skilled office and manual	32.6	15.8	87.0	16.1	301.1	19.2	653.7	18.4
Unskilled	80.4	39.1	223.6	41.3	736.7	46.9	1,491.9	42.1
Total	205.5	100.0	541.3	100.0	1,570.8	100.0	3,548.3	100.0

Note:
[a]Figures for 1985 are forecasts made in 1983. See note to Table 8.2.
Source: Serageldin *et al.* 1983: 51.

Table 8.8. *Estimates of Indian immigrants (persons born in India) by occupational category; selected countries in developed and developing regions, 1981*

Region and country	Number of immigrants in labour force (1,000)	% in			
		Professional, technical, and kindred workers	Managers and administrators	Sales, clerical, craft, and operatives	Labourers and service workers
Developed regions					
United Kingdom	160.0	15.0	0.9	50.0	34.1
United States	94.0	77.4	6.5	11.7	4.4
Canada	46.0	52.6	5.0	34.8	7.6
Western Europe	37.0	75.4	6.2	11.4	7.0
Australia	16.0	77.5	6.2	11.9	4.4
Total	353.0	45.7	3.7	32.0	18.6
Developing regions					
Middle East	599.5	9.0	0.9	50.0	40.1
Malaysia	167.5	6.0	1.5	35.8	56.7
Singapore	25.0	8.0	2.0	40.0	50.0
Nigeria	9.0	55.5	0.0	11.1	33.3
Hong Kong	5.5	9.1	1.8	54.5	34.6
Total	806.5	8.9	1.0	46.4	43.7
Grand total	1,159.5	20.1	1.9	42.0	36.0

Source: Author's calculations with data from Madhavan, 1985: 465.

migrants, also, have a comparatively high number of dependants with them, but this seems to cause only minor social problems. The ethnic composition of the host countries is influenced by immigration policy: there is substantial change in the UAE, and Qatar, where most of the new immigrants are Asians, compared to Saudi Arabia, with its relatively large indigenous population and its preference for Arab workers.

For the individual worker who intends to migrate, possibilities of illegal migration also determine his prospects of employment, especially if the governments of potential host countries apply more rigid immigration policies, as is now the case in most labour-importing countries, particularly Saudi Arabia. This gives a comparative advantage to Pakistanis, who can enter the country illegally by sea. Furthermore, being Muslim, people from Pakistan, Bangladesh and to a certain extent, India, have the possibility of entering the country as *hajjis*.

Conclusion

Obviously, South Asian labour is hardly able to compete on an individual basis in the Middle East, where East Asian companies are taking over an increasing share of the market. A completely new strategy for South Asia would be the formation of companies which deal in package migration. It is, however, more than questionable whether they could successfully enter into competition with East Asian enterprises which are already well established in the Middle East and possess many years of experience. Only private Indian firms, which are supported by the government, seem to try to take up package contracts to any significant extent. In 1981, a conference on joint ventures and sub-contracting firms was held in New Delhi with the objective of replicating existing firms which have successful operations in the Middle East (Ling 1984: 35).

As wages in East Asia, especially in Korea and Taiwan, have risen substantially in recent years, the domestic labour force of these countries is, however, no longer cheap enough to be attractive for the Middle East. Consequently, Korean firms have to look for other sources of labour for their package programmes. There may be a chance for South Asian countries to stay in the market if they turn directly to Korean and other East Asian companies. Another possibility for South Asians is migration to Arab countries which have already sent a large part of their own labour to the Middle East, as, for example, Yemen and Jordan. Replacement migration of Pakistanis into Jordan is already subject to inter-governmental agreement.

In the foreseeable future labour export on a large scale will be increasingly difficult for South Asian countries. The prospects for emigration of unskilled workers and rural labourers, whose educational levels tends to compare poorly with inhabitants of urban areas, will worsen. The outlook is better for the few highly skilled and technical workers and professionals. Their emigration, however, involves high costs for the exporting countries, especially Pakistan and Bangladesh.

References

Abella, M.I. 1984. 'Labour migration from South and South-East Asia: some policy issues', *International Labor Review*, 123, 4: 492–506.
Addleton, J. 1984. 'The impact of international migration on economic development in Pakistan', *Asian Survey*, 24: 574–96.
Bangladesh Bureau of Statistics 1985. *Statistical Yearbook of Bangladesh 1984–85*, Dhaka.
Birks, J.S. and C.A. Sinclair 1980. *International Migration and Development in the Arab Region*, Geneva: International Labour Organisation.
Bundesstelle für Aussenhandelsinformation/NfA(k) 1985. *Kommentar zu Saudi-Arabiens Entwicklungsplan*, Bonn, 21 May.
1985. *Schwerpunkte in Saudi-Arabiens Fünfjahresplanung*, Bonn, 9 May.
1986. *Saudi-Arabien fördert Privatsektor*, Bonn, 18 February.
Gulati, L. 1986. 'The impact on the family of male migration to the Middle East: some evidence from Kerala', in *Asian Labor Migration*, ed. F. Arnold, Boulder, Colorado: 194–211.
International Labour Office 1985. *World Labour Report*, Geneva.
International Monetary Fund 1986. *International Financial Statistics*, Washington.
Kim, Kyong-Dong and Lee On-Jook 1983. 'Social psychological implications of international labour migration. The case of Korean workers in the Middle East and their families', Paper presented for the Conference on Asian Labour Migration to the Middle East, the East-West Center, University of Hawaii, Honolulu, 19–21 September, 1983.
Knerr, B. 1989 'The effects of international labour migration on the economic growth of Bangladesh', in *Work for Wages in South Asia*, ed. M. Holmström, New Delhi: Manohar Publications.
Ling, L.H.-M. 1984. 'East Asian migration to the Middle East – causes, consequences and considerations', *International Migration Review*, 18: 19–36.
La Porte, R. 1984. 'The ability of South and East Asia to meet the labour demands of the Middle East and North Africa', *The Middle East Journal*, 38, 4: 699–711.
Madhavan, M.C. 1985. 'Indian emigrants: numbers, characteristics, impact', *Population and Development Review*, 11, 3: 457–81.
Petroleum Economist (ed.) 1986. *World Energy Outlook to 2000*, London: Petroleum Press Bureau Ltd.
Raj, K.N. and M. Tharakan 1983. 'Agrarian reform in Kerala and its impact on the rural economy', in *Agrarian Reform in Contemporary Developing Countries*, ed. A.K. Ghose, New York: Croom Helm.
Schürmann, H.J. 1986. 'Entwicklungstendenzen in der Energieversorgung – ein aktueller Rückblick und ein offener Vorblick', in *Zeitschrift für Energiewirtschaft*, 4, 86: 235–49.

1985. 'Internationale Entwicklung', *Zeitschrift für Energiewirtschaft*, 3, 85.
Serageldin, I., St P Socknat, B.L. Birks, and C.A. Sinclair 1983. *Manpower and international migration in the Middle East and North Africa*, Oxford: World Bank.
Shaw, P.R. 1979. 'Migration and employment in the Arab World: construction as a key policy variable', *International Labour Review*, 118: 589–605.
    1981. 'Manpower and educational structure in the Arab World: an interim strategy', *World Development*, 9, 7: 637–55.
Sherbing, Maiem A. 1984. 'Expatriate labour flows to the Arab oil countries in the 1980s, *The Middle East Journal*, 38, 4.
Statistisches Bundesamt (ed.) 1985. *Statistik des Auslandes*, Vereinigte Arabische Emirate, Wiesbaden.
    1986. Indien, Wiesbaden.
    1986. Pakistan, Wiesbaden.
Tsakok, E. 1982. 'The export of manpower from Pakistan to the Middle East, 1975–1985', *World Development*, 10, 4: 319–25.
UN/ESCAP 1984. 'Remittances from international labour migration: a summary of findings and issues for labour-exporting developing countries of the ESCAP region', *Economic Bulletin for Asia and the Pacific*, 34, 2.
World Bank *World Development Reports*, Washington.
VIZ (ed.) *Vereinigung für Internationale Zusammenarbeit* 1985. Oman, Wiesbaden.
    1983. Vereinigte Arabische Emirate, Wiesbaden.
    1987. Indien, Wiesbaden.
    1987. Pakistan, Wiesbaden.

9

Asian Indians in the United States: a geographic appraisal

Surinder M. Bhardwaj and N. Madhusudana Rao

Spatial configuration of the 'Asian Indians' in the United States at different geographic scales, regional, metropolitan, and intra-metropolitan, shows that they are more evenly distributed than most other Asian ethnic groups. They do not seem to have formed ethnic neighbourhood clusters. This relatively distinctive geographic pattern has probably resulted from the confluence of a variety of factors.

Focus on the immigrants from India, as a component of the American 'ethnic mosaic', has sharpened only since the late 1970s due to their demand for and subsequent successful achievement of a distinct nomenclature: 'Asian Indians'. They were enumerated as an ethnic group for the first time in the 1980 US Census. Prior to the major policy changes in US immigration in 1965, most studies of Indian immigrants were concerned with the Punjabi settlers of California (Brown 1975, 1982; Tinker 1977). Increasing numbers of sociological studies related to the Asian Indians are being carried out in the wake of the immigration of Asians in general since 1965 (Saran and Eames 1980; Fisher 1980; Melendy 1977; Saran 1985).

Temporal aspect: an overview

Pre-1965 trend

From 1820, when a solitary Indian was admitted to the United States, through the next half a century, fewer than ten Asian Indians arrived per year on average (Chandrasekhar 1982: 87). This trickle of Indians, all told, amounted to fewer than 700 over a period of 80 years from 1820 to 1900. In fact, no Asian Indian was admitted to the United States between 1893 and 1898. During the early years of the twentieth century the number of Indian immigrants increased from a mere 9 in 1900 to over 1,000 in 1907. By 1910, this number was deemed alarming enough that the Asiatic Exclusion League and the American Federation of Labor began to brand the immigrant Indians variously as a 'Tide of Turbans', 'ragheads' and even a distinct 'menace' (Brown 1975: 88–9; 1982: 41). The Indian immigrants, irrespective of their religious affiliation, were defined by the generic term Hindu or Hindoo (Brown 1982: 41). Most (nearly 90%) of these Hindoos were from Punjabi Jat farming families, and belonged to the Sikh faith (Jensen 1980: 298). Many of these early Sikh immigrants worked on the Western Pacific Railroad and later moved into the rural areas of the Central Valley of California reasserting their agricultural tradition (Jensen 1980: 298). Scholarly interest in the Sikhs of California has intensified in recent years due partly to the visibility of the Asian Indians on the American scene (La Brack 1983; Gonzales Jr 1986), but also because of the turmoil in the Sikh heartland of Punjab and its national and even international implications (*India Abroad* 1987a).

The number of Asian immigrants to the United States gradually declined after 1910, reaching minuscule numbers during the 1930s and early 1940s. Even the number of students from India in American universities was small during this time (Shridharani 1941: 72).

Post-1965 trend

After the 1940s a slow, fluctuating, but upward immigration trend ensued for the next two decades to about 1965, when the repeal of the Immigration and Nationality Act of 1965 triggered a major upward surge, unequalled in the history of Asian Indian immigration to the United States (Immigration and Naturalization Service, Annual Reports, 1964–80). This act came as a boon to many of the professionally qualified Indians, because the first Commonwealth Immigrants Act, 1962, passed by the British parliament had restricted the entry of Indians to those who were able to obtain employment vouchers (Jones and Smith 1970; Allen 1971). The White Paper of 1965 further specified an annual maximum of 8,500 work vouchers (Tinker 1977). Concurrently, the United States, with its new immigration law based on the preferential treatment of highly trained professionals, attracted well qualified persons. The first, second, fourth and fifth preferences of the 1965 Immigration Act, which allots 74% of the country quotas to family unification, has further enhanced incentives to migrate to the United States.

Thus, whereas in 1965 fewer than 600 Asian Indian immigrants arrived in the United States, close to 10,000 came in 1970. These Asian Indians were only part of the broader trend in which the European immigrant rates greatly declined whereas the non-European rates of immigration jumped (Reimers 1981: 9–11). In the fiscal year 1984, admitted immigrants of Asian origin were four times those of European origin (Gardner *et al.* 1985: 10). Thus, Asian immigrants have increasingly become part of the

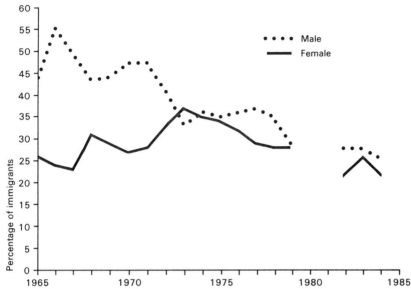

Figure 9.1   Indian immigrants by sex, 20–39 age group (comparable data for 1980 and 1981 not available)

'visible' US minorities; this visibility is shared by the Asian Indians as well. The number of Asian Indian immigrants per year is usually much smaller than Korean, Chinese and Filipinos. However, it reached as high as 97,484 during the 1976–80 quinquennial, and has fluctuated annually between about 15,000 and 22,000. In 1965 there were no more than 582 Asian Indians entering the United States, whereas 1980 recorded over 20,000. In one year they outnumbered the *total* before 1965 (US Bureau of the Census 1980). Most entering Indian immigrants were young males (Figure 9.1), but during 1972–6 females outnumbered them as the already admitted immigrant males began to bring in Indian brides.

The reasons for the Asian Indian immigration of the post-1965 era have had more to do probably with the American 'pull' than with the Indian 'push' factors. The kind of immigrants who came to the United States from India were not the poor and the wretched. Instead, they belonged to the educated, professional elite who, although Indian by the fact of birth, belonged to the various worldwide professional cultures. The American economy was in the process of unprecedented expansion as well as transformation. The race for technological supremacy was in full swing, demanding in its wake engineers, scientists and college teachers. The rapid expansion of the health industry during the 1960s needed a great number of physicians (CCME 1976). In fact, the broad spectrum transformation

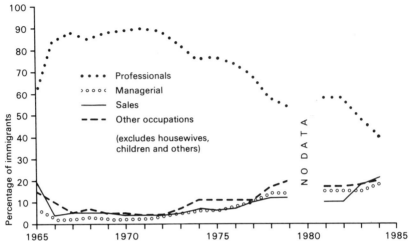

Figure 9.2   Asian Indian immigrants by occupation (comparable data for 1980 and 1981 not available)

of the American economy generated a powerful pull on the technological cultures of the developing world, India included. It helped skim, some allege drain, some of the most resourceful young professionals from India. Since Indian professionals had been trained in their respective fields through the medium of the English language (Krauter and Davis 1978: 93), their integration in the professional culture of the United States was relatively easy. In fact, many already westernised and urban immigrants may have been partial aliens in their own predominantly rural motherland. Owing to the built-in restrictions of the 1965 immigration laws, only the most talented and highly educated professionals could enter the United States. It is no surprise that between 1966 and 1973 well over 80% of Indian immigrants under occupational preference belonged to the category of 'professional, technical and kindred workers' (Figure 9.2), reaching a peak of 90% in 1971, but substantially declining since then. During the 1960s and early 1970s, Indian immigrants considerably outnumbered other nations in the professional category of engineers and medical graduates, natural and social scientists (Bhagwati and Dellalfer: 1976). Indians may still be the best educated of all immigrants, but their average level of education has been falling in recent years, due to their extensive use of the 'preference system' to bring to the United States their immediate, non-professional relatives (Bouvier and Gardner 1986: 23). Overall, the Indian immigrants after 1965 were very different in their occupational background compared to many earlier ethnic groups – European or Asian.

Table 9.1. *Relative regional concentration of America's Asian populations compared to total US population*

		Census Regions			
		Northeast	Northcentral	South	West
Relative regional concentration[a]		0.78	0.47	0.42	2.95
Chinese	%	26.80	9.20	11.30	52.70
	RRC	1.23	0.35	0.34	2.75
Filipino	%	9.90	10.40	11.00	68.80
	RRC	0.45	0.40	0.33	3.60
Japanese	%	6.50	6.50	6.60	80.30
	RRC	0.29	0.25	0.19	4.20
Korean	%	19.10	18.10	19.90	42.90
	RRC	0.88	0.69	0.59	2.24
Asian Indian	%	34.20	23.10	23.40	19.20
	RRC	1.57	0.88	0.70	0.99
Vietnamese	%	9.00	13.40	31.40	46.20
	RRC	0.41	0.51	0.94	2.42
1. Total US (%)		21.70	26.00	33.30	19.10
2. Total Asian (%)		17.10	12.30	14.20	56.40

Note: The phrase 'America's Asian Population' is used in this paper following Peter I. Rose, in preference to the more common phrase 'Asian Americans'.
[a]Relative regional concentration (RRC) is the ratio between the Asian group's percentage and the US percentages for the same region.
Source: US Department of Commerce, Bureau of the Census. Asian and Pacific Islander Population by State: 1980; Supplementary Report (P.C. 80-S1-12), December 1983.

Spatial distribution of Asian Indians

The spatial distribution of Asian Indians is examined at three levels: regional, metropolitan and intra-metropolitan. At the intra-metropolitan level some aspects of Asian Indian ethnicity are examined taking Akron SMSA (now MSA – Metropolitan Statistical Area) as an example. Comparisons with other Asian ethnic groups are made at the regional and metropolitan levels to point up the distinctive aspects of Asian Indians.

Regional

Considering the four US census regions, the Asian Indians are remarkably evenly distributed as compared to other Asian groups (Table 9.1). The highest census regional concentration of Asian Indians is in the Northeast (34.2%), whereas over 80% of the Japanese, about 69% of the

Filipinos, and over half of the Chinese are situated in the West. The Koreans and Vietnamese also show a clear gravitation toward the West, albeit less dramatically than the Japanese. The present comparatively balanced overall regional distribution of the Asian Indians appears somewhat anomalous when we recollect that, like the Chinese, Japanese and the Filipinos, the first important concentration of the Asian Indians, too, was in the West census region. Whereas the other Asian groups have continued to maintain a significant regional bias in favour of their initial concentration in the Western states, Asian Indians have broken the mould; or, more accurately, have developed a Northeast bias (Map 9.1).

This somewhat distinctive behaviour of the Asian Indians is probably due to the fact that the earliest Indian immigrants (mostly Sikhs) had their roots in one specific linguistic region of India. Asian Indians who emigrated after 1965 were, of course, from the various linguistic areas of India. Thus, the early Punjabi Sikh concentration in the Western United States was of marginal attraction to the vast majority of new immigrants – most of them from non-Punjabi areas. In addition, the post-1965 Asian Indians brought their professional occupational orientations to an America which was itself in the process of change from an industrial to a post-industrial service-dominant society. The lifestyle of the new immigrants had little in common with that of the early Indian community of California with its agrarian orientation, predominance of illiterate males, and willingness to get married to non-Indians, especially poor Hispanics (La Brack 1983: 222).

The regional distribution of Asian Indians may also be viewed in comparison to the total US population in each region (Table 9.1). The relative regional concentration of Asian Indians shows that they 'prefer' the Northeast more than the general population of the United States. It is also clear that all the Asian groups tend to avoid the South (census region) to a considerable degree. The Asian Indians, however (except the special case of the resettled Vietnamese refugees), come closest to being distributed proportionately to the US population in the South.

The relatively lower gravitation of the Asians to the South has, in fact, a precedent in the European migrations of the nineteenth and early twentieth century, which had also tended to avoid the South in general for economic and institutional reasons related to the southern agrarian and plantation way of life. The fact that the Asian Indian population is closer to the percentage of the US population in this region than to other Asian groups, in spite of this region's rather negative inter-racial image, is not clearly understood. Asian Indians who have moved to the South have done so probably in response to the newer industrial developments.

The distribution of Asian Indians on the basis of census regions masks

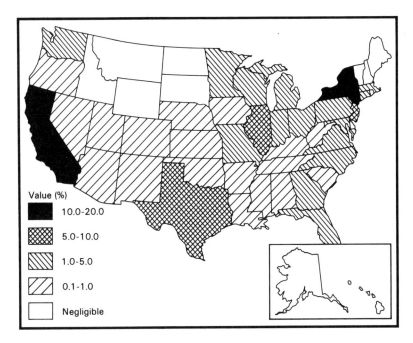

Map 9.1   Percent distribution of US Asian Indians, 1980

some geographic realities by ignoring the functional relationships of states and areas belonging to two different census regions. 'Megalopolis' is a case in point. The component states of the megalopolis, parts of which form this major functional urban region, account for almost 40% of the Asian Indian population in the United States. If three other related urban industrial states (Ohio, Michigan and Illinois) are added, the geographic region so formed has almost 60% of all the Asian Indians in the United States.

If, instead of the census region South, we consider the less urbanised, less industrialised states of the 'Inland South' (Alabama, Mississippi, Tennessee, Arkansas), the paucity of Asian Indian population there will immediately become noticeable. In the Asian Indian mind, these states are perceived as regions of racial prejudice, poverty and little opportunity. Thus, few Asian Indians are found in South Carolina, Alabama, Mississippi, Tennessee, Arkansas, Kentucky and West Virginia. However, southern states with opportunities in engineering, commerce, tourism, real estate, science and medicine have not been shunned by the Asian Indians. Such states include Texas, Georgia and Florida.

Whatever distinctive religious and political ideology and values the

Asian Indians might otherwise profess as symbols of their ethnic identity, one thing that stands out is their full participation in American material culture; they are driven by the same economic and social imperatives as the white American upper-middle class. Following the lifestyle and aspirations of this class, it should not come as a surprise if their spatial distribution is also similar to the general American population.

Metropolitan areas
Asian Indians, like other Asian American groups (such as the Chinese, Filipinos, Japanese, and Koreans) are preponderantly metropolitan. It is not a matter of coincidence that almost 70% of the Asian Indians live in the eight major industrial-urban states – New York, California, New Jersey, Texas, Pennsylvania, Michigan, Illinois and Ohio. As a group, they are much more concentrated into metropolitan areas than the general American population. This is to be expected because most are 'recent' immigrants and are employed in the industrial and service sectors of the economy. About 50% of all Asian Indians in the United States live in the top twelve standard metropolitan statistical areas (MSAs). In fact, about a third of the Asian Indians, according to the 1980 census, lived in only four MSAs – New York, Chicago, Los Angeles and Washington, DC (Table 9.2).

Although the states constituting the Pacific census division (Washington, Oregon and California) have over 17% of America's *Asian Indian* population, the latter form a small proportion of the *total Asian* population – usually 6% or less in the major metropolitan areas. The MSAs of the Mountain division have a somewhat higher component of Asian Indians than the West Coast MSAs. For example, Salt Lake City, Ogden, Denver and Phoenix had respectively 6.1%, 9.5% and 10.1% of their Asian populations comprised of Asian Indians. This somewhat higher proportion is not because of the larger absolute numbers of Asian Indians, but rather because other Asians gravitate more to the West Coast states. Over 80% of the Asian Indians of Colorado and Utah live in one MSA of each state, showing how closely their activities are linked with the major urban centres.

Moving eastwards toward the mid-section of the country (the West North Central, and West South Central divisions) the MSAs show a higher proportion of Asian Indians in the Asian populations, varying from about 10% in San Antonio to about 23% in the Houston MSA. High technology-related industry of the West North Central division and petroleum mining and refining industries of the West South Central division attracted many Indian scientists, engineers, technologists and health professionals. Decline in oil production and the depressed oil-

Table 9.2. *SMSAs with over 5,000 Asian Indians each (1980 Census)*

SMSA	Number	% of all Asian Indians in the US (N = 387,223)	Cumulative %
1 New York	55,815	14.41	14.41
2 Chicago	33,541	8.66	23.07
3 Los Angeles	18,770	4.85	27.92
4 Washington, DC	15,698	4.05	31.97
5 San Francisco	12.782	3.30	35.27
6 Houston	11,805	3.05	38.32
7 Philadelphia	10,951	2.83	41.15
8 Detroit	10,274	2.65	43.80
9 Newark	8,317	2.15	45.95
10 Nassau-Suffolk	5,868	1.52	47.47
11 Boston	5,864	1.52	48.99
12 Anaheim-Santa Ana	5.222	1.35	50.34
13 San Jose	5,187	1.34	51.68
14 Jersey City	5,127	1.32	53.00
15 Dallas-Fort Worth	5,095	1.32	54.32

Source: Calculated from 1980 US Census of Population:
(*a*) Supplementary Report PC80-S1-5, October, 1981 Standard Metropolitan Statistical Areas and Standard Consolidated Statistical Areas; Tables 1 and 4.
(*b*) General Social and Economic Characteristics, Part 1, United States Summary PC80-1-C1, December 1983, Tables 160 and 248.

related job market in the early 1980s, however, caused much unemployment among Indian engineers in the MSAs of this region. Outmigration, especially from Houston, was rather dramatic.

Major MSAs of the traditional American industrial heartland (Table 9.3) attracted Asian Indian engineers to the steel and automobile related engineering industries during the late 1960s and early 1970s. Increasing demand for health professionals by a dense and affluent population in this American Midwest resulted in the immigration of many physicians from India from 1965 to about 1975. These 'recent' Indian immigrants, with their professional orientation and ability to adapt through fluency in the English language, became established rather rapidly. Many have adjusted to life in this region's major cities in spite of the industrial problems of the last ten years, partly because of the nature of their occupations (e.g. physicians), but also by developing flexibility through acquiring additional degrees in business management or law. Had the Asian Indians been in the traditional 'blue-collar' occupations of this manufacturing

Table 9.3. *Asian Indians in the American Midwest, 1980*

SMSA (selected)	Asian Indians (number)	Asian Indians as % of Asian Americans
Chicago	33,541	23.7
Detroit	10,274	30.8
Cleveland	4,165	31.6
Pittsburgh	3,409	36.1
Buffalo	2,068	35.0
Columbus	1,497	21.5
Indianapolis	1,170	21.5
Akron	1,091	36.2
Toledo	1,015	29.7
Dayton	960	14.9

Source: same as Table 9.2.

belt, the effects of technological transformation on them could have been devastating. The economic diversity of the Midwest, and the adaptability of the Asian Indians, has prevented a massive outmigration, in contrast with areas with a limited or specialised economic base.

The MSAs of the Megalopolis, because of the great diversity of employment opportunities, including those for independent business, have been attractive to the Asian Indians. To many Asian Indians, New York symbolised America. It is not a coincidence that in 1980 there were over 55,000 Asian Indians in the New York MSA. By providing an early 'threshold' population for the Asian Indian community, New York MSA served as a major acculturating ground for later arrivals. It must be noted, however, that the proportion of Asian Indians among all Asians in the megalopolis area is significantly less than in the 'American Heartland', because of proportionately fewer opportunities in engineering-related fields, except in industrial cities such as Newark (where their proportion is higher).

The MSAs of the South have attracted Indians due to the same reasons as the industrial cities of the Midwest, in spite of the negative perception of the South in the Indian mind. Asian Indians formed a varying proportion of the total Asian American population from a low of 2.4% in Norfolk, Virginia Beach MSA, to a high of 43.8% in Charlotte-Gastonia MSA in North Carolina, with its high-technology industries. However, the absolute number of Asian Indians in the southern metropolitan areas was, and continues to remain, modest.

In general, the large and economically diversified MSAs, where building

Table 9.4. *Population in the centre city, selected MSAs, 1980*

MSA	% of respective group's total		
	White	Asian Indian	Black
Atlanta	9.1	15.0	56.7
Boston	15.6	17.3	78.7
Chicago	28.6	35.2	83.8
Houston	46.3	58.5	83.3
Los Angeles	35.8	40.5	53.5
New York	70.2	82.6	91.9
Philadelphia	26.5	32.1	72.3
San Francisco	22.5	24.7	62.8
Washington, DC	8.3	6.0	52.6

Source: Based on US Census, 1980.

activity or manufacturing was strong, attracted Indians because of their engineering and technical training. In addition, real estate and tourism, as in Miami, Florida, have been attractive to many Indians. According to a recent estimate in the *Wall Street Journal* (27 January 1987), 28% of the 53,629 motels (mostly small ones) in the United States were Indian owned – many by persons of Gujarati origin. In fact, there is a high correlation between Patels and Indian owned motels, to the extent that the *Times of India* carried an article with the catchy title 'No motel without a Patel' (Sharma 1984).

Overall, except for the metropolitan areas of the Far West, where the proportion of Asian Indians is small (Los Angeles 4.33%), they form over a fifth of the total Asian populations in the major MSAs of the nation (New York 29.6%, Chicago 23.7%, Houston 23%).

Intra-metropolitan distribution and the nature of Indian ethnicity
The distribution of Asian Indians within American metropolitan areas at present is in contrast to their encapsulation and experience of marginality in Britain (Robinson 1984). Jan Pillai's observation quoted in the *Wall Street Journal* (27 January 1987), that 'we've scattered all over; we don't have Indian towns', is more or less descriptive of the intra-metropolitan distribution pattern of Asian Indians, at least as the self-image of the majority of Asian Indians.

Contrast between the Asian Indians' intra-metropolitan distribution and that of the blacks (the most numerous minority) is clear enough (Table 9.4). Whites and Asian Indians form a closely comparable, and usually small, proportion of their respective populations in the central city segments of the major MSAs. Most of the Asian Indian population, as of the whites, is suburban.

The Asian Indian intra-metropolitan population distribution is more similar to that of the whites, even when compared to the other Asian ethnic groups, although most of these groups themselves have a population distribution that is dissimilar to the non-Asian minority groups (such as blacks, Puerto Ricans and Mexicans). In order to compare the overall intra-metropolitan distribution of the major Asian ethnic groups with the white population, an index of dissimilarity, D, was calculated, based upon the work of Duncan and Duncan (1955), following its use by Peach (1975), White (1986) and others. This is represented as:

$$D = \tfrac{1}{2} \sum_{i=1}^{I} \left| \frac{n_{ij}}{N_j} - \frac{n_{ik}}{N_k} \right|$$

Where i indexes cities
I = total number of cities
j = white population
k = individual Asian American ethnic groups
n_{ij} = number of white persons in a particular city i
N_j = total white population of all the cities
n_{ik} = number of Asian Americans in a particular city i
N_k = total Asian American population of all the cities.

Included in the analysis were all the twenty-two MSAs, each with a minimum population of 1,000 for each of the Asian ethnic groups. These groups were: Japanese, Chinese, Filipino, Korean, Asian Indian and Vietnamese. The value of the index of dissimilarity, D, ranges from zero to 100. The MSAs included were Anaheim, Atlanta, Baltimore, Boston, Chicago, Dallas, Denver, Detroit, Houston, Kansas City, Los Angeles, Minneapolis, New York, Philadelphia, Phoenix, Portland, Riverside, Sacramento, San Diego, San Francisco, San Jose and Washington DC.

The D values for the different Asian ethnic groups are shown in Table 9.5. Whether we take the central city or the non-central city population of the MSAs, the distribution of the Asian Indians comes closest to that of the white population compared to other Asian groups. This relationship is also shown graphically in the Lorenz Curves (Figure 9.3). Thus, the broadly held perception of Asian Indians regarding their dispersed spatial distribution has some basis in reality. There are some basic interrelated reasons for such a spatial distribution.

America's Asian Indians (unlike their countrymen in Britain), did not come in response to demand at the bottom end of the occupational

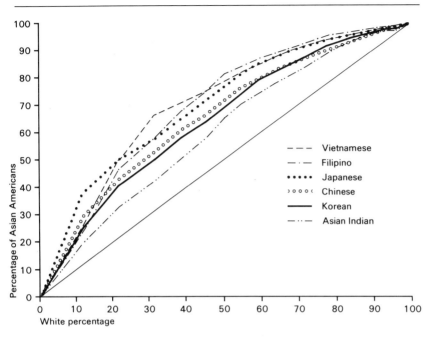

Figure 9.3   Lorenz Curves to show distributional relationship between whites and Asians and other selected US minorities (data for 22 selected MSAs)

structure (Peach 1984: 220; Robinson 1986). They came at a time when America badly needed already trained or rapidly trainable cohorts of scientists, engineers, teachers, health professionals and others, belonging to the general census category of managerial and professional speciality occupations. The hectic technological race in the United States had no time to wait until only homegrown cohorts would be ready to fill all the needed positions. In any case, this would be out of character with the American ethos of seeking instantaneous solutions. Due to the nature of their occupations and high income levels, most Asian Indians had a wide choice in locating themselves in the urban and suburban areas. This is generally in contrast to the South Asian Indian experience in Britain (Robinson: chapter 12). Their generally high levels of education and income prevented them from being pigeonholed into the ethnic social or spatial categories of an earlier era.

Americans, especially in the populous industrial Midwest and the dynamic Megalopolis, had little historical negativism about Asian Indians. Even California, with its earlier history of vociferous anti-Asian attitudes – and exclusionary legislation – had been transformed by the mid-1960s. Consequently, there was little overt racial prejudice that the

Table 9.5. *Index of dissimilarity with whites for 22 selected MSAs*

Ethnic group	Central city	Non-central city
Asian Indian	26.2	26.1
Chinese	38.8	43.3
Filipino	46.8	45.4
Japanese	46.7	48.0
Korean	30.1	29.0
Vietnamese	42.4	40.7

Asian Indians had to endure in their search for residential location. Combined with this is the fact that most Asian Indians were not competing for blue-collar jobs or for the very old housing stock (except as investment property). They were thus able to avoid the potential ire of the American working class, as well as avoiding a ghettoisation process.

The expanding US economy during the 1960s assured a vast and growing housing market away from the central cities. Coupled with this was the availability of home mortgages, at rates unheard of in India, and the invitingly small down payments. Any one with the painful experience (or aspiration) of home ownership in any major city in India would jump at the opportunity of home ownership in an American metropolitan area. Early home ownership for Asian Indians was tantamount to achieving a symbol of the good life. In addition, there appears to have been the transference of Indian status derived from the ownership of what, in India, is termed as 'immovable property'. The combination of American opportunity and Indian aspiration and values has meant a very high rate of home ownership in the suburban areas.

Whereas in Britain Indians were former subjects, in the United States there was no such perception by either the 'core culture' (Robinson 1984) or the immigrants. The lack of such hierarchical social categories also ultimately translated into the lack of evolution of similar spatial categories. Thus, spatial 'encapsulation and marginality' have not so far occurred on the American scene for Asian Indians due to external pressure from the majority.

There are some relative concentrations of Asian Indians within the metropolitan areas and some clearly avoided areas. Thus, Queens county, New York, has the single largest concentration of Asian Indians, proclaiming its Indianness in part by at least two major Hindu temples and a Sikh Gurdwara (temple). Raj Mathur's excellent (c. 1985) map of Asian Indians in Southern California clearly shows that they are rather widely distributed in Los Angeles and Orange counties, but have avoided areas such as Watts, Willowbrook and Vernon, all rather poor residential areas. The two largest concentrations of Asian Indians outside of San Diego (1,046) are in Hollywood (710) and Cerritos (973), and yet together, these two suburbs account for only 9% of the Asian Indian population of Los Angeles county. Thus ethnic ghettos or even ethnic neighbourhoods, where a majority of people is of Asian Indian origin, simply do not exist at present.

For Asian Indians spatial proximity to other Indians appears to be a lesser consideration than the desirability of a given residential area on other grounds – such as the value of home and the location of the area. Since the problems of 'acculturation' for the Asian Indians were relatively few, and dependence upon others for initial support was usually for a limited time, the need for, or desire to, form ethnic clusters seems to have been minimal. Some change in this situation may occur, however, as secondary, less educated and elderly relatives arrive sponsored by the primary immigrants. In addition, occasional recent acts of violence with strong ethnic overtones may cause a local Indian community to react by increased 'encapsulation' (*India Abroad* 1987b: 6).

Religion and Asian Indian ethnicity

An important reason for the lack of ethnic concentration or ethnic neighbourhood development of the Asian Indians in American cities may have to do with the very limited role of Hinduism as a religion. The majority of Asian Indians are Hindus, but Hinduism has a very different religious organisation from Christian denominations, Islam, or Sikhism. The various Christian churches played an important role among European immigrants during the nineteenth and early twentieth centuries in developing both religious and social networks which helped to ease the acculturation process (Abramson 1980: 869, 873). Much of this immigration, of course, occurred before suburbanisation in America turned into an urban explosion.

Hinduism has no church hierarchy comparable to Christian denominations, nor do Hindu sects generally play any significant non-religious function. In essence, Hinduism, even in an immigrant situation in the United States, remains to a great extent an individual-oriented rather than a congregational religion. In addition, unlike European ethnic groups, Hindus are characterised by great linguistic diversity. Thus, religion has not been able to help generate or foster Hindu ethnic neighbourhoods. Hindu temples are important as places in which to worship rather than as places from which the community is controlled, though Hindu temples have a significant influence in language-based ethnic identification

(Bhardwaj and Rao 1983). Hindu temples are symbols of an emergent ethnicity, but as yet lack the sophisticated institutional framework to spatially affect the Hindu population's reorientation or redistribution. In short, the fact that Hindu religious locus is still the home means that the ethnogenic influence of the temple on Hindus as a whole is very limited, resulting in a lack of strong intra-metropolitan spatial concentration.

Thus, historical, socio-economic and religious aspects have all collectively contributed toward an absence of ethnic neighborhood clustering by the Hindus from India. However, a significant exception is the clustering of Indian owned stores in some of the major metropolitan communities such as New York and Chicago. Such shopping enterprises can be successful on the basis of rather large Indian population thresholds, in cities like New York, Chicago, Los Angeles and San Francisco (and Toronto and Vancouver, in Canada). Elsewhere, Indian-owned stores can hardly depend on the Indian community alone for their survival as business enterprises. Thus, a business clustering that could serve as the nucleus of residential clustering has also not generally materialised, with the exception of a Flushing (New York) or a Girard Street (Toronto). Since the occupational composition of the Indian community is changing, there may, in the future, be a growth of residential-cum-business agglomerations of Asian Indians in the large cities.

Diversity and ethnicity

The 'Asian Indians', though apparently homogeneous to the outsiders, are, in fact, internally highly diversified in terms of region of origin, religion and language. Such diversity is clearly expressed at the intra-metropolitan level, even in a medium-sized MSA such as Akron (Ohio). Some idea of the internal diversity of the Asian Indians can be obtained by examining the state of origin information in the 'Directory of India Community' in the Akron MSA (Table 9.6). Maharashtra and Gujarat together accounted for about 37% of the Asian Indian families in the Akron MSA, though these two states make up only about 14% of India's population. On the other hand, only 8.7% of the Asian Indian families were from UP and Bihar, the two most populous Hindi-speaking states which together form over 26% of India's population. Punjab and the Union Territory of Delhi are greatly 'over represented' in the Akron MSA population. Asian Indians from the four Dravidian-language speaking states (Andhra, Karnataka, Kerala and Tamilnadu) make up a somewhat larger proportion (26.6) of the total Asian Indians in Akron than they do in respect to the total (23.9) population of India. In general, it

Table 9.6. *Akron area: origin of Asian Indians*

State of origin	Number[a]	%
1 Maharashtra	47	22.8
2 Gujarat	29	14.1
3 Tamilnadu	24	11.6
4 Punjab	21	10.2
5 Karnataka	14	6.8
6 West Bengal	14	6.8
7 Andhra Pradesh	11	5.3
8 Uttar Pradesh	11	5.3
9 Delhi	9	4.3
10 Bihar	7	3.4
11 Kerala	6	2.9
12 Other state or country[b]	13	6.3

Notes:
[a]Eleven entries in the *Directory of Indian Community* did not indicate place of origin.
[b]Includes Madhya Pradesh (3), Rajasthan (3), Kashmir (2), one each for Sind, Guyana, Laos, Assam and Sri Lanka.
Source: *Directory of Indian Community* (Akron: India Community Center Committee, 1984)

appears that India's states with low levels of literacy are also the ones from which fewer people migrated to the United States.

The India Community Directory of Akron also provided information about the city of origin of the Asian Indians. Bombay alone accounted for about 19% of the listings. Six large cities of India (Bombay, Madras, Calcutta, Delhi, Bangalore and Hyderabad) made up almost 44% of the listings. This high proportion from so few cities is at least partly due to the location of the US embassy at New Delhi and the consulates at Bombay, Calcutta and Madras. Caution must be exercised in interpreting these data, since people who listed their origin as a large metropolitan area such as Bombay could linguistically be Sindhi, Punjabi, or from the southern states of India. One conclusion is inescapable, namely, the process of migration to the United States, since the mid-1960s brought from India mostly those people who already had urban backgrounds, quite unlike Helweg's (1979: 22) 'Jandialians', who went 'phoren' (Indians who went foreign) to England, or the California Punjabis of the 1900s. Tottathil and Saran's (1980) sample of 194 respondents from the New York metropolitan area showed 73% came from an urban background. In Bhardwaj's (1982) study of the Shri Venkateswara Temple's pilgrims, over 77% of the respondents indicated a major Indian city as their place of origin.

The lack of Asian Indian spatial concentrations discussed earlier and their diversity in the United States should not convey the impression that ethnic identity is not developing at all. When (or where) the population of Asian Indians was small, the binding factor for Indians of diverse regional and linguistic origin was Indian nationality. In other words 'fusion' was probably the dominant ethnogenetic motif at such a stage. However, with increasing populations from the many distinct regions of India, thresholds have been reached for regrouping on the basis of language, regional religious symbolism, and even strong regional social categories. Thus, with increasing population, we observe a process of 'fission' as an ethnogenetic motif. Simultaneously, there is the official recognition of a nationwide 'Asian Indian' ethnic identity. The process of Asian Indian identity formation is thus proceeding apace at several levels; at some levels 'fusion' and at others 'fission' appears to be dominant. The internal diversity of the Asian Indians makes it hard for language-based regional groups to form at smaller localities, but it also makes a true Indian ethnicity difficult to develop. In the larger cities, however, regional/ linguistic associations are already active.

It is not as yet clear whether the many regional populations from India will, in the long run, de-emphasize their Indianness in favour of their linguistic or religious identity, leading to distinct ethnic identities in the United States. Some groups, notably the Sikhs and to a lesser extent the Tamils, Gujaratis and Bengalis, have, through their various associations, expressed a tendency toward religious and/or linguistic regional and cultural consciousness. How far this process might go is not clear, but it will be surprising if it did not significantly and persistently intensify. Such a process will, no doubt, be affected by what happens on the Indian political scene, because the Indian overseas populations of today are not as isolated from their original homeland as were the nineteenth-century indentured Indian labourers. For many, otherwise widely separated Asian Indians in the United States, the high technology of today provides instant linkage, especially in the large metropolitan areas where most of them live. In modern information culture, spatial non-proximity is less consequential for many types of interaction. The development of ethnogenetic linkage among Asian Indians (including the regional groups) does not require the same conditions of spatial proximity which obtained in the America of the early twentieth century. Annual conferences of some of the more culturally conscious linguistic populations indicate efforts at ethnic articulation.

In several of the major American cities, the Hindu temples exhibit a clear distinction between the Northern and Southern Indian cultural tradition, symbolised by their distinctive architecture, deities, mode of worship, languages, and even the organisational style of temple management. Where an accommodation has been reached between the local Northern and Southern Indian religious communities, the temple microspace clearly shows such signs. There are several other ways in which ethnogenesis is taking place, but those processes, such as intermarriage, social interaction (or lack thereof) between Americans and Asian Indians, and even between various Asian–Indian groups themselves, is beyond the scope of this chapter. Within the very diversity of the Asian Indian population lie the seeds of future ethnic formation. Whether that will result in spatial-ethnic concentrations within the metropolitan areas is an open question. Social rather than spatial 'encapsulation' is more likely – if at all – to develop at the intra-metropolitan level. Up to the present, the prominent attributes of the Asian Indians, and the economy and society of which they have become an integral part, militate against the development of their ethnic spatial clustering. Other spatial configurations are of course possible, if economic and political changes occur.

Envoi

It is difficult to escape the general conclusion that whatever the geographic scale – regional, metropolitan or intra-metropolitan – the Asian Indians (except for their 'visibility') are closer to the spatial categories of the American middle class than to groups subjected to any internal or exogenous restrictions. This spatial configuration has resulted from the confluence of many factors, some peculiar to the American ethos and the socio-technological state of the American system, and some specific to the highly selective immigration process which produces Indian immigrants of selected occupational categories. The nature of the time, the place and the interaction between a dynamic America and an equally eager Asian Indian community, have all resulted in a rather happy spatial and social configuration so far, certainly for the Asian Indians.

Cognizant of the fact that the future could be different, the Asian Indians are deeply concerned about the next generation – the American born, culturally American children who may not follow the narrow professional orientation, and even the mother tongue, of their parents. It is inevitable that the demographic and socio-economic profiles of Asian Indians will change in time. Will these changes mean a radical transformation of the present spatial configuration? Probably not in the near future, but it appears that language and religion will eventually become more not less important as symbols of Indian or other identities that are likely to emerge.

References

Abramson, H.J. 1980. 'Religion', in *Harvard Encyclopedia of American Ethnic Groups*, eds. S. Thernstrom, A. Orlov, and O. Handlin, Cambridge: Harvard University Press, 869–75.

Allen, Sheila 1971. *New Minorities, Old Conflicts: Asia and West Indian Migrants in Britain*, New York: Harper and Row.

Bhagwati, J.N. and W. Dellalfar 1976. 'The brain drain and income taxation: the United States', in *Taxing the Brain Drain: A Proposal*, ed. J.N. Bhagwati and M. Partington, Amsterdam: North-Holland Publishing Company.

Bhardwaj, S.M. 1982. Unpublished survey data on the visitors to the Sri Venkateswara Temple, Monroeville, Pittsburgh, Pennsylvania.

Bhardwaj, S.M. and N.M. Rao 1983. 'Religious reknitting of ethnic Hindus in the "New World"'. A Paper presented at the 79th Annual Meeting of the Association of American Geographers, Colorado (USA): Denver, 24–27 April 1983.

Bouvier, L.F. and R.W. Gardner 1986. 'Immigration to the U.S.: the unfinished story', *Population Bulletin*, 41, 4: 1–51.

Brown, Emily C. 1975. *Har Dayal: Hindu Revolutionary and Rationalist*, Tucson: The University of Arizona Press.

   1982. 'Revolution in India: Made in America', in *From India to America*, ed. S. Chandrasekhar, La Jolla: Population Review Publications, 41–7.

Coordinating Council on Medical Education 1976. 'Physician manpower and distribution; the role of the foreign medical graduate', *JAMA*, 236, 26: 3049–55.

Chandrasekhar, S. 1982. 'Some Statistics on Asian Indian Immigration to the United States of America', in *From India to America*, ed. S. Chandrasekhar, La Jolla: Population Review Publications, 86–92.

Duncan, O.D. and Duncan, B. 1955. 'A methodological analysis of segregation indexes', *American Sociological Review*, 20, 2: 210–17.

Fisher, M.P. 1980. *The Indians of New York City*, Columbia, Mo.: South Asia Books.

Gardner, R.W., B. Robey and P.C. Smith 1985. *Asian Americans Growth, Change, and Diversity*, Washington DC: Population Reference Bureau.

Gonzales Jr, J.L. 1986. 'Asian Indian immigration patterns: the origins of the Sikh community in California', *International Migration Review*, 20, 1: 40–54.

Helweg, A.W. 1979. *Sikhs in England: The Development of a Migrant Community*, New Delhi: Oxford University Press.

India Abroad 1987a. 'Sikhs of Yuba city', B. Vora. *India Abroad*, 27 February.

India Abroad 1987b. 'New ethnic coalition to fight racism', *India Abroad*, 4 December.

Immigration and Naturalization Service 1964–80. Annual Reports.

Jensen, J.M. 1980. 'East Indians', in *Harvard Encyclopedia of American Ethnic Groups*, ed. S. Thernstrom, A. Orlov and O. Handlin, Cambridge: Harvard University Press, 296–301.

Jones, K. and A.D. Smith 1970. *The Economic Impact of Commonwealth Immigration*, Cambridge University Press.

Krauter, J.F. and M. Davis 1978. *Minority Canadians: Ethnic Groups*, Toronto: Methuen.

La Brack, B. 1983. 'The reconstitution of Sikh Society in rural California', in

Overseas Indians: a study in adaptation, ed. G. Kurian and R.P. Srivastava, New Delhi: Vikas, 215–40.

Mathur, R. 1985. 'Asian Indians in Southern California' (map only). Diamond Bar (California): Cultural Map Service.

Melendy, H.B. 1977. *Asians in America: Filipinos, Koreans, and East Indians*, Boston: Twayne Publishers.

Peach, C. (ed.) 1975. *Urban Social Segregation*, London: Longman.

1984. 'The force of West Indian Island Identity in Britain' in *Geography and Ethnic Pluralism*, ed. C. Clarke, D. Ley and C. Peach, London: Allen and Unwin, 214–30.

Reimers, D.M. 1981. 'Post-World War II immigration to the United States: America's latest newcomers', *Annals, American Academy of Political and Social Sciences*, 454: 1–12.

Robinson, V. 1984. 'Asians in Britain: a study in encapsulation and marginality', in *Geography and Ethnic Pluralism*, ed., C. Clarke, D. Ley and C. Peach, London: Allen and Unwin, 231–57.

1986. *Transients, Settlers and Refugees: Asians in Britain*, Oxford: Clarendon Press.

Rose, P.I. 1985. 'Asian Americans from pariahs to paragons', in *Clamor at the Gates*, ed. N. Glazer, San Francisco: Institute for Comparative Studies Press, 181–212.

Saran, P. 1985. *The Asian Indian Experience in the United States*, Cambridge, Mass.: Schenkman Publishing Company, Inc.

Saran, P. and Eames, E. (eds.) 1980. *The New Ethnics: Asian Indians in the United States*, New York: Praeger Publishers.

Sharma, D.R. 1984. 'No motel without a Patel', in *Times of India (Sunday Review)*, 6 May, section IV, 3–8.

Shridharani, K. 1941. *My India, My America*, New York: Duell, Sloan and Pearce.

Thottathil, P.A. and P. Saran 1980. 'An economic profile of Asian Indians', in *The New ethnics*, ed. P. Saran and E. Eames, New York: Praeger Publishers.

Tinker, Hugh 1977. *The Banyan tree: Overseas Emigrants from India, Pakistan and Bangladesh*, London: Oxford University Press.

US Bureau of the Census 1964–1977. *Immigration and Naturalization Service: Annual Reports*, Washington DC: US Department of Justice.

1978 to 1984. *Statistical Year Book of the Immigration and Naturalization Service*, Washington DC: US Department of Justice.

1980. *Statistical Abstract of the United States: 1980*, Washington DC.

1981. *1980 Census of Population, Standard Metropolitan Statistical Areas and Standard Consolidated Statistical Areas: 1980*, (PC80-S1-5), Washington DC: Superintendent of Documents.

1983. *Census of Population, Asian and Pacific Islander: population by states, 1980*, (PC80-S1-12), Washington DC: Superintendent of Documents.

US Bureau of the Census, Department of Commerce (1983), *General Social and Economic Characteristics, Part 1, United States Summary*, (PC80-1-cl), Washington DC: Superintendent of Documents.

The Wall Street Journal 1987. Tuesday, 27 January.

White, Michael J. 1986. 'Segregation and Diversity Measures in Population Distribution', *Population Index*, 52, 2: 198–221.

10

Migration and kinship: the differential effect of marriage rules on the processes of Punjabi migration to Britain

Roger Ballard

Now that Britain's South Asian population has grown to include well over a million people, it has become dangerously misleading to regard all its members as forming a single homogeneous social group. To be sure, all Britons of Indian, Pakistani and Bangladeshi descent have something in common. On the one hand, they all share – thanks to the routine use of skin colour as a social marker by their white fellow citizens – the experience of racial exclusion; and on the other, they also share certain cultural commonalities, especially in domestic contexts. Varied and changing though their personal lifestyles may be, their preferences are still inspired at least as much by their roots in the sub-continent as by their more local, British, experience. Yet even though 'Asians' may consequently appear to constitute – at least from the outside – a more or less distinctive social category in Britain's increasingly polyethnic society, it does not follow that it is appropriate to regard them all as belonging to a single community.

Firstly, these broad commonalities are but rarely used as vehicles for corporate action: real communities are invariably much more restrictively organised. This is hardly surprising. Even though they share common origins in the sub-continent, South Asian settlers in Britain are of diverse regional, linguistic, religious, caste and class origins; and it was around these specificities – reinforced by the even more tightly parochial loyalties of kinship – that networks of social solidarity and mutual support were, and continue to be, constructed. So, even when large numbers of people of South Asian origin live in a particular area, it does not follow that they will necessarily form a single monolithic community. On the contrary, most such settlements include a multiplicity of caste and kin-based networks, whose members in turn compete almost as much as they cooperate. Moreover, most such networks are relatively small: few include more than a few score households, even in the midst of settlements many thousands strong.

Where such networks are composed of people of similar backgrounds – in two neighbouring villages, for example – the differences between them will usually be comparatively small, especially if everyone has adapted to life in Britain in very similar ways; so, even though members of rival networks may *feel* themselves to differ, their structural position in the wider social order may actually be virtually identical. But that is by no means always so. Since those of differing origins – whether by caste, class, region or previous migratory experience – brought with them varying sets of skills, goals and competences, the survival strategies which they have devised to cope with their new and largely hostile environment are by no means always identical. Quite the contrary. As it becomes increasingly obvious that settlers of differing backgrounds are following varied, and often sharply contrasting, social trajectories, so it is becoming steadily more difficult, and indeed increasingly inappropriate, to make generalisations which are valid for all 'Asians' in Britain.

How, though, can the source and significance of these variations best be explored? So great is their number, and so wide the differences in outcome – as, for instance, between wealthy East African Patidars in Leicester, and poverty-stricken Sylhetis in Tower Hamlets – that a comprehensive analysis of all dimensions of difference is way beyond the scope of a single chapter. So, to keep the number of variables to a more manageable level, I have opted, instead, for a comparative approach, restricting my attention here to just two groups: to Sikh Jullunduris on the one hand, and to Muslim Mirpuris on the other.[1]

An analysis which focuses so exclusively on these two very specific groups – originating as they do in two small districts in the broad sweep of the sub-continent – might seem, at first sight, to be of very limited interest and significance. But this is most misleading; not only are at least two-thirds, and possibly as many as three-quarters of all British South Asians of Punjabi origin, but the great majority of British Punjabis can in turn trace their roots (in approximately equal numbers) either to the Jullundur Doab in India, or to Mirpur District in Azad (Pakistani-held) Kashmir (see map 10.1); indeed as many as three-quarters of British Punjabis may well be either Jullunduris or Mirpuris.[2] Given their very large proportional presence, together with the complex patterns of similarity and difference between them, it follows that a detailed comparative analysis is not only extremely illuminating, but of *general* significance to all those concerned with the implications of the South Asian presence in Britain.

Map 10.1   The Punjab

The Punjabi presence in Britain

The similarities between Jullunduris and Mirpuris are obvious enough. Not only were the majority of migrants from both areas drawn from small peasant farming families, but they all shared – as Punjabis – strong cultural, social and linguistic commonalities. But there were major differences, too. In terms of religious affiliation, Mirpuris are virtually all Moslem, while British Jullunduris are predominantly, although by no means exclusively, Sikh; more prosaically, Jullundur's local economy is, and long has been, in much better shape than Mirpur's. What relationship, though, might all this have to the equally complex patterns of similarity and difference in the trajectories which members of the two groups have followed since arrival?

Although the very earliest pioneers found their way to Britain by different routes – Jullunduris as pedlars during the 1930s (Ballard and Ballard 1977), and Mirpuris as stranded merchant seamen (Dahya 1974) – both were drawn into industrial jobs during the Second World War. Following the close of hostilities many stayed on; and it was these pioneers who, when the postwar boom and its accompanying labour shortages took off, were able to act as bridgeheads for the mass inflow which followed. To be sure, the only jobs available were those which the native English would not take, usually because they were hot, hard, heavy and relatively low-paid. But to young men from peasant farming families in both Jullundur and Mirpur they offered an opportunity to make money more quickly than had ever been possible before. So, once channels of communication were open, chain migration – where relatives called over relatives, who in turn called over *their* relatives – soon took off. Large numbers of Jullunduris and Mirpuris began to find their way to Britain.[3]

Migrants from both areas set out with much the same objectives: to earn and save as much money as possible as quickly as possible before returning home. Most, in fact, stayed on for much longer than they originally intended, but all encountered similar obstacles. Whatever their prior skills and qualifications, they only had access to the jobs which the white natives did not want. In struggling to establish themselves in their new environment, all faced similar structures of constraint: routine racial discrimination, the introduction of racially biased and ever more restrictive immigration laws, and finally, the collapse, in the late seventies, of the textile and heavy engineering industries in which so many of them originally came to work. Yet their responses to these experiences have differed markedly.

Patterns of family reunion

One of the most salient contradictions encountered by all long-distance labour migrants is that between the emotional imperatives of family relationships and the financial imperatives arising from their position in the labour market. Hence, Punjabi migrants in Britain were by no means unique in finding that, although their principal aim was to improve the material welfare of their families, fulfilling that goal simultaneously cut them off from their nearest and dearest; nor in finding that, despite all the pain of separation, the temptation continually to postpone their return in order to earn and save still more was yet more powerful still. The migrants' dilemma was clear: their emotional commitment to their families stood in stark contradiction to their growing economic dependence on the British labour market.

Even though members of both groups faced the same dilemma, they coped with it in different ways. The Sikhs chose family reunion. By the late 1950s Sikh women began to join their husbands in Britain, and a few years later this became routine. So, although Sikh men continued to come to Britain in search of work until they were stopped by changes in the immigration rules in the mid-sixties, by then few waited for much longer than a year or so – during which they paid off outstanding debts and saved enough to buy and furnish a small terraced house – before calling their wives and children to join them.

By contrast, most Mirpuris opted to become international commuters. The typical pattern was for a man to work in Britain for several years before making an extended visit back home, taking his accumulated savings with him, before returning to work in Britain once again. This cycle was often repeated several times over. It was not until the early seventies that Mirpuri women began to join their husbands overseas, and only at the end of the decade did this become routine. In consequence there are, at present, substantial differences in the demographic character of the two communities. Since most Sikh families were reunited the best part of two decades ago, a British-born second generation has now reached adulthood; British-born Mirpuris are, by contrast, only just beginning to leave school.

Patterns of upward mobility

Although the Mirpuris are only just beginning to enter a terrain which has long since been occupied by the Sikhs, it is quite wrong to assume that they will necessarily follow the same social trajectory as their predecessors: indeed, the differences between them, even allowing for the delay, have now become almost as striking as the commonalities. While the majority of Sikhs can now be described as having become broadly middle class in their lifestyles and aspirations,[4] the Mirpuris have, as yet, been much less successful; the two groups thus currently find themselves standing in very different positions in the social order.

Most saliently, the overwhelming majority of Mirpuris continued to work in semi- and unskilled positions in heavy engineering and textiles right up to the end of the seventies. As a result they were disproportionately vulnerable to the impact of the recession of the late seventies, for it was precisely those industrial sectors in which they were overwhelmingly concentrated that were most severely hit. In the last few years well over half of all middle-aged Mirpuri men have lost their jobs, and many are still unemployed. Most Sikhs have, by contrast, survived the eighties in much better shape. While those still working in the more vulnerable industrial sectors could not escape redundancy, by the time the recession struck many had moved up into more secure and better paid jobs, often as craftsmen and technicians, in more prosperous and more buoyant sections of the labour market; meanwhile, a significant minority had opted out of waged labour completely, and started their own businesses instead.[5]

However, this shift towards small business and self-employment among South Asians was by no means solely a result of the recession, even though it certainly made the option more attractive. As the early pioneers had long since discovered, while Britain's white natives might routinely discriminate against them in the employment market, it was still possible to make a living – and potentially a much more profitable living – in the marketplace proper. Provided that they could offer sought-after goods and services at a keen price, as well as at the right place and time, white people would buy, regardless of the colour of the seller's skin. Taking advantage of this chink in the armour of racism, many of the earliest pioneers became pedlars, selling clothes from door to door. Since then, the size and scope of Punjabi business enterprises have grown by leaps and bounds: apart from ubiquitous corner groceries, these now include taxi services and restaurants, post offices and supermarkets, as well as garages, clothing manufacturers and building contractors. And because it offers an opportunity partially to circumvent the worst effects of racial discrimination, itself made sharper by the recession, starting a business has become an increasingly attractive option.

Even though Mirpuris as well as Sikhs have opted for self-employment in ever-growing numbers, there are still marked differences between them: Sikh businesses tend to be a great deal larger, and thus much more profitable. The same is true in the housing market, where many, if not all, Sikh families have now sold – often to Mirpuri buyers – the cheap inner-city terraced houses in which they originally settled, and have moved on into suburban semis. The most successful of all are eagerly buying even more expensive detached houses in the outer suburbs. Meanwhile, in the educational sphere Sikh children's levels of academic achievement are now akin to those of the indigenous middle class (Ballard and Vellins 1984; Ballard and Driver 1979).

British Mirpuris present a very different picture. Though no less ambitious for themselves and their children than their Sikh counterparts, they have generally achieved much less in the way of occupational, residential and educational mobility, not least because the niche in the employment market on which they had come to rely collapsed at just the time when they were facing the heavy additional expense of family reunion. Very few have been able to emulate their Sikh counterparts by moving upwards and outwards, with the result that in residential terms they are still overwhelmingly concentrated in under-resourced inner-city areas. In broad terms Mirpuris are very much more 'deprived' than Sikhs.

How are these increasingly salient differences in patterns of employment, residence and educational achievement, as well as in the speed of family reunion, best accounted for? Is it that Mirpuris are in some way more parochially minded, and hence more 'traditionalist' than their Jullunduri Sikh counterparts? Or is it that these differences are better understood as a product of differences in the material conditions which they experienced prior to emigration? As I have argued elsewhere (Ballard 1983a, 1986, 1987) the latter perspective, which seeks to relate these differences to the widely differing economic and political histories of the two areas, has much to recommend it. Let me summarise.

Prosperous Jullundur . . .

Economically the Jullundur Doab has a great deal going for it. Located in a fertile and easily irrigable part of the Punjab plain, its population, even in rural areas, has long enjoyed access to a well developed system of infrastructural resources: a network of roads, railways and irrigation canals, as well as of schools and basic health care facilities, was laid down during a century of British rule. Since Independence in 1947 the infrastructure has been extended yet further, and East Punjab has become a by-word for rural prosperity. And although Sikhs – who dominate Punjab socially and politically, even though they only form a bare majority of the state's population – often assert that this prosperity is primarily an outcome of their own energy and entrepreneurial commitment, there is little evidence that they have a monopoly of these qualities.

On the contrary, they are characteristic of *every* section of Punjab's population, regardless of religious affiliation.

Material factors provide a better foundation for the explanation of Punjab's economic growth. Thanks to relatively high agricultural prices, as well as the (post-Independence) Government of India's policy of protecting indigenous manufacturers, both Hindu and Sikh Punjabis (all Moslems in the region having fled to Pakistan) were fortunate to find themselves in an environment in which an extremely effective and profitable symbiosis between industrial and agricultural growth has taken place. Not only has Punjab become India's richest state, but Jullundur is one of its most affluent Districts. And so far, at least, it has remained so, despite the severe tensions that have been associated with the recent rise in Sikh militancy and state repression.

... and stagnating Mirpur

Mirpur has been much less fortunate. Located in an area of low hills just above the plains proper, it enjoys a higher annual rainfall than Jullundur, but is much more densely populated per cultivable acre. In the past its broken terrain provided some shelter from marauding invaders, but today that is only a hindrance. Communications are poor, and although the land is fertile, irrigation is difficult: despite its location in a bowl between the Jhelum and Poonch rivers, virtually all agriculture in Mirpur was and remains *barani* or rain-fed. Historically the District was severely disadvantaged by its incorporation into the Maharaja of Kashmir's notoriously exploitative kingdom. Not only were his subjects more heavily taxed than their directly ruled neighbours in British India, but infrastructural investment was minimal. In 1947 there were no metalled roads, and only two high schools in the whole District; and in the war which followed (for Kashmir was disputed territory) its two most important *qasbahs* (they were hardly towns) were bombed by the Indian air force, while the small local bourgeoisie (who were overwhelmingly Sikh and Hindu) fled to India. Nor has the District fared much better since then. Nationally, Pakistan has been far less successful than India in identifying a secure path to economic growth; and the more deeply it has slipped into dependency, the more its rural economies, especially in areas of heavy overseas migration, have stagnated. To cap it all, much of Mirpur's most fertile land has disappeared beneath the waters of the Mangla Dam, a huge power and irrigation project which was completed in 1966. As in so many other such projects, the dam has brought many benefits to the people living downstream in Pakistani Punjab, while those living upstream in Mirpur have had to bear the brunt of its environmental costs.

Jullunduris and Mirpuris in Britain

Given these wide ranging differences, it is hardly surprising that Jullunduri settlers should have been more swiftly upwardly mobile than their Mirpuri counterparts. Thanks to the greater prosperity of their home villages, Jullunduris were much more likely to possess marketable craft and business skills, and also to be literate at least in Punjabi, and sometimes in English too. Indeed a small but very significant section of the Sikh inflow were college graduates. Their higher levels of skill and education have proved invaluable in the struggle to obtain better jobs, while even in less well educated families the success of others in the kinship network has provided both a goal and a role model, as well as an understanding of the kind of support and encouragement that their children would need if they were to force their way upward through the educational system. But given the relative economic backwardness of Azad Kashmir, these skills and understandings were much attenuated among the first generation of Mirpuris. As a result most were content to remain in the same, largely unskilled, jobs in heavy engineering and textiles in which they first began.

For many years this was a far from unreasonable strategy. Basic wages were low, but those prepared to work long hours of overtime could still earn a reasonable income. However, the massive industrial recession of the early 1980s changed all that, for this niche in the employment market virtually disappeared. Unemployment rates soared, so that it was soon more common for middle-aged Mirpuri men to be out of work than in it. Given the scarcity of new jobs, let alone their poor command of English and routine discrimination, their chances of finding another job have remained disappearingly small.

In the wake of such experiences, it is scarcely surprising that Mirpuris are a great deal more socially disadvantaged than the Sikhs. Not only are they still overwhelmingly concentrated in those parts of the country which provided the largest and longest-lasting demand for unskilled labour, such as Birmingham, Sheffield and the textile towns on both sides of the Pennines; within those areas they are yet further concentrated in inner-city areas, and very often in those where, thanks both to the scale of their presence and to the extent of white flight, they now dominate both physically and numerically. Membership of these residential concentrations most certainly brings some benefits – for there is safety in numbers, while the very density of settlement promotes the establishment of particularly strong communal networks. But there are disadvantages too. Not only is the quality of public services invariably inferior to those in the more suburban areas to which most Sikhs have now shifted, but the very poverty of most Mirpuris families makes it impossible for them to contemplate making a similar move upwards and outwards.

These residential concentrations – which are particularly marked in the textile towns on both sides of the Pennines – have all sorts of consequences, and not least in linguistic terms. Although most Sikh parents are keen that their children should be reasonably fluent in Punjabi, their residential circumstances are such that their children are invariably in routine contact with English-speaking children. Most Sikh children are therefore more fluent in English than Punjabi. Not so Mirpuri children. If, as is very often the case, they live in a neighbourhood which is exclusively Asian, if their parents speak little or no English, and if the schools which they attend are again dominated by Punjabi speakers like themselves, they will have very few opportunities to acquire fluent English from face-to-face contact with fluent English speakers. No wonder, then, that the many Mirpuri (and Bangladeshi) children who grow up in such circumstances, and who receive little or no relevant educational assistance to enhance their linguistic competence, tend to fare much less well in examinations than do their Sikh counterparts.

Although the generally poor and relatively unsophisticated Mirpuris have consequently gained a reputation for 'backwardness' amongst their fellow South Asian settlers, and although some outside observers are also beginning to reach the same conclusion, it must be emphasised that these differences are no way innate. It is not that Mirpuris have any less of an appetite, or a capacity, for upward mobility than the Sikhs: it is their starting points which differ. Consequently, by far the simplest and most plausible way of explaining most aspects of currently observable differences between Jullunduris and Mirpuris is that they are an outcome of the strikingly different histories and political economies of their home bases. Yet however useful and necessary it may be to begin with such a perspective, the time has come to insist that it does not provide a *sufficient* basis for understanding all dimensions of difference. Specifically, such materialist arguments cannot explain why Mirpuris – in common with most other Moslems – should have taken so much longer to reunite their families than did Sikhs and Hindus; nor why Mirpuris – again in common with most other Moslems – tend to sustain much tighter and more inward-looking social networks, even in the diaspora, than do Sikhs or Hindus.

Could cultural – and, more specifically, religious – variables be a partial determinant of such differences? It is, after all, quite frequently asserted that Islam is more 'authoritarian', and less 'open-minded', than either Hinduism or Sikhism; and there clearly *is* a correlation between patterns of family and community organisation on the one hand, and religion on the other. Could the relationship be causal? It is an argument that I find myself approaching with great caution, for the dangers are clear. Any explanation which rests on sweeping, and inevitably stereotypical, assertions about the allegedly 'conservative' or 'liberal' character of the two religious traditions must be rejected as unhelpful and unilluminating. Nevertheless, I have become increasingly convinced that there *are* some very significant issues at stake here, which are indeed broadly associated with religion; however, if the analysis is to have any validity, and stereotypes are to be avoided, all arguments must show, in a very specific way, just *how* difference has been precipitated. With this in mind it is worth exploring the implications of three very specific areas of difference:

(i)   *In marriage rules*: while Sikhs, like Hindus, are barred from marrying their close kin, Moslems are permitted, and indeed encouraged to do so.

(ii)   *In gender rules*: given the conventions of *purdah*, Moslem women's public mobility is much more tightly restricted than is the case among Sikhs and Hindus.

(iii)   *In mortuary rites*: while Moslems bury their dead, Sikhs, like Hindus, opt for cremation.

Esoteric though these differences may seem, they have had, I would argue, a very substantial differential impact on both the character of kinship structures in Punjab and on processes of overseas migration.

Kinship and marriage in Punjab

We must begin, though, by getting to grips with the character of the broad arena within which these differences occur. All Punjabis – Hindu, Sikh and Moslem – follow much the same basic kinship conventions, in which patrilineal descent and patri-virilocal residence are the guiding principles.[6] Each family (*ghar*) – which ideally includes a man, his sons, and his sons' sons, together with their wives and unmarried daughters – is a strongly corporate group, whose members are expected to live cooperatively together under the same roof while jointly exploiting their common assets and property. As well as being the arena within which the most intense personal relationships are sustained, such units also provide the basic building blocks for the local social structure. It is above all as members of their families, rather than as lone individuals, that Punjabis participate in the wider world.

While relationships within the family are both more demanding, and more supportive, than all others, they by no means exhaust the universe of kinship. Within each caste (*zat*) and descent group (variously *got*, *qom*, *patti, biraderi* or *tabbar*) families are linked by an equally complex, although less overwhelmingly binding, network of extra-familial kinship ties: and it is in this extra-familial sphere that differences in marriage rules have a decisive impact.

Agnates and affines

In Punjab extra-familial kin are conceptually divided into two categories: agnates – members of families with whom one shares common patrilineal descent; and affines – those with whom a relationship has been established by marriage. Each set of relationships has its own distinctive character.

Since residence is normally patri-virilocal, neighbours usually belong to the same descent group. But, although such brothers, whether real or classificatory, expect to sustain a strong sense of mutual loyalty, their relationship always has a strongly competitive edge, for they are simultaneously allies and rivals. Ties of affinity, by contrast, are socially and physically more distant, and also firmly *non*-reciprocal. In Punjab as elsewhere in Northern India, bride-givers stand in a position of social inferiority to bride-receivers. But, in the absence of the competitive undercurrent which is so characteristic of agnatic ties, affinal links provide a neat counterpoint to those of descent, for men invariably maintain particularly close and affectionate ties with their sisters, and through them with her children: relationships between mothers' brothers and their sisters' sons are thus uniquely close.

Marriage rules

Up to this point the conventions of family and kinship organisation used by Hindus, Moslems and Sikhs are virtually identical: where they differ radically, however, is with respect to marriage rules. While both Hindus and Sikhs expect marriage to be caste-endogamous (i.e., one must marry into one's own caste), they also follow equally strict rules of exogamy. Marriage into one's father's, mother's, father's mother's and mother's mother's *got* (clan or descent group) is generally prohibited, as is the exchange of women between two families. Since all members of the same caste in any given village usually belong to the same *got*, it follows that brides must expect to move from one village to another when they go to join their husbands, and that they will normally have no prior ties of kinship with either their mother-in-law or their sisters-in-law.

Conversion to Islam has, however, had a dramatic impact on the structure of these networks, for in Moslem law, marriage is restricted only by the incest taboo: this excludes only immediate consanguines – parents, siblings, and parents' siblings – as potential spouses. And following a practice which is widespread in the Islamic world, many Punjabi Moslems have not only abandoned the principle of clan exogamy, but adopted an active *preference* for marriage with cousins. Just why conversion should have precipitated such a radical change in marriage strategies is most unclear. One common suggestion is that it is a tactical response to the Islamic law of inheritance, which makes daughters heirs as well as sons: by routinely marrying patrilateral cousins, men can ensure that property does not slip beyond control of the descent group. But plausible though this may seem in principle, it is in fact virtually unheard of for Moslem women even to try to claim their share of the patrimony – whoever they may have married. In Mirpur, as in most of the rest of Pakistan, what seems to be far more important is that the absence of the necessity for exogamy has reinforced the strength of sibling ties. Brothers and sisters now *expect* to be given right of first refusal in offers of marriage for each others' children, so much so that the rejection causes great offence: it is often regarded as a repudiation of the obligations of siblingship itself.

This does not mean that Mirpuri marriages are *always* arranged between close kin. Spouses of the right age and sex may not be available, and even if they are, acute conflicts between siblings can lead to such obligations being deliberately, if temporarily, repudiated. Moreover, most families find it strategically advantageous to make at least *some* external marriage alliances. Nevertheless my observations suggest that well over half of all marriages in Mirpur are contracted between first cousins, and that even when matches are arranged with non-relatives, they are rarely left in isolation. When followed up by further matches, two previously unconnected families can soon find themselves bound together in a single network.

This has many consequences. Because of the high level of *biraderi* endogamy, kinship networks in Mirpur are much less geographically extensive than those of the Jullunduri Sikhs; and although the conceptual distinction between agnates and affines has not been abandoned, most *biraderi* members are related to each other several times over by entirely different routes. Relationships within such networks are consequently far more in-turned and all-embracing than in those where exogamy is the rule. For men, the loyalties and obligations of agnation are supplemented and reinforced by those of affinity, while for women the whole experience of marriage is fundamentally transformed. Rarely does a bride join a household of strangers: more often than not either her mother-in-law and/or her sisters-in-law are already closely related to her.

This, I will argue, has had a major impact on processes of migration to

Britain; but before considering how, we must explore the two other major dimensions of difference.

Purdah

In the domestic domain, all Punjabis – Hindu, Sikh and Moslem – employ broadly similar patterns of gender expectations. While women are expected to behave with circumspection when men are present – and so, for example, to keep their faces well covered with a *chuni* (headscarf) in the presence of their husbands' elder male kin – they are by no means wholly withdrawn from the productive process, at least in peasant farming families. Women perform a wide range of domestic tasks which, although largely performed in and around the house and its courtyard, by no means confine them wholly to those limits. On the contrary they regularly move about the village to fetch water, wash clothes, feed animals, and – especially during the busiest periods in the agricultural cycle – to work in the fields.

However, specifically Moslem rules of *purdah* (which are, in fact, followed with particular strictness in Mirpur) have a dramatic impact on women's behaviour in the public domain.[7] Adult women, with the partial exception of those who have long since passed the menopause, are expected to avoid all public places, including the bazaar. As a result all shopping in Mirpur is normally done by men, except when itinerant pedlars – of whom there are many – come directly to the courtyard. When women travel beyond the confines of the villages – to visit kin or a shrine, for example – they are particularly circumspect. In the past they usually wrapped themselves in a *chaddar* (a large shawl), but it is now more fashionable, and more prestigious, to wear a *burka*, a light but long-sleeved coat, from whose hood two panels of fine material can be pulled down to completely cover the face. Women's spatial mobility is thus tightly restricted, as is their involvement in public events.

Although the use of the *burka* by women travelling outside their immediate home neighbourhood – among whose inhabitants such strict *purdah* is not kept – is a relatively novel phenomenon in Mirpur, its adoption, which implies an increase in the level of seclusion to which women are subjected, reflects an important current in the contemporary Pakistani social order. Not only is the seclusion of women regarded as prestigious, at least in peasant families aspiring to join the lower middle class, but it is a practice which receives constant ideological reinforcement from both state and mosque. The contrast with Jullundur could hardly be sharper. In India both the state and the educational system have a strongly secular emphasis. And although gender is still marked – so wearing a *chuni* remains a mark of respectability – restrictions on women's mobility are far less severe. While the prospect of a respectable young woman travelling a long distance alone in India might still cause some concern, no-one would suggest that women should not go to the bazaar alone, nor that it might be socially demeaning for them to take up paid employment.

Funeral rites

The final issue whose implications we must explore is that of funeral rites; for while Moslems bury the dead, the Sikhs, like the Hindus, cremate. While these practices reflect the differing perspectives on the afterlife adopted by each faith, it is not their theological under-pinnings, but rather their practical consequences that I want to high-light here. The point is simple: while cremation leaves no physical memorial, burial does. Why, though, should this matter?

A striking aspect of the rural scene in Mirpur is the way in which each little *biraderi* has its own carefully tended graveyard, in which everyone gradually reassembles after death. And although Islam allows no cult of the ancestors, the graveyard itself not only provides a strong physical expression of the *biraderi*'s corporate character, but gives it a very strong sense of rootedness. Hence when deaths occur in Britain – as is now becoming increasingly frequent – most families go to great and very expensive lengths to fly the body back to Pakistan for an appropriately located burial. By contrast, location exerts no pressure on either Sikhs or Hindus, for cremation, which should take place within twenty-four hours, can be carried out anywhere. And although the ashes should ideally be subsequently scattered in the sacred river Ganges, other rivers can serve as substitutes. So although many British Hindus, and at least some Sikhs, still take their elders' ashes back to Hardwar or Benares, a local river – the Thames is much favoured – can be used instead. Cremation does not generate ties to a particular local-ity, as burial does for Moslems.

Taken in isolation, this difference would be trivial; where it gains significance, however, is from its place in a more general pattern, for these otherwise disparate differences in marriage rules, *purdah*, and mortuary rites all reinforce the same tendency. Thanks to their com-bined impact, Moslem kinship networks tend not only to be much more tightly knit than those of Sikhs and Hindus, but also to have a much stronger local focus, as well as inhibiting the physical mobility of Moslem women. This greater degree of tight-knittedness has, in turn, greatly affected patterns of migration to and settlement in Britain.

Kinship, migration and settlement

Settlement in Britain has, of course, been strongly mediated by kinship. Not only did virtually all migrants set off with the support and encouragement of their extended families – for it was they who usually financed the cost of a ticket and passport – but only the very earliest pioneers lacked prior contacts overseas. Thereafter everyone joined kinsmen and acquaintances who were already established overseas. Thus despite their location thousands of miles from home, most migrants continued to live and work alongside their kinsmen and fellow villagers. Nor did emigration necessarily undermine the structure of the extended family. Taking a well-paid job abroad was not just seen as bringing personal benefits: on the contrary, those who did so were perceived, and perceived themselves, as fulfilling their most basic obligation as a family member – to make the maximum possible contribution to the collective resources of the group.

However, even though there was no question about migrants' continued family membership, their very initiative soon began to precipitate all sorts of tensions and contradictions. Migrants, for example, often felt that while those who stayed at home reaped an immediate benefit from their remittances, they often failed to appreciate how much hardship had been faced in generating them. And although sending money home gave migrants great satisfaction, most also felt that they should, given their greatly enhanced contribution to the group's collective resources, have a larger voice in family affairs, despite their youth and formal juniority. But if, thanks to these changes in the balance of power, those who stayed behind soon began both to fear and to half-expect such challenges to their authority, they were far from lacking resources with which to contest them. It was they who still controlled the family's patrimonial resources, and especially its land; moreover, migrants' wives and children were effectively in their custody.

Nor was it just in this sphere that contradictions arose, for the longer they stayed abroad, the more migrants began to miss regular contact with their wives and children; I was told many poignant stories about children being unable to recognise their fathers on their return from lengthy spells of work abroad. On the other hand, few wished to abandon the material advantages that arose from working in Britain. How were the contradictions to be resolved? For migrants to bring their wives and children to join them was an obvious option, for it reduced tensions in the domestic and conjugal sphere, even if it also tended to exacerbate those within the wider extended family. Indeed such reunions could seem to threaten its very existence.

Processes of dissidence within Punjabi families

Although founded on expectations of unlimited reciprocity and solidarity, all Punjabi extended families, at home, no less than in the diaspora, are also riven by internal tensions. As we have already noted, siblingship contains its own contradictions, for brothers are at once the closest of allies and the most bitter of rivals; and these contradictions are further exacerbated by marriage. Not only do in-marrying wives, especially if unrelated, have their own separate interests, but the more brothers, as husbands, become emotionally committed to their own wives and children, the more the principle of agnatic solidarity will be challenged.

This contradiction is incorporated into the very rituals of marriage itself, no less amongst Moslems than Sikhs and Hindus. Overtly, the ideal of jointness is both emphasised and much celebrated: it is into her in-laws' household, of which her husband is but a junior member, that the bride is formally incorporated. Yet at the same time the bride's all-important dowry quietly provides a symbolic counterpoint. Besides her personal jewellery, a dowry should include everything – beds, bedding, furniture and a complete range of household utensils – which the bride and her husband would need to establish their own independent household. For although the prospect of partition receives no public stress, the possibility of its occurrence is no secret. Indeed, once couples have established themselves economically, and have been blessed with the offspring needed to secure their future, it has long been commonplace – even in the most 'traditional' of rural contexts – for a gradual process of domestic separation to take place, even if a formal division of family property rarely occurs before the patriarch's death (Kessinger 1975).

For a conjugal pair to seek greater autonomy within the joint family by partially separating themselves from it is not, therefore, an unusual or unexpected event: such developments – however much they may be opposed by its remaining members – are routine. Nevertheless the dynamics of that process differ substantially as between Moslems on the one hand and Sikhs and Hindus on the other. Where wives have no prior ties of kinship, they can only be expected to have a very limited interest in the maintenance of jointness; and again because of their unrelatedness, each also provides her husband with his own unique network of affinal kin. Thus when brothers (or even fathers and sons) fall out, each has access to at least some degree of support and encouragement from an external ally. By contrast, the close interweaving of agnatic and affinal links found in most Moslem *biraderi*s leaves men with much less in the way of individuating support; meanwhile, if mothers-in-law, sisters-in-law and daughters-in-law are kin, they may well have *their* own reasons for staying together. So even though most conjugal couples do eventually seek a greater degree of autonomy for themselves, moves in that direction tend to proceed a good deal more slowly amongst Moslems than Sikhs.

Doubts and uncertainties

Thus while men who called their wives and children to join them in Britain may, in so doing, have undermined the residential unity of the extended family, they were not doing anything new. Similar developments might well have occurred had everyone stayed back in Punjab, and in any case they developed along an established fault-line within the family structure. Nevertheless many settlers have very mixed feelings about the consequences of making such a move. Clear though the emotional benefits might be, most were equally conscious of the possible costs. Since it was far more expensive to maintain a family in Britain, their propensity to save, and to remit, dropped sharply; their dreams of going home for good were thus pushed yet further into abeyance. Dangers were also perceived to be lurking in other spheres for, impressed though they were by Britain's material prosperity, most Punjabi migrants' evaluation of the *moral* quality of native British lifestyles was quite the reverse. Indeed it was precisely in order to protect their families from what they perceived as the 'corrupting' influence of English ways that many of the early settlers concluded that for safety's sake their wives and children were best left at home.[8]

But widespread though these fears may have been at the outset, once ethnic colonies became larger and more secure, so generating a social arena within which a Punjabi moral order could be reproduced, doubts began to fade. Led by the Sikhs and Hindus, Punjabi settlers gradually began to feel that it was both safe and sensible to bring their wives and children to join them in Britain.

The collapse of inter-continental commuting

While the Mirpuris eventually reached the same conclusion, they were a great deal more cautious: it took them the best part of fifteen years to change their minds. Thus from the late fifties right up till the early seventies most Mirpuris became international commuters. Travel was expensive, and so was not undertaken lightly: most men worked in Britain for anything between one and four years, and then went home for a period that might last just as long. Besides enjoying a well-earned rest, they spent their time investing in such projects as building new houses, buying more land, digging wells and planting orchards, or celebrating their own, or their sisters' or their daughters' marriages. Many also awaited the successful conclusion of their wife's next pregnancy before returning to the industrial treadmill. During this period Britain was, in effect, little more than an income producing way-station; it was not, for them, their domicile.

During the seventies, however, this strategy became increasingly difficult to sustain. Before the recession set in, when most mills and foundries were chronically short of labour, extended leave of absence had been easy to negotiate. But as levels of unemployment rose this ceased. Not only did those who absented themselves for lengthy periods find it impossible to get their old jobs back, but new ones were virtually unavailable. International commuting was, in other words, no longer a viable option. Yet if family reunion thereby became much more attractive, it was, by the late seventies, a much more difficult move to implement, thanks largely to the impact of Britain's ever-tightening immigration laws.

The impact of immigration control

Although the principal object of two decades of changes in the immigration rules has been to reduce the number of non-European settlers to the lowest possible level, their impact on processes of chain migration has often produced paradoxical outcomes. So, for example, while the 1962 Immigration Act curtailed Commonwealth citizens' previously automatic right of entry by insisting that settlers must first obtain employment vouchers, it hardly curbed the volume of inflow. Since the demand for additional labour, especially in heavy engineering and textiles, was still acute, many Punjabis, only too aware that the window of opportunity might soon close, obtained as many vouchers as they could for their kinsmen back home. The scheme may or may not have reduced the total inflow, but it most certainly greatly reinforced the process of chain migration.

Subsequent measures have had a similar effect. Following the withdrawal of the voucher scheme in 1965, it became extremely difficult for men from the sub-continent to come to Britain to work. Yet there was still a demand for their labour, and at comparatively high wages: for enterprising young men in Jullundur and Mirpur, the British labour market remained as attractive as ever. But how could they take advantage of the opportunity? Other than illegal entry, only two routes were available: either boys on the verge of adulthood could be brought in as dependants provided that their fathers had already established residence rights in Britain; or alternatively, young men could marry girls whose parents had already taken them to Britain, and gain entry as their husbands.

Jullunduris and Mirpuris have, however, followed rather different courses through the thickets of immigration control, largely because of their differing strategies of family reunion. Jullunduris, since they started earlier, ran into fewer obstacles. When they began to appear at Heathrow with their families – as they did in rapidly increasing numbers from the early sixties onwards – they encountered few problems. Until the early seventies, by which time most Sikhs had already reunited their families, it was adult male 'primary immigrants', rather than established settlers' dependants, who were the principal targets of immigration control. Hence wives and children were usually allowed to enter after answering a few straightforward questions. Since then, however, much has changed. Although all Commonwealth citizens who have gained a right of abode in Britain still have the same right, at least in principle, to reunite their families, the seventies and eighties have witnessed the introduction of an ever larger battery of administrative obstacles, aimed, quite deliberately, at minimising the number doing so. This has led to the development of a complex game of cat and mouse between the immigration authorities and potential settlers.

In the late sixties, for example, an increasing number of Mirpuri men began, following one of their periodic trips home, to bring their fourteen and fifteen-year-old sons back with them to Britain. Young enough to be permitted to enter as dependants – and thus avoiding the bar on adult males – it would not be long before they left school and started work. But, seeing this as a 'loophole' which should be closed, immigration officers began to insist that if dependants were to enter, the whole family must come. One way round that was, of course, to bring everyone over, and then to send one's wife and daughters back to Pakistan again after a brief visit to Britain. Despite the very considerable cost a few men did just that; but for many more these developments simply provided yet another impetus towards a change in strategy. Not only were the family contradictions outlined earlier sharpening around them, but inter-continental commuting was becoming ever more difficult in practice. Even though changes in the immigration rules may only have been a contributory factor, they provided Mirpuris with yet another incentive to switch their domestic domicile to Britain.

By the late seventies, family reunion had indeed become the goal of most British Mirpuris; but by then the goalposts had been shifted once again. Though their rights of entry were, in principle, unchanged, entry certificates had become increasingly hard to get. Families were forced to wait (and often still have to wait) for a year or more before getting their first interview, or more accurately, undergoing their first interrogation. Husbands and wives (and any other available family members) are questioned separately, and must convince the Entry Certificate Officer that they are indeed the persons they claim to be, that they are legally married, that each of the children they claim as theirs is indeed the child of that marriage. They must also satisfactorily explain any discrepancies between their verbal statements, the extensive documentation that they are required to present, and the evidence of 'linked files' – the records of previous interrogations carried out when other members of their families applied to go to Britain. Faced with this obstacle course, in which confusion is compounded by the immense linguistic and conceptual gulf between English bureaucrats and Punjabi villagers, applications can take years to process. And despite expensive reapplications and appeals, many have found themselves unjustly, but quite deliberately, excluded (Commission for Racial Equality 1985).

The maintenance of roots in Mirpur

In analysing the process of family reunion, however, it is not sufficient simply to set the prospective material and social advantages of reunions against the obstacles – primarily arising from immigration control – which stand in the way of their fulfilment. What must also be explored is the positive attraction of maintaining roots back home. Why then, did Mirpuris continue to make so many return visits, continue to remit such a substantial proportion of their earnings, and continue to invest so much in extending and embellishing their houses back home, even though they were becoming ever more tightly bound into the British employment market?

In the first place the simple pleasures of returning to a place where the climate is warm, vegetables fresh, one's friends and family are all around and where life is easygoing – in marked contrast to the pressures, hostilities and sheer barrenness of life in inner-urban Britain – should never be underestimated. But there were many other factors too. Given the nature of Punjabi society, competition for *izzat* (honour) was inevitably of critical importance, for as long as some people kept returning to extend their houses, and to equip them with televisions and refrigerators, for example, all their neighbours, and especially their fellow kinsmen, found themselves under pressure to do the same if loss of face was to be avoided. But since considerations of this kind apply with just as much force to Sikhs as to Moslems, we need to identify a further dimension to explain delays in family reunion, and in my view differences in the structure of kinship networks provide the most plausible answer.

As suggested earlier, the very structure of the family itself generates a contradiction between the interests of young men working overseas and the elders who stayed at home: the more the former could be locked into making repeated visits back home, the longer the latter could take advantage of the continued arrival of remittances, while still sustaining their position of dominance. Moreover, the opportunities for doing so were a good deal more extensive where close kin marriage was practised. Various strategies were available. For unmarried sons, delay was a powerful constraint, since it was only when parents arranged the ceremony that the usually long since agreed upon marriage could actually take place. In these circumstances it was easy to insist that financing the celebrations to the appropriate degree of splendour required yet another spell of work abroad.

Even when marriage did take place, it often proved much more difficult for Mirpuri men to successfully challenge the conventions of co-residence, and thus to bring their wives to Britain. Quite apart from Moslem conventions of *purdah*, which could be used to oppose the swift removal of a bride overseas, Mirpuri women themselves tended to be much less interested in making such a move. Unlike their Sikh counterparts, who, thanks to the rules of exogamy, are thrust by marriage into the company of strangers, most Mirpuri brides are already related to their new affinal kin. Failing that, other kinswomen invariably live nearby. Not only do they have much less of an immediate interest in achieving greater domestic autonomy; on the contrary, they may well positively welcome the prospect of staying put.

Thus, despite the many similarities in the basic cultural premises used by both Jullunduris and Mirpuris, a whole series of minor differences – of cousin marriage and the consequent construction of kinship networks containing fewer ready-made cleavages, of the tighter limits on women's spacial mobility imposed by the rules of *purdah*, and of necessarily unshiftable family graveyards which provide a physical focus for the *biraderi* – have served to tie Mirpuris much more firmly than Jullunduris to their localities of origin. It is in terms of these considerations, alongside the changing character of the British labour market and the increasingly restrictive impact of the immigration rules, that Mirpuris' relatively slow rate of family reunion is best understood.

Differing trajectories in the post-migratory period

Even though the great majority of Mirpuris have now, at long last, managed to reunite their families in Britain, they are by no means following identical social trajectories to those of their Jullunduri predecessors. And although, as suggested earlier, many aspects of those differences can be attributed to the relative lack of economic development in Mirpur, as well as the much more restricted set of opportunities currently available in Britain's recession-ridden economy, by no means everything can be so explained.

Two issues are worth noting as we pass: first in terms of employment, where Moslem women's participation in the formal labour market has, thus far at least, been much more limited than that of their Sikh and Hindu counterparts. The reasons are not hard to identify: given their stronger commitment to seclusion, Moslem women – and most especially those born and brought up in rural Pakistan – have been exceedingly reluctant to take up jobs outside their homes. However they are very far from being economically inactive, for since the recession has rendered so many of their husbands unemployed, the great majority now do out-work at home. Technically self-employed (and so overlooked in most surveys of economic activity), they receive minimal wages for long hours of work in atrocious conditions; but for many, these earnings now provide a crucial supplement to their family income (Mitter 1986).

A second very significant difference is in fertility levels, which, thus far at least, are much higher among Moslems than Sikhs (Ballard 1983b). This, once again, has a religious foundation. In general, Sikhs are unworried about using contraceptives. By contrast, popular Islam not only tends to promote rather stronger reservations about the legitimacy of human intervention in the God-given blessing of fertility, but Moslem rules of seclusion also tend to make it more difficult for women to gain access to family planning services. That said, it is not the case that these differences will necessarily be permanent. Most young British-born Mirpuri women now look forward to earning incomes of their own, and like their Sikh counterparts, are much more determined to limit their fertility.

Important though the social effects of employment and fertility may be, marriage patterns – especially when there is an option of marrying overseas – can have an even more enduring impact; and here, once again, the two groups have followed strikingly different courses.

The Sikhs' post-settlement marriage strategies

Given the rule of exogamy, Sikh parents have no prior obligation to make or accept any particular offer of *riste* (marriage); since every match is arranged from scratch, the choice for each child is open. At the beginning of the settlement process most British-based Sikhs continued, when it came to finding spouses for their offspring, to follow the strategies which they would have employed had they stayed at home: matches were arranged into families living in villages near to their own. Although this was not their primary purpose, such practices had the effect of yet further increasing the volume of immigration. Not only did Punjab-based brides, following tradition, invariably come to join their husbands' families in Britain, but in the inverse case, where British-based girls married Punjabi boys, their husbands almost always took advantage of the opportunity to shift their residence to Britain too. But with the passage of time, preferences have changed. Amongst British Sikhs, locally arranged marriages have now become the norm.

That change has, however, by no means been straightforward. For a long time it was widely felt that girls brought up in Britain were likely, thanks to their contact with English ways, to prove less dutiful and obedient as daughters-in-law than those who had been brought up in Punjab. Hence parents frequently favoured the latter over the former. And precisely because of this tendency – reinforced by the 'leakage' of potential grooms precipitated by the much greater propensity of Sikh boys to throw over the traces by establishing relationships with English girls – British Sikhs with daughters on their hands have found themselves in an increasingly competitive marriage market. In the absence of a large and tempting dowry, good locally based grooms were often hard to find. But getting a groom from Punjab was much easier: since such matches offered the opportunity of settlement in Britain, they seemed most attractive to both young men and their parents.

Nevertheless, there has been a growing realisation on all sides that such matches tend to be much more conflict ridden than most. Many, though not all, British-bred girls were disturbed, to say the least, by the prospect of trying to establish relationships with men whom they felt were unsophisticated and rustic; meanwhile those same men were equally unhappy about the apparent 'forwardness' of their wives. In the inverse case, where it was the bride rather than the groom who was brought from India, problems of compatibility tended to be less severe: the conventional hierarchy of gender was less directly threatened. Even so, most Sikh boys have now joined their sisters in regarding such matches with disfavour. So despite the frequent receipt of offers of *riste* from India, which some parents – and especially those having difficulty in finding suitable matches for their daughters – may be tempted to accept, their children invariably strongly oppose them. And in doing so, young Sikhs have the advantage of knowing that their parents are under no prior obligation to accept any given offer. Hence the vast majority of Sikh marriages are either locally arranged, or at least contracted elsewhere in the overseas Sikh diaspora.

Mirpuris' post-migration marriage strategies

Amongst the Mirpuris, however, marriages with Pakistan-based partners remain much more frequent, for even though they have proved as tension-prone as those amongst the Sikhs, parents find themselves under much more intense pressure to accept offers of *riste* from their Mirpur-based kin. It is not hard to see why. When it comes to arranging their children's marriages, those Mirpuris with British-resident siblings – and so large has the scale of emigration been that very few are not in that position – invariably seek to remind their relatives of their familial responsibilities. Not only are their British-resident nephews and nieces precisely those to whom they would have expected to marry their children in the absence of emigration, but they also feel that the advantages which accrue from residence in Britain redouble their kinsmen's obligations in this sphere. Those lucky enough to have made it ought, as a matter of principle, to do everything in their power to share their blessings with their less fortunate kin. Many British Mirpuris often find these pressures and expectations hard to resist. Over and above their genuine feelings of loyalty to and affection for their now-distant kin, they are very conscious that a persistent rejection of all offers of *riste* will inevitably be perceived by those at home as mean, unjustified and unnecessary; and that having been so put down, their slighted kinsfolk may well take every opportunity to blacken their name – a major sanction in a society where *izzat* is so crucial.

Yet although the majority of British Mirpuri marriages are still *biraderi*-endogamous, it does not follow that all such marriages involve Pakistan-based partners; many are arranged between British-resident couples. Nevertheless although many younger British Mirpuris have now grown almost as doubtful about the viability of matches with spouses from back home as have their Sikh counterparts, their parents often find their hands are much more closely tied, feeling duty-bound to consider offers of *riste* from Pakistan-based *biraderi* members just as seriously as those proposed by local residents. In consequence the incidence of trans-continental marriage is not only much higher amongst Mirpuris than Jullunduris, but seems likely to remain so for quite some time to come, despite all the obstacles which have now been introduced by the immigration authorities.

The continuing importance of trans-continental links

Standing back for a moment to take a broader view, it should by now be clear why the increasingly popular demand – at least among members of the white majority – that all further (non-European) immigration should be halted is proving so difficult to achieve. However draconian the curbs on further movement that may be introduced, migrants – and especially those as heavily involved in their kinship networks as are South Asians – will be strongly committed to maintaining links with other members of their community, wherever they may live. Marriage and family reunion are only the most obvious ways in which such trans-continental links are sustained, for the underlying ties of interest, affection, obligation and loyalty are also manifested in a wide variety of other ways: letters, message-filled audio- and video-cassettes as well as telephone calls stream back and forth, while visits, again in both directions, are much looked forward to.

The conclusion that must be drawn is that migration is not, and cannot be made to be, a single time-limited event: rather it creates a series of umbilical links between geographically separated communities. Having recognised this, the issue most worthy of exploration is not so much the continued existence of such links, but their dynamics, for if ties of interest and affection keep drawing people together, economic and political obstacles, wherever they occur, keep driving them apart. How then can British South Asians' ties with their homelands best be characterised? Once again we find some major differences.

In Mirpur . . .

While most Mirpuris still maintain close links with their home villages, the character of those links is slowly changing. So, for example, while visits back home are still made almost as frequently as ever, since lengthy stays are no longer a viable option for wage-earners, brief emergency visits, precipitated by accident, illness or death have become more commonplace.

In recent years, however, a new development has emerged. Faced, during the early eighties, with recession, redundancy, and the prospect of long-term unemployment, the prospect of going home for good became increasingly attractive to many middle-aged Mirpuris. Having sold their houses to realise all their available capital, such returnees hoped to invest their savings in a profitable business back home. A few have indeed managed to do so with great success; but the experience of most has been very different. Given the stagnation of Mirpur's rural economy, together with their lack of the all important connections with the administrative and political elite, the great majority of returnees have not been able to find a secure and profitable home for their savings. They have been forced, instead, to live on their capital. Many have now exhausted their savings, only to be confronted with the uncomfortable realisation that the best available option is to return, now penniless and homeless, to the bottom of the ladder in Britain.[9]

A few returnees do better, most notably those whose links with Britain, in the form of a pension, for example, give them a secure income. What is clear, however, is that although the Mirpuris have invested a great deal, no less in emotional than in financial terms, in maintaining links with their home villages, the stagnation of the rural economy has, through no fault of their own, largely vitiated their efforts to sustain a physical base there.

. . . and in Jullundur

The Sikhs, by contrast, face a very different set of options. In principle Jullundur, with its thriving local economy, is a much more attractive proposition for potential returnees, and in the early eighties there was indeed the beginnings of a return. But that has now ceased, and instead many families are only too keen to liquidate their investments in Punjab. The reasons are not hard to identify. Since 'Operation Bluestar' in 1984, when the Indian Army took the Golden Temple in Amritsar by force, life in Punjab has become increasingly insecure: violence is now commonplace and social polarisation vicious. Worse still many government officials tend to identify Sikhs, and most especially overseas Sikhs, as potentially seditious. Even obtaining a visa to visit Punjab was made very difficult. Given that overseas Sikhs now widely (if erroneously) perceive Punjab as being subject to enemy occupation, it is hardly surprising that very few now seek to return for anything more than the briefest of visits. This is unlikely to change until and unless current tensions are resolved.

Global connections

It is also worth emphasising that where migrant groups have established a multiplicity of beach-heads overseas, those considering moving on are often able to explore a much wider set of options than the simple polar choice between staying put and going back. The Sikhs, for example, now work within a global diaspora. Thus while well educated and professionally qualified young Sikhs who have grown disillusioned by the lack of opportunities in racist and industrially declining Britain may have little interest, at least at present, in going back to Punjab or in joining their relatives who have settled in Southeast Asia and East Africa, the opportunities available in Canada and the United States, where well-established Sikh communities are also to be found, are much more attractive. In consequence a great deal of re-emigration across the Atlantic is currently taking place.

The Mirpuris once again present a contrast, for although they too have established a diaspora, it is much less extensive. Few have yet found their way to North America, although they do have a significant presence in Saudi Arabia and the Gulf, as well as in Scandinavia and West Germany. But they, too, are taking advantage of those connections. Given the higher wages and lower levels of unemployment, even for those with the most basic skills, now found in continental Europe, many Mirpuris are now taking advantage of EEC regulations to get there.

Conclusion: South Asian differentiation in Britain

International migration is therefore a much more complex process than is often supposed. Rarely does it entail a simple bilateral movement from one country to another, for not only do those caught up in migrant diasporas tend to have a very comprehensive knowledge of the range of opportunities available in the global labour market, but their kinship networks greatly facilitate their ability to take advantage of those opportunities. Nor is migration a one-off population transfer of a kind that might have, or be brought to, a finite and clearly delineated end. Rather, it sets in train an on-going *process*, in which members of a multiplicity of geographically separated but socially interlinked communities use and indeed continually readjust all the resources – human and cultural no less than material – available to them, both to advance their interests, and to circumvent any obstacles they encounter.

Once viewed in such dialectic terms, it follows that as a result of variations in their deployable resources, it is only to be expected that those of differing origins will follow different trajectories. Hence my approach in this chapter, where I have sought to show how a specific set of politico-economic differences on the one hand, together with an equally specific set of religio-cultural differences on the other, have interacted with the changes in the state of the British labour market as well as in the immigration rules to produce a strikingly varied set of outcomes. 'Asians' are by no means all the same.

Yet, even though my central aim in this chapter has been to highlight the extent and the complexity of some of the differences so produced, I am still very conscious of the extent to which I have been forced to simplify while setting forward my analysis. First, I have treated both 'Sikhs' and 'Mirpuris' as if they formed two internally homogeneous groups. But in the Sikh case this could be regarded as most misleading, for the community is actually strongly differentiated in terms of both class and caste. Members of the Jat (peasant-farmer), Ramgarhia (craftsman) and Bhatia (pedlar) castes have not only formed their own networks, but have also set off on strikingly different trajectories.[10] Second, I have ignored the immense complexity of the Punjabi presence in Britain, for by no means all Jullunduris are Sikh, nor are British Pakistanis all Mirpuri; and although it is particularly illuminating to contrast, at least for heuristic purposes, the strikingly different social trajectories of these two groups, it would be quite wrong to assume, for example, that all other Punjabi Moslems behave in the same way as the Mirpuris. In fact those from *nehri* areas such as Sialkot and Faisalabad have followed equally complex trajectories which fall somewhere between those which have been highlighted here, while the small community of Jullunduri Moslems – and especially those members of the Arain caste who have moved into the clothing business – have now become at least as affluent as the Sikhs.

To those unfamiliar with the complexities of the Punjabi social order, it may well seem extremely tempting to overlook all these apparently obscure and esoteric dimensions of social and cultural variation. But the consequences of doing so are clear: in the absence of an awareness of such diversities, statements about 'Asians', 'Punjabis' and 'Sikhs' will be reduced to a broadly generalised mean. This is a grave mistake. Anyone who wishes to come fully to terms with the nature of the South Asian presence in Britain, both in terms of the increasingly salient variations in the quality of its members' lifestyles, and of the causes and consequences of those variations, has no alternative but to take these complexities aboard.

Notes

1 Most of the empirical material presented in this chapter is based on my own personal fieldwork observations. These have not only focused on the Jullunduri and Mirpuri population in West Yorkshire, but also on migrants' villages of origin in Punjab. I carried out extensive fieldwork in both areas in 1972/3, 1981, and again in 1984/5 (and during the final period with support from an ESRC grant).

2 Since an 'ethnic question' was not asked in the 1981 Census, making an estimate of the size of Britain's minority population is a complex enough task (Ballard 1983b); estimating the size of the various components of the Punjabi presence presents many more problems, and these figures are no more than my own informed guesses.

3 There is now an extensive literature on the process of Punjabi migration to and settlement in Britain. Besides my own work, Saifullah-Khan (1976a, 1976b, 1977) has written extensively about Mirpuris, and Aurora (1967), James (1974) and Helweg (1979) about Sikhs. Shaw (1988) presents a very valuable comprehensive account of the Punjabi Moslem presence in Oxford, and Anwar (1979) of that in Rochdale.

4 Bhachu (1985, 1988) presents a very graphic account of the extent of upward social mobility among (predominantly East African Ramgarhia) Sikhs in West London.

248   *Roger Ballard*

---

5 According to the Labour Force Survey (1986), no less than 20% of adult male Indians (not all of whom are Sikhs, of course) were self-employed when the survey was carried out; only 16% of Pakistanis and Bangladeshis were in the same position. Meanwhile the unemployment rate amongst Pakistanis and Bangladeshis was then 30%, as compared to 15% for Indians and only 11% for whites.
6 Detailed accounts of Punjabi family and kinship organisation in Punjab can be found in Alavi (1972), Ballard (1982), Eglar (1960), Hershman (1981) and Kessinger (1975).
7 Saifullah-Khan (1976a) presents a very detailed account of the practice of *purdah*.
8 Aurora's account (1967) of life during the early phase of the Sikh settlement in Southall is particularly illuminating with respect to these assumptions.
9 The personal and domestic contradictions often encountered by returnees to Mirpur from Britain are discussed in much greater detail in Ballard (1986).
10 For an analysis of the extent and significance of internal differentiation amongst British Sikhs, see Ballard (1989).

References

33
3
Aurora, G. 1967. *The New Frontiersmen*, Bombay: Popular Prakashan.
Alavi, H. 1972. 'Kinship in West Punjab Villages', in *Contributions to Indian Sociology*, n.s., 6: 57–89.
Anwar, M. 1979. *The Myth of Return*, London: Heineman Educational Books.
Ballard, R. 1982. 'South Asian families: structure and process', in *Families in Britain*, ed. R.N. Rapoport, M.P. Fogarty, and R. Rapoport, pp. 174–204, London: Routledge.
    1983a. 'Emigration in a wider context: Jullundur and Mirpur compared', in *New Community*, 10: 117–36.
    1983b. 'Race and the census: what an "ethnic question" would show', in *New Society*, 12 May, 212–14.
    1986. The Context and Consequences of Emigration from Northern Pakistan, a Final Report to ESRC.
    1987. 'Political economy of migration: Pakistan, Britain and the Middle East', in *Migration, Workers and the Social Order*, ed. J.S. Eades, pp. 17–41, London: Tavistock.
    1989. 'Differentiation and disjunction amongst the Sikhs in Britain', in *The Sikh Diaspora*, ed. Gerald Barrier and Verne Dusenberry, pp. 200–34, Delhi: Manohar.
Ballard, R. and C. Ballard 1977. 'The Sikhs', in *Between Two Cultures: Migrants and Minorities in Britain*, ed. J.L. Watson, pp. 21–56, Oxford: Basil Blackwell.
Ballard, R. and G. Driver, 1979. 'Comparing performance in multi-racial schools: South Asians at 16 +', in *New Community*, 8: 143–53.
Ballard, R. and S. Vellins 1984. 'South Asian students in British universities: a comparative note', in *New Community*, 12: 260–5.
Bhachu, P. 1986. *Twice Migrants*, London: Tavistock.
    1988. '*Apni Marzi Kardi*', in *Enterprising Women*, ed. P.S. Westwood, P. Bhachu, pp. 76–102, London: Routledge.
Commission for Racial Equality 1985. *Immigration Control Procedures: Report of a Formal Investigation*, London: CRE.

Dahya, B. 1974. 'Pakistani ethnicity in industrial cities in Britain', in *Urban Ethnicity*, ed. A. Cohen, pp. 77–118, London: Tavistock.

Eglar, Z. 1960. *A Punjabi Village in Pakistan*, New York: Columbia University Press.

Helweg, A.W. 1979, *The Sikhs in England*, Bombay: Oxford University Press.

Hershman, P. 1981. *Punjabi Kinship and Marriage*, Delhi: Hindustan Publishing.

James, A. 1974. *Sikh Children in Britain*, Oxford: Oxford University Press.

Kessinger, T. 1975. *Vilayatpur 1848–1968*, Berkeley: University of California Press.

Labour Force Survey 1986. London: HMSO.

Mitter, S. 1986. 'Industrial restructuring and manufacturing homework: immigrant women in the UK clothing industry', *Capital and Class*, 27: 37–58.

Saifullah-Khan, V. 1976a. 'Purdah in the British situation', in *Dependency and Exploitation in Work and Marriage*, ed. D.L. Barker and S. Allen, pp. 244–45, London: Longmans.

1976b. 'Perceptions of a population: Pakistanis in Britain', *New Community*, 5: 222–9.

1977. 'The Pakistanis' in *Between Two Cultures*, ed. J.L. Watson, pp. 57–89, Oxford: Blackwell.

Shaw, A. 1988. *A Pakistani Community in Britain*, Oxford: Blackwell.

11

Transcontinental families – Gujarat and Lancashire: a comparative study of social policy

Elinor Kelly

Transcontinental families:

It was during my first visit to India in the autumn of 1985, that I coined the term 'transcontinental families'. I was staying in the Bharuch district of the state of Gujarat (Map Intro. 3), with the kin of Asian immigrants who had settled in the county of Lancashire in England. While in Gujarat, I was introduced to migrant workers who were home on long visits from Africa, the Middle East and Britain or who had returned in order to take up the lives they had left while working abroad. As word spread that an English woman professor was staying, the migrant visitors were eager to come and talk to me. Gradually, as they told their stories and discussed the pros and cons of the different countries where they worked, I realised that Britain was not the centre of their world and that my country was only one of a number of options which they would consider in order to earn the cash which should flow as remittances into their villages.

In addition, sitting in a rather bewildered and exhausted posture, surrounded by the family, kin and neighbours of my hosts, I soon realised that I was experiencing something else which all the literature on Asian communities in Britain had somehow failed to convey. The 'myth of return' (Anwar 1979) seemed to be less of a myth and more of an actuality. The connections between kin in the different countries appeared to be well able to withstand long periods of absence. They were closely observed and checked by, for instance, grandparents who did not give up their residential status in India, but flew to join their sons and daughters on extended visits. It is true that this was not possible in all countries – I was told that the Gulf states, for instance, do not permit family visits or settlement. Also, fears were expressed about the increasing restrictions on travel in and out of Britain. But, even so, I could witness the international swirl in the social life which developed during the 'visiting season'.

251

Some of the flurry was undoubtedly more noticeable at the time I was there because I was visiting during the winter months when the weather in Gujarat is balmy and relaxing for both the villagers and their overseas visitors. Had I been there during the months of the monsoon, I would surely have found the villages much quieter and certainly there would have been few of the stylishly dressed young visitors in whom the villagers took such pride. But my experience was by no means unique; as I travelled round Gujarat, I met other visitors from England who were themselves doing the full round of sightseeing and family visits. Sitting on the bus or train, we would compare notes on which people and places we knew best in Britain and send greetings to our respective friends in Lancashire towns.

These first observations of 'transcontinental families' influenced me greatly and have caused me to make some adjustments in my thinking about their British context and how it compares with the situations they inhabit in other countries. It seems to me that I should, as it were, follow the lead of the Bharuchis and develop more of a genuinely comparative perspective in which to study the economic, social and political contexts which they enter as migrants and settlers. In this chapter I am embarking on this approach by focusing on the 'ethnic' contexts in which the Bharuchis find themselves in Gujarat and in Lancashire.

Bharuchi Muslims in Gujarat:

The village through which I was first introduced to the kinsfolk of my Lancashire friends lies 53 km south of the city of Baroda, close to the railway line which runs down the western coast of India to Bombay and beside one of the national trunk roads which carries huge amounts of freight and passenger traffic between the major cities, as well as servicing the thousands of villages on either side.

The local economy is still dominated by agriculture; the village is one of 1,217 in the local district of Bharuch. Cotton accounts for about 50% of the area under crops, then jowar (12%), pulses (10%) and fodder crops (7%), along with wheat, rice and vegetables. But there are signs that this village is changing towards greater dependency on cash wages; certainly a number of the farmers to whom I spoke hope that the next generation will escape a life of gruelling work in the fields. They are sending their sons to work in the local towns of Bharuch and Baroda; and brothers, cousins and uncles are sending remittances from abroad, particularly from England and the Gulf States.

Living in a village such as this and visiting the kin of my contacts, it would have been easy to forget that the Muslims are a minority, because I rarely met or was introduced to a Hindu. If I visited Bharuch, Baroda or even Bombay I was taken straight through town to the Muslim quarters where my friends would find me a place to stay. I learnt to use the minarets of the local mosques as landmarks when travelling alone in either rural or urban areas. I visited Muslim schools. I was introduced to Muslim dignitaries and the Gujarati which I learnt was rich in greetings which are spoken between Muslims. It was only when we went shopping in the towns that I began to meet Hindus such as the market traders and the booksellers – and embarrassed my friends by using the wrong greetings! In Gujarat, the Bharuchi Muslims live in enclaves which are remarkably self-contained. The social lives of my contacts, whether in town or village, are dominated by visits and activities shared among people who are close kin and/or neighbours. When I asked who was who, I would be answered with reference either to kin ties or to the village in which that person held land or lived. When I travelled to Bombay I was taken to the mosque rest-house run by Bharuchi Muslim kin in a Muslim quarter of the city; this was the domestic base for labour migrants who commuted on a weekly basis from Gujarat, as well as being a hostel for long-distance travellers.

In pursuit of comparative material, I studied the indicators of 'ethnic' context which can be traced in the official statistics of the Indian national census. These 'indicators' need to be handled carefully because, in secular India, political sensitivities about communal issues are so great that the statistics are published in ways which block detailed study of the economic conditions of the different communities. None the less, for my purposes, the census data were sufficient to set some crude parameters for analysing my field notes and to clarify the minority situation of the Bharuchi Muslims.

Muslims account for only 9% of the total population of Gujarat – a proportion which is exceeded in eight other states in India. Moreover, in only four of the nineteen Gujarat administrative districts do Muslims amount to more than one-in-ten of the local population. Bharuch happens to be one of those districts – 15% of its population are Muslim.

Muslims are not an undifferentiated mass; they are stratified by caste-like formations, denominational divisions, social class and occupational differences (Misra 1964; Kamat 1981). In Bharuch district, many Muslims own land in their villages and are thus classified in Indian statistics as 'cultivators'. These cultivators have little in common with the landless poor who are crushed into the teeming slums of Gujarat's urban areas – even though many of these slum-dwellers happen to be Muslim (Engineer 1982a, 1982b).

If one looks at the language details published for Bharuch District there is another clue. The 1971 Census of India enumerated among the district's 1,109,601 inhabitants a total of sixty-two languages as mother tongue: 'the language spoken in childhood by the person's mother to the person'. In the census 91% of these persons gave Gujarati as mother tongue, 5% Bhili/Bhilodi, 2% Urdu, 1% Marathi and another 1% Hindi. Gujarati and Marathi are regional languages, Hindi is one of the national languages of India, Urdu is the language of the educated Muslim classes and Bhili is the language of one of the tribes which make up 45% of Bharuch district's population. The Muslims, in other words, are not the only minority in Bharuch or Gujarat. They are outnumbered by tribal peoples – the 'tribals' who form 14%, and the 'untouchables' who are 7% of Gujarat's population.

In day-to-day living in the village, no reference was made to these inter-ethnic differences and I could have remained oblivious to their significance had it not been for several significant, and revealing, developments during my field trips. In 1984, for instance, I slipped away for a solitary walk through village paths and had to be rescued by my hosts from a hostile crowd in the dingy huts on the edge of the village. When I asked about the people living outside the village and why they had been so hostile, I was told that they were 'BC', backward classes. When I sought some clarification of this term, my informants did not wish to amplify; they simply repeated their admonitions about keeping strictly to the parts of the village to which they had introduced me. It was only in 1985 (when everyone was shaken by the scale and ferocity of the rioting which broke out in Gujarati cities and the topic of 'reservations' dominated the newspapers and radio broadcasts) that my informants became more forthcoming and talked about the contemporary history of inter-communal relations and government policies in relation to the backward classes – the tribal people and the untouchables. They also explained their own resentment and sense of injustice about being excluded from the reservation measures when many people who were better off than themselves could enjoy protected status in education and jobs.

In Britain, programmes to eradicate discrimination against minority ethnic groups in society and to promote 'equal opportunities' in public institutions are a recent phenomenon, initiated with reference to similar programmes in the USA. At no time has there been any public acknowledgement of the fact that in India there is a long history of protective legislation and positive discrimination or that the British themselves initiated such measures when they still ruled India. It was therefore with a sense of anticipation that I embarked on my enquiries into the backward classes, the reservation policies, their impact on the people at the centre of my field studies and the tensions and conflicts of interest into which the policies are now meshed.

In India the political authorities and the judiciary have been firm in their resolve to sustain policies of protective measures for the untouchables and the tribals – who have endured centuries of discrimination. Article 341 of the Indian Constitution authorises the president of India to specify 'castes, races or tribes or parts of or groups within castes, races or tribes which shall for the purpose of this Constitution be deemed to be Scheduled'. Scheduled castes and tribes qualify for reserved places in political representation, at both state and union level – currently 79 out of 542 of the seats in national parliament and 541 out of 3,977 seats in state assemblies are reserved for the scheduled castes. They also qualify for reserved places in education and employment and each state can make adjustments in the lists of groups which qualify as scheduled and in the reservations to which they are entitled. In Gujarat, twenty-nine tribes or tribal groupings have been listed as scheduled tribes in the 1981 census, plus thirty scheduled castes or caste groupings. Together the two lists account for 21.4% of the state's population. In the villages where I stayed, scheduled castes accounted for 6% of the local population and tribals for 11% according to the 1961 Census of India, and it was they who were described to me as the 'backward classes'.

Both at Union and state level, the reservation policies have had effect and some individuals and communities of scheduled-caste and scheduled-tribe origin have succeeded in breaking out of the grinding poverty and political exclusion which would otherwise have remained their historical lot. Some indeed have established themselves as wealthy and influential class factions, creaming off the benefits which were intended to be spread more widely and leaving behind the mass of other scheduled caste and tribal people. The dangers in this situation have been recognised by the Supreme Court of India, the guardian of the spirit and intent of the constitution. Since the 1970s there has been a number of cases in which the court has gradually inserted income ceilings on the rights of individuals to claim the benefits of reservations, and in 1985 the new policy was enshrined in the case of Vasanth Kumar (*All India Reporter* 1985). The scale of poverty among the tribal and untouchable people of India is still so massive that this adjustment by the Supreme Court will have limited effect, dependent as it is on existing practices being challenged by politically astute individuals. It is also resented bitterly by the people who must give up their privileges.

At the same time, the 'scheduling' of tribal and untouchable people, and their related reservations, have been much envied by other caste and communal factions, many of whom are themselves desperately poor. They have lobbied and fought their way into recognition as 'other backward classes' (OBCs) who then qualify for their own reserved seats in education and employment. Even in Gujarat, one of the wealthier states of India, the state government's own estimate is that 60% of the population are living below the poverty line and several administrations have set up commissions of inquiry to report on which communities should be listed as OBCs and by what criteria. In 1980, for instance, the Gujarat government accepted the report of a commission which recommended that another 82 communities should be classified as OBCs and thus be given reserved seats in education and state employment. Among these communities, 22 were Muslim caste groupings, and Muslims were thus drawn closer into the fray of the politics of reservations in Gujarat.

The combination of threat to the privileges of the upper-class factions, the increased competition for scarce resources among a rapidly growing and increasingly impoverished population, and the lobbying for protected status as OBCs is a volatile mix. When, in addition, Muslim groups are among those lobbying for OBC status, then the historical well of distrust between Hindus and Muslims can be tapped to heighten the conflict between competing claims of classes, castes and factions.

Recently in Gujarat there have been changes in the balance of political power which have brought the issue onto the agenda (Sanghavi 1982), and since 1981 the contest about reservations has reached extremes of agitation and violence. It is at first difficult to grasp the reason why this should be so, because, from an all-India perspective, the Gujarat government has not been particularly radical in its policies – south Indian states, such as Madras, Mysore, Karnataka and Tamil Nadu have all done more by way of reservation of jobs in government employment. Moreover, in the south the whole operation has gone more smoothly (Mandal Commission 1980). Even though the 1980 Gujarat government lists encompassed 60% of the population, the places which were reserved for competition by the designated tribes, castes and classes amounted to only 25% of the total available. Moreover, the groups which qualified for reserved places were barred from competing for the remaining 75% of places.

There appears to be little immediate advantage for any of the groups which joined the lists. However, it is not simply numbers and proportions which count; the issue of reservations comes alive when sensitive niches in the economy are penetrated. The education places and the jobs which are demarcated by the reservation policies are highly desirable and subject to fierce competition because they can promise entry to a resource which is extremely scarce in an economy such as that of Gujarat, namely white-collar and professional posts (Alavi 1985).

It is the government and municipal sectors in the 'other workers' category which have been the target of the reservation policies, and it is the effect on specific niches within this category which triggered one hostile response. The labour market of Gujarat, like all other aspects of society, is stratified into complex sectional and communal interests which restrict competition and seek to perpetuate the status quo by ensuring that all recruitment to jobs, of whatever kind, is done by 'word of mouth', via the networks of people already employed or with influence over those making decisions. Reservation policies drive a wedge into word of mouth recruiting by demanding advertising of posts, preference to be given to candidates of specified reservation status, and, in many instances, refusal to allow any substitute if an appropriate and suitable candidate is not found. Instead the post remains vacant.

It was places in higher education which became the catalyst of the recent disturbances in Gujarat. Demonstrations against reservation of places in postgraduate medical school sparked off riots which lasted thirty days in nine of Gujarat's nineteen districts including Bharuch and resulted in thirty-four deaths and fifty-two persons injured and the destruction of the livelihood of many hundreds of people (Bose 1981). Gujarat has one of the highest rates of literacy in India, so the struggles had a material base – there would be candidates suitably qualified to take the reserved places. The threat was such that an alliance of middle-class caste Hindus formed the All-Gujarat Education Reforms Agitation (AGERA) to lead and maintain the struggle against reservations (Gandhi 1985). From the college campuses, where students were agitating, often backed by their families in AGERA, the demonstrations spread into the poorest quarters of the cities. Here, in turn, serious conflicts were inflamed, feeding off the intensity of competition and power struggles among people who were eking out precarious existences in the overcrowded urban environment (Desai 1981). Crowds and mobs were mobilised as 'Muslim' and 'Hindu'.

The violence was worst in the slums, but it did spill over into other parts of town, and to other cities, so that its impact was widespread and caused considerable alarm even in the rural areas. The Bharuchi Muslim cultivators have to date escaped unscathed. They have been protected by the fact that they are spatially separated not only from caste Hindus, tribals and the impure castes – including the untouchables – but also from other Muslims who were caught up in the mob violence. Their kin in the towns were not so fortunate and, for one of the transcontinental families in my study, the reservation riots were a contributing factor in their decision about further migration to Blackburn.

The Bharuchi Muslims in Blackburn

Blackburn is a town of 140,000 inhabitants which is located 40 km from Manchester in the north-west of England. Long before the Gujaratis started to migrate to England, Blackburn was integrally involved in trading connections with India through the cotton-textile industry which had been the mainstay of its local economy. Like other Lancashire cotton towns it has known periods of enormous expansion and equally drastic decline. Most recently it has succeeded in diversifying its industrial base into engineering and electronics, regenerating its commercial and shopping facilities, and upgrading the quality of much of its housing stock (Robinson 1986).

Migration from Gujarat and other parts of the Asian sub-continent began in the late 1950s and early 1960s and gained momentum as the textile industry experienced another of its periodic labour shortages. Initially it was mainly men who migrated, as workers, and left their families in their home towns and villages, but, in the late 1960s and early 1970s, wives and children began to travel to join their menfolk and to settle with them in Blackburn. One of my contacts, for instance, arrived in Blackburn to work in a local mill, having been told about such opportunities while working as a cleaner in hotels in Scandinavia. His wife came to join him in 1970 and all their children have been born in Blackburn.

Where do the Bharuchis figure in local statistics? For my purposes the national census in Britain is even less informative than that of India because neither mother-tongue nor religious statistics are collected. Instead, the most effective indicators must be sought in extrapolation from details about 'place of birth' of individuals and of heads of households. In 1981, the census figures for Blackburn showed that 13% of the local population had been born outside the United Kingdom, 2,189 in Éire, and 15,000 in the 'New Commonwealth' – 8,339 in India, 5,692 in Pakistan, 1,131 in East Africa, and several hundred in Hong Kong and the Caribbean. Also settled in the town were Jewish, Ukrainian and Polish people, mostly refugees fleeing the genocide and repressions of war-time Europe (*Lancashire Evening Telegraph* 1958). There were also Italian migrants, and several hundred Chinese refugees from Vietnam.

At first sight, it would seem as if the ethnic horizon of the Bharuchis in Blackburn is dominated by the indigenous majority of Lancashire-born, predominantly working-class people, but also embraces a whole range of minorities who are new to them and who would, in turn, influence their adaptation to the British context. At the neighbourhood level, the inter-ethnic relations of the Bharuchis are indeed different from what they knew in Gujarat, but they do not approximate at all to the 'melting-pot' pluralism on which British social policy was based until recently. The Bharuchis have settled in the inner wards of the town where cheap housing was for sale. They, their kin and other Gujarati Muslims, from India and East Africa, now live in streets where the majority of their neighbours are not native Lancastrians, but co-religionists from Pakistani Punjab, and where they have been able to establish the essential infrastructure of enclave living around their mosques.

By migrating to Britain, the Bharuchis have left behind many of the sub-castes and communities of Gujarat and the scheduled caste and tribal people who are mostly too poor to migrate overseas. By settling in Blackburn they have been able to form an enclave which is shared with other Muslims who come from a neighbouring part of the Asian sub-continent. Their ethnic horizon has, if anything, become more closely circumscribed as a result of their migration and settlement.

What then are the chances of the Bharuchi enclave dispersing beyond kin boundaries? As migrants, the Bharuchis are intent on seeking out the best opportunities in the local economy and their settlement has coincided with the rise of unemployment in Lancashire and the consequent closing of many options. By 1986, unemployment had climbed to 14% across Lancashire and to 38% in the neighbourhoods where migrant households are concentrated (*Lancashire Monitor* January 1986). Many of the closures have been in the large factories where the workforce comprised people from the different communities. The local councils of Lancashire and Blackburn are major sources of employment for all grades of worker from manual to executive; together they have workforces totalling 57,000 but, by 1986 only 100 employees were known to be of New Commonwealth descent (Kelly 1986). Very few migrants from the Indian sub-continent, however well qualified at the time of departure for Britain, have penetrated the professions, finance or public administration. For the most part their jobs are characterised by irregular hours, low pay and heavy physical demands (Robinson 1986: 137).

The chances of the Bharuchis interacting much with people outside their enclave have been reduced and the economic advantages in drawing on the skills and resources of the extended family as an income-generating network have increased. The 'ethnic economy' (Westwood and Bhachu 1988) of textile outwork on home-based sewing machines is flourishing in Blackburn. Also, as Muslims they can draw on an extraordinarily rich repertoire of encapsulating resources, as pointed out in other chapters in this volume. Their marriage preferences create multiplex affinal ties among agnates and these overlapping ties reinforce each other so that kin are bound together particularly tightly (Ballard: chapter 10). Islam is a religion with congregational tendencies which lend themselves better than the domestic centred practices of Hinduism to residential clustering and organisational order (Bhardwaj and Rao: chapter 9). Islamic phenomena alter less, are less pliable, than those of Hinduism (Vertovec: chapter 4). It would seem as if Islam has lent itself repeatedly to the maintenance of communal ties among Asian communities throughout the world. Neither Gujarat nor Lancashire are exceptions to this general trend.

So what have been the responses of the local people and the authorities to the arrival and settlement of the Bharuchis and other migrants in the town? Blackburn has a history of resentment towards immigrant workers recruited to work in the mills. In the mid nineteenth century, for instance, there was a strike at a local mill in protest against migrant workers from Coventry (*Blackburn Standard* 1860) and I have anecdotal accounts of the resentment felt against the Irish migrants who have been arriving in Lancashire for more than a hundred years. We also know that the circumstances in which the migrants first came from the Indian sub-continent were not propitious. Although there was a temporary shortage of labour, resulting from the new shift system in the mills, 'the staple textile industry had been savaged by foreign competition . . . the housing stock had been largely untouched since its creation in the 1880s . . . the town was suffering a haemorrhage of young and educated people who left behind them a physically and psychologically aged population' (Robinson 1986: 16). In other words, a proud indigenous working-class tradition was in decline and many local people were extremely suspicious about the migrants and their role in the local economy.

These factors in themselves would have been sufficient basis for tension but many of the people of Blackburn have also absorbed the full flavour of war-time nationalism and imperialist attitudes to colonial peoples, exacerbated rather than eased as the colonies achieved political independence. When the migrants first began to arrive from the sub-continent they did not enter a conceptual vacuum; instead, they were greeted by a powerful and even inflammatory set of preconceptions about Asians, their alien habits and tendencies (Seabrook 1971: 43–5). These ideas were hardly likely to subside as the textile trade and the local economy went into further decline and as unemployment began to mount. Right-wing organisations, such as the National Front, with programmes and slogans blatantly antagonistic to 'Paki immigrants', found fertile ground on which to mobilise and to win support in one textile town after another. The very term 'Paki' which could not exist before Partition, is indicative of the force of feeling – it has become the single most commonly used form of reference and abuse in relation to all people of South Asian appearance.

Much less noisy but equally effective are the petty annoyances and everyday discriminations which exclude New Commonwealth migrants from the mainstream of economic and political life in the town. Until the Race Relations Acts of 1965, 1968 and 1976, racial discrimination was quite openly practised in the form of the colour bar against black and Asian people. The Race Relations Acts had the effect of clearing the streets of the most overt forms of discrimination, such as notices in the windows of lodgings stating 'Room to Let, No Blacks'. But they had minimal impact on the labour market or political systems which remained firmly resistant to the entry of the 'immigrants'. Discrimination against people of New Commonwealth descent – black people – has persisted. Writing in 1984, Brown commented 'For the most part, Britain's well-established black population is still occupying the precarious and unattractive position of the earlier immigrants. We have moved, over a period of eighteen years, from studying the circumstances of immigrants to studying the black population of Britain only to find that we are still looking at the same thing' (1984: 323).

The first response of the governments of the 1960s to the facts of racial disadvantage and to the inflammatory dangers of racial tensions was to adopt a stance of neglect, relying on a balance between limiting the numbers of immigrants, cleansing the most overt forms of discrimination from public places, and expecting the immigrants to assimilate. Then, in the 1970s, the Labour government launched a series of programmes of urban aid to alleviate the poverty of areas most affected by immigration. The mainstream politicians in all parties combined to exclude any form of racially explicit vocabulary in political discourse and to maintain a set of euphemisms which blurred the purpose and intent of what was clearly 'positive' intervention by government intended to improve race relations (Edwards and Batley 1978: 25). Not surprisingly, the programmes failed to shift discrimination which was based on steady and unspoken resistance. Many of the posts which were specially created for work with 'the immigrants' were actually filled by indigenous English. Central government initiatives became means of enlarging municipal resources, rather than of creating change and eliminating racial prejudice (Kelly 1986).

Now, however, in the late 1980s, the combination of constant pressure and protest by minority organisations and the urgent impetus of repeated and serious racial disturbances in British cities (Joshua and Wallace 1983) has resulted in a significant change in political perspective – one municipality after another has declared openly that it is pursuing 'equal opportunities' policies as employer and provider of services. The 1976 Race Relations Act cleared the statutory ground when it not only made all forms of direct and indirect racial discrimination illegal, but also placed specific duties on local authorities 'to make appropriate arrangements with a view to ensuring that their various functions are carried out with due regard to the need to eliminate unlawful racial discrimination and to promote equality of opportunity and good relations between persons of different racial groups'. These duties are not policed by central government and have been left as exhortation and admonition rather than statutory requirement. But gradually local councils have begun to make moves towards adopting the principles of the act into their administrative systems. They have established the appropriate data-collecting and monitoring mechanisms; they have adjusted the procedures by which staff are selected and promoted; in particular they have put an end to the time-honoured systems of word-of-mouth recruitment in the manual and basic service grades, which did so much to shore up the employment opportunities for local people.

'Municipal pluralism' is a recent development in British local government, particularly in Lancashire where the 'immigrants' have not exercised as much political muscle as in the metropolitan conurbations of London and the Midlands. How far the politicians and their officers are willing and able to sustain the programmes they have launched is the matter of key debate for many groups and organisations. Now that resources are being made available, other minority groups are claiming 'ethnic status' (*Blackburn Citizen* 1987) and increasing the competition for scarce resources. There is no unity of view among South Asians, some of whom are profoundly sceptical about what will result from all the noisy debate. The indigenous Lancastrians are viewed warily by the politicians who talk with some trepidation about 'white backlash'. By undertaking these programmes, the municipal politicians have launched themselves into fields of tension in which feelings run high on all sides.

The local councils in Britain have taken so long to respond to the intentions of the 1976 Race Relations Act that they are now initiating change in a form which originated in an era of mainstream political consensus, but at a time when a radical right-wing government has been in power for nine years. Government ministers in Britain today do not feel the same inhibitions as their predecessors about implementing measures, such as the 1981 Nationality Act and tighter restrictions on immigration, which are blatantly discriminatory in intent. Also, they are giving voice to fears about the 'swamping of British culture' which were formerly consigned to the political sidelines (Barker 1981; Rushdie 1982; Sivanandan 1986). The disjuncture between belated local government action and central government intentions is one which is certain to inflame rather than cool conflicts, and the very low level of representation of the New Commonwealth minorities at any level of the political process is one which raises questions about the capacities of local government to keep themselves informed about developments among the minority communities or to sustain a controversial and fractious momentum.

One of the ways in which councils have sought to accommodate the pluralist forces which they have unleashed is to adopt as wide-ranging an approach as possible. Lancashire County Council, for instance, adopted an equal opportunity policy in October 1985 which stated that 'Lancashire County Council as an equal opportunity employer intends that no job applicant or employee shall receive less favourable treatment because of his or her sex, marital status, race, colour, nationality, national origin, ethnic origin, sexual orientation or disability, nor be disadvantaged by any other condition or requirement which cannot be shown to be justifiable.' In their attempt to accommodate pressure groups Lancashire County Council has blurred its commitment to implementing the Race Relations Act and created a set of 'disadvantaged' categories which have very different meanings and which sit uneasily within the class traditions which have played such a significant part in local politics.

Another mechanism adopted by the council was to create new posts to which they could recruit staff who were actually drawn from the groups they had identified as disadvantaged. In this way they could delay the necessity for tackling the far more difficult matter of intruding into the restrictive practices which had developed in their workforce. Word of mouth recruiting functions at all grades of council employment, but is more easily detected in the manual grades where there is the greatest turnover of staff. As councils have found, to their cost, in other parts of Britain, intervening in the protectionist custom and practice of long-established networks of recruitment meets with considerable resistance.

The council's policies have raised expectations among various sections of the minority groups they identified, and have multiplied the pressures on them to sustain the momentum. Now, however, the equal opportunities programme is in serious difficulties because council budgets have been drastically reduced by central government and there is not the same room for financial manoeuvre as in the past. The politicians cannot continue to create new posts and they must now decide whether they are capable of forcing their policies deeper into their own administrative systems.

The analogy with the backward classes and the 'other backward classes' is irresistible. If the councillors do follow their intent, then they will challenge the class interests of the native Lancastrians – sections of whom have enjoyed some degree of protection of their interests through restrictive and discriminatory practices in council employment. If the councils do not challenge these interests, then they will have raised expectations among a range of minority groups who would feel embittered and betrayed by failed promises.

Conclusion

When I was working in Gujarat, one of my most helpful inform-ants was a young man, Iqbal. His father, son of Bharuchi cultivators, had attained educational qualifications and achieved the esteemed status of headmaster in a Muslim primary school in the city of Baroda. He was ambitious for Iqbal and had financed him through the first year of his university studies, in the hope that he would eventually find himself a salaried post, perhaps in a bank. However, Iqbal's studies had been suspended while the university was closed during all the demonstrations against the reservation policies, and his family reviewed his situation, deciding that he had limited prospects of ever completing his studies, still less of finding a good job, and that a radical change of plans was required.

Iqbal began to train in home tailoring, a reliable source of income in the ethnic economy of Baroda, or anywhere else that he might settle where he could be protected by the extended network of his kin. Then a marriage was arranged with his father's sister's daughter in Blackburn. The possibility that they could make a home for themselves in Baroda was not one which they could view with any optimism – the housing problems in the city are overwhelming for a low-paid worker, the seriousness of the communal tensions within the reservation riots had instilled anxiety about his future prospects as a Muslim, and he had little chance of ever completing his studies. By moving to Lancashire, he would join kinsfolk that he knew well, be assured of work, find housing of a quality way beyond his reach in India and even renew his studies. Various members of the Blackburn family, including his fiancée, flew across to Gujarat to visit, to make the ritual preparations and to assist him in the arrangements for his exit from India and entry to Britain. In June 1988, the last stage of the marriage rituals was completed in Blackburn and he is now settled with his wife.

By moving to Blackburn, Iqbal has experienced both familiarity and contrast. On the one hand he is very much 'at home', living among Bharuchi kinsfolk, speaking his mother tongue, praying in the mosque just minutes away, earning his keep as a tailor while he waits to qualify for admission to the local college. On the other, he is learning every day about the differences he must absorb in his new context. It has come as something of a shock to realise that there is a deal of hostility in the town to immigrants such as himself, that there is little social mixing between the minorities and with the Lancashire majority and that, as an Asian, he is counted among the 'backward classes' in Britain. If he stays within the enclave, he is secure in a familiar context and can visit kin in many other towns and cities, perhaps even find some other work through them. If he succeeds in leaving the Bharuchi enclave in order to pursue his studies, he will learn even more about racially discriminatory restrictions and constraints on his ambitions to achieve a worthwhile career.

Iqbal's personal history graphically illustrates the comparative perspective to which I was drawn by my experience of the visiting season for the 'transcontinental families' of Gujarat. When I paid my first visit to the village, I thought that my work would follow the path conventional for a British social anthropologist and focus on some aspects of the migration of villagers from an essentially rural domain to the startling contrast of the urban context of Blackburn. By now, it must be clear that I was disabused of any notion I may have had that the Bharuchi villages were discrete rural systems which had no connection with urban settings or with issues which are normally assumed to be 'urban' – such as intercommunal/racial relations. At every level of engagement with the pluralist system of Gujarat, the Bharuchis are acutely aware of their minority status and experience the impact of reservation policies on a day to day basis, whether in town or countryside. Their responses to the reservation policies are particularly acute because, as cultivators, they are excluded from the protective provisions and resent the fact that they do not qualify for educational seats and financial aid, and cannot enter the restricted routes to government employment.

I was travelling in Gujarat at a time when communal tensions were unusually heightened, and it was this fact which drew my attention to the minority context of the Bharuchis. However, now that I have shifted perspective, I suggest that there are lessons to learn from Gujarat. The history of Iqbal and his fellow Bharuchis makes it clear that there are considerable advantages for them in settling in that town and drawing on the rich resources which they have in their enclave, so long as the racial tensions of the town remain at a low level. In principle, it would seem as if the advantages of staying in Blackburn should increase as a result of the equal opportunities policies of the council, not least because of the range of special posts for which Asians are especially encouraged to apply. But in Gujarat lies a cautionary tale: on the one hand, sectional interests can dominate among the groups targeted for protectionist measures, on the other, groups excluded from the measures will begin to express their resentments.

Britain's involvement, as ruler in India, with the racial and ethnic minorities of the sub-continent is not something which is usually seen as relevant to discussion about 'race relations' in Britain. With the Bharuchi

and other migrants from Gujarat, whether Muslim or Hindu, the connections are direct because they come from and arrive in societies where
relations between communities are strained and where the authorities are
intervening in order to ease both popular and institutionalised discrimination amongst minorities. The minority-majority tensions in Lancashire
have not, as yet, developed into anything on the same scale or intensity as
in Gujarat, but it is now clear that there are important lessons to learn
from study of the history of reservations in India and application of this
study to equal opportunity policies in Britain.

References

I am very grateful to Werner Menski of the School of Oriental and African Studies,
University of London for his comments on an earlier draft of this paper.

Alavi, H. 1985. 'Pakistan and Islam: ethnicity and ideology', Paper for the Middle
East Discussion Group, Oxford.
Ali, N. 1988. 'Growing communalism in India', *Asian Times*, 5 February.
The All India Reporter 1985. Vol. 72, Supreme Court Section.
Anwar, M. 1979. *The Myth of Return: Pakistanis in Britain*, London: Heinemann.
Barker, M. 1981. *The New Racism: Conservatives and the Ideology of the Tribe*,
London: Junction Books.
Blackburn Citizen 1987. 'Irish community "ethnic minority"', 17 April.
Blackburn Standard 1860. 'The Colne strike and strike at Moorgate Fold', 8
August.
Bose, P.K. 1981. 'Social mobility and caste violence. A study of the Gujarat riots',
Economic and Political Weekly, 16: 713–16.
Brown, C. 1984. *Black and White Britain: The Third PSI Survey*, London: Policy
Studies Institute and Heinemann.
Desai, I.P. 1981. 'Anti-reservation agitation and structure of Gujarat society',
Economic and Political Weekly, 16: 819–23.
Edwards, J. and R. Batley 1978. *The Politics of Positive Discrimination. An
Evaluation of the Urban Programme, 1967–77*, London: Tavistock.
Engineer, A.A. 1982a. 'Gujarat – communal violence in Ahmedabad', *Economic
and Political Weekly*, 17: 100.
    1982b. 'Baroda riots – wages of political corruption', *Economic and Political
Weekly*, 17: 1845–6.
Gaborieau, M. 1985. 'From Al-Beruni to Jinnah. Idiom, ritual and ideology of the
Hindu-Muslim confrontation in South Asia', *Anthropology Today*, 1 (3):
7–14.
Gandhi, N. 1985. 'Women in the Gujarat agitation', *Outwrite*, 41, November.
Gordon, P. 1986. *Racial Violence and Harassment*, London: The Runnymede
Trust.
Hiro, D. 1982. *The Untouchables of India*, London: Minority Rights Group.
Joshua, H. and T. Wallace 1983. *To Ride the Storm: The 1980 Bristol 'Riot' and the
State*, London: Heinemann.
Kamat, A.R. 1981. 'Literacy and education of Muslims. A note', *Economic and
Political Weekly*, 26: 1031–3.
Kelly, E. 1986. 'Ten years on – racial equality and local authorities in the north of

Britain', Paper for the seminar Race and the Elected Member, Manchester University, September 1986.

1987. 'Pupils, racial groups and behaviour in school', in *Racism in Schools – New Research Evidence*, A Multicultural Education Pamphlet, Trentham Books.

Lancashire Evening Telegraph 1958. 'Patriotic Poles still dream of home', 16 July.

Lancashire Monitor 1986. 'A planning and industrial information bulletin for Lancashire', prepared by the County Planning Department, no. 38, January.

The Mandal Commission 1980. *Report of the Backward Classes Commission, Part 1, vols 1 and 2*, Government of India.

Misra, S.C. 1963. *The Rise of Muslim Power in Gujarat. A History of Gujarat from 1298 to 1442*, Bombay and London: Asia Publishing House.

1964. *Muslim Communities in Gujarat. Preliminary studies in their history and social organisation*, Baroda: Department of History, Maharaja Sayajirao University of Baroda.

Robinson, V. 1986. *Transients, Migrants and Settlers: Asians in Britain*, Oxford University Press.

Rushdie, S. 1982. 'The New Empire within Britain', *New Society*, December, 417–20.

Sanghavi, N. 1982. 'Gujarat: impending realignments', *Economic and Political Weekly*, 17: 1947.

Seabrook, J. 1971. *City Close-Up*, Harmondsworth: Penguin Books.

Sheth, 1985. 'Communalism in India', *India Today*, 15 May.

Sivanandan, A. 1986. *From Resistance to Rebellion: Asian and Afro-Caribbean Struggles in Britain*, Race and Class Pamphlet no. 1, London: Institute of Race Relations.

Watson, J.L. (ed.) 1977. *Between Two Cultures: Migrants and Minorities in Britain*, Oxford: Basil Blackwell.

Westwood, S. and P. Bhachu, (eds.) 1988. *Enterprising Women: ethnicity, economy and gender relations*, London: Routledge.

12

Boom and gloom: the success and failure of South Asians in Britain

Vaughan Robinson

The introduction to this book draws attention to the issue of scale in the study of South Asian populations overseas and subsequent chapters provide examples of the two main levels of analysis. On one level, analysts seek to articulate the broad position of South Asians in relation to the societal structures of those countries in which they have settled. On the other, they tease out the detail of identities and social relations *within* those same Asian populations, and some workers even draw the conclusion from this that there are no meaningful aggregates which can be labelled as South Asian communities overseas. Religious, caste and regional identities are simply too independent and mutually exclusive to allow generalisations which could apply to all South Asian groups within a given overseas satellite. Although these two contrasting scales of analysis are really no more than the manifestation of differing disciplinary philosophies, there is an unfortunate tendency to regard them as mutually incompatible. Indeed, on occasions, the reader is left with the distinct impression that proponents of the two scales of analysis may not even have grasped that their objects of study are one and the same. An anthropologist may thus reject a detailed statistical analysis of South Asian disadvantage in the UK because the conclusions derived from it do not apply to the thirty households in Leicester who act as his respondents. Conversely, a sociologist may interpret levels of Asian self-employment in the UK purely in terms of racial discrimination in the labour market, without acknowledging the significance of antecedents such as group-specific merchant ideologies or previous experience as dukawallas in East Africa.

At present then, there is a clear difficulty in meshing together what could be complementary approaches because of disciplinary enmities and methodological antagonism. But clearly without such a *rapprochement* our understanding will never be more than partial or partisan. My own

269

attempt to set the particular within the general grew out of a need to make sense of a detailed study of the many South Asian communities in one northern textile town, Blackburn (Robinson 1986). However, one of the many weaknesses of that first attempt was that it was essentially static. Despite the development of a diachronic typology of Asian settlement in British cities – designed specifically to place Blackburn in a broader context – the analysis assumed an unchanging pattern of social and economic opportunities, and therefore concentrated upon how different South Asian sub-groups might opt to gain access to them. Since 1977 (when the fieldwork for the Blackburn study began) such an assumption has become increasingly indefensible. The last ten years have seen the culmination of a postwar process of demographic, economic and social restructuring which has completely redrawn the opportunity pattern on offer to every one of Britain's residents, regardless of ethnicity. South Asians in Britain now exist within a context very different from that which prevailed thirty years ago at the peak of their mass migration. Inevitably, changing national circumstances have touched elements of the South Asian population in different ways, but no group has been unaffected. This chapter attempts to elucidate the process of societal transformation and chart its impact upon the South Asian population as a whole. It is left to others to relate their detailed studies of different communities to these overarching processes, but if they choose to ignore the most significant transformation of British society for a century and a half they do so at their peril.

The winds of change

In the past thirty years or so, Britain has become a post-industrial society with major changes to almost all facets of the space-economy. Central to this has been a shift from an economy producing saleable commodities to one providing invisible services. The manufacturing sector fell in size by 44% between 1971 and 1984 with a loss of some 3.6 million jobs. Gains in the service sector (up 25% and 2.7 million jobs) have been insufficient to make up for this and the net effect has been both a reduction and sectoral redistribution of employment. Even within sectors, employment opportunities have not remained static as different industries have reacted to restructuring and recession in different ways. Some industries, textiles and engineering included, have been particularly vulnerable. In the former, employment has fallen from over 2 million in 1945 to 517,000 in 1986. In the latter, job loss has been a more recent phenomenon but has been no less severe: over 1 million jobs have disappeared in the last fifteen years. Even some service sectors have experienced reshaping, with transport and communications recording a net loss of 200,000 jobs between 1971 and 1986. Clearly then, the postwar period has seen a radical reshaping of the British economy and a shift to a service-based economy in which service workers outnumber those in manufacturing by three to one.

Given the varying fortunes of economic sectors and indeed of particular industries, it is hardly surprising that restructuring has had a differential impact upon population groups and parts of the country. Green and Owen (1985) have, for example, written of the 'technologisation' of the workforce. They describe how, with capital investment in new manufacturing processes, those jobs which remain are either highly specialised management functions or semi-skilled machine minding. The jobs which are lost are those for junior non-manual, skilled manual and unskilled manual workers. Indeed over the decade 1971–81, three-quarters of all job loss within manufacturing was concentrated into these three socio-economic groups. In contrast, the same period saw a net gain of 85,000 intermediate and senior white-collar jobs within manufacturing. There is also parallel evidence to indicate that the cost of restructuring is being shared unevenly between regions. There has been massive job loss in certain regions such as the North West (-16% 1979–86), Yorkshire (-12%), Wales (-17%) and the West Midlands (-10%), whilst others such as East Anglia ($+9\%$), the South West (-2%) and the South East (-2%) have broadly maintained or even marginally expanded their economic base. At a different spatial scale, job loss has also varied between conurbations, major cities, small towns and rural areas. Major conurbations and particularly their inner areas were especially vulnerable. London has lost 50% of its manufacturing employment since the 1960s and the other conurbations have recorded losses in excess of 40%. Conversely, the new jobs created by growth, relocation and the birth of new enterprises have clustered in the small and medium towns in a crescent 30 to 100 km from London (Champion *et al.* 1987). The generation of new employment has also had a selective impact on the sexes, with many of the new jobs being part-time service employment for women. Female employment in the service sector rose by almost 30% between 1971 and 1984, and two-thirds of this growth was made up of part-time employees (*Social Trends* 1987). In total then, the restructuring of the British economy has seen an overall reduction in economic opportunities, and their redistribution away from established regions, cities, sectors and industries.

In response to this changing pattern of opportunities, there has been a parallel redistribution of people, a process aided by rising postwar levels of personal mobility. Again it has been the major conurbations and their cores which have borne the brunt of this change. Some began to lose population before others, but by 1971 all six English conurbations were on a downward population trajectory. Greater London, for example, saw its population fall by 20% between 1951 and 1985 whilst the West Midlands experienced a fall of 7% in the fourteen-year period 1971–85. *Within* these conurbations, rates of loss were even more marked: Tower Hamlets in inner London experienced a 75% fall in population between 1901 and 1985. Further analysis of the combined process of suburbanisation and de-urbanisation which underlies such dramatic figures reveals that population loss was a problem in terms not only of quantity but also of its demographic selectivity. Research indicates that the young, white-collar workers, and decision makers were all over-represented in the movement out of the conurbations and that the groups left behind were the unskilled, the welfare-dependent, and those regarded as socially marginal. The movers overwhelmingly settled in small and medium free-standing towns and even in previously isolated rural areas. On the whole, population growth was concentrated south of a line linking the Severn and the Wash. Public and private investment would also tend to gravitate to these centres of growth and expansion.

The combined effect of these economic, social and demographic changes has been to sharpen significantly the degree of polarisation within Britain. The evidence for this can be found at all levels. Spatial analysts are again discussing regional disparities and are generalising these into a North–South divide (Champion *et al.* 1987), although there is also evidence of disparities between West and East as a result of the impact of North Sea oil (Champion and Green 1985). At finer spatial scales, other commentators are noting that urban-rural contrasts are becoming more pronounced as indeed are disparities between the suburbs and the inner city (Archbishop of Canterbury's Commission on Urban Priority Areas 1985). In the economy, too, signs of polarisation are more evident, with booming consumer and producer services but relatively stagnant manufacturing industry. Individuals and households are also finding themselves on diverging trajectories which explains the paradox of historically high unemployment at a time of unparalleled consumer spending, particularly on luxury commodities. Housing too is becoming more polarised, not only between owner-occupiers and a residual council sector, but also between those who own a home in areas experiencing rapid increases in property values and those who own homes in areas where property is almost unsaleable. And finally there is ample confirmation that income distribution in the UK is becoming more unequal, with the most affluent 20% of households gaining in their relative share of the country's wealth, whilst the least affluent 20% are losing despite differential taxing and transfer payments (*Social Trends* 1988). Indeed, these tendencies have been so marked and so consistent between a number of advanced western economies that they have led certain commentators to postulate a new social order with newly formed classes. Whether there really has been a 'new class' (Bruce-Biggs 1979) or simply realignments within existing classes is still unclear (Hacker 1979; Bell 1979), although at least one British commentator feels that middle-class values have been totally rewritten with a new emphasis upon instantaneous gratification and self-indulgent consumption (Samuel 1982).

In short then, national restructuring has offered a new range of opportunities to certain regions and groups of people whilst simultaneously withdrawing pre-existing opportunities from others. The result has been a more unequal society

> as between a majority in secure attachment to a still prosperous country and a minority in marginal economic and social conditions, the former moving into the suburban locations of the newer economy of a 'green and pleasant land', the latter tending to be trapped into the old provincial industrial cities and their displaced fragments of peripheral council housing estates.
>
> (Halsey 1987: 19)

Britain's South Asians: their migration and societal role

Two major accounts now exist of the growth of Britain's South Asian population (Visram 1986; Fryer 1984). Both stress that Indian migration to Britain has not just been a twentieth-century phenomenon, for an Indian population has been part of metropolitan society for almost 300 years. Visram, in particular, shows how during this period Indians have been merchant seamen, domestic servants, politicians, barristers, doctors and social celebrities. Indeed, prior to the 1950s, Indians in Britain might reasonably be described as a middle-class group with a preponderance of doctors (Kondapi 1949), students (Kanitkar 1972) and international businessmen (Desai 1963).

However, the scale and nature of Indian settlement altered radically in the 1950s, with the development of mass chain migration. South Asians were no longer migrating in search of qualifications and professional experience but to fill gaps in the lower orders of the British labour market. Migrants were largely unskilled and were drawn from specific areas of origin, sometimes even groups of villages. They were young, often single, labour migrants seeking to meet financial targets set by the head of the extended family before returning to the village of origin. They regarded themselves as economic transients and had a somewhat unfavourable opinion of British cultural and moral values (Robinson 1986). Between 1955 and 1962, 146,300 (net) Indian and Pakistani workers entered Britain, the timing of their migration being influenced by the varying fortunes of the UK economy (Robinson 1980a). However in 1962, the British government reacted to unregulated immigration and the increasing politicisation of the race relations issue by imposing restrictions on unskilled labour migration. This fundamentally altered both the nature of South Asian migration and the permanence of the resulting settlement. Migration was increasingly of (female) dependants and for marriage, and South Asian settlement became more permanent and family orientated. Subsequent legislation, designed to further restrict immigration, has strengthened these tendencies, whilst the youthful age structure of the South Asian population and its higher (albeit declining) fertility rates have ensured both a steady growth in numbers and an indigenisation of the population. Growth was also stimulated by the arrival of East African Asian refugees in the late 1960s and early 1970s (Robinson 1986). The most reliable government statistics now indicate that the South Asian population in Britain numbers some 1,140,000 of whom 760,000 are ethnic Indians and 380,000 are ethnic Pakistanis (OPCS 1986a). Of these totals, 35% and 40% respectively are now UK-born second generation. In total, the South Asian population constitutes 2.2% of the British population. Fertility rates still exceed those of the white population with total period fertility rates of 5.6 births for Pakistanis/Bangladeshis, 2.9 births for Indians and 1.7 births for Britons as a whole.

Inevitably, therefore, the South Asian population will form a growing proportion of the nation's people with government estimating that there may be up to 1.5 million ethnic South Asians in the UK by 1991 (OPCS 1979). Finally, it is important to note that demographically the South Asian population is actually an amalgam of sometimes contrasting constituents. The process of family reunion and reorientation to permanent settlement has not yet been uniform across the population. Gujarati Hindus and Sikhs, for example, have embraced both processes, while other groups such as the Bangladeshis and Pakistani Muslims are still in an earlier phase of development. These internal differences show clearly in statistics for such features as age structures, fertility rates and family sizes.

While internal differences between South Asian groups are of considerable interest, their study must be set within the broader context of how the encompassing society evaluates and behaves towards *all* South Asians. Rex (1970) argues that this can only really be understood in relation to the conditions which prevailed when the two groups first experienced sustained contact. In the case of Indians and Britons, this was under colonialism, during which Britain was in direct conflict with the Indian people and later subjugated them politically, economically and militarily. In the resulting hierarchy, Indians were seen as an inferior and conquered people and in time colour became a shorthand signifier of these characteristics. Although Rex is less convincing on how such attitudes and stereotypes were transferred from the limited number of Britons in India to the mass of the population in the UK, he argued that, eventually, they became internalised in the culture and institutions of the metropolitan society. Lawrence (1974) also suggested that the educational system played a key role in the process of transferral and internalisation, whilst others point to the importance of the media, the Church and popular literature. The net effect, however, was that generations of Britons learned that 'black people were different, that we were their masters and teachers, and that they were naturally subordinate to us' (Lawrence 1974: 55).

If anything, these views hardened rather than softened during the period of mass migration because members of the indigenous British working class were placed in a position where people whom they had traditionally regarded as inherently inferior were suddenly living next door to them, working in the same factories or even renting rooms in the same house. Status insecurity could only be avoided by social distancing and further stereotyping. South Asians became not only vanquished peasants but also people who overcrowded and failed to maintain good property, had dubious standards of personal hygiene, were social security scroungers, but simultaneously took all the 'good' jobs, ate cat and dog food, and poached local white girls (Seabrook 1971). These and pre-existing colonial stereotypes ensured that attitudes towards South Asians in the UK were at best grudging acceptance and at worst outright rejection (see Robinson 1987a for a study of attitudinal change and variation).

The net effect of this attitudinal context was to allocate a very specific role to South Asians in the UK. They were relegated to a position as an excluded underclass which would be allowed access to valued resources only in so far as it enhanced their value as marginal labour (Robinson 1986). Phillips (1986; 1987) has shown how access to 'good' housing has been restricted by both direct and indirect racial discrimination, while both Jenkins (1986) and Brennon and McGeevor (1987) indicate the strength of exclusion from a broader range of employment. The Home Affairs Committee (1986) discusses racial attacks and harassment and this, too, might be seen as a way of containing Asians within a particular (spatial) niche.

However, in order to fully understand the position of South Asians in

Britain, it is necessary to explore their role in the labour market in greater detail, since their migration was economically motivated. Given the antipathy which exists in Britain towards South Asians, there must have been clear reasons why, in the 1950s and 1960s, employers and government colluded in their acquiescence to immigration. Four such reasons can be identified all of which relate to differing aspects of the need for labour. Peach (1968) has argued that black immigration was allowed, and even in some cases encouraged, because of an absolute shortage of labour in the UK brought about by economic expansion. The success of the British economy had created new jobs both in new and existing industry. In certain regions the expansion of employment opportunities simply outstripped the availability of local labour and black labour was introduced to fill these vacancies. In other cases the process was somewhat less direct: successful industries had new vacancies which were attracting workers from other employers where the pay and conditions were less attractive. Again black labour was sought, but in this case for the old jobs vacated by white workers moving up the industrial hierarchy. For Peach then, black labour was used directly and indirectly to fill new vacancies generated by economic expansion. Fevre (1984) does not disagree, but proposes two further sets of circumstances where the immigration of black labour may be beneficial. Both cases involve changes in existing jobs rather than the addition of new ones. In one scenario, employers seeking to restructure in the face of declining competitiveness would invest capital in production processes which would degrade certain occupations to the point where white labour might either choose or be forced to withdraw. The example he cites of this is the instigation of night shifts in the wool textile industry. Here the cost of new machinery made twenty-four-hour running essential and operatives were required to supervise more machines. White women who could not legally be redeployed onto night shifts left the industry and were replaced by Asian men. In the second scenario, employers might attempt to reduce their unit labour costs rather than embark on restructuring. Here wages would not be maintained to the level necessary to attract white labour in the full knowledge that all vacancies would still be filled by Asians. In both these cases then, the use of Asian labour facilitated the painful and expensive process of adjusting to revised market conditions.

South Asians in the early 1970s

Professionals and East African refugees aside, Asian migration to Britain was thus motivated and sanctioned by the need for unskilled labour to fuel economic expansion or industrial transformation. And this is clearly reflected in the data on the position of Britain's South Asians at the start of the 1970s, prior to the real onset of recession. Heath and Ridge (1983) and Smith (1974), for example, investigated the de-statusing of black (mainly Asian) immigrants both as a consequence of migration and the lowly position accorded black workers in Britain. The latter discovered that 31% of those who had been partly skilled manual workers prior to migration had been downgraded into unskilled workers after migration. And an overwhelming 90% of those who had previously been white-collar workers had been forced to take manual employment. Indeed it was not unknown for Indians with degrees to work as labourers in foundries.

Table 12.1 provides a more detailed description of the socio-economic status of South Asians at that time. It reveals a number of points: first, regardless of sex, all three groups are under-represented in white-collar occupations; second, the degree and type of that under-representation varies, with Indian men, for example, being under-represented on aggregate despite having a greater relative presence in the professions than whites; third, Pakistani men have the weakest overall profile, despite being less recent arrivals than East Africans; and fourth, Asian manual employment is more often of the unskilled and semi-skilled type than is the case for whites.

Analysis of the industrial distribution of South Asian workers in 1971 also reveals a profile of marginality and vulnerability. Pakistanis were concentrated into textiles (18.9%), engineering and metal goods (17.8%), metal manufacturing and chemicals (11.3%) and transport and communications (6.8%). The same industries were also important for Indians although their relative order was different (6.8%, 17.7%, 11.3% and 10.5%, respectively). In addition Indians had a strong presence in professional and scientific employment (9.9%).

Chain migration from particular regions and villages, and the concentration of industrial sectors within parts of the UK ensured a high degree of spatial clustering of South Asians in the early 1970s. Indeed the 1971 Census found 65% of Pakistanis and 58% of Indians to be concentrated into the six English conurbations alone; these consist of Greater London, West Midlands, Greater Manchester, Merseyside, Tyneside and West Yorkshire. Within these, London was the dominant centre for both groups (with 33% of Indians and 22% of Pakistanis), followed by the West Midlands (14% and 17% respectively), and in the case of Pakistanis, West Yorkshire (16%) (Robinson 1988a). Lower down the urban hierarchy, South Asian settlement was prominent in the textile towns and heavy engineering towns, and was relatively absent from service centres and newer industrial settlements (Robinson 1986). In fact,

Table 12.1. *Socio-economic status of South Asians in the UK, 1971*

	Males				Females			
	Whites	Indians	Pakistanis	East Africans	Whites	Indians	Pakistanis	East Africans
Professionals	5	10	3 ⎫	10	1	4	7 ⎫	2
Employers/managers	13	6	4 ⎬	20	5	3	3 ⎬	38
Junior non-manual	18	15	5		50	43	45	
Total non-manual	36	31	12	30	56	50	55	40
Skilled manual	40	32	25	44	8	9	12	12
Semi-skilled	16	24	38	24	27	34	29	41
Unskilled manual	18	13	25	2	8	6	3	7
Total manual	74	69	88	70	43	49	44	60

Note: East African Asian data relate to 1974.
Sources: 1971 National Census, and Smith (1974).

only one of the twenty largest Asian settlements in 1971 could be described as being located in a city which was dependent upon an essentially twentieth-century economic base.

Within these centres, patterns of residential concentration also reflected the economic nature of migration. A range of empirical studies has demonstrated a remarkable degree of uniformity in the scale and form of Asian segregation in the early 1970s. Asians characteristically lived in those districts which encircled the commercial heart of the city, where they were in close proximity both to public transport and to places of work such as foundries or textile mills. A combination of exclusion from large parts of the housing market and a desire to retain community encapsulation ensured levels of segregation which exceeded those for most other ethnic groups. What is more, Asian segregation appeared to be rising at a time when, for example, West Indian levels were falling. In Blackburn, the Index of Dissimilarity for Asian-white segregation rose from 50.37 in 1968 to 54.74 in 1973 (Robinson 1980b). These high levels of concentration undoubtedly helped the development of community facilities such as shops, evening classes and places of worship, but they were also synonymous with the spatial marginalisation of the Asian population. Areas of Asian residence had some of the poorest housing and environmental conditions in Britain. Indeed, Smith (1974) found that the housing of Asians was inferior to that of whites on all counts.

In the early 1970s the Asian population in Britain was thus a utilitarian phenomenon, recruited to fulfil a specific function and allocated resources only in so far as was necessary to undertake this function. At the time, this role might not have been entirely alien or distasteful to Asians who had fulfilled similar functions elsewhere in the world quite profitably. Indeed, given the avowed aim of many of the labour migrants to return home to the sub-continent once their immediate financial targets had been met, the somewhat ascetic and undistracting nature of residence in the UK might not have been unwelcome.

Moving up and moving out?

As we have seen, the 1970s and 1980s marked the culmination of a period of profound change in the UK which has affected every one of the country's residents. Certain industries, regions and groups gained from this change while others lost. The critical question for South Asians is whether *they* were among the former or the latter.

The Office of Population Census and Survey (OPCS) Longitudinal Study (see Brown and Fox 1984) provides an indication of the socio-economic progress of a sample of ethnic South Asians between 1971 and

Table 12.2a. *Social mobility of ethnic Pakistanis, 1971–81 (%)*

		Social class in 1981[a]						
Social class in 1971		I	II	IIIN	IIIM	IV	V	Total
I	Prof and managerial	2.3	0.9	0.3	0.1			3.6
II	Employers and managers	0.1	3.7		0.6	0.4	0.1	5.0
IIIN	Junior non-manual	0.1	2.0	2.6	0.6	0.3		5.6
IIIM	Skilled manual		2.3	1.3	13.0	8.5	2.1	27.2
IV	Semi-skilled manual		3.4	2.1	10.8	18.1	6.0	40.4
V	Unskilled manual		0.6	0.3	4.0	7.6	7.6	18.1
Total		2.6	12.9	6.6	29.1	34.9	13.9	100

Note: England and Wales only; (*a*) N = 697.
Source: Calculated from specially commissioned table ASVR301 of Longitudinal Study.

Table 12.2b. *Social mobility of ethnic Indians, 1971–81 (%)*

		Social class in 1981[a]						
Social class in 1971		I	II	IIIN	IIIM	IV	V	Total
I	Prof and managerial	5.2	1.3	0.5	0.3			7.4
II	Employers and managers	0.9	8.2	1.4	0.6	0.6	0.1	11.8
IIIN	Junior non-manual	0.6	3.6	8.3	0.8	0.9	0.2	14.5
IIIM	Skilled manual	0.3	2.5	1.3	15.6	6.4	1.7	27.8
IV	Semi-skilled manual	0.2	3.4	2.7	7.4	13.7	2.4	29.7
V	Unskilled manual		0.4	0.4	2.5	2.7	2.7	8.7
Total		7.2	19.5	14.7	27.1	24.4	7.1	99.9

Note: England and Wales only.
Source: Calculated from specially commissioned table ASVR301 of Longitudinal Study.

1981. These data relate only to intra-generational social mobility not to that between generations. Table 12.2a and 12.2b contain special tabulations from this source. They reveal a number of points; first, that upward mobility exceeds downward mobility for both groups, although in each case about half the group (net) has remained static; second, that there has been little growth or diminution of the professional class; third, that one of the most notable changes has been significant movement into the professional/managerial class from skilled and semi-skilled manual work

(Pakistanis) and junior non-manual work (Indians); fourth, that as expected, given models of social mobility, the junior non-manual class has experienced some inflow from blue-collar employment and some out-flow to more senior white-collar employment; fifth, that in both cases the manual classes have declined in size especially within the semi-skilled category; and lastly, that there is considerable movement between the manual classes. In total, these findings suggest an upwardly mobile South Asian population which is making progress out of semi-skilled and unskilled manual employment into white-collar (self-) employment.

However, as Halsey (1987) has pointed out, such analyses are potentially flawed since they take no overt account of those who have become unemployed. In the Longitudinal Study data, this is of some significance, since unemployment within the sample rose from 3.1% to 13.0% (Indians) and 4.2% to 19.4% (Pakistanis). When this factor is included the analysis appears somewhat different. In both cases, white-collar numbers have increased, by 14% (Indians) or 35% (Pakistanis). Skilled and semi-skilled employment has declined (down by 17% for Indians and 18% for Pakistanis). And the most socially and economically marginal groups – the unskilled and the unemployed – have expanded greatly (46% for Indians and 32% for Pakistanis). This indicates strongly that the South Asian population, like the population as a whole, has become more polarised under the influence of restructuring and recession. Those people who have remained in employment have gained from these trends, but others have lost their positions in the labour market entirely. Clearly the overall pattern has changed (cf. Heath and Ridge 1983). Table 12.3 draws together the analysis and illustrates the national picture which now exists for those in employment. Again, though, it excludes the sizeable number of blue-collar workers who have experienced downward mobility into unemployment.

Changes in industrial classifications prevent definitive statements about the impact of restructuring upon ethnic industrial concentration. Those data which do exist suggest an essentially static picture over the last decade and a half. Brown's (1984) data indicate continued Indian concentration in transport services, engineering/metal goods, vehicles, textiles and metal manufacture. Pakistanis retained their concentrations in textiles, engineering/metal goods, vehicles, metal manufacture and transport services. The most recent Labour Force Surveys (OPCS 1986c) are in general accord with Brown's earlier findings for inner city South Asians. However, they do reveal one inconsistency which is entirely in line with those trends in social class identified above, that is, a significant expansion of both Indians and Pakistanis into the retail, distribution and catering fields. According to OPCS, approximately one-third of each of the groups

Table 12.3. *Socio-economic status of South Asians in the UK, 1984*

	Males				Females			
	Whites	Indians	Pakistanis/ Bangladeshis	East Africans	Whites	Indians	Pakistanis/ Bangladeshis[a]	East Africans
Professionals	7	10	5 ⎱	} 22	1	5		} 7
Employers/managers	19	20	12 ⎰		8	6		
Junior non-manual	17	15	10	21	52	40		52
Total non-manual	43	45	27	43	61	51		59
Skilled manual	38	33	42	31	8	11		3
Semi-skilled	13	17	23	22	22	33		36
Unskilled manual	5	4	7	3	8	4		3
Total manual	56	54	72	56	38	48		42

Note: [a] Pakistani/Bangladeshi female sample too small to allow accurate calculations; East African Asian data relate to 1983.
Sources: OPCS (1986b) and Brown (1984).

is now found within this sector, no doubt as a result of the shift to self-employment. OPCS are however the first to admit that sampling errors for the Labour Force Survey are high.

Fortunately, the evidence for changes in the spatial distribution of Britain's South Asian population is much richer. This is perhaps because space and spatial distribution is the central concern of only one discipline (see Robinson 1987b for a review of the last thirty years research by British geographers of ethnic relations). At the coarsest level, this work has demonstrated that South Asians are indeed still concentrated into limited parts of the country. Analysis of unpublished 1981 Census data for all of England and Wales' 140,000 Enumeration Districts (EDs) reveals that 62%, 75%, 85% and 94% of those administrative units had no residents born in India, East Africa, Pakistan and Bangladesh, respectively. South Asian settlement is still, therefore, an unusual phenomenon for the majority of the country. However, closer analysis of the same data set indicates that South Asian settlement cannot be so easily summarised. Table 12.4 looks at the clustering of the different South Asian birthplace groups into Enumeration Districts containing varying concentrations of those same groups. It demonstrates that between 18% (Pakistanis) and 33% (East Africans) of South Asians live in districts in which they are likely to be the only such family or in which there might possibly be one other. At the other extreme, between 2% (Indians) and 6% (Bangladeshis) of these groups live in EDs where they are the majority birthplace group. Taken together, and even allowing for the problem of whites born in the Indian sub-continent, these data indicate three points; first, that the majority of the country is devoid of Asian settlement; second, that areas of marked clustering still exist with, for example, one-in-four Pakistanis living in EDs where that birthplace group forms more than 20% of the population; but that, third, intermediate areas also exist where Asians are living at very low densities in essentially white districts. Undoubtedly this latter group of Asians contains both the elite, who will always have been residentially dispersed in prestigious neighbourhoods, and those families who have begun to disperse from ethnic colonies during the 1970s. Regardless of this distinction, the data point to a situation in which polarisation is now present between those who remain in ethnic clusters and those who have left them.

Mention of the term 'dispersal' here could be very misleading. It implies wholesale movement out of inner-city ethnic colonies either to the suburbs or to exurban locations, and therefore a radical relocation of a group's centre of gravity. This is not an image which is consonant with a discussion of South Asian dispersal because the underlying trend in the settlement of that group has been stability. Indeed the hierarchy of Asian

Table 12.4. *Residential concentration of South Asian born people in Britain, 1981*

No. of people in an ED born in a particular South Asian country	% of average ED population	% of			
		Indians	Pakistanis	Bangladeshis	E. African Asians
1–5 people	0.1–1	25.0	17.6	26.5	33.5
6–45 people	1.1–10	41.7	39.6	43.1	51.7
46–90 people	10.1–20	14.1	18.2	13.7	13.3
91–135 people	20.1–30	8.4	10.7	4.8	1.4
136–180 people	30.1–40	5.6	7.4	3.8	0.0
181–225 people	40.1–50	2.7	2.9	1.9	0.0
225 + people	50.1 +	2.1	3.5	6.2	0.0

Note: column 2 assumes an average ED size of 450 people.
Sources: calculated from unpublished tabulations of 1981 Census data.

settlement was essentially fixed by 1971 and has simply endured in a modified form over the last seventeen years. The major conurbations have, for example, increased their importance for South Asian settlement over the period 1971 to 1985. Indian concentration in the six English conurbations rose from 58% to 65% and that of Pakistanis increased from 65% to 71%. Lower down the urban hierarchy, the picture is also one of stability despite restructuring and recession. Many existing centres of settlement have retained or even increased their importance (Figure 12.1). However within this essentially static gross picture there do appear to have been significant changes, already hinted at in the previous paragraph. Figure 12.1 and Table 12.5 allow a more explicit consideration of their nature. They demonstrate the strengthening position of the textile centres, but more importantly the pioneering of new territory particularly within London. There, the inner areas have experienced relative decline to the benefit of the suburbs and those boroughs with service-based economies. Similar trends may also have been apparent within Greater Manchester and the West Midlands, had disaggregated data been available. And finally, outside the conurbations, there is evidence of relatively rapid growth in suburban and service centres such as Milton Keynes, Solihull, Basingstoke, Aylesbury and St Albans.

To summarise then, the last decade and a half has not seen a radical reshaping of South Asian settlement patterns despite the tumultuous restructuring of the space-economy. Rather, existing cities have retained their absolute dominance through a combination of natural increase and family reunion. Within the rank order some cities have fared better than others, but the major element of change has been an undercurrent of short-range, often intra-urban mobility of South Asian families out of ethnic areas into adjacent or nearby 'white' areas. As they have dispersed, they have 'joined' – although not necessarily in a physical or geographical sense – those middle-class Asians who had always resided outside ethnic territory. Again, contrasts within the population have been strengthened rather than weakened.

This same finding of increased diversification within the South Asian population has also come from the literature on intra-urban segregation. Few longitudinal studies of segregation in British cities exist, but among those which do there is consensus that South Asian segregation has declined since the early 1970s. Data for Wolverhampton, for example, show the Index of Dissimilarity falling from 51.7 in 1971 to 42.3 in 1981 when measured at the ward level. Table 12.6 charts the decline of segregation in Blackburn from its high point in 1973 to its current figure of just over 52; a fall of 11% in as many years. Although there are exceptions to this pattern of falling segregation (Peach 1987), it does point to the

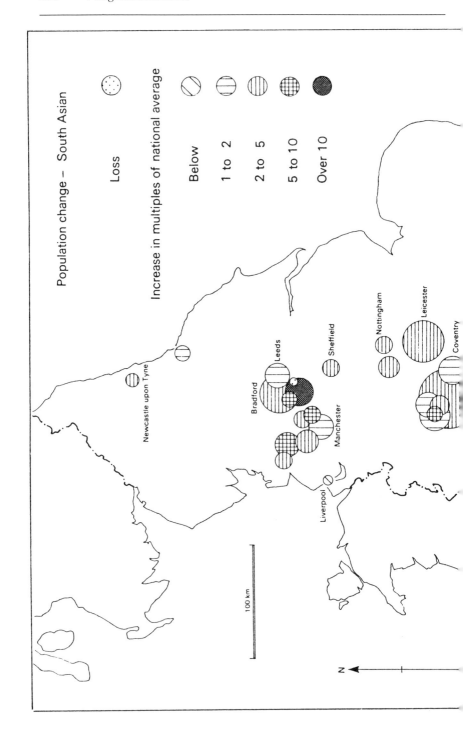

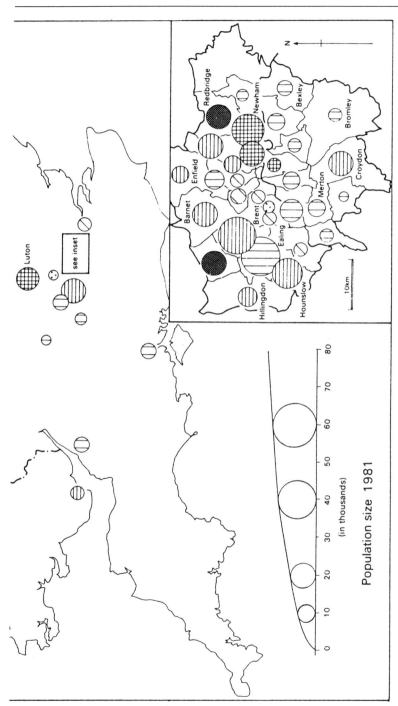

Map 12.1 Urban distribution of Britain's South Asian population and its change, 1971–81

Table 12.5. *The South Asian urban system in Britain, 1971–81*

Urban type	% S. Asian population 1971	% S. Asian population 1981	Average % growth 1971–81	Average change of rank within urban hierarchy 1971–81
I *London*				
traditional industrial areas	4.6	4.4	137	+ 4.6
new industrial areas	2.4	1.6	67	− 15.0
inner areas	19.9	16.5	58	− 11.6
suburbs mixed	10.1	11.7	155	+ 4.1
suburbs exclusive	3.3	3.1	108	− 0.7
service	8.6	10.3	159	+ 3.9
II *Conurbations*				
traditional industrial areas	10.1	10.8	144	0.0
service/port areas	0.9	0.8	92	+ 2.0
service/textile areas	4.9	4.7	118	0.0
III *Service centres*				
commercial	1.9	1.6	92	+ 0.8
professional/administration	1.1	1.1	95	− 1.0
IV *Industrial centres*				
textiles	11.9	14.0	166	+ 3.9
textiles/service	5.9	6.9	161	+ 4.0
engineering/commerce	0.4	0.5	212	+ 1.0
engineering/railways	5.2	5.1	134	+ 0.7
heavy engineering	8.6	6.7	148	− 3.0

Note: typology taken from Robinson (1986). Data from national Censuses.

Table 12.6. *Residential segregation of South Asians in Blackburn,*
1973–85

Year	Index of dissimilarity	Year	Index of dissimilarity
1973	58.74	1979	54.98
1974	56.96	1980	55.67
1975	55.96	1981	53.58
1976	56.14	1982	53.34
1977	55.39	1983	52.87
1978	56.92	1984	51.80
		1985	52.20

Source: calculated from name counts off the electoral register.

pioneering of new areas by Asians. Several reasons can be suggested for
this: first, the desire to create space to facilitate the process of communal
fission after an initial period of fusion. Robinson (1979; 1986) and Phillips
(1982) have discovered evidence of this tendency in Blackburn and
Leicester respectively, whilst Bhardwaj and Rao elsewhere in this volume
comment on a similar trend in the US (chapter 9). Second, the movement
of South Asians into public housing – which was previously closed either
because of its unsuitability or its lack of availability – has again provided
access to new residential neighbourhoods (Robinson 1980c); and finally,
as elements within the South Asian population have gained upward social
mobility, so they have sought out better areas of residence in the suburbs.
Werbner (1979) provides an excellent account of this latter tendency
among Pakistanis in Manchester; this group has also been researched by
Nowikowski and Ward (1979) and Ward *et al.* (1982).

The final manifestation of the social fragmentation of the South Asian
population can be found in the profile of that population's distribution
across different neighbourhood types and, in parallel, the characteristics
of their housing within these. Previous research has been unable to
provide a summary measure of neighbourhood type which can be generalised to allow comparisons across the country. Recently, however,
researchers at the Newcastle Centre for Urban and Regional Development Studies have allocated each of England and Wales' EDs to one of
twenty-two neighbourhood types. These neighbourhood types provide a
nationally comparable summary of socio-economic and residential characteristics and therefore offer a general overview of the life-chances
enjoyed by residents within each neighbourhood type. For this chapter,
the types have been used in conjunction with unpublished birthplace data
from the census for each of the 140,431 EDs in England and Wales. The

Table 12.7. *National profile of neighbourhood types by ethnic group, 1981*

Neighbourhood type	Total population	Indians	Pakistanis	E. Africans	Bangladeshis
A	100	57	22	60	18
B	100	59	26	56	21
C	100	293	200	411	232
D	100	370	598	268	472
E	100	104	204	77	204
F	100	33	22	31	26
G	100	27	15	31	19
H	100	83	80	114	234
J	100	25	9	29	8

Note: all South Asian figures are index numbers which are designed to show over-representation or under-representation in a category relative to the white population.

Key to neighbourhood types:
A. Suburban, professional-managerial population, large detached or semi-detached houses.
B. Average sized semi-detached, white-collar population.
C. Flats, largely white-collar workers, singles or young families.
D. Owner-occupied/rented terraces, manual workers.
E. Converted bedsits, unskilled population, high unemployment.
F. Council houses, skilled manual population, low population turnover.
G. Council flats, skilled manual and OAPs, low population turnover.
H. Council flats, unskilled, high unemployment, large families, one-parent families.
J. Rural, farming and retirement/second home areas.
Source: calculated from unpublished census data using Openshaw's neighbourhood typology.

results can be found in Table 12.7, where they are shown as index numbers which relate South Asian values to those of the respective white populations. The table can be interpreted at two levels. First, that all the South Asian groups are concentrated in a narrow range of neighbourhood types. All four groups are over-represented in working-class terraced neighbourhoods and in districts where properties are undergoing transition and subdivision into self-contained rented flats. In addition, Pakistanis and Bangladeshis are over-represented in transitional working-class bedsit areas, and the latter group also has a strong presence in areas of unattractive council accommodation of the flatted variety. None of this is surprising given the exclusionary closure of white society, and the desire both for community proximity and access to inner-area employment and transport facilities on the part of many South Asians. At the second level of interpretation, however, the results *are* somewhat surprising. Given the unremitting concentration of academic research on working-class Asians in Britain, it can become difficult to accommodate the notion of successful upper-middle-class Indians or Pakistanis. Yet the data show that around 19% of both Indians and East Africans live in *the* most affluent suburban or exurban locations, while a further 12% reside in comfortable semi-detached suburbia. Even amongst Pakistanis and Bangladeshis – the groups most often stereotyped as poor manual labourers – between 7 and 10% of the population live in neighbourhood types A and B. Clearly then, in each of these groups there are individuals who are reaping the rewards of their success. What is also of some interest is that these successful families are not solely concentrated within London.

Doctors and patients

The analysis so far has indicated the existence, within the South Asian population, of a more varied range of social statuses than has hitherto been claimed. In particular, the population appears increasingly polarised into those who have already exceeded a certain threshold of success and are therefore likely to have benefited from broader societal trends, and those at the very base of the social pyramid whose lot will have worsened under the impact of recession and restructuring. Although there are undoubtedly intermediate groups between these polar extremes, it is the latter which are of greatest interest since their experience over the last decade has been so divergent. The final section of this chapter attempts to illustrate these polar extremes by providing brief descriptions of exemplars, namely the Bangladeshis and the Indian middle class.

Since at least the middle of the nineteenth century there has been an Indian middle class in Britain, made up of doctors, students, barristers, merchants and academics. Visram (1986) notes, for example, the cases of a nineteenth-century professor of Hindustani at University College London, an eighteenth-century physician, and the Liberal MP Dadabhai Naoroji. She also describes the growth of the student body from 4 in 1845 to 1,800 in 1931, at which time its members formed the largest number of foreign students in the country. Others have pointed to medical communities and a business elite. Even so, the literature on the Indian middle class in Britain is still very underdeveloped. Both Werbner (1979) and Ward *et al.* (1982) have provided introductory studies but neither claims to be comprehensive or exhaustive.

Recently, however, a new data source has become available which allows researchers to describe some of the basic socio-demographic characteristics of a selection of 'elite' Indians. Pande and Pande's (1985) *Indians in Britain Who's Who* is, as the name implies, a compendium of brief biographies of leading Indians in the UK. The sampling methods prevent it being in any way representative of all Indian members of the middle class (Robinson 1988b), but it is nevertheless valuable. To date, two studies based on the 1985 data have appeared (Robinson 1988b; Robinson 1988c) and these provide basic descriptive socio-demographic profiles. The average age of the sample was forty-six years, and over half had entered Britain during the 1960s. Others predated the 1962 legislation, but nearly a quarter had migrated during the tightly controlled 1970s. Clearly the fact that many had skills which are in short supply in Britain allowed them to enter Britain under the voucher system. Most came direct from the subcontinent although one-in-five had spent time in East Africa. Others had come to the UK from elsewhere in the Indian diaspora such as Fiji, Guyana, Trinidad and Malaysia. Regardless, their contribution was very varied with the 392 respondents listing 28 different occupations or reasons for inclusion in *Who's Who*. There were GPs, medical consultants, psychologists, dentists, opticians, businessmen, accountants, engineers, research scientists, university lecturers, authors, poets, barristers, solicitors, civil servants and an architect. What all these shared was a dedication to education and formal qualifications; 86% already had qualifications before arrival in the UK but a staggering 64% went on to take further qualifications. This had obviously been rewarded, since 71% had gained their first post in their present occupation after arrival in the UK. The group was considerably more spatially dispersed than their working-class counterparts, with a significant presence in areas not noted for South Asian settlement such as Wales, Merseyside, South Yorkshire and the outer South East. Within these and other areas, respondents appeared to reside in more prestigious locations, such as Stroud, Southport, Sale, Wilmslow, Thames Ditton, Solihull, Bath and Worcester. Despite their social (and presumably economic) success, the group had not abandoned their 'roots'; 73% had married another Indian (cf. Robinson 1980d) and almost 40% were members of ethnic or cultural associations. This brief profile indicates that at least some members of the Indian middle class can be firmly placed within the 'new' class – if such a thing really exists – that has been a major recipient from the restructuring of economic opportunities. They are in the very information occupations which Bell (1973) put at the heart of the 'post-industrial' society, and they are likely to be within those income brackets which have improved their relative position over the last decade. Jaffe-Pearce (1988) confirms this, with her profile of successful and upwardly mobile Patels.

At the opposite end of the social spectrum in the UK are the Bangladeshis. For them, life is not a matter of social mobility but of harsh existence in an environment which offers few opportunities and numerous pitfalls for the unwary. They are the most recent arrivals within the South

Asian population and are still undergoing the process of family reunion and extension. Population growth is therefore rapid and half the group is less than fifteen years of age (Home Affairs Committee, 1986). They are heavily spatially concentrated, effectively into only twenty conurbations and cities. Within these, London is by far the largest with approximately 45% of the total Bangladeshi population of the UK. And even within London, there is marked concentration, with perhaps 26,000 Bangladeshis in West Tower Hamlets. There, the group faces a series of acute problems which prompted the Home Affairs Committee (1986b) to label them as the most disadvantaged ethnic group in Britain. At the root of this disadvantage are three causes: first, the very recent immigration from an essentially peasant economy to an urban industrial society; second, low levels of fluency in English, with 50% of male Bangladeshis speaking English not at all or only slightly; and third, discrimination. In combination these causes tend to reshape the entire opportunity structure available to Bangladeshis in Britain. In Tower Hamlets, they have access only to the poorest accommodation, usually within the public sector; 90% of the Borough's homeless and 80% of their bed-and-breakfast families are Bangladeshis, for example, and those who are offered permanent council accommodation get only the worst flatted properties on the least desirable estates (Phillips 1986). There they face regular racial harassment and attacks, the impact of which was summarised by another Home Affairs Committee Report (1986a: vi):

> the reality which lies behind all of these cases – an individual or family living in fear, subject to humiliation, stress and physical danger, frequently too terrified for their safety to allow children to play outside, driven to tranquillisers and sleeping pills, constantly at the alert wondering if tonight will bring a brick through the window, or tomorrow morning the letters 'NF – Pakis go home!' on their front door. Family life is destroyed as the parents and children, almost invariably, show their frustration, anger and fear to each other. What was a home becomes a prison . . . [and] . . . options are reduced as lives are re-organised to minimise the number of dangerous journeys and offers of housing are refused on estates where attacks are feared.

Despite a flurry of self-employment, prospects are little better in economic terms; 45% of Oldham's male Bangladeshis are unemployed, while in Tower Hamlets almost 70% of those in work are either unskilled or semi-skilled labourers. In the clothing industry the Bangladeshis get access only to the worst jobs, and those who have moved into the catering trade might expect to work ten to fifteen hours per day seven days a week (Carey and Shukur 1985). Even so, Bangladeshi income levels are the lowest of any of the black or Asian groups (Brown 1984). Problems of language fluency further reduce opportunities by debarring equal access to services such as education and health care. The Home Affairs Committee Report on the Bangladeshis (1986b: xiii) commented on the high incidence of physical illness within the group because of a failure to fully utilise medical services and also of problems which doctors had in diagnosing diseases in the absence of complete information. It also described the underachievement of Bangladeshi children in British schools and concluded that 'it is an educational and social disaster of profound significance for the future of Britain's Bangladeshi community that 74% of 15-year-old Bengali speakers were not fluent in English'.

Clearly the prospects for Bangladeshis in Britain reflect the coincidence of their shift from transience to permanent settlement at a time of restructuring and recession. They are marooned in declining parts of declining cities where services are underfunded and unresponsive. They seek housing at a time when investment in the inner city and more particularly in council housing is at a postwar low. They are looking for work in a labour market awash with potential employees. And they are sharing territory with whites who have also suffered from restructuring and who find it all too easy to blame 'the Pakis' for the deterioration in their own prospects. For them, recent changes in the British space-economy have simply exacerbated pre-existing difficulties and ensured a continuing and painful position on the social and economic margins of British society.

Conclusion

The last thirty years have seen Britain metamorphosed from an industrial to a post-industrial society and this change has reshaped the opportunity structure on offer to each and every resident. Some regions, industries, settlements and population groups have undoubtedly benefited whilst others have not. These processes might appear remote to those researching the internal dynamics of specific South Asian groups in one particular city, but they cannot be ignored no matter what the scale of analysis. The shift to a post-industrial society has strengthened the position of certain Asians who are clearly members of the upwardly mobile and increasingly affluent 'new' class, which some commentators feel now exists. Other South Asians have not been so fortunate. They have seen their already weak position progressively undermined by social and economic change. For them, the post-industrial future is bleak, caught as they are on the wrong end of a new international division of labour in a country that does not care.

Acknowledgement

I am indebted both to the ESRC Data Archive and the Social Statistics Research Unit at City University for supplying data. They are not, however, to be held responsible for the analysis and interpretation of these. All Longitudinal Study data remain Crown Copyright. I should also like to thank Ceri Peach and St Catherine's College, Oxford for providing me with the sabbatical facilities which allowed me to research this chapter.

References

Archbishop of Canterbury's Commission on Urban Priority Areas 1985. *Faith in the City*, London: Church House.
Bell, D. 1973. *The Coming of Post-industrial Society*, New York: Basic Books.
    1979. 'The new class: a muddled concept', in *The New Class*, ed. D. Bruce-Biggs, New Brunswick: Transaction Books.
Brennan, J. and P. McGeevor 1987. *Employment of Graduates from Ethnic Minorities*, London: Commission for Racial Equality.
Brown, A. and J. Fox 1984. 'OPCS Longitudinal Study; ten years on', *Population Trends*, London, 37: 20–2.
Brown, C. 1984. *Black and White Britain*, London: Heinemann.
Bruce-Biggs, D. 1979. *The New Class*, New Brunswick: Transaction Books.
Carey, S. and A. Shukur 1985. 'A profile of the Bangladeshi community in East London', *New Community*, London, 12, 3: 405–17.
Champion, A. and A. Green 1985. *In Search of Britain's Booming Towns*, Newcastle: CURDS.
Champion, A. *et al.* 1987. *Changing Places: Britain's Demographic, Economic and Social Complexion*, London: Edward Arnold.
Desai, R. 1963. *Indian Immigrants in Britain*, London: Oxford University Press.
Fevre, R. 1984. *Cheap Labour and Racial Discrimination*, Aldershot: Gower.
Fryer, P. 1984. *Staying Power*, London: Pluto.
Green, A. and D. Owen 1985. 'The changing spatial distribution of socio-economic groups employed in manufacturing in Great Britain', *Geoforum*, London, 16, 4: 387–402.
Hacker, A. 1979. 'Two new classes or none', in *The New Class*, ed. D. Bruce-Biggs, New Brunswick: Transaction Books.
Halsey, A. 1987. 'Social trends since World War 2', *Social Trends*, 17: 11–19.
Heath, A. and J. Ridge 1983. 'Social mobility of ethnic minorities', *Journal of Biosocial Science*, 8: 169–84.
House of Commons Home Affairs Committee 1986a. *Racial attacks and harassment*, London: HMSO.
    1986b. *Bangladeshis in Britain*, London: HMSO.
Jaffe-Pearce, M. 1988. 'The English family Patel', *Sunday Times*, 7 February.
Jenkins, R. 1986. *Racism and Recruitment*, Cambridge University Press.
Kanitkar, H. 1972. 'An Indian elite in Britain', *New Community*, 1: 378–83.
Kondapi, C. 1949. *Indians Overseas, 1838–1949*, New Delhi: Indian Council of World Affairs.
Lawrence, D. 1974. *Black Migrants: White Natives*, Cambridge University Press.
Nowikowski, S. and R. Ward 1978. 'Middle class and British', *New Community*, 7: 1–11.

Office of Population Censuses and Surveys 1979. 'Population of New Common-wealth and Pakistani ethnic origin', *Population Trends*, 16.
  1986a. Ethnic minority populations in Great Britain', *Population Trends*, 45.
  1986b. *Monitor LFS 86/2*, London: OPCS.
Pande, G. and G. Pande 1985. *Indians in Britain. Who's Who*, Swansea: Computers and Geotechnics.
Peach, C. 1968. *West Indian Migration to Britain*, London: Oxford University Press.
  1987. 'Immigration and segregation in Western Europe since 1945', in *Foreign Minorities in Continental European Cities*, ed. G. Glebe and J. O'Loughlin, Stuttgart: Fritz Steiner.
Phillips, D. 1982. 'The social and spatial segregation of Asians in Leicester', in *Social Interaction and Ethnic Segregation*, ed. P. Jackson and S. Smith, London: Academic Press.
  1986. *What Price Equality?*, London: Greater London Council.
  1987. 'Searching for a decent home', *New Community*, 14.
Rex, J. 1970. *Race Relations in Sociological Theory*, London: Weidenfeld and Nicholson.
Robinson, V. 1979. *Segregation of Asians in a British City*, Oxford: Oxford University, School of Geography.
  1980a. 'Correlates of Asian immigration to Britain', *New Community*, 8.
  1980b. 'Lieberson's P* index: a case-study evaluation', *Area*, 12.
  1980c. 'Asians and council housing', *Urban Studies*, 17.
  1980d. 'Patterns of South Asian ethnic exogamy in Britain', *Ethnic and Racial Studies*, 3.
  1986. *Transients, Settlers and Refugees: Asians in Britain*, Oxford: Clarendon Press.
  1987a. 'Spatial variability in attitudes towards race in the UK', in *Race and Racism*, ed. P. Jackson, London: Allen and Unwin.
  1987b. 'Race, space and place: the geographical study of UK ethnic relations', *New Community*, 14.
  1988a. 'Economic restructuring, the urban crisis and Britain's black population', in *Social Problems and the City*, ed. D. Herbert and D. Smith, Oxford University Press.
  1988b. 'Who's Who, Who's What, Who's Where: an Indian elite in Britain', in *Indians in Britain Who's Who* (2nd edn), ed. G. Pande and G. Pande, Swansea: Computers and Geotechnics.
  1988c. 'An Indian middle class in Britain: their origins, characteristics and geographical patterns of settlement', *Ethnic and Racial Studies*, London.
Samuel, R. 1982. 'The SDP and the new political class', *New Society*, 22.
Seabrook, J. 1971. *City Close Up*, Harmondsworth: Penguin.
Smith, D.J. 1974. *Racial Disadvantage in Employment*, London: Political and Economic Planning.
Social Trends 1987. London: HMSO.
  1988. London: HMSO.
Visram, R. 1986. *Ayahs, Lascars and Princes*, London: Pluto Press.
Ward, R. *et al.* 1982. 'Middle class Asians and their settlement in Britain', in *Migrants Workers in Metropolitan Cities*, ed. J. Solomos, Strasbourg: European Science Foundation.
Werbner, P. 1979. 'Avoiding the ghetto: Pakistani migrants and settlement shifts in Manchester', *New Society*, 7, 376–89.

13

The participation of Asians in the British political system
Muhammad Anwar

Introduction

Over the last forty years people from the New Commonwealth countries and Pakistan, whose colour differs from that of the majority indigenous population, have exercised their right to come to this country. This freedom of movement was restricted after the Commonwealth Immigrants Act came into force in 1962. The estimated present-day number of these ethnic minorities is 2.6 million or about 5% of the total population of the Great Britain (54 million). The term 'ethnic minority' is used in this chapter for those people whose origin is mainly from the New Commonwealth countries and Pakistan. The two main groups of ethnic minorities in Britain are the Asians and Afro-Caribbeans. It is estimated that just over half (55%) of the ethnic minority population is of Asian origin (1.4 million). They can no longer be considered 'immigrants' since almost half of them are now British-born; many more came as children and have spent almost all their formative years in this country. Most of the other Asians have British nationality. They are here to stay, and Britain is now permanently a multiracial and multicultural society.

Over the centuries, Britain has received and absorbed a large number of immigrants from other countries (Anwar 1979). However, what makes the recent ethnic minorities different from, and more visible than, the earlier migrations is their colour. And it is because of this and their newness and different cultural backgrounds that the ethnic minorities face racial disadvantage and racial discrimination. It is a fact of daily life for many ethnic minorities. But despite these difficulties, ethnic minorities are playing an important role in British life, including the British political system. Table 13.1 shows the Asian and other ethnic minority population in 1984.

Table 13.1. *Population by ethnic group, distinguishing the population born in the UK, 1984*

Ethnic group	All persons (1,000)	Persons born in the UK (1,000)	% UK born
White	50,895	48,871	96.0
West Indian or Guyanese	529	281	53.1
Indian	807	290	35.9
Pakistani	371	151	40.7
Bangladeshi	93	30	32.2
Chinese	109	24	22.0
African	109	35	32.1
Arab	63	5	7.9
Mixed	205	146	71.2
Other	75	19	25.3
Not stated	829	549	66.2
All ethnic groups	54,084	50,400	93.1

Source: Labour Force Survey (LFS) 85/1, OPCS 1985.

Settlement patterns

The Asian and other ethnic minorities are not evenly distributed throughout the country. They are mainly concentrated in inner-city and industrial areas, most of them having come to Britain as economic migrants. For example, in 1981, 56% of ethnic minorities were found in London and the South East, 23% in the Midlands, 16% in the North and North West, 4% in the South West and Wales, with relatively few (2%) in Scotland (OPCS 1983). The contrast between the general population in Greater London and the South East (31%) and the ethnic minority population (56%) is particularly marked. However, they are heavily concentrated within these regions in certain local wards and parliamentary constituencies, which makes them statistically significant in the political process.

Further analysis of the 1981 census shows that almost half of those of Indian origin were living in the South East as were 57% of Bangladeshis and 65% of East African Asians, but only 31% of Pakistanis. Almost two-thirds of the total population of Pakistani origin live in the conurbations of the West Midlands (22%), Yorkshire and Humberside (21%), and the North West (16%). The settlement pattern of Pakistanis in these regions, in some cities and towns within these areas and, on a smaller scale, within towns on the basis of their home origin, is not a chance phenomenon. It came about as a result of the active kin-friend 'chain migration' (Anwar 1979). But, generally, the settlement pattern of Asians was clearly determined by the availability of work in different areas, as most of them initially came as economic migrants.

Therefore, the position of Asians in the labour market is a fundamental aspect of their position in British society. The type of work available to them not merely governs their incomes, it also helps to determine the areas in which they settle, where their children go to school, how they interact with the indigenous population generally, their chances of participation in civic life, and their overall status in society. If Asians are granted access to only a limited range of occupations upon arrival, there will be concentrations in certain factories and certain industrial sectors, and consequently, depending on their location, in certain towns, cities, and regions.

The importance of the Asian vote

The participation of Asians in the British political process is an important indication of their involvement in the society. Because of the historical links of Asians with Britain they, as British and Commonwealth citizens living in this country, have a legal right to participate fully in politics. This includes the right to vote and to be a candidate in elections. However, such participation is not new. Three MPs from the Indian sub-continent had been elected to the House of Commons before the Second World War. The first, Dadabhai Naoroji, was elected as long ago as 1892 as a Liberal with a majority of five at Finsbury Central. The second, Sir Mancherjee Bhownagree, was twice elected as a Conservative for Bethnal Green North East, in 1895 and 1900. The third, Shapurji Saklatvala, was twice elected for Battersea North, as a Labour candidate in 1922 and as a Communist in 1924. In the House of Lords, there was one member from the Indian sub-continent, Lord Sinha of Raipur (1863–1928). However, since the Second World War there had been no Asian MPs until 1987, although there is at present one member of the House of Lords, Lord Chitnis. There have been a number of parliamentary candidates who belonged to the Asian communities (Anwar 1986). These included both those who have stood as candidates for the main political parties and those who have come forward for the minor political parties or have stood as independents.

On the other hand, what has been the impact of Asian voters upon British politics? Are there many such voters? Do they occupy a strategic position in the elections, especially in inner-city marginal constituencies? The answer to the last question is yes. There are several reasons for this. Asians are not randomly distributed throughout the country. Their concentration in particular conurbations means that, at least in statistical terms, they are in a position to influence the voting strength in those areas. Within these conurbations, they are even further concentrated in some parliamentary constituencies and local election wards, and are therefore in a position to make an impact on the overall voting turnout in those inner-city areas. For example, according to the 1981 census, there were fifty-eight constituencies with more than 15% of the total population living in households with heads born in the New Commonwealth and Pakistan; the majority were of Asian origin. Nineteen of them had more than 25% and seven had over 33% (with three approaching almost half: Birmingham Ladywood, Brent South and Ealing Southall). There are many others with an ethnic minority population of between 10 and 15%. These figures do not take into account ethnic minorities where the head of household was born in this country. However, it is estimated that in 1987 there are about 100 parliamentary constituencies in England with an ethnic minority population of over 10%.

As far as the local election wards are concerned, there are now several hundred with more than 15% ethnic minority population, and several with almost 50%. The highest ethnic minority (Asian) population of 85.4% was in Northcote ward in the Borough of Ealing, where it was estimated that almost 76% of electors in 1981 were Asians out of a total of 8,148 on the register. Glebe ward in the same borough had almost 60% Asian electors. It must be pointed out, however, that counting Asian names on the register is an under-estimation of their actual numbers in the population as some Asians do have anglicised names. There is also under-registration among Asians compared with whites. It was estimated that in 1983 almost one-fifth of the Asians in some areas were not on the register.

It is worth stressing again that it is not only the actual number of Asian electors in the constituencies that makes them 'important', but also their relative concentration in these constituencies that places them in a position to influence the outcome of elections. For example, at the time of the 1979 general election, our analysis showed that in some constituencies there were roughly as many Asian electors on the electoral register as were recorded in the 1971 census. For instance, there were 11,000 Asian names on the register in Leicester South constituency, about 10,000 in Birmingham Sparkbrook, almost 12,000 in Bradford West, and so on (Anwar 1980). When we look at the proportion of the total electorate in individual constituencies or wards who are Asian, the importance of the 'Asian vote' becomes even clearer (Table 13.2). By 1987 the numbers had increased further.

The level of political awareness among Asians and other ethnic minori-

Table 13.2. *A select list of wards where over half of the population was composed of ethnic minorities, mainly Asians, based on 1981 census*

Ward	Borough/District	% population with head of household born in NCWP
Northcote	Ealing	85.4
Soho	Birmingham	71.7
Glebe	Ealing	71.0
University	Bradford	67.6
Brookhouse	Blackburn	66.1
Wycliffe	Leicester	65.7
Spitalsfield	Tower Hamlets	63.1
Spinney Hill	Leicester	61.8
Mount Pleasant	Ealing	58.8
Sparkbrook	Birmingham	55.0
Upton	Newham	55.0
Kennington	Newham	55.0
Handsworth	Birmingham	54.0
Wembley Central	Brent	53.3
Kensal Rise	Brent	52.9
Sparkhill	Birmingham	52.6
Aston	Birmingham	51.0

ties has also increased over the past two decades. This is partly because they have recognised that their sense of security in this country can be buttressed by such an awareness, and partly because an increasing number of Asian organisations are articulating issues such as race relations and immigration controls which impinge on their sense of security. The Asian press has also played an important role in the creation of this awareness. In this regard, they are responding to speeches and comments that are widely disseminated by the mass media including the Asian press, particularly during election campaigns, and are thus in a position to take action individually or through the organisations to which they belong to guarantee their own future in this country.

The presence of National Front and other anti-immigrant candidates in elections has increased their awareness of the political issues, and contributed towards an increasing degree of political mobilisation and, indeed, participation in elections in order to counter the anti-immigrant propaganda. There is also the response of the major political parties. These parties have not only felt the need to take steps to involve Asians in their activities and campaigns, but have openly sought their votes in various elections between 1974 and the general election in 1983. This pattern also applied to local elections including the May 1986 elections (Anwar and Kohler 1975; Anwar 1975; Anwar 1980; Anwar 1984). The participation of Asians and other ethnic minorities in the political process depends on various factors, including whether they appear on the Electoral Register, and, if they do, whether they come out to vote. It is also necessary to look at how they compare with other ethnic minorities, and white people, in this respect.

Registration

Registration on the Electoral Register is a fundamental pre-requisite for participation in British local, general and European Assembly elections. In 1974 a sample survey of 227 Asians showed that 27% of Asians, compared with 37% of Afro-Caribbeans and 6% of whites from the same areas, were not registered (Anwar and Kohler 1975). In 1976 checks in two areas where field work had taken place in 1974, showed a great improvement in the registration level of Asians. In Birmingham it was found that 5% of Asians and 13% of Afro-Caribbeans were not on the register compared with 4% of whites. In Bradford, 9% of Asians were not registered as against 5% of whites from the same areas.

At the 1979 general election a survey in twenty-four constituencies spread throughout the country, however, showed that 23% of Asians, 19% of Afro-Caribbeans and 7% of whites were not registered (Anwar 1980). Compared with the 1974 survey referred to above, the level of registration among Afro-Caribbeans rose by 18% (from 63% in 1974 to 81% in 1979), while among Asians it increased marginally from 73% in 1974 to 77%. Among the white population it remained virtually constant (94% in 1974 and 93% in 1979). However, it is relevant to point out that for Asians the results showed wide variations from area to area. Part of such variation was linked with the policies of local electoral registration offices and with the interest taken by the political parties and Asian organisations in persuading and helping Asians to register.

The results of the 1979 survey were confirmed by an OPCS study undertaken in 1981 at the time of the census (Todd and Butcher 1982). The study showed that in Inner London both the Asian and Afro-Caribbean people had about double the non-registration rate of white people (27 and 24% as opposed to 12%). I again monitored registration in 1983 in the same areas as in 1979 (Anwar 1986). This survey showed that, among those qualified to be registered, Asians' level of registration had increased from 77% to 79%. But the level of registration among Afro-Caribbeans had fallen in 1983 from 81% in 1979 to 76% (Table 13.3). The fieldwork for the survey was undertaken in inner city wards where registration levels are generally low.

Table 13.3. *Registration by racial groups: comparison of general elections, 1974–83 (%)*

	White			Total ethnic minority			Afro-Caribbean			Asian			Other ethnic minority		
	1983	1979	1974	1983	1979	1974	1983	1979	1974	1983	1979	1974	1983	1979	1974
Sample	(994)	(1,041)	(150)	(1,020)	(774)	(183)	(152)	(145)	(41)	(822)	(570)	(142)	(46)	(59)	
Registered (%)	81	93	94	78	77	70	76	81	63	79	77	73	78	73	
Not registered (%)	19	7	6	22	23	30	24	19	27	21	23	27	22	27	

When I looked at the 1983 survey results at constituency level, it showed that there was quite a lot of variation in registration levels as far as Asians and other ethnic minorities were concerned. For example, particularly low levels of registration (60% or less) were recorded among ethnic minorities in Ealing Southall, Croydon North-East, Hackney North and Stoke Newington, Norwood, and Walsall South constituencies. On the other hand, Wolverhampton South-West, Preston, Rochdale, Sheffield Heeley, Leicester South, Manchester Gorton, Birmingham Sparkbrook, and Battersea constituencies had over 80% registration among ethnic minorities (Anwar 1986). Although steady improvement had taken place in the registration levels of Asians in the last ten years, the high level of non-registration among ethnic minorities and also now among whites in the inner cities is alarming and needs action.

Reasons for non-registration include the newness, the language difficulty that Asians and some other ethnic groups face, the general alienation of some groups, and feared harassment and racial attacks from the National Front and other such organisations, who could identify Asians from their names on the register. There is also the fear of 'fishing expeditions' by immigration authorities. Finally, it could be the administrative inefficiency of the Registration offices. Research is needed to find out the precise reasons for non-registration among different groups. However, in the meantime, steps are being taken to reduce the high level of non-registration among ethnic minorities. Several areas now use either special leaflets designed for ethnic minorities in several languages which go with Form A or a translation of Form A into different languages. Some registration offices – Ealing, for example – now employ fulltime, year-round field-workers who visit homes from which no Form A has been received during the previous year. Among others, Lambeth and Haringey in London, Birmingham and Bradford have made special efforts. Hackney in London started a special registration campaign. The Home Office has issued a Code of Practice for EROs which is also relevant in this context. The ethnic minority press has been used, and ethnic programmes on radio and television have also helped to make people aware of the importance and the timing of registration. Political parties in some local areas, some ethnic minority organisations, and some local Community Relations Councils have also put in special efforts to increase registration among Asians and other ethnic minorities. It is due to such efforts, and an increasing awareness among Asians and other ethnic minorities of the political process, that their registration level is edging nearer that of white people. But do those who register come out to vote at elections?

Turnout

Several studies of the rates of turnout in the last thirteen years, at the time of various local and general elections, have shown that on average Asian turnout is always higher than non-Asians from the same areas. For example, at the October 1974 general election a survey in Bradford and Rochdale showed that the turnout rate among Asians was 57.7% compared with 54.6% for non-Asians (Anwar 1980).

At the 1979 general election turnout rates at certain polling stations in nineteen constituencies were calculated for Asians and non-Asian voters. In eighteen of the nineteen areas, the Asian turnout was higher compared with that of non-Asians. On average it was 65% for Asians and 61% for non-Asians. Further, in order to see whether this pattern applied to polling stations within constituencies, eight selected polling stations in the three constituencies of Bradford West, Burnley and Rochdale were covered at the same election. Once again, it was confirmed that the level of turnout among Asians was higher than that of non-Asian voters (73.1% compared with 56.5%) (Table 13.4).

To look at this trend, for Asians' higher rates of turnout than non-Asians, I monitored another type of election, the European Parliamentary election in June 1979. Again it was discovered that the Asian turnout in Bradford and Burnley (for four polling stations) was higher than non-Asians – 38.5% compared to 21.3%. It is indeed significant that, while the turnout rate among all electors nationally for the European Parliament election was lower than their turnout rate for the general election a month earlier, the turnout rate among Asians was not only higher than that of their non-Asian neighbours who voted at the same polling stations, but also higher than the national turnout rate of 32.1%. Their turnout rate of 38.5% was almost twice that of their non-Asian neighbours and this was achieved at an election which the general electorate clearly did not consider to be as important as the general election held a month previously (Le Lohe 1984).

Some further work at the 1980–2 local elections also confirmed this trend. For example, in Ealing in one ward at the 1981 local election the turnout rate among Asians was 59.1% compared to 32.8% for non-Asians. In 1982 in Bradford, results for one ward showed that the Asian turnout was 58.4% compared with 23.1% for non-Asians.

Twenty constituencies were monitored at the 1983 general election as part of a Commission for Racial Equality (CRE) survey to look at the turnout of different ethnic groups. Some of these constituencies were those that were covered in the 1979 survey referred to above. Interviews recorded the total number of voters leaving the polling stations, as well as

Table 13.4. *Asian and non-Asian turnout in Bradford West, Burnley and Rochdale, 1979 general election*

Polling Station	Asian electors	Non-Asian electors	Asian proportion %	Asian voters	Asian turnout %	Non-Asian voters	Non-Asian turnout %
Bradford Drummond	773	398	66.0	531	68.9	206	51.8
Bradford Grange	1,692	1,894	47.2	1,333	78.8	998	52.7
Bradford St Andrew	332	253	56.7	185	55.7	162	64.0
Bradford Southbrook	1,093	2,006	35.3	821	75.1	905	45.1
Total Bradford	3,890	4,551	46.1	2,870	73.8	2,271	49.9
Burnley Stoneyholme	472	1,038	31.2	355	75.2	729	70.2
Rochdale West St	326	285	53.4	199	61.0	187	65.6
Rochdale Silver St	137	1,135	10.8	112	81.8	735	64.8
Rochdale Shepherd	581	477	54.9	415	71.4	308	64.6
Total	5,406	7,486	42.0	3,951	73.1	4,230	56.5

their ethnic group. At this election, 81% of Asian voters turned out compared to 60% for non-Asians. Almost a quarter of the electors on the register in the areas surveyed were Asian, and the greater likelihood of their turning out to vote suggests that they had a significant impact on the final outcome in each constituency. In eighteen of the twenty constituencies covered, turnout among Asian voters was higher than among non-Asians. In 1979 the Asian turnout was higher in eighteen of the nineteen constituencies monitored compared with that of non-Asian voters (Anwar 1986).

All these results show that Asians are capable of being more reliable voters and are consequently in a better position to influence the outcome of elections where they vote. But who do they vote for?

Voting patterns

The voting patterns of Asians, other ethnic groups and whites are examined for two general elections, 1979 and 1983. It must be pointed out that the CRE surveys in 1979 and 1983 were mainly undertaken in inner city areas where support for the Labour Party is usually higher.

At the 1979 general election a sample of voters from twenty-four constituencies was asked to record (on duplicate 'ballot' papers) the way they voted in the polling stations. The 'ballot' papers were similar to those used in the real election, except that they were marked by the interviewers to record the voter's ethnic group. The 'ballot' papers were placed in a box by the voters as they left the polling booth. Out of a total sample of 3,225 voters involved in this exercise, 1,205 were from ethnic minority groups. The results show that the majority of ethnic minority voters voted for the Labour Party. While 50% of whites voted Labour, 90% of Afro-Caribbeans and 86% of Asians in the sample did so.

Among whites in the sample, Labour had an 11% lead over the Conservatives compared with a 78% lead among Asians and 85% among Afro-Caribbeans. Comparing the results of the 1979 survey with another undertaken in 1974, we find that in the wards in seven constituencies where comparisons of voting are possible, it appeared that the Conservative vote among ethnic minorities, particularly Asians, had increased. Ethnic minority 'swings' to the Conservative Party were largely accounted for by the voting pattern of Asian voters as against Afro-Caribbean voters. Whereas Afro-Caribbean voters solidly backed the Labour Party, Asian voters spread their votes between the Labour and Conservative Parties in such a way that higher proportions voted for the Conservative Party in some constituences than in others. In seven constituencies out of the twenty-four surveyed, over 15% of Asian voters cast their votes for the

Table 13.5. *Support among Asians for Conservative and Labour candidates in selected constituencies, 1979 general election*

Constituency	% vote for Conservative	% vote for Labour
Lambeth Norwood	40	60
Hornsey Haringey	33	67
Glasgow Central	31	69
Croydon North East	30	60
Ealing Acton	19	81
Newcastle North	18	77
Brent East	16	79

Conservative Party (Table 13.5). The CRE's exit poll of the 1983 general election, based on 4,240 voters in twenty-five constituencies, showed that 71% Asians voted Labour, 5% Conservative and 11% for the Alliance (Table 13.6).

As a group, 70% of ethnic minorities voted Labour. It must be pointed out that most of the twenty-five constituencies covered in this survey were Labour-held at the time of the 1983 general election and this obviously had a bearing on these results. The national exit poll, which was conducted by the Harris Research Centre for ITN, showed that the majority of ethnic minorities had voted Labour (57%) but 24% and 16% had voted Conservative and Alliance respectively. The Gallup polls at the 1983 general election also showed 21% of ethnic minorities supporting the Conservative Party, compared with 64% and 15% supporting Labour and the Alliance respectively.

Comparison of the two CRE surveys showed that the Asian support for Labour decreased from 86% in 1979 to 71% in 1983. Another survey showed that 21% of ethnic minority voters who had voted for the Labour Party in 1979 switched from Labour to other parties at the 1983 election (*The Guardian* 1983). In comparison, the Labour vote remained strongest among Afro-Caribbeans. Only the Liberal/SDP Alliance had substantially increased its share of the vote in these constituencies among both white and ethnic minority voters. The highest recorded ethnic minority vote for the Labour Party was in Bristol East (93%), for the Conservatives in Croydon North-East (27%), and for the Alliance in Rochdale (54%), the last two with predominantly Asian electorates. This pattern was consistent with the CRE survey of the 1979 general election referred to above. Monitoring of these three constituencies has shown that the personal popularity of the respective candi-

Table 13.6. *Voting patterns by ethnic group; 1983 general election (%)*

	Total	White	All ethnic minority	Afro-Caribbean	Asian	Other EM
Sample	(4,240)	(2,190)	(2,050)	(603)	(1,375)	(72)
Labour	48	35	70	72	71	49
Conservative	20	29	6	6	5	22
Alliance	14	17	9	4	11	9
Others	1	1	1	1	1	
Refused	16	18	13	17	12	19

dates for these parties was one of the key factors in attracting the Asian vote.

A survey conducted by the Harris Research Centre during the 1987 general election campaign (25–29 May) about the voting intentions of Afro-Caribbeans and Asians showed that 86.8% of Afro-Caribbeans and 66.8% of Asians intended to vote for the Labour Party compared with 5.7% and 22.7% respectively for the Conservative Party; 10% of Asians and 7% Afro-Caribbeans intended to vote for the Alliance. No white electors were included in the survey. As these were only intentions it is impossible to know how these ethnic minorities actually voted on the polling day (*Asian Times* 1987).

Another poll conducted by the Harris Research Centre in London between 8–9 June 1987, however, showed that 64% of ethnic minorities intended to vote Labour, 23% Conservative and 11% Alliance. On the other hand, 32% whites intended to vote Labour, 45% Conservative and 23% for the Alliance.

An indication of Asian voting patterns at the 1987 general election came from an ITN exit poll also conducted by the Harris Research Centre. It showed that 61% of Asians and 92% of Afro-Caribbeans had voted for Labour compared with 31% of whites. On the other hand 20% Asians, 6% Afro-Caribbeans and 43% whites had voted for the Conservative Party. The Alliance received 17% of Asian votes, and 24% from whites, but none from Afro-Caribbeans in the sample. It must be pointed out that these results were based on a small sample of ethnic minorities (Harris Research Centre 1987).

The voting patterns of Asians depend on many factors. It appears that regular contacts between political parties and Asians, the organisation and mobilisation of Asians at the elections, the candidates' personal familiarity with the Asian electors, their party policies generally and about race and immigration issues in particular, and the presence of Asian candidates, are important factors in attracting Asian votes. Recent research shows that an overwhelming majority of Asians vote on party lines and not on ethnic lines (Anwar 1986).

Political parties' response

The policies and initiatives taken by the political parties to encourage Asian participation in mainstream politics are important. Leaders of the major political parties have openly sought Asian voters' support in the last few years without the fear of losing white voters. Some political parties have special set-ups to attract Asian and other ethnic minorities support. For example, the Conservative Party has had an ethnic minority unit in the Conservative Central Office's Department of Community Affairs since 1976. Its objective is to make party members aware of the growing electoral importance of Asian and Afro-Caribbean electors and to influence party policy to improve the image of the party among ethnic minorities and, thus, attract their support. The unit helped form an Anglo-Asian Conservative Society through which to recruit Asians directly into the party. This was followed by the formation of an Anglo-West Indian Conservative Society with the same objective. These societies had representation on the area and national committees of the National Union of Conservative and Unionist Associations. The Anglo-Asian Conservative Society had over twenty-seven branches throughout the country. Among its other activities the society arranged meetings between Conservative candidates and Asian groups at election times. These societies have now been replaced by the 'One Nation Forum' which is also serviced by the Central Office.

The Labour Party Race and Action Group (LPRAG) was set up in 1975 as a pressure group to educate and advise the party on relevant issues. More recently, Labour's NEC set up a Black and Asian Advisory Committee similar to the party's women's and local government committees, to attract ethnic minority support for the party.

The Liberal Party does not have special arrangements for Asians and other ethnic minorities within its constitutional framework, but it has a Community Relations Panel which has Asian and other ethnic minority members. It meets regularly to discuss issues relevant to the ethnic minorities and also to formulate policies which the party implements to attract ethnic minority members, as well as to devise campaign strategies at elections specially directed at them.

Like the former Liberal party, the SDP has not got any special arrangements for ethnic minorities within the party's constitution.

However, it encourages ethnic minority candidates for its National Council. In 1987 there were two directly elected ethnic minority members on the council. The SDP has started a Campaign for Racial Justice which has been asked to nominate two ethnic minority members to the council to make it more reflective of the composition of the membership.

Another way to examine the response of the political parties to the question of Asian participation is to look at the number of candidates adopted by the main political parties in the last few years. What sort of constituencies have they contested? What support did these candidates receive from the party machinery? What success rate did the Asian candidates achieve? Why did a lot of 'independent' and 'fringe' party Asian candidates stand at elections? Do they succeed and how does their success rate compare with that of Asian candidates who stand for the main political parties?

At the February 1974 general election, the Labour Party put forward a Pakistani, Councillor Bashir Maan from Glasgow to contest East Fife. Dhani Prem (Coventry South East) stood for the Liberals and there were two Independent Asian candidates. None of them had any chance of winning. No Asian candidates stood for any of the main political parties in the October 1974 general election. Only one Asian stood as an Independent candidate. In the 1979 general election out of the five ethnic minority candidates put forward by the three main political parties, three were Asians (seven others stood for the minor parties). Two Asians were selected by the Conservative party and one by the Liberal party. This was the first time since 1945 that the Conservative Party had nominated ethnic minority candidates. In the event, all the Asians lost – and this includes all the other ethnic minority candidates – because they contested seats where they had no chance of winning.

Two-thirds of the eighteen ethnic minority candidates who stood for the major (four) parties in 1983 were Asian. How did they perform as candidates? Most of the Asian and other ethnic minority candidates performed like any other candidate for their respective parties. For example, in seventeen of the eighteen constituencies contested, where comparison with the notional party position in 1979 is possible, the parties' position was unchanged. However, as in 1979, no Asian candidate contested a 'winnable' or 'safe' seat.

As far as the Independent or fringe party Asian and other ethnic minority candidates are concerned, thirty stood in general elections between 1950 and 1983. The analysis of their results shows that their performance, on the whole, has been 'poor' compared with those who stood for the main political parties. But why did these candidates stand for election? A close examination of their campaigns shows that some, like other fringe or Independent candidates, stood because they wanted to air certain issues, others to represent small parties, and still others because they wanted to protest at the lack of ethnic minority representation in the House of Commons.

However, it must be pointed out that factors affecting the performance of Asian candidates are complex. There may be many factors at work, and these may vary according to party label, characteristics of the area contested, personal popularity of a candidate, rejection by some white voters on grounds of colour, and whether the seat is 'safe' or 'winnable'. Some of these could equally apply to a white candidate. However, there is enough evidence to indicate that in the 1980s Asian candidates have succeeded as never before. For example, in the Greater London borough elections in May 1986, sixty-four Asian councillors were elected. Outside London, others were elected in Leicester, Bradford and Birmingham, to mention a few areas.

The main political parties have continued their efforts to attract Asian electoral support, and selected twenty-seven ethnic minority candidates at the 1987 general election, eighteen of whom were Asian. However, only one of them, Keith Vaz (Leicester East), was returned – for the Labour Party. Several Asians were elected in the 1988 local elections, thus continuing the trend towards their increasing participation. Some Asians have also become mayors and one has recently been elected Lord Mayor; others occupy important positions on committees of local councils.

The Asians' response

Looking at the Asian response over a decade, their membership of the political parties has increased, they have participated fully in the campaigns of the 1974, 1979, 1983 and 1987 general elections, and also been involved in several local elections. Asians have participated in the elections individually, through their organisations, and also through the Asian press. It is clear from the recent pattern of participation, both as activists and as voters, that in the future their influence in the political life of Britain is likely to increase. However, they still face an uphill task to participate fully without any fear of rejection or discrimination.

Conclusion

The participation of Asians in the political process must be seen in the wider context of British society in which racial disadvantage and racial discrimination are a daily reality for far too many Asians and other ethnic minority groups. Similarly, political parties, as part of society, are not free of prejudice and discrimination on the part of their members against the ethnic minorities. This can be conscious or unconscious. However, the political parties need to educate their own members and to try to stamp out any racial prejudice and racial discrimination within the parties. They ought also to set an example to others by promoting racial equality and good relations. This would encourage Asians to join the political parties and become integrated into the political process without any fear of harassment or less favourable treatment. The importance of Asians in the political process is unquestionable; however, their integration into the political process requires 'effective' representation and involvement and not 'tokenism' as has happened so far. They need to feel equal and to participate fully in the decision-making process. This will, in turn, make them feel that they are accepted as full citizens of this country, rather than a 'problem' which is to be 'deplored'. How can this be achieved?

The process obviously has to be a two-way effort: the political parties have to open their doors to Asians and welcome them as members by removing all obstacles; and the Asians have to feel free to join the political parties and take initiatives without any fear of rejection or prejudice. The political parties need to make sure that their Asian members get an equal chance to represent the party at all levels to make their representation effective. Lessons need to be learned from the United States, where concerted efforts in the 1970s both by the parties and the blacks helped to achieve a breakthrough in the political process. As a result, the representation of blacks increased dramatically (Cavanagh 1984).

In Britain, Jews, not more than half a million in number, provide a good example of success in politics. There were twenty-eight Jewish MPs in 1983 and twenty-three were elected at the 1987 general election (Alderman 1987). Several Jews are in the House of Lords, some are members of the cabinet, and several have become members of the European Parliament (MEPs). It is a great achievement for a small community, and a good example of political integration.

Although most Jews initially joined the Liberal and then the Labour Party, slowly the majority have now moved to the Conservative and other political parties. The 1983 general election was the first time in British political history that more professing Jewish MPs were elected for the Conservatives (seventeen) than for the Labour Party (eleven). At the 1987 general election sixteen were elected for the Conservative Party and seven for Labour (Alderman, 1987). The highest number of Jewish MPs ever elected (46) was in 1974. The majority of them belonged to the Labour Party (thirty-five) (Alderman 1983). The same shift has applied to the Jews' voting patterns. In the recent past the Jews voted overwhelmingly for Labour, but now their votes are divided between the main political parties.

As far as Asians in Britain are concerned, their occupational trends and other values, such as ownership and emphasis on family life, are believed to be more relevant to the Conservative Party philosophy. They are, therefore, seen as 'natural' Conservatives. Due to these factors and the efforts of the Conservative Central Office, as with the Jewish community, the original tendency towards Labour is being eroded as Asians perceive their increasing affinity with the Conservative Party. But it must be mentioned that they are also joining and supporting the Liberal and SDP parties. This pattern of support applies, to some extent, to other ethnic communities as well.

On the other hand, to increase Asian representation in the political process (Jewish experience is once more instructive in this connection), Asians need to join the political parties in greater numbers, to seek office, and work hard through the political parties' hierarchy to become candidates, and get elected. They also need to get involved actively in trade unions, as many MPs for the Labour Party are sponsored. The process of political party membership among Asians has actively started in several areas, for example, Bradford, Leicester, Birmingham and Southall. Political parties must become accessible to Asians and other ethnic minorities; since they are numerous and are concentrated, their vote does count. Political parties cannot afford to ignore this fact any longer. Furthermore, the positive involvement of ethnic minorities in the political process, and all aspects of British public life, is the genuine long-term solution to racial disadvantage and discrimination at every level.

References

Alderman, G. 1983. *The Jewish Community in British Politics*, Oxford: Clarendon Press.
1987. 'London Jews and the 1987 General Election', *Jewish Quarterly*, 34, 3.
Anwar, M. 1975. 'Asian participation in the 1974 autumn election', *New Community*, 3, 4.
1979. *The Myth of Return*, London: Heinemann.
1980. *Votes and Policies*, London: Commission for Racial Equality.
1984. *Ethnic Minorities and the 1983 General Election*, London: Commission for Racial Equality.
1986. *Race and Politics*, London: Tavistock.
Anwar, M. and D. Kohler 1975. *Participation of Ethnic Minorities in the General Election, October, 1974*, London: Community Relations Commission.
The *Asian Times*.
Cavanagh, T.E. 1984. *The Impact of Black Electorate*, Washington DC: Joint Center for Political Studies.
The Guardian 1983. 13 June.

Harris Research Centre 1987. Surveys conducted between 25–29 May and 8–9 June 1987 and an exit poll for ITN on the polling day.
Le Lohe, M. 1984. *Ethnic Minority Participation in Local Elections*, University of Bradford.
Office of Population Census and Survey (OPCS) 1983. *Census 1981, Country of Birth, Great Britain*, London: HMSO and Registrar General Scotland, Census 1981.
    1985. *Labour Force Survey.*
Todd, J. and B. Butcher 1982. *Electoral Registration in 1981*, London: Office of Population Census and Survey.

14

Bangladeshi community organisation and leadership in Tower Hamlets, East London

John Eade

The discussion of South Asian community leadership in Britain is undergoing a significant transformation reflecting both changes within those communities and wider influences emanating especially from the political system. Whereas earlier studies emphasised the role played by 'traditional' leaders who drew upon kinship and village solidarities, for example, and by community representatives who pursued professional careers or were wealthy businessmen (Bentley 1972–3; Anwar 1973–4; Khan 1976), more recent studies of local ethnic minority groups have examined the increasing professionalisation of community representation and the emergence of young activists who are employed in state institutions or in local organisations which receive public funds (Peggie 1979; Werbner 1985; Eade 1986). These professional activists have posed a serious threat to the claims of other leaders to represent 'their community' and their rise to prominence is important to any examination of the processes of change involving Britain's South Asian minorities during the last fifteen years. There is also a growing awareness of the ways in which state institutions and white outsiders have influenced political and community developments among local ethnic minority groups (Solomos *et al.* 1982; Werbner 1985; Ben Tovim *et al.* 1986; Eade 1989).

The following discussion will examine the relationship between the Bangladeshi community in Tower Hamlets and local political and administrative institutions in order to explore the complexity of political representation and the definitions of such collectivities as the 'Bangladeshi community' and the 'working class'.

Bangladeshi settlement and Tower Hamlets

Studies of South Asian community leadership and political involvement have concentrated largely on Punjabi and Gujarati settlers from India and upon those who have migrated from Pakistan. The comparatively small Bangladeshi population has been virtually ignored until recently (Bentley 1972–3; Carey and Shukur 1985–6; Eade 1986, 1987, 1989). The most recent authoritative survey of Bangladeshi settlement nationally – the Home Affairs Committee report 'Bangladeshis in Britain' – claimed that by 1985 approximately 100,000 had settled in the country (Home Affairs Committee 1986–7, vol. 1: v).

Bangladeshis were scattered across Britain's urban, industrial centres: Bradford, Manchester, Oldham, Glasgow, Luton and London. Their largest concentration was to be found in the East London borough of Tower Hamlets; almost a fifth of those born in Bangladesh had settled there, although they still constituted, according to the 1981 Census at least, a small proportion of the borough's residents (7%), 12,600 persons or 7% of the population (see Home Affairs Committee, 1986–7). A borough council report in 1984 claimed that the Bangladeshis constituted 10% to 13% of the total population (see *A Short Report on the Asian Population* 1984: 10), while some Bangladeshi community groups maintained that their compatriots constituted almost a quarter of the borough's total population.

Bangladeshis in Tower Hamlets were more similar to the Pakistani Mirpuris discussed by Ballard elsewhere in this volume (chapter 10) than to the Jullunduri Sikhs or Manchester Pakistanis. The first generation migrants came predominantly from small landowning families in the district of Sylhet which was well outside the political and economic heartland of Bangladesh. They were mainly illiterate and had entered unskilled or semi-skilled jobs mostly in the garment industry, the hotel and catering trade and the small shopkeeping sector. In a borough which contained a very high proportion of council housing, Bangladeshis had been largely confined to whatever privately rented accommodation was available or to council estates which were unpopular among white residents. Movement by Bangladeshis into accommodation favoured by white people sometimes led to violence, adding to the grim record of harassment experienced by a number of Bangladeshis in the borough. Competition for housing was exacerbated by the slow process of family formation, as Bangladeshi males struggled to bring their relatives, wives and dependents into Britain.

Only a small proportion of settlers possessed a mastery of standard Bengali, and conversations among Bangladeshis in Tower Hamlets were usually conducted in various shades of Sylheti dialect. Although there was a small Hindu minority in Sylhet, migrants in Tower Hamlets at least were predominantly Muslims of the Sunni persuasion. Two mosques had long been established in the west of the borough – the Jamme Masjid on Brick Lane and the East London Mosque which, since 1986, occupied a fine new building on the Whitechapel Road. Although the Bangladeshi population still constituted only a very small proportion of the borough's total population, large concentrations had developed in certain wards. By the early 1980s Bangladeshis formed the majority of Spitalfields' inhabitants, while substantial settlements had developed in several other wards such as St Katharine's, St Mary's, Shadwell, St Dunstan's and Weavers.

There appeared to be very few wealthy Bangladeshi entrepreneurs in the textile industry, but a substantial number of businessmen had emerged as owners of the various ethnic shops, restaurants, travel agencies and taxi firms in Tower Hamlets and further afield. These entrepreneurs and the few professionals (doctors, accountants and teachers, for example) who pursued their careers in the borough, frequently owned their own homes outside Tower Hamlets. In several respects, therefore, their social and economic situation differed sharply from that experienced by the large proportion of unskilled and semi-skilled Bangladeshi workers in the borough.

Community organisation and representation before May 1982

The first generation of Bangladeshi settlers was usually represented by businessmen whose organisational base was the Pakistan Welfare Association which was founded in 1952. The Association moved to its current premises near the Jamme Masjid in Spitalfields in 1965, but its offices had been periodically closed during disputes in which first generation businessmen were the principal contestants.

Leadership of what became the Bangladesh Welfare Association (BWA) in 1973 brought local prestige and influence as well as useful contacts with officials in the Bangladesh High Commission and in Bangladesh itself. Local businessmen in Tower Hamlets mobilised support among BWA members in the periodic elections and disputes by drawing on patron-client relations with local Bangladeshi workers whom they sometimes helped in their difficulties with British officials.

This system of community organisation and representation began to change during the late 1970s as voluntary workers from the second generation started to assert themselves. Leaders of youth groups began to compete with the older businessmen as providers of assistance to Bangladeshi residents in their dealings with outsiders, especially officials, and they began to take a keen interest in local politics. They discussed the spread of National Front activities in the area with white activists in local trade union and political organisations, and when a young Bangladeshi worker in the textile industry was killed on the night of the 1978 borough election, they joined with the older businessmen in mobilising support for large-scale protests.

The experience of the political events in 1978 encouraged the younger activists to assert themselves further, and two years later they entered the contest for BWA posts for the first time with an agreed slate of candidates. They gained election to some of the offices once the older businessmen had won the key positions of president and general secretary, but soon decided to form their own power base through the establishment of a national Federation of Bangladesh Youth Organisations (FBYO). The new organisation set up its offices in Spitalfields and was soon in receipt of public funds. When a dispute broke over the election of the BWA president at the beginning of 1982, the FBYO youth leadership was well placed to benefit from the prolonged closure of the BWA's offices as the dispute dragged on. Not only could they strengthen their claim to be the more effective representatives of their community, but they were also in a position to form an alliance with one of the disputants, the general secretary, who ran a travel agency in St Katharine's ward.

The development of Bangladeshi community organisation and leadership during the late 1970s and early 1980s revealed the internal resourcefulness of a rapidly expanding population, as the first generation of settlers was strengthened by a second generation of dependants. At the same time, however, the emergence of new community groups and leaders was partly an indication of the increasing influence of outside political and administrative systems through which funds were allocated to Bangladeshi and other local voluntary projects. Spitalfields gained the lion's share of public funding on account of the acute social and environmental problems in the ward, which, by 1982, contained the UK's largest number of Bangladeshi community organisations and the highest proportion of Bangladeshi residents. Nevertheless, the establishment of substantial Bangladeshi concentrations in other wards encouraged community activists to seek public funding for similar voluntary organisations, and various official bodies such as the Department of the Environment, the Home Office, the GLC, ILEA and the borough council were prepared to make some contribution to many of these groups. The extent to which local voluntary organisations had grown through the combination of internal community and external official forces can be judged by ILEA's list of 112 groups in the borough – the majority were run by Bangladeshis and were based in Spitalfields.

The professionalisation of community activism was encouraged by the requirements which official bodies laid down when allocating their grants. The voluntary groups had to manage their affairs efficiently and their officers had to be accountable to their members and to the funding body for the spending of the moneys received. Community leaders became adept at dealing with white politicians and bureaucrats and were also engaged in a multitude of local meetings as voluntary organisations competed for public funding or forged temporary alliances with each other in order to pressurise local and central government institutions into satisfying their demands. By 1982 some of these community activists were being appointed to junior posts within the very public bodies which they sought to pressurise. The GLC was particularly active in recruiting personnel from Bangladeshi and other minority groups after the 1981 metropolitan election resulted in the establishment of a Labour Majority Group, which began to introduce 'anti-racist' policies.

Although the Bangladesh Welfare Association remained the largest and most prestigious of the community's voluntary groups and its leaders were able to gain funding for its welfare services, the proliferation of local pressure groups and the professionalisation of community activism put an end to the dominant position which the association and its business leaders had enjoyed until the mid-1970s. Second generation activists vigorously challenged the claims of businessmen and professionals to represent the Bangladeshi community, and they were able to take advantage of factional conflicts among the BWA's leaders, who, in turn, sought to exploit the differences between their younger opponents. By 1982 community disputes began to involve not only Bangladeshi groups but also white outsiders and conflicts within the wider political system.

Political developments and community organisation from 1982 to 1987

During the 1970s Bangladeshi voters and activists had made little obvious impact on local politics apart from the protest campaigns surrounding the 1978 borough election. Very few Bangladeshis joined local political organisations, and most white politicians did not address themselves closely to Bangladeshi interests. Bangladeshi activists felt particularly alienated from the Labour Party, which had long been the dominant force in local politics, and only one Bangladeshi candidate was selected to represent the party in the 1982 borough election. The nine other Bangladeshis who contested the election campaigned as Independents or as representatives of the new Social Democratic Party (SDP).

These ten Bangladeshi contestants were a mixture of first and second generation community workers and businessmen. The first Bangladeshi councillors – the Labour Party's candidate in St Katharine's and an Independent in Spitalfields – were community workers from the first generation and from districts outside Sylhet. Bangladeshi community organisations played a prominent role in Spitalfields at least through their formal support of the Independent councillor who ran in tandem with a second generation Sylheti community worker.

The 1982 borough election was marked by a development of more general import than the entry of Bangladeshi candidates into local electoral politics. White working-class disenchantment with the Labour Party had an even greater impact on the election, benefiting the Liberal Party whose seats on the council rose from seven to fifteen. As white voters turned away from the Labour Party, radical white Labour activists, particularly in the western wards, began to encourage Bangladeshi recruitment. This strategy, which was frequently described as 'anti-racist', threatened to alienate white voters even more, and the 1986 borough election saw the Labour Party lose control to the Liberal/SDP Alliance in an area which Labour had dominated long before the formation of Tower Hamlets in 1964.

Between the 1982 and 1986 borough elections, a small number of Bangladeshi activists rose to positions of responsibility within ward Labour Parties and at other levels of the local party structure. Their rising political fortunes antagonised other Bangladeshi community workers, but those who campaigned outside the Labour Party in the 1986 borough elections were defeated even in Spitalfields, where the lone Bangladeshi Independent councillor lost his seat. Five Bangladeshi Labour Party candidates were elected in wards with substantial proportions of Bangladeshi residents (Spitalfields, St Katharine's and St Dunstan's). The importance of the Bangladeshi vote and of Bangladeshi activists was assumed to have become so considerable that some Bangladeshi members began to talk about a future selection of a Bangladeshi parliamentary candidate in the borough, and the success of four 'black' Labour candidates in the May 1987 general election encouraged their hopes.

These political developments between 1982 and 1987 had a substantial impact on Bangladeshi community organisation. Local groups were encouraged to look for public funding from Labour-controlled authorities – the GLC and ILEA as well as the borough council – and to cooperate with white left-wingers in the process. An authority's failure to respond to local applications could be blamed on an insufficient commitment to anti-racist and socialist policies. A number of community workers entered local authority employment as the borough, GLC, ILEA and the central government introduced posts to cater for the special needs of Bangladeshis and other racial minorities.

Although a variety of political and administrative institutions were involved in the provision of community group funding and job opportunities, the left-wing leaders of the GLC and ILEA encouraged Bangladeshi activists to look to them for support. During the detailed negotiations over GLC and ILEA projects in Tower Hamlets, however, rivalry between Bangladeshi groups threatened to polarise into a struggle between the FBYO and the BWA: the 1985 Spitalfields by-election, for example, was heavily influenced by the competition between those two particular organisations. Several Bangladeshi activists argued that the conflict between community organisations had been exacerbated by the process of lobbying for local authority support, and some went further to explain the divisions in terms of a 'divide and rule' strategy pursued by white politicians and officers. It was clear, however, that the increasing involvement of Bangladeshi activists in wider political and administrative structures had resulted in party political struggles overlapping with intra-communal conflicts.

In 1986 the demise of the GLC threatened the expansion of Bangladeshi opportunities as did the victory of the Liberal/SDP Alliance in the borough election. The five Bangladeshi councillors who were elected to the borough council in 1986 were unable to protect the interests of Bangladeshi organisations as the Liberal/SDP Alliance Majority Group began to cut back the funding of many local pressure groups. Resources began to be directed away from Spitalfields and other areas favoured during the Labour Party's regime. The return of a Conservative government in the 1987 general election and the continuing decline of the Labour Party's majorities in the borough's two parliamentary constituencies brought no solace to Bangladeshi community leaders within the Labour Party. The economic and residential transformation taking place in the southern wards of the borough made it even less certain that a Bangladeshi Labour candidate would in future be victorious in either of the two parliamentary constituencies.

Community representation, political rhetoric and the 1985 Spitalfields by-election

As Bangladeshi activists became involved in local politics they began to engage in public debate about who should be chosen as the representatives of various political constituencies. In these debates they frequently referred to the Bangladeshi community and to the political representation of that community's interests. Community was defined in this context in terms of nationality and country of origin. However, it was evident that political contests between Bangladeshi candidates in local elections involved other considerations, such as more specific affiliations based upon kinship, village and district, as well as evaluations about the character and influence of particular candidates.

Community groups usually described themselves in terms of their country of origin – Bangladesh. The events surrounding the break-up of Pakistan and the creation of an independent Bangladesh in 1971 had deeply influenced many first and second generation settlers. Nationalist celebrations reinforced Bangladeshi consciousness and helped parents to hand on to their children a variety of images about a country which many in the growing third generation had visited only briefly.

Most migrants had come from Sylhet and as the population expanded Sylhetis began to defend their interests against those who had come from other districts in Bangladesh or from the Indian state of West Bengal. Most of the Bangladeshis who contested local elections between 1982 and 1986 came from Sylhet or were the offspring of Sylheti migrants. However, because they campaigned on rival political platforms, appeals to district solidarity were of limited value; votes had to be mobilised partly through kinship, village and friendship ties among Sylheti residents. The 1985 by-election in the Spitalfields ward particularly highlighted the increasing involvement of Sylheti residents in the local political process and the way in which factional divisions among them overlapped with political conflicts.

The defeat of one of the Spitalfields Labour Party's white candidates by Nurul Huque, a non-Sylheti Independent, in the 1982 borough elections had encouraged the ward party's leaders to expand Bangladeshi recruitment. When the veteran Spitalfields councillor, Annie Elboz, died in 1985, a young Bangladeshi community worker and ILEA employee, Abbas Uddin, was selected to defend the seat. The party's choice soon found himself challenged by another young Sylheti activist, Abdul Hannan, who had left the Labour Party with a number of other Bangladeshi recruits after a complicated dispute involving the leadership of the ward party. Although a young white Conservative also entered the by-election, most activists believed that the main threat to Abbas Uddin's prospects would come from his Bangladeshi rival, and the election result confirmed their opinion since the Labour Party candidate defeated Abdul Hannan by only nine votes. Party activists were considerably relieved to have held on to the seat, given the threat which Bangladeshi Independents had posed in the 1982 election and the special circumstances surrounding ward by-elections.

As both Bangladeshi candidates came from Sylhet it quickly became clear that votes would be mobilised partly through kinship, village and friendship ties. For the many Sylheti voters who were personally linked to the candidates, however, the election also raised the issues of respectability and influence in which Bangladeshi norms played a major role. The candidates had to convince Sylheti residents that they were respectable young members of the Bangladeshi community as well as people of note in political and administrative institutions outside that community.

In spite of Abbas Uddin's community work in the area, for example, some of his Bangladeshi supporters claimed that many residents had never met him and were impressed by his rival's reputation as a highly educated person. Abdul Hannan's election material tried to take advantage of his educational achievements in Sylhet, Dacca (the capital of Bangladesh) and London. His first electoral address, published in standard Bengali, concentrated on his academic qualifications and community activities rather than on conventional political issues. Hannan also received the support of the Bangladesh Welfare Association for whom he was working at the time. The Association's business leaders sought to impress upon their Bangladeshi employees and clients the importance of voting for a young Sylheti community worker whom they trusted and who had challenged the power of white 'extremists' in the local Labour Party.

Hannan also received the support of the ward's Independent councillor, Nurul Huque, who came from a district outside Sylhet. The young Sylheti candidate based his English language address on a document which Nurul Huque had distributed during the 1982 election. This address conformed much more to election conventions than the Bengali language statement. Hannan's educational and community achievements were replaced by a list of demands concerning local social, economic and political issues and an appeal to 'the local working-class people of Spitalfields'.

The appeals to different audiences through English and Bengali election addresses indicated that the election was being fought on two different levels: the level of formal politics where policies concerning the provision and distribution of scarce material resources were the prime consideration, and the level of informal lobbying and gossip among Sylheti residents who were concerned about the social background and respectability of the respective candidates as members of their particular community. The Bengali addresses implicitly acknowledged that the candidates had to take account of both levels: the two young Sylhetis were presented as dedicated community workers who could fight for the interests of both the community and the 'local working class'. Conflicts over the allocation of resources between Sylhetis and other sections of the local population were conveniently ignored in these electoral materials.

The first Bengali-language address on behalf of the Independent candidate, Abdul Hannan, was the only local public document which drew attention to the contestant's Sylheti background. However, a discussion of the election campaign by a white Spitalfields Labour activist in the weekly newspaper, *Labour Herald*, revealed that members of the ward party were ready to acknowledge publicly the impact of cultural and political forces within a particular ethnic minority upon this particular contest.

The by-election was presented as a struggle between the representative of a reformed, popular ward party and an Independent candidate who was receiving the tacit support of the Liberal/SDP Alliance and the open favour of the Bangladesh Welfare Association. The campaign had been 'complicated because voting intentions may not be dictated by loyalty to the Labour Party but by bonds inherent to Bengali culture'. According to the article, Abdul Hannan was arguing that Bangladeshi voters should 'be loyal to the village areas with which they have family ties in Bangladesh'. He was being championed by the BWA, which was described as the 'community face of businessmen and elders'. The association's tightly controlled advice and welfare work in the area 'has encouraged loyalty and deference in return'.

In contrast to this narrow emphasis on traditional ethnic community ties the Spitalfields Labour Party sought to represent the interests of all the local population through a multi-racial campaign. The party was described as 'fighting on the platform of a united community'. Moreover, canvassing was 'organised so that Bengali and non-Bengali members are together on the doorsteps'.

In practice the situation was more complicated. Bengali members did indeed canvass with white colleagues on a number of evenings and helped with public meetings on weekends, but the main burden was shouldered by a small band of activists which included only one Bengali who neither hailed from Sylhet nor belonged to powerful Bangladeshi community organisations. Furthermore, Abbas Uddin spent little time with this small group of activists, preferring to rely on Bengali supporters who were unknown to the white leadership and who, in some cases, did not belong to the ward party.

Significantly, the *Labour Herald* article attempted to link the entry of a Bangladeshi Independent candidate to the machinations of the Labour Party's main opponents, the Liberal/SDP Alliance, in the local political arena. Even though the informal level of ethnic community norms and the influence of community organisations was recognised, the author's perception was largely determined by the formal level of party politics and ideological debates.

Whatever may have been the truth of the claim about Liberal/SDP Alliance involvement during the 1985 Spitalfields by-election, the selection of several Sylheti community activists by the SDP to fight the 1982 and 1986 borough elections confirmed the ability of the Labour Party's opponents to take advantage of the overlap between community and political factionalism. Like Abdul Hannan, some of the SDP's Bangladeshi candidates in the 1986 election were Sylheti activists who had left the Labour Party as a result of disputes involving other Sylheti community workers and white left-wing party leaders. Their lack of success, and the defeat of the only Bangladeshi Independent councillor, appeared to confirm the popular view that most Bangladeshi voters supported the Labour Party and that personal ties to particular Sylheti candidates were less important than debates between British parties in the formal political arena about the provision and distribution of scarce resources.

Conclusion

Although Bangladeshis in Tower Hamlets still constitute only a small proportion of the borough's total population, they have already made a deep impact on local political and community developments. The emergence of a second generation of community activists was facilitated by the expansion of publicly funded welfare posts, and some of these activists were quick to challenge the claims of both first generation businessmen and white political representatives to speak for the Bangladeshi community. They encouraged Bangladeshi residents to become involved in formal British political debates and electoral politics and to seek the furtherance of their interests through the formal political arena. A lively debate developed, therefore, between competing groups of political and community activists, the conflicts between whom increased in intensity and scope as public funds became available from borough, metropolitan and central government sources.

The expansion of the Bangladeshi population was associated, it would appear, with the growth of fissiparous tendencies evident among other South Asian communities elsewhere (Bhardwaj and Rao: chapter 9). Solidarities could be based on friendship, kinship, village, district, nation, gender, class and race, for example, and could be politically mobilised during electoral contests. Yet, as the Spitalfields by-election demonstrated, only certain solidarities were selected for formal political discussion. References were made to community defined in terms of nation (the 'Bangladeshi community') or to class (the 'local working class') while people were sometimes described as 'black' or 'white' members of the working class. More particularistic ties among the 'Bangladeshi community' were rarely discussed in the political rhetoric of the electoral addresses, even though it was clear that Bangladeshi voters were keenly interested in the Sylheti backgrounds and the moral worth of the two young candidates.

It was evident, however, that the fissiparous tendencies within the Bangladeshi community were not solely associated with internal growth. Local and central government agencies encouraged, directly or indirectly, the development of community organisations, and applications for public funds led to fierce competition between community workers and their organisations. Similar developments have been reported by Werbner in the case of Pakistani Muslim settlers in Manchester (chapter 15). Furthermore, in Tower Hamlets at least, struggles between community organisations have overlapped with political party factionalism and with contests between parties producing, for example, *adhoc* alliances between white, left-wing Labour activists and a small number of second generation Sylheti community workers.

The entry of Bangladeshis into borough and parliamentary elections as representatives of other major parties or as Independents has stimulated Bangladeshi residents to engage with current British political and ideological debates (see Anwar 1986 and his discussion in chapter 13), and Bangladeshi support for the Labour Party in the borough could no longer be taken for granted. The demise of the Labour-controlled GLC and the party's defeat in the 1986 borough election were serious blows to attempts by Bangladeshi Labour activists to represent the interests of their supporters in the competition with white outsiders for scarce material resources. These political developments encouraged Bangladeshi residents to consider the policies of other parties, and the blandishments of Bangladeshi businessmen whose major community forum, the Bangladeshi Welfare Association, was still a potent local force as the Spitalfields by-election demonstrated.

The manifold divisions within community and political institutions reflected to a considerable extent the social and cultural diversity of the local population. However, community and political activists frequently spoke as though they represented unitary groups which had clearly established needs (Werbner 1985). The electoral addresses which were published during the 1985 Spitalfields by-election, for instance, appealed to voters in terms of the Bangladeshi community and the working class. The use of different languages enabled the activists to construct constituencies in separate contexts and to fudge the issue of whether the interests of Bangladeshi and non-Bangladeshi residents in the ward were in conflict.

The employment of standard Bengali in electoral addresses neatly illustrated how the ideological construction of a community as a unitary group was at variance with the complexity of social divisions among residents. Most Bangladeshi voters from the first generation spoke various shades of Sylheti dialect and could neither read nor write standard Bengali. Despite the development of Sylheti assertiveness among community workers in Tower Hamlets the 'Bangladeshi community' could not be simply defined as the 'Sylheti community' because local ties were established which set networks of Sylheti residents against each other in political contests. There was no fundamental social group whose interests could be articulated through the process of political representation – rather, ideological constructions of unitary communities and classes coexisted with political, administrative and community organisational practices which mobilised particular networks at various levels of social affiliation. The foregoing discussion is offered as a contribution to our expanding knowledge about the way in which the coexistence of ideological constructions and various practices is expressed in the context of a specific ethnic minority within a particular locality.

References

Anwar, M. 1973–4. 'Pakistani participation in the 1973 Rochdale local elections', *New Community*, 3, 1–2, 69–72.
    1986. *Race and Politics*, London: Tavistock.
Bentley, S. 1972–3. 'Intergroup relations in local elections: Pakistanis and Bangladeshis', *New Community*, 2, 1: 44–8.
Ben Tovim, G. *et al.* 1986. *The Local Politics of Race*, London: Macmillan.
Carey, S. and Shukur, A. 1985–6. 'A profile of the Bangladeshi community in East London', *New Community*, 12, 3: 405–17.
Eade, J. 1986. 'The politics of community: the Bangladeshi community in East London'. Unpublished thesis, University of London.
    1987. 'The political representation of a South Asian minority in a working-class area: the Bangladeshi community in Tower Hamlets, East London', *South Asia Research*, 7, 1: 55–69.
    1989. *The Politics of Community: The Banglideshi Community in East London*, Aldershot: Gower.
Home Affairs Committee 1986–7. 'Bangladeshis in Britain', vol. 1, London: HMSO.
Khan, V.S. 1976. 'Pakistanis in Britain: perceptions of a population', *New Community*, 5, 3: 222–9.
Peggie, A. 1979. 'Minority Youth Politics in Southall', *New Community*, 8, 2: 170–7.
Solomos, J. *et al.* 1982. *The Empire Strikes Back*, London: Hutchinson.
Tower Hamlets' Directorate of Development 1984. 'A short report on the Asian population of Tower Hamlets'.
Werbner, P. 1985. 'The organization of giving and ethnic elites: voluntary associations amongst Manchester Pakistanis', *Ethnic and Racial Studies*, 8, 3: 368–88.

15

Manchester Pakistanis: division and unity

Pnina Werbner

Parallel migration flows

Cross-continental migratory movements may sometimes be composed of relatively homogeneous migrant populations. This was probably a feature of the indentured labour population movement during its early phases. *Voluntary* migration is more often, however, a highly complex social movement, in which the migration population is recruited from various classes and economic sectors within the migrants' societies of origin. Such migrants come with different aspirations and often follow – at least for a period – different economic strategies. In major British cities such as Manchester, this complexity of the migrant population is exemplified in the different historical roots of sub-sections of the Asian community in the city, and the different economic careers they have pursued.

In her research on Asian suburban residents in Manchester, Susan Nowikowski (1984) identified three major Asian groups resident in the city's more affluent suburbs: 'the professionals', 'the business bourgoisie', and 'the urban lower-middle class and rural middle strata'. These three groups, she argues, responded to different pressures to migrate in South Asia, and occupy different economic niches within British society. In extending her argument further, I propose to show that the different social locations of different sub-groups within the migrant population have a critical effect on the way the community, seen as a whole, develops over time. I argue, moreover, that such historically located social divisions come to be, in the space of a generation, cut across by other segmentary and horizontal divisions. The emergent patterns of segmentation and alliance may be regarded as both divisive and cohesive. In any case, the emergence of other significant bases for segmentation tends over time to minimise earlier historical divisions between the different sectors of the migrant community.

331

Pakistani migration to Manchester may be regarded as composed of three parallel yet distinct migratory movements or flows. For a while, during the late 1950s and early 1960s, the three movements appeared as one. Yet in reality, the arriving migrants followed distinct migratory patterns.

The 'trader' migrants

A well-documented feature of Asian migration to Britain was the pre-war arrival of migrants from the Punjab who became door-to-door pedlars. It is noteworthy that these migrants settled in the larger cities: in London, Birmingham, Manchester, Leeds, Glasgow or Newcastle. The question *why* they became pedlars is not usually raised. It is likely, however, that like Jewish and Irish pedlars before them, they had very little option. The British economy was in deep recession and there were few jobs open to them. In Manchester such pedlars are known to have arrived in the 1930s and most continued to struggle for many years, operating on a tiny scale until the early 1950s. Ironically, however, it is this no-option depressed economy, which these early pedlars encountered, that set the basis for the economic fortunes of one major group of Manchester migrants. These migrants, arriving from the late 1940s onwards, tended to work in factories for a brief period only, long enough to pay back their fares and accumulate the initial capital (often a very small sum) needed to start trading. They thus entered almost immediately after their arrival into different sectors of the clothing and garment trade (Werbner 1990a).

Within this general category of 'trader' migrant there were three major sub-groups, each composed of a *biraderi* – a localised marriage-cum-caste group – in the city. One group was that of East Punjabis, mainly from the Jullundur area, and mainly of the Arain *zat* (Muslim caste). After the Partition of India and Pakistan in 1947, this group moved as refugees into the Canal Colonies in the Punjab – to the Sahiwal and Bahavarpur areas, and to the large cities – Lahore, Rawalpindi, Faisalabad and Karachi (Map Intro. 3). At the same time that some were moving as refugees into the newly formed state of Pakistan, other members of the group began arriving in Manchester in quite large numbers, following a pattern of chain migration. Most became market traders, and later wholesalers, in the garment trade. They started by selling stockings (the cheapest item on the market) but quickly branched into knitwear as well. Later they diversified into other types of fashionwear. Some of the largest wholesalers and manufacturers in the city today come from this group.

A second *biraderi*, following a similar pattern, was also originally from

East Punjab. The family was already established in trading and the kin group extended into Singapore and Malaysia. After Partition members of the kindred, of the Rawal *biraderi*, settled in Wazirabad and Gujranwala, while some began migrating to Manchester. They too entered successfully into market trading and shopkeeping. One prominent branch of this family owns a successful small hotel, another is a large wholesaler.

A third *biraderi*, also with international trading links in the Far East, came somewhat later, in the 1950s. Many members of this kindred were tailors by occupation. They too originated from Gujranwala, but mainly from Gujranwala town itself and its surrounding villages. Several members of this family had served in the British army, either as tailors or in other administrative capacities. They were discharged after the independence of Cyprus in 1960. One of the first major Pakistani clothing factories, and later one of the largest knitwear factories, appear to have belonged to members of this group. Many today are successful manufacturers, a few are wholesalers as well.

Members of all three groups, and especially the two Gujranawala *biraderis* were literate and educated to high school or college level, while a few prominent members of the Gujranwala *biraderis* had university degrees. This, despite the fact that most came of village or small town origin. They were all Punjabis, and they incorporated newcomers from their groups into trading and manufacturing after very brief periods in factory wage-employment.

The students

The second major migrant flow to Manchester was that of students. Like other major British cities, postwar Manchester attracted a large number of students to its educational institutions. Education at that time was free, visas were not required. The most successful of these students completed their studies and returned to Pakistan to occupy choice positions within the emerging – and as yet tiny – elite. Many students, however, remained in the city, either to practise (as accountants or doctors) or to go into business. They were in any case mostly born in India, and most were Punjabis, although there were some Urdu speakers from Delhi, Lucknow, and other parts of Uttar Pradesh, and a few Gujarati speakers from Karachi. The families of most of these students had moved into the cities of Pakistan after Partition. Virtually all belonged to higher castes, and while forming a sub-group, many had connections to the 'trader' East Punjabi migrants. In any case, the community in those days was very small, and concentrated residentially in certain areas of the city around the University (Werbner 1979), all of which made for links between the two groups.

The 'worker' migrants

The third flow of migrants to the city occurred after the other two groups were well established. During the late 1950s and early 1960s the pattern of migration to the city changed. While the East Punjabis and students were bringing over wives and families, young bachelor men from West Punjab – primarily from the Gujrat and Jhelum Districts – began arriving in Manchester. These men did not come from refugee families but from smallholder families and *biraderis* with deep extensive roots in their village localities. Moreover, the traditional supplementary occupations in these *barani* (rainfed) areas were of service in the army and the police. Although most of the men were literate and educated, some to high school level, there was no tradition of trading in their families. They came to Manchester to work in local factories or in public transport services (the buses and railways), and they remained wage earners until the most recent economic recession and its associated factory closures and cut backs of the mid or late 1970s. These migrants were not connected to the trading families and only a small minority attempted to move into market trading, shopkeeping or manufacturing. Like the earlier pedlars, however, this enterprising minority was to lay the foundation for this group's entry into business in the 1980s. As in the other two migratory flows, caste membership was related to area of origin. Hence, while the 'worker' flow was made up of migrants from a variety of castes, including some service *kammi* castes, the vast majority appear to have originated from the Gujjer and Rajput landowning castes. They were not, however, from a single *biraderi*, but from several discrete *biraderis*. It has thus taken them some time to acknowledge links across the different kindreds, even within the same caste. We see then that although in the 1960s there seemed to be a single flow of Pakistani labour migrants into the city, in reality this flow – seen in social terms – was a highly heterogeneous one.

Although the movement of migrant 'workers' has been the most recent, they appear to be the largest group numerically (there are no statistics on this matter, and I base this statement on mobilisation events). Their numbers have been augmented recently by migrants shifting into Manchester from other parts of Lancashire and South Yorkshire. Most of these migrants – who should, perhaps, be regarded as constituting a fourth, internal, migratory flow – appear also to originate from Jhelum and are linked by prior ties to the local Jhelum migrants.

There is no real parallel among Pakistanis to the wealthy Indian textile merchants, Nowikowski's 'business bourgoisie', although one of the foremost textile merchants in the city is a Gujarati Muslim from Karachi. His lone presence in this occupational enclave only serves, however, to underline Pakistanis' virtual absence from this category. Most Pakistanis in the city are still concentrated in the food, services and fashion industries, or are professionals – doctors, accountants and solicitors. Other immigrant business enclaves are now emerging – property, hotels and taxi driving being perhaps the most noteworthy recent areas of economic expansion. In a manner typical of immigrant settlers, Pakistanis tend to 'capture' economic enclaves as their experience and success in specific economic sectors precipitates the entry of fellow migrants into this sector (Werbner 1987).

Origin and social identity

The sources of personal identity and group affiliation conferred by migrants' past background point to the beginnings of an emergent complexity. As refugees, many first-generation migrants have social and familial roots stemming both from their place of birth in India and from their place of current domicile in Pakistan. We find, moreover, that while caste affiliation tends to coincide with regional divisions – dominant landowning castes in South Asia typically concentrate regionally (Beck 1976) – it may also cut across these regional divisions. Often this stems from a move from the countryside to the city. Among those living in Manchester it is not only refugee families but also indigenous West Pakistanis who have shifted to urban centres. Sometimes their work careers prior to their migration to Britain precipitated a move from their villages. In many cases they have relocated themselves in towns *after* their migration to Britain (in such cases the relocation is usually to the urban centre closest to their village). There are various reasons for this dual migratory or dual urbanisation trend. The primary reason appears to be that local migrants think it more sensible to invest their remittances in urban centres where property retains its value, and where it is possible to open a business.

Past background is in any case only one source of personal identity. Current residence and work are equally, if not more, important. Paralleling the migration flows have been residential shifts within Manchester itself (Werbner 1979). There are three major Pakistani residential concentrations in the city today, one in the north of the city, two in the south, all located within two miles of the city centre. Beyond these residential enclaves Pakistanis live scattered throughout South Manchester and its suburbs (Werbner 1990a). The number of Pakistanis in the city is constantly being augmented by internal migration from surrounding areas of the North West, and by the high birth rate in Pakistani families. It is thus difficult to estimate the current size of the local community. Community leaders claim there are 40,000 Pakistanis resident today in the Manchester city metropolitan district. The 1981 population census points, however, to somewhat lower numbers. According to figures derived from the census, there were in 1981 about 15,000 Pakistanis resident in the three metropolitan districts of Manchester, Stockport and Trafford, out of an estimated Asian population of 22,000 in these three, primarily southern, districts. (The number of Asians in Greater Manchester is much higher, as there are large Asian concentrations in Ashton, Oldham, Rochdale, Bury and Bolton – all originally mill towns.)

Although the 'trader' migrants lived initially near the city centre, they have shifted since to the inner suburbs of the city, where most still live in small detached and semi-detached houses. Here they mingle with the ex-student population and other more recent newcomers to the city. Many of the more successful traders and professionals have moved to the outer suburbs, the wealthiest to very exclusive and expensive homes. Although Asians live scattered in these suburbs, their aggregate number is increasing steadily.

Migrants of the later 'worker' flow are more concentrated in and around the three residential enclaves. They live in somewhat cheaper semi-detached and terraced housing. Nevertheless this pattern is merely a tendency. At the neighbourhood level migrants from the different migratory flows intermingle, and as time passes, local residence becomes an increasingly important source of personal and social identity.

Regarded territorially, then, the community can be classed in terms of its members' area of birth, current domicile in South Asia, and residence in Manchester. The emergent picture has been represented schematically in Figures 15.1 and 15.2.

In Nowikowski's schema, the parallel flows of migration *remained* parallel and discrete in Britain since, in her words, 'each of these migrant flows has complemented specific structural developments of British postwar capital' (1984: 158). This type of analysis assumes that sub-groups within a migrant population can, and will, remain encapsulated after migration. The picture in Manchester denies this simple social continuity. From the start, as we saw, many of the students arriving in Manchester moved into business. There were thus links between the professionals and the trading elites and they tended to control most communal associations – including the central mosque – jointly (Werbner 1985). There has been a further move by the 'workers' and their children into the trading community, and by some of the children of both established traders and workers

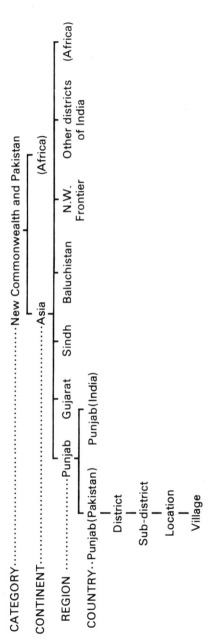

Figure 15.1 Area of origin/birth of Manchester Pakistanis

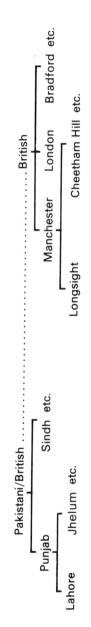

Figure 15.2 Current nationality/domicile of British Pakistanis

into professional occupations. In other words, the foundation laid by the early pedlars and traders created a basis for entrepreneurship for groups beyond their immediate family members and *biraderis*. The 'entrepreneurial chains' which were generated reached out to other groups through ties of friendship, neighbourliness and common associational activities.

In other respects too, the early divisions have been cut across by emergent divisions. Hence, while differentials in wealth within the community have increased, they do not simply reflect the three migratory flows. Some traders have prospered while others continue to struggle. Some of the workers who entered into manufacturing and market trading in the late 1970s have done remarkably well within a relatively short space of time. Their move into trading and business has gathered momentum with the maturation of their families and the greater availability of family labour (Werbner 1987). Their networks beyond the city allow them to mobilise clothing machinists – always a scarce resource – within a wider region. At the same time it is among the 'worker' families that one finds most unemployed, 'retired' men in their late forties and early fifties. These men, although not wealthy, spend a great deal of time in communal activity and are heavily involved in local social affairs within the residential enclaves where most of them live. They can thus gather political influence despite their relatively modest incomes, and their impact on communal affairs is increasing rather than decreasing.

Religion and community

Complicating the picture even further are religious and ideological divisions and alliances. These have been a major source of internal conflict within the community. The Muslim community in Manchester is divided by nationality (such as Pakistani, Bangladeshi, 'Arab', Iranian), and along major denominational lines (Sunni, Shia, Wahabi and so on). Each of these groups has its own national-cum-denominational mosques. Among the Pakistanis, Sunnis form a large majority. There are, however, a minority of Shia and a group of Ahmedia. Each group has its own mosque and religious organisations. Within the Sunni majority, most Pakistanis adhere to fundamentalist forms of Islam. They adhere closely to the Koran and Hadith (sayings of the Prophet) and few, if any, 'modernists' exist within the local religious establishment.

The important divisions within Sunni fundamentalist Islam in India and Pakistan are, however, reflected in religious politics and organisation in Britain. Hence, during the 1960s and 1970s the major division around which Central Mosque politics revolved was that between the Deoband

and Barelvi religious schools. Deoband is the name of a town and religious seminary in North India which produces graduates qualified to act as religious instructors and officials. The school's stress is on religious scholarship and adherence to the Sha'ariya – the laws of Islam. Central to the school's beliefs is the fact that knowledge contained in the Koran is accessible to all and can be disseminated through teaching and publication. The Barelvi school, by contrast, is founded upon the belief in the ineffable mysteries of the Koran. The Barelvi movement, named after a town in India where its founder was born, is a local label for the recent Sufi revivalist movement in India and Pakistan. Here the stress is on practice rather than scholarship, and on personal intercession through Sufi saints or 'Pirs' as they are known locally. Fundamental to Sufism is the idea that the Koran contains inexplicable mysteries, passed on 'chest to chest' through a chain, 'silsila', of holy men, saints or Pirs who can intercede between the Saint's followers and God.

The Sufi orders, or *tariqa*, are organised as 'regional cults' (R.P. Werbner 1977). Werbner argues that regional cults are 'cults of the middle range – more far-reaching than any parochial cult of the little community, yet less inclusive in belief and membership than a world religion in its most universal form' (1977: ix). For Pakistanis the Pir is the figure around which the universality of Islam gains its specific localised mystical authority. He and his followers form the centre of a regional organisation which has its branches in a large number of cities and towns in Britain. Each Pir who heads an order visits his different centres regularly, on a monthly basis, for the monthly communal commensal meal held in the mosque and known as *gayarwin sharif*. This meal is said to commemorate the eleventh day of each month, the day, according to tradition, when the founder of the order was born. Once a month the Pir's *mureeds* (disciples) come from all the branches affiliated to him for a similar meal at his mosque or *khanqa*. During the annual religious festival commemorating the birth of the Prophet (*Id milad el Nabi*), processions are held in all the major centres of the order, attended by the Pir and by delegations from the order's other branches. The month is opened with a major procession in the Pir's city, attended by delegations from all his branches. Together they join in a single procession which moves through the city streets carrying green Islamic flags embroidered with the *Kalimah*, which is led by the Pir himself. In each case the procession ends with a commensal meal at the mosque.

Finally, once a year each Pir holds a three day *Urs* for all his disciples and followers, and for the general public, including anyone who has been cured through his powers of healing. During the *Urs* the whole congregation receives food and fruit which – like in the other commensal meals – is thought to be imbued with the Pir's *barkat* (divine blessing).

In Manchester the focus of religious disputation has shifted from one between the so-called Barelvi or Sufi adherents and adherents of the Deoband school (as well as other puritanically inclined fundamentalists) to a division between two Sufi regional cults (in this particular case, between followers of the Qadriya and Naqshbandi orders). Hence, the earlier conflicts between the Deoband and Barelvi schools ended during the late 1970s with the takeover of the Central Mosque by Barelvi followers. The various other puritanical or fundamentalist schools (Deoband, UK Islamic Mission and Tabliqi Islam) now have separate, relatively small mosques located in different neighbourhoods. The two major mosques in the south are of the two competing *tariqa*, and they form the major locus of current power struggles.

Within the local Pakistani community the vast majority profess to be either indifferent and puzzled by these religious disputes or to prefer Sufi practices which tend to be less rigid and puritanical, open to women and in general more sociable. On the other hand, there is a sizeable minority who deny the powers of the various Pirs, and claim they need no intercession with God. They argue that the Koran provides the basis for all the knowledge they seek and that they can pray directly to God for help and succour. Most Pirs are regarded by non-supporters as money-seeking manipulators and opportunists. Only disciples and adherents believe in their purity and mystical privileged power and knowledge. Nevertheless, it must also be said that most Pakistanis believe that saintliness, mystical power and knowledge are, and can be, in the possession of truly pure persons. These, however, they argue, usually remain hidden from the public eye.

Hence, although Pakistanis claim a unitary identity as 'British Muslims', the Muslim community is, not surprisingly perhaps, represented by a large number of ideological streams, separate organisations and mosques. The religious divisions within the Muslim community may be represented schematically as shown in Figure 15.3 and the wider religious and linguistic divisions as set out in Figure 15.4. The choice of which mosque to attend is, for most Pakistanis, as much a matter of convenience as religious conviction. Major communal conflicts tend to focus, however, upon the Central *Jamia* Mosque, controlled during the 1980s by a follower of a Pir based in London and claiming affiliation to the Qadriya Sufi order.

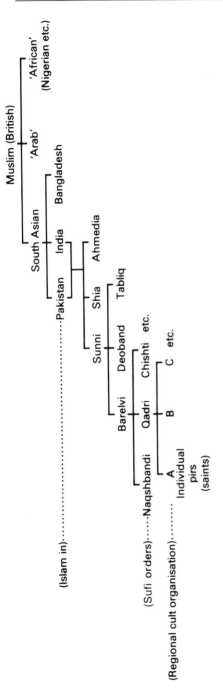

Figure 15.3 Religion/nationality/country of origin of British Muslims

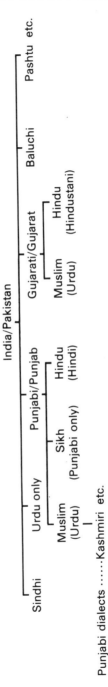

Figure 15.4 Region/religion/language of British South Asians

Community and identity

Clearly, then, there are several salient communal identities which Pakistanis can choose to highlight, depending on the political context and the particular aims of an association or group. Although a stress on identity is always situational, depending on a particular interactional context, in the political arena three primary identities are most frequently mobilised. First is the claim to be 'British Muslims' – often regarded by Pakistanis as the most *positive* of their self-attributed identities. The stress on religious affiliation is, moreover, also important politically for many of the battles fought in the wider context are religious battles: for special Muslim burial practices, for the provision of ritually slaughtered meat in schools, over the appropriate dress for girls in school, regarding the continued need for single-sex high schools, over the granting of planning permission for new mosques, regarding the provision of support for afternoon Koran studies, and so on.

The second collective identity frequently raised is that of 'British Pakistanis'. Pakistanis sometimes deny that this is still a salient social identity since, they claim, most Pakistanis are here, in Britain, for good. All their activities, however, point to its continuing saliency for them. Few important events are complete without the presence of the Pakistani Consul, Ambassador or some other dignitary from Pakistan. The visit of the Pakistani cricket team to Manchester generated intense excitement and extreme competition over the privilege of hosting the team to costly festive dinners. The strategies and political aspirations of local communal leaders are regarded by most Pakistanis as oriented towards Pakistan, and the status or economic advantages which, they claim, office in key Manchester associations confers there.

The third salient collective identity claimed in the public arena is that of British 'Asians' or, more controversially, British 'black'. Inherent in this identity is the recognition of the common problems faced by Britain's most recent immigrants, and the fact that they appear to be exacerbated by racial bias. Most Pakistanis describe themselves, ironically and somewhat bitterly, as 'black'. Only a minority of communal representatives and brokers embrace this label wholeheartedly. Nevertheless, the experience of racism and underprivilege is widely accepted as a basis for unified action, and thus for a common identity.

Each of these salient communal identities has its own central institutional arena. In the religious arena, the Central Mosque, dominated by Pakistani Sunnis, is regarded as the prize forum to be captured and controlled. In the 'national' arena, the newly built Pakistani Community Centre has replaced the Pakistan Society and welfare associations –

almost moribund by now – as the central forum to be 'captured'. In the race relations arena, the City Council Race Sub-Committee – an advisory body with some influence on council policy – has probably replaced the local Community Relations Council as the central political arena where representatives from different ethnic groups meet and act jointly. Here the competition is over gaining a seat as a community representative. The seats are defined territorially, and over the years Pakistanis have successfully claimed four seats, representing four separate residential concentrations.

The emergence of these three arenas in the late 1980s as the most significant is tied to the fact that in each arena regular public elections are held on an annual or bi-annual basis. The elections follow a cycle, with community representatives to the Race Sub-Committee being elected on a *territorial* basis (Longsight/Levenshulme, Whalley Range/Chorlton, 'Central' and Cheetham Hill) in June, the Community Centre elections taking place in January and the Central Mosque elections being held bi-annually, in August. Each election provides a testing ground for aspiring political contenders, and is the basis for the emergence of factional politics.

Communal factions and alliances

It might be expected that since these three arenas – the mosque, the community centre and the Race Sub-Committee – represent essentially different 'communities' (the 'Muslim' community, the 'Pakistani' community and the 'black' community) there would be no connection between them. Each, after all, is concerned with quite different issues, each has a different financial basis and the objectives of each forum differ radically. In reality, however, the three arenas – as well as all other significant Pakistani associations – are closely interlinked. This is so both empirically, from an observational standpoint, and in the minds of the chief protagonists. The key forum – the prize of all successful political aspirants – is the control of the Central Mosque Management Committee. This is regarded as the position carrying decisive influence and power, as well as great kudos, and hence financial benefit, in Pakistan. Most communal politics ultimately revolve around the Central Mosque, while those in control of the Central Mosque attempt, in turn, to extend their ambit of control to as many significant communal organisations as possible (Werbner 1990b).

Historically, the Central Mosque and Pakistan Society were both controlled by the early 'trader' migrants from East Punjab. Whatever internal divisions there were within this group remained suppressed, and

344 *Pnina Werbner*

the group as a whole presented a united front in mosque politics. Behind the scenes the controlling faction was dominated by a large, successful wholesaler family, of which the senior partner was a founding member of the community and a patron to many later traders.

The collapse of this wholesaler's firm during the early 1980s revealed a significant factional split within this trader group itself, with the largest competitor wholesaler (a distant relative) assuming both dominance and control. The ensuing dispute within this trader group and its close allies mobilised migrants from the third 'worker' migrant group, now traders themselves, and for the first time they assumed positions of some influence on the Management Committee. The history of the dispute is complex and cannot be dealt with here (see *Arabia* 1985). Nor is it possible to document in detail the pattern of alliances formed by Pakistanis in the city during subsequent years. What is fascinating – and indeed quite unexpected – is that these alliances tend to conform to the factional alliance model outlined by Barth for the Pakhtun in Swat (Barth 1959).

Barth recognised that alliances among the Pakhtun did not conform to a segmentary model of fission and fusion, presumed to typify alliance patterns in unilineal descent groups. Instead, the division between close, *low level*, segments was given continued saliency in broader arenas. Alliance took the form of two competing coalitions made up of opposed low-level segments.

Although the Manchester case is not one of a unilineal descent group, a similar principle appears to underlie Manchester Pakistani political alliances. The primary opposing factions in each arena align across the different arenas, rather than uniting against ideologically more distant groups. The operative principle is that of 'my enemy's enemy is my friend', rather than 'me against my cousin, me and my cousin against our more distant cousins'. This second pattern does sometimes occur, but only in very special circumstances. Schematically, the alliance pattern has been represented in Figure 15.5. While shifts may sometimes occur across the blocks, there are, as Barth, too, found, always *two* blocks, and they *cut across*, rather than reinforce, high level segmentary divisions.

The implications of this pattern are very interesting. Alliances within the Pakistani community tend to be farreaching and extensive, as leaders seek potential allies in different arenas. The alliances link together groups which might otherwise remain discrete. In this respect, although not in others, such alliances unify the community even as they divide it. Discrete territories, separate mosques, unlike political associations, all get intermeshed in a single complex of political manoeuvrings. Oldtimers and newcomers, traders and 'retired' workers, religious zealots and Labour Party activists are drawn, almost despite themselves, into a single complex political arena.

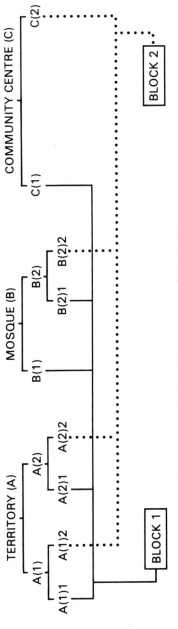

Figure 15.5   The pattern of Manchester Pakistanis' communal political alliances

Leaders know, or know of, each other. The communication network is comprehensive and extensive. In this sense the community is a unitary one with a single boundary. Yet the boundary is highly permeable. The arena is politically *divisive*, so that internal divisions constantly surface in inter-action with other communities (Werbner 1990b; 1990c). Leaders and groups rarely present a united front; Barth's view that interethnic analysis should focus on the 'boundary', rather than the stuff within it (Barth 1969), is thus far too simplistic.

The pattern of political alliances also has negative implications which make this case very different from the Swat factional model. Many local Pakistanis find the constant disputes and continuous conflicts in the political arena extremely distasteful, and respond by withdrawing alto-gether from arenas where confrontations are likely to occur. There is a large silent majority in the community which avoids public meetings and large-scale events such as elections, because people fear possible violence or unpleasantness. Moreover, as I argue more fully elsewhere (Werbner 1990b), confrontation politics tend to create very little that is tangible or of lasting value. Most culturally innovative organisations and institutions in the community have been built up by small cadres of enthusiasts who try to avoid publicity for as long as possible, for fear that the involvement of political activisits will undermine their project even before it has been fully launched. Alliances are wide reaching but fundamentally competitive and negative. Creative power is necessarily in the hands of smaller, cohesive groups sharing a common ideology.

Conclusion

Understanding the historical roots of an ethnic community is only a first step towards an analysis of community formation. It is, indeed, important to recognise that a community of labour migrants can be highly heterogeneous in its social composition, seen in terms of the skills, knowledge, experience and aspirations of its members. Migrants may come from different class backgrounds and be able to mobilise different resources (Light 1984). Over time, however, these resources come to be available to other, less privileged members of the migrant community. This is so because the sub-groups within the community do not remain fully encapsulated. In this chapter I have analysed the ways in which different sections of the Manchester Pakistani community create links and alliances beyond the boundaries of their separate groups. I have argued, further, that divisions within the community, while they create cleavages at one level, lead to a larger unity and an interdependence between discrete domains and arenas.

Although Pakistanis in Manchester claim membership in different 'communities', each with its own domain of activity, in reality communal politics form a single complex arena. While the setting varies from one event to another, the significance of each event can only be understood in relation to a wider totality of such events.

References

Arabia 1985. 'Old differences make a new start in Eid violence', *Arabia*, 5, 50.

Barth, Frederik 1959. 'Segmentary opposition and the theory of games', *Journal of the Royal Anthropological Institute*, 89, 1: 5–22.

—— 1969. 'Introduction' in *Ethnic Groups and Boundaries*, ed. F. Barth, London: George Allen and Unwin.

Beck, Brenda 1976. 'Centres and boundaries of regional caste systems: towards a general model', in *Regional Analysis: Social Systems*, vol. II, ed Carol A. Smith, New York: Academic Press, 255–86.

Light, Ivan 1984. 'Immigrant and ethnic enterprise in North America', *Ethnic and Racial Studies*, 7, 2: 195–216.

Nowikowski, Susan 1984. 'Snakes and ladders: Asian business in Britain', in *Ethnic Communities in Business*, ed. Robin Ward and Richard Jenkins, Cambridge University Press.

Werbner, Pnina 1979. 'Avoiding the ghetto: Pakistani migrants and settlement shifts in Manchester', *New Community*, 7: 376–89.

—— 1984. 'Business on trust: Pakistani entrepreneurship in the Manchester garment trade', in *Ethnic Communities in Business: Strategies for Economic Survival*, ed. Robin Ward and Richard Jenkins, Cambridge University Press, 189–210.

—— 1985. 'The organisation of giving and ethnic elites', *Ethnic and Racial Studies*, 8, 3: 368–88.

—— 1987. 'Enclave economies and family firms: Pakistani traders in a British city', in *Migration, Labour and Social Order*, ed. Jeremy S. Eades, ASA Monographs 25, London: Tavistock.

—— 1990a. *The Migration Process: Capital, Gifts and Offerings among British Pakistanis*, Explorations in Anthropology Series, Oxford: Berg Publishers Ltd.

—— 1990b. 'The fiction of unity in ethnic politics: aspects of representation and the state among British Pakistanis', to appear in *Black and Ethnic Leaderships in Britain: the cultural dimensions of political action*, ed., Muhammad Anwar and Pnina Werbner, London: Routledge.

—— 1990c. 'Factionalism and violence in British Pakistani communal politics', in *Global Migrants, Pakistani Cities: Economy and Culture in a Muslim Society*, ed. Pnina Werbner and Hastings Donnan, London: Macmillan.

Werbner, R.P. (ed.) 1977. *Regional Cults*, ASA Monograph No. 16, London, New York: Academic Press.

Author index

Note: References to present volume are indicated by 'present vol,'.

Subject index

Toledo, USA *206*
Tongaat, Natal 135
Tora, Apisai 114
Toronto 212
tourist trade, US 203, 207
Tower Hamlets, Bangladeshi community in
171, 293, 317–29; activists 171, 317,
319–21; Asian vote *301*; divisions 171,
328–9; elections 321–7; funding, public
319, 322, 323, 327–8; leaders 171, 317,
319–21; nationalism 324; occupations
293, 318, 319; representation 317,
319–27; size of population 272, 318;
see also: St Katharine's Ward;
Spitalfields; Sylhetis
traders, Indian 19, 23, 181–2, 193, 318;
Britain 332–3, 336, 343–4; East Africa
151–2, 156, 158, 160; South Africa
131, 134–5, 136, 137, 145; USA 212
transport: Britain 271, 334; French
colonies 81; Trinidad 94; see also
railways
Transvaal 132, 133, 134, 136, 142;
Transvaal Anti-SAIC Committee 143;
Transvaal Indian Congress 37, 143
Trinidad 35–6, 89–111
Africans 92, 96, 101, 106
agriculture 90, 91, 105, 106
Black Power movement 92
caste 93, 94
Christians, Indian 92
class 91, 92, 99
commerce 91
communality 94, 99, 107
consumer boom 101, 102–3
culture, Indian 35–6, 93–5, 103, 106
Democratic Labour Party 15
Development and Environmental Works
Division (DEWD) 92–3, 96, 99, 101
discrimination, ethnic 82, 92, 93
diversity, ethnic 90, 91
domestic relief programmes 96
education 94, 98
elections 92, 93
employment 92, 93, 98, *100*, 101–2, 105
family structure 93, 94, 103, 106
Fertilisers of Trinidad and Tobago Ltd
105
five-year plans 92
generation gap 103
GNP 96, *97*
government racial policies 92–3, 96,
98–9, 101, 102, 106
Hinduism 15, 93, 94, 100, 103, 106
housing 102
identity, ethnic 106, 107

indenture system 9, 33, 91
independence 91
Indian commissioner 11
industrialisation programme 96, 104–5,
106
investment, Indian capital 98
Iron and Steel Company of Trinidad and
Tobago (Iscott) 105
Islam 93
land ownership 91
language 93
mobility, social 94, 98
occupations 91, 99, 105
oil boom 95–100, 100–3, 106, (years
before) 90–5
organisations, welfare 106
patronage networks 98
Penal Rock Road 100–3, 105–6
People's National Movement 92–3, 98–9
Point Lisas industrial estate 96
politics, racial 15, 106
poverty 92, 9
racism, institutionalised 96, 101, 106
re-indenture 91
recession 104–6, 106–7
rice cultivation 100, 102, 105
rural populations 35, 91
St Patrick County Council 101–2
size of S Asian population 2, 33, 90
strikes 108
sugar cultivation 90–1, 95, 98, 100,
101, 102, 105; prices 98, 99,
101
tension, ethnic 92, 93, 108
transport 94
twice-migrants to UK 292
unemployment 96, 105
United Labour Front 15, 101–2
wealth and poverty 91
women 72, 93, 102
Tripura 46
Tun Razak 53
Tungku Abdul Rahman 51, 52, 53
twice-migrants 17–18; East Africa to UK
19, 37, 167, 168, 269, 274, 292, (Sikhs)
161; Sikhs from UK to N. America
245
Tyneside 277

U Nu 45
U Saw 43
Uganda: Africanisation 14; Asian–African
relations 16, 157, 167; coup (1985)
150; expulsions 17, 19, 33, 37, 150,
157, 158, 167; indenture system 9;
Ismailis 159; Mombasa railway 160,

Uganda (*cont.*)
161; Nubians 158; residual Asian
communities 150; traders C19th 153
Ukrainians in Blackburn 258
Umzinto, South Africa 138
unemployment 54, 204–5; *see also under*
Britain
Union of Soviet Socialist Republics 123
unions, trade 5, 7, 14, 90, 314, 319
United Arab Emirates: development
priorities 186; ethnic composition 194;
migrant workers in 175, 177, *178*, *179*,
186; migration to USA 188
United Nations 132
United States of America 18, 168, 197–217
'Asian Indian' identity 197
Asiatic Exclusion League 197–8
Bengalis 214
British Asians contrasted 209
Central Intelligence Agency 123
Chinese 199, 201, 208, *209*
culture; Indian North–South divide
214–15
demand for labour 199–200, 209
discrimination 23
distribution 201–11, 215
diversity within Asian group 212–13,
215
education 198, 205, 209
Egyptians 189
encapsulation 210–11, 215
equal opportunities policies 254
family reunion 198, 200, 211
Federation of Labor 197–8
Filipinos 201, 202, 203, 208, *209*
fusion/fission 214–15
Gujaratis 207, 214
health sector 199, 205
Hinduism 21, 214–15
housing 209–10
immigration policies 21, 168, 197, 198,
200, 215
Immigration Act (1965) 198, 200
integration 168, 170, 205, 207–11, 215,
289
Japanese 201, 203, 208, *209*
Koreans 199, 201, 203, 208, *209*
language 205, 214, 215
marriage, immigration for 199
missionaries in Malaya 49
occupations 21, 192, *193*, 199–200, 203,
205, 207, 212 (*see also* professionals
below)
oil companies 95
Patels 207
political involvement 313

professionals 168, *188*, 198, 202, 205–6,
209, 215
race relations 209, 210
railways 168, 198
religion 211–12, 214, 215
second generation 215
Sikhs 168, 202, 214, 245
size of S Asian population 2
skilled labour 168
suburban residence 210
Tamils 214
ties with S Asia 214
unemployment 204–5
urban backgrounds, migrants with 213
Vietnamese 201, 202, 203, 208, 209
violence, recent racial 211
women migrants 199
see also individual states and towns
universities: Indians at 198, 333–4, 336;
Middle East 187; South African 136,
145–6
Untouchables 254–5
urban background, migrants with 6, 213,
335
urban residence 5; East Africa 16, 156, 157;
French colonies 35, 78, 81; Malaysia
54; South Africa 131, 133, 138; *see
also* Britain (settlement geography)
Urdu language 19, 85, 254, 333
Utah, USA 204
Uttar Pradesh 11, 91, 212, 213, 333

Vaishnavism 11, 93
Vancouver 212
Varendra language 13
Vaz, Keith, MP 312
Vellach (indentured woman worker, Natal)
67–8
venereal disease 68
Vereeniging, South Africa 132
Verulam, Natal 69, 135, 138
Vietnamese in USA 201, 202, 203, 208, *209*
violence, racial 16, 23, 211, 245, 261, 318;
see also harassment
visits, family 244, 251, 252
voluntary migration 159, 160, 331
voluntary welfare workers 319, 327
vote, British Asian *see* Britain (elections)
vouchers, work 198, 237, 292

Walsall 304
wars: First World, aftermath of, 155–6;
Indo-Pakistani 226; Naning 47;
Second World: burma 43–4; Fiji 119;
industrialisation 160; immigration
restricted after 156–7; Malaya 50;